THE VISIBLE CONFEDERACY

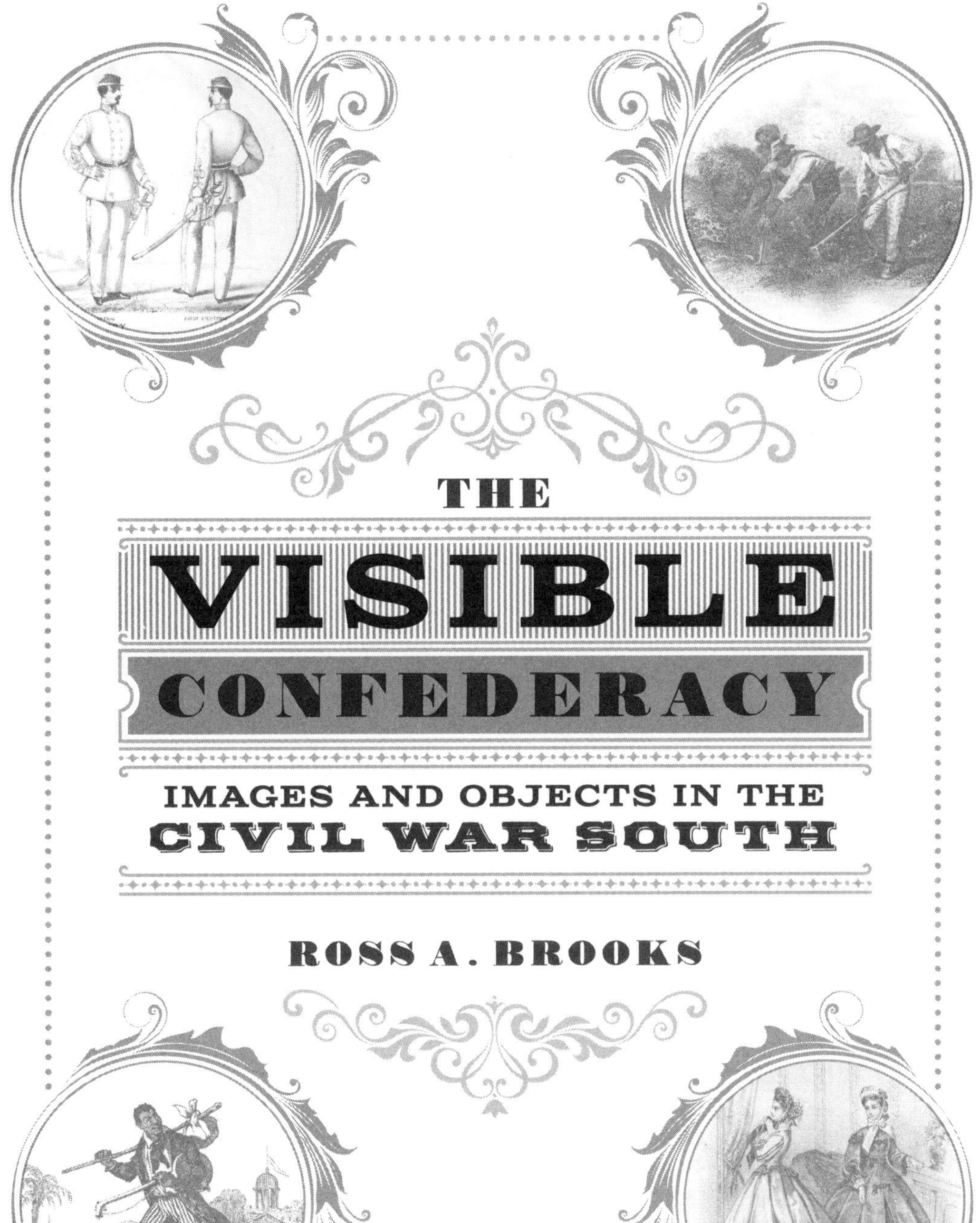

THE VISIBLE CONFEDERACY

IMAGES AND OBJECTS IN THE CIVIL WAR SOUTH

ROSS A. BROOKS

LOUISIANA STATE UNIVERSITY PRESS BATON ROUGE

Published by Louisiana State University Press

Manufactured in the United States of America
First printing

DESIGNER: *Mandy McDonald Scallan*
TYPEFACE: *Whitman*
PRINTER AND BINDER: *Sheridan Books, Inc.*

Library of Congress Cataloging-in-Publication Data

Names: Brooks, Ross A. (Ross Andrew), 1958– author.
Title: The visible Confederacy : images and objects in the Civil War South / Ross A. Brooks.
Description: Baton Rouge : Louisiana State University Press, [2019] | Includes bibliographical references and index.
Identifiers: LCCN 2019018885 | ISBN 978-0-8071-7196-7 (cloth : alk. paper)
Subjects: LCSH: Material culture—Confederate States of America—History. | United States—History—Civil War, 1861–1865—Antiquities. | United States—History—Civil War, 1861–1865—Art and the war.
Classification: LCC E646.5 .B76 2019 | DDC 973.7—dc23

The paper in this book meets the guidelines for permanence and durability of the Committee on Production Guidelines for Book Longevity of the Council on Library Resources.♾

To my parents, Valma and Richard

CONTENTS

ACKNOWLEDGMENTS ix

Introduction 1

CHAPTER 1
Iconography of the Confederate Government 9

CHAPTER 2
Nativism and Depictions of Race 32

CHAPTER 3
The Southern Defense of Slavery 55

CHAPTER 4
Manufacturing and Southern Autonomy 77

CHAPTER 5
The Photographic and Graphic Print Industries 93

CHAPTER 6
The Meanings of Confederate Military Clothing 115

CHAPTER 7
Visualizing the War for the People 132

CHAPTER 8
Representations of Womanhood 162

CHAPTER 9
Picturing Hierarchies of Manhood 187

Epilogue 211

APPENDIX:
The Origins of Vignettes Used on Confederate Currency 215

NOTES 219

BIBLIOGRAPHY 281

INDEX 313

ACKNOWLEDGMENTS

This book exists because of the ongoing support and input of many wonderful and generous people, some for many years and others for shorter periods. The most fundamental to its genesis and development is the late Warren Ellem of La Trobe University. Warren saw more than interesting snippets in my research and more than a tourist in my interest in history. His questions and knowledge of American history are deeply embedded in this work. I am so grateful for his continuous encouragement and am glad that he knew of Louisiana State University Press's interest in this work before his passing. Thanks also to Timothy Minchin, who supervised my postgraduate candidature and who has supported this project all along.

I am very grateful for the assistance I received in the latter stages of the manuscript's publication from a range of people. The list starts with two great historians: Giselle Roberts, who throughout the process contributed sage advice concerning my readings of women and the Confederacy's visual and material culture; and Keith Wilson, who unstintingly expended time and exercised his scholarship in reviewing the entire manuscript. I also acknowledge Sean Young, Dale Blair, Barry Crompton of the Archer Library, and Michael Adcock, who at stages of this book's writing have all shared their knowledge and wisdom. I thank Rand Dotson and Catherine Kadair for their patient support of this project. Especial thanks to Elizabeth Gratch, who so sensitively and thoroughly copyedited the manuscript.

From its inception to now, the world of the researcher has benefited from incredible change. To access the earliest primary sources used in this work required a combination of correspondence, guesswork, and visits to collections. I am grateful to all the curators, from those like the late Norm Simmons of the Pensacola Historical Society, Robert Hancock of the American Civil War Museum, and Caldwell Delaney of the Mobile's Museum of History, who helped me when this project was little more than curiosity, to those like Sarah Tignor of the Johnson Collection and Michelle McDonald of the East Tennessee Historical Museum, whose assistance in the later stages has materially improved this work. Additionally, as I began my postgraduate studies at La Trobe University, Jonelle Bradley and the Borchardt Library's interlibrary loans department searched out and delivered hard-to-find sources. More recently, thanks to the generosity and foresight of many institutions, many of these and more are now available through the internet. For sources not freely available at that time, the web has led me to collectors, like Confederate currency specialists Pierre Fricke and Richie Self and Confederate firearms collector E. Larry Jackson, who have kindly shared images of pieces in their collections to use in this work.

Finally, I would like to acknowledge the debt that I owe to my family. To my parents Val and Dick, for sparking an interest in history and a passion for language. To my children, Riley, William, and Mahalia, who grew up sharing their lives and our household with "Dad's book." They started merely as onlookers and have grown into participants in my writing. And at the heart of all this Greta. More than a steadfast source of support and encouragement, she has provided everything possible to enable me to find and shape my own voice.

THE VISIBLE CONFEDERACY

Introduction

Early in spring 1865, Richmond's besieged citizens viewed two new paintings by artist John Adams Elder in the window of Bidgood's bookstore. The first, *The Scout's Prize,* depicted a winter scene with a galloping Southern cavalryman leading the mount of a Federal officer he had just killed. The second, larger work, *The Battle of the Crater, Morning after the Explosion,* showed the moment eight months earlier when Confederate troops repelled a major Union incursion into their defenses at nearby Petersburg. Amid a broken landscape, strewn with bodies and the detritus of war, it showed Confederates coming to the aid of a lone comrade battling black and white Northerners. Both impacted viewers. Richmond's *Whig* praised each work's "high artistic merit," and the *Enquirer* called *The Battle of the Crater* "a faultless representation."[1] In less than three weeks, Richmond lay a smoldering ruin, the two paintings destroyed, and the Confederate government and its armies were on the run.[2] But in that instant, Elder represented ideas that resonated with Confederates in their struggle for independence.

Although the nation Elder had depicted collapsed within weeks, it remains a presence in human minds. Posterity considers this American proto-nation in various ways, from revulsion to reverence. For me, it is intriguing that my world's most powerful democracy fractured within a lifetime and engaged in such a protracted and destructive war. It raises questions regarding not only national identity and government systems but also what prompted and sustained the Southern attempt at independence. This long interest led me to examine the Confederacy through its visual objects, to investigate the state and individuals who generated this visual matter and to understand the messages it conveyed. This work results from that study. Examining these images and objects provides a window on Confederate minds and an opportunity to reconstitute glimpses of the ways they saw their world.

The images and objects created by the Confederacy offer insights into the quest for identity that accompanied its citizens' bid for independence. Romantic nationalists, they sought to set up a reactionary, exclusivist state for a people convinced that the federal government no longer represented them.[3] For decades, historians have examined the Confederacy's intentions and ideologies and debated how much popular support this nation enjoyed. In the late twentieth century, historiographers such as Kenneth Stampp, Paul Escott, and Richard E. Beringer explored centrifugal ideas that eroded and cleft the nation.[4] In recent times, writers such as Drew Gilpin Faust, Gary Gallagher, Anne Sarah Rubin, and Michael Bernath have advanced our understanding of what drew and sustained Southerners' allegiance to the Confederacy.[5]

This work's focus is on the visual realm of Confederate images and objects. Before the 1990s, few historians used the insights granted by these artifacts to study their attempt at building national commonality.[6] One prominent work on Confederate graphic print culture stated bluntly that in "terms of visual representation the Cause was lost by 1862."[7] Additionally, another considered that "few Southern artworks were seen publicly."[8] Such writing creates the impression that the Confederacy left little visual and material culture and, therefore, that an in-depth study faces a dearth of matter with which to work.

Deeper research shows the limitations of such notions. While the Confederacy's production of visual matter was small in comparison to the North, in contrast to the antebellum South's output, it was significant. The experience of Memphis, Tennessee, provides an example. In early July 1861, the editor of Memphis's *Daily Appeal* cast an approving eye over a fresco of fruit and flowers painted for an ice cream saloon by Samuel Tosi (1828/32–85). He enthused, "A painting is a thing we rarely see—a new one of merit never."[9] However, over the next seven months, the *Appeal* detailed four new artworks, each of which related to the Confederate cause.[10] Patriotism spurred production and patronage in cities like Memphis. But like Elder's paintings, many of the originals are lost, and only written descriptions provide a way of picturing them.[11] Collating these and extant pieces provides the over one thousand examples of Confederate-made commercial imagery and objects that form the basis of this book.[12] Additionally, original wartime dramas performed a fictive Confederacy for audiences. In all, this study includes works produced within the Confederacy by manufacturers, artists, engravers and lithographers, photographers, theatrical impresarios, and playwrights.[13] Created for the government or for commercial purposes, these were objects made mindful of needs and popular opinion. Those who made them included patriots, closet Unionists, and slaves seeking to survive in the Civil War South. As a whole, these items reveal a richer, if still fragmentary, visual world than some have suggested.[14] Examining the evidence of what remains shows that while never matching the North in quality or quantity of visual matter, Confederates established and sustained local producers of imagery suited to their sensibilities during the conflict. These products provide access to an artery of ideas that fed their sense of national identity until Appomattox.

While the practical need to meet demand for goods drove Confederate manufacturing, commercial imagery performed no such pragmatic service. Rather, like wartime literature, Southerners' desire for their own cultural expressions influenced its creation. Coleman Hutchison and Michael Bernath's respective investigations into wartime fiction and print media show Confederate cultural nationalists' efforts to create an independent literature. This undertaking led to an increase in books, journals, and pamphlets that embodied their national ideals and myths.[15] Additionally, it prompted an upsurge in domestic theater with Southern nationalist themes.[16] Collectively this expressed a desire to convey a distinctly Confederate worldview. Recent examinations of flag culture, currency, and patriotic envelopes find streams of thought expressed by Confederates about subjects such as slavery, their Northern opponents, their military, and Americanism.[17] This work builds on and deepens these studies.

The historiography of the Confederate South is extensive and underpins this work. It provides understanding of the historic context and helps discern the meanings and messages of these products. Besides those previously cited, the inquiries of historians such as George Rable, Paul Quigley, Colin Woodward, and Chandra Manning have been essential. Their works highlight major themes in Confederate thinking and not only enhance this work but are, in turn, reinforced and nuanced by it.[18]

Confederate creators responded to market forces and mass culture. They prized knowing and catering to their audiences. Entrepreneurial individuals recognized the profitability of combining entertainment and patriotism. Theater owners, aware that the populace craved stimulation, produced a variety of shows. Publishers capitalized on not only soldiers' boredom in camp and women's desire for escapist literature but also their readers' prejudices.[19] Yet the Confederate experience presented examples of the fickleness of the Southern marketplace. Works filled with the appropriate emotional hooks triggered patriotic responses and brought patronage. Artists and other creatives who misjudged popular taste faced destitution or even violence.[20] In essence, the notion that these commercial creators crafted items to suit the taste of their audience is fundamental to this study.

Confederates shared likings in common with other Westerners. This included visual and material culture. Jean-Louis Comolli described Confederates and their contemporaries as having lived at a time with a "frenzy for the visible" that spanned high and low cultures.[21] Fine arts provided a marker of cultivation. The bourgeois studied artworks, and the powerful owned them. Moreover, emerging technologies offered more democratic access to imagery through reprography and public performances. These vehicles offered working people greater opportunities to view or purchase reproductions of scenes and personalities. Although laden with cultural content and vehicles for spreading stereotypical representations, audiences viewed them as objective images revealing their subjects' psychological truths.[22]

More specifically to the Confederate South, visual stimuli possessed a significant potential. Although a powerful force for building a national consciousness, the printed word required a literate society. With the South's literacy rates a tenth of those in the North, however, uneducated citizens lacked this avenue to cultural nationalists' ideas.[23] In less educated societies, nonverbal communication of information and ideas gains greater importance.[24] Still or dynamic imagery, such as Confederate theatrical productions, attracted audiences from every level of civilian and military society.[25] It enabled the less learned in Southern society access to Confederate ideology in obvious or more subtle ways.

Locked into their matter and manufactures are the needs, values, ideas, attitudes, and assumptions of the society that produced them. The studies of visual and material culture offer methods to decode and unpack these messages. Significantly, Peter Burke and Francis Haskell's work concerning imagery reminds us that representations give access to the makers' construction of their world. Particularly, by considering their context and scanning them not only for themes and inclusions but also exclusions, we gain insight into that world.[26] Beyond this, identifying and analyzing an object's maker and its making help us further discern contemporaneous beliefs and values.[27] Therefore, studying both object and maker in relationship to their parent culture builds a greater understanding of each.[28]

Confederate visual culture enabled Southerners to see a world filtered to their taste and contributed to an imagined Confederacy. In his study of aesthetics, *Simulation and Simulacrum,* Jean Baudrillard describes the process by which the representation of reality and its reproduction transform depictions into a hyperreality—a simulacrum, an image divorced from the actual and only existing within itself, or what Michael Camille terms a "false likeness."[29] Although Baudrillard suggests that this condition emerged more recently, Confederate imagery indicates that processes at least similar to those he described functioned in the Civil War South.[30] Examining their representations of African Americans, their enemies, and themselves shows the degree and way Confederates replaced reality with visual rhetoric. In written or visual form, their simulacra brought both potential strengths and weaknesses.

Like many nations, Confederates used contrast to try to differentiate themselves as a group. Peter Sahlins writes, "Confronted by an alien 'Them,' an otherwise diverse community can become a reassuring or disparate 'Us.'"[31] Confederates' imagery and objects contributed to this process, making visible, normalizing, and spreading the values and beliefs the nation used to construct simulacra of "us" and "them."

With their reliance on stereotype and ridicule, cartoons provided an effective instrument for distinguishing insider from outsider. While dried by time of whatever capacity to produce laughter they once possessed, these innocuous objects once identified Confederate insiders and outsiders. Sigmund Freud noted that by making others "small, contemptible, or comical" vehicles for jokes, humor vanquished the object and bribed third parties with laughter to take the creator's side.[32] Their mirth bonded audience and author, as it reinforced their prejudices and the gulf between them and those they considered objectionable. Cartoons became another way for Southerners to distance themselves from Northerners, slaves, and disloyal "them's." However, they possessed adverse side effects. Like most cartoons, the jokes in the Confederate versions were conservative and channeled hostility downward through society. Consequently, this led various groups to experience direct or collateral ridicule. So, while humor helped define and unify the people, it also threatened to divide.[33]

Other Confederate creations influenced individuals in other ways. Their literature and dramatic productions not only built national identity but also provided an escape from the realities of a losing war.[34] The psychological process of transportation narratives—created alternate realities through word, picture, or setting, emotive characters and plots—drew their audiences' focus and released them from the real world. As a result, plays and dioramic entertainments moved people's attitudes more than still imagery.[35] Despite the concerns some expressed, most Confederates valued their theater.[36] Without understanding the subconscious impact of theatrical performances, they noted the positive effects of escapism the theater provided and praised the morale-boosting properties of its original dramas.[37]

Confederate visual culture also used more deliberate techniques that are less obvious to the casual contemporary reader: messages depicted in the topography of faces by their makers. Based on the popular pseudoscience of physiognomy, that imagined link between facial features and personality, artists utilized a face's details to represent character. Moreover, theories such as this dovetailed neatly with equally spurious racist-driven anthropology and ethnology, and Confederate artists could draw on all of it when fashioning semblances to convey personality, morals, and intellect. Mary Cowling's study of this quasi-science and its influence on nineteenth-century art, *The Artist as Anthropologist*, provides a guidebook for reading Confederate artists' use of physiognomy in their engravings and paintings.[38]

The ways producers delivered and distributed their creations both enabled and limited their works' ability to create Confederate hyperrealities. Circulation of imagery in print, onstage, or as visual art started on the streets of major cities. Newsboys hawked Southern illustrated journals and flyers for performances, and shop windows displayed paintings and prints. In addition, the South's transport infrastructure conveyed these packages of Confederate propaganda to points across the country on rail, road, and river. Of these, trains emerged as the fastest and most efficient form of transport. Until the war's end, railways carried men and goods. These physical things made the Confederacy appear more tangible.[39]

Historians have revealed a Confederate world that contained a variety of patterns or themes: sacrifice, faith in their military ability, demonizing the enemy, defending racial slavery, defining their independence, and who they were. Through these they sought to justify and legitimize their actions, working to establish lasting independence for the nation they had created. Within Confederate imagery and objects, the themes interweave and interrelate. This work's structure reflects this complexity. The idea of "Yankees," for example, enters the chapters on race, industry, martial nature, and gender. Convictions regarding sacrifice and suffering emerge in the chapters on industry, uniforms, and gender. However, the visual and written evidence is not always in accord.

In contrast to these common domestic themes, works featuring Confederates' spiritual world or the one outside their borders are almost entirely absent from Confederate visual creations. With regards to their faith, officially, only the motto chosen for the great seal—"Deo Vindice" (translated commonly as "With God our vindicator")—made obvious visual reference to the Deity.[40] In the public field, evidence of Confederate-created religious imagery is limited. Searching contemporary sources has revealed the following: two short-lived panoramas; a painting; the decorations of two Augusta, Georgia, churches; several Southern-made engravings in the first issue of *Children's Friend;* and the reused prewar woodcuts that appeared in each issue of the *Child's Index*, a Baptist periodical published from late 1862. These were slender offerings for a nation that prided itself on its godliness.[41] Similarly, despite the importance of international recognition, only a handful of images conveyed Southerners' frustration over the failure of Confederate diplomacy.[42] The themes of mercenary and calculating European powers letting the South battle alone, conveyed in Armistead Hurdle's cartoon "Recognition," is typical (fig. I.1). Notwithstanding these concerns, Confederates saw tantalizing promises of overseas support in the English-made uniforms, Europeans arms and equipment issued to their soldiers, and reports of the British-built ships in their navy. However, more commonly in Confederate imagery, other matters provided the focus.

When compared to the other subjects in Confederate imagery, the lack of works concerned with spirituality or the world outside the South is clear. Rather war, race,

FIG. I.1. "Recognition," by Armistead Uriah Hurdle, *Southern Illustrated News*, Sept. 5, 1863. From *GenealogyBank.com*, a leading online genealogical resource from NewsBank, Inc.

autonomy, and a wish to create a sense of commonality saturate Confederate visual and material culture. This study shows that the way Confederates represented their world fostered both homogeneity and division within the society. Chapter 1 examines imagery and objects the government used as it attempted to present itself domestically and internationally as a substantial and modern political entity. This complements later chapters that look at the unifying and divisive qualities of works constructed by private institutions and individuals. Chapters 2 and 3 use these visual artifacts to assay the role race and slavery played in establishing an identity and mission for the Confederate nation. It finds pictures fueled by delusions and prejudices. Chapters 4 and 5 examine the impact of manufacturing and the reprographic industry on Confederates' sense of independence. Rapid change brought the South both benefits and significant costs. Chapters 6 and 7 study Confederate martial iconography, iconology, and identity. Through uniforms and both still and dynamic imagery, they reveal the possibilities and limitations of Confederate attempts to use imagery and objects to create both icons and imagine their military struggle. Finally, chapters 8 and 9 consider how Confederates visualized gender. Confederate products such as cartoons, theatrical performances, and uniforms show that the war exerted pressures that challenged traditional concepts of masculinity and femininity. As a whole, this book recognizes the conservative nature of the Southern nation. Moreover, it emphasizes the Confederacy's complexity and shows some of the divisions and tensions that contributed to the failure of its attempt to form a nation.

Soon after the war, Elder used his memory and resources to re-create versions of his paintings of *The Scout's Prize* and *The Battle of Crater.*[43] One of the earliest creatives to feed on and represent the Confederacy, his endeavors joined other peddlers of the "Lost Cause." Rather than acknowledging the Confederacy's complexities and flaws, these individuals worked the nation's values and beliefs into a collection of myths that declared the virtues of the prewar South and cast the war as a heroic battle against the odds. Within a lifetime, the efforts of these individuals erased the Confederacy's political, economic, and social tensions and left a sanitized shell of a struggle for states' rights and a land of contented slaves and a unified population. In 1882 former soldier Carlton McCarthy explained what the Confederates battled against: Union government "backed by a treasury that turned out money by the ton . . . [Northern] factory and foundry chimney [that] made a pillar of smoke by day and of fire by night . . . tons of quartermaster stores . . . illustrated papers, to cheer the 'Boys in Blue' with sketches of the glorious deeds they did not do . . . plus swarms of men, the refuse of the earth."[44] Writers like McCarthy swept many of the Confederacy's problematic ideas out of public awareness or debate. In doing so, they also obscured the Confederate story, ignoring or downplaying those areas that complicated their narrative. Scrutinizing Confederate visual and material artifacts helps reveal the nation that the Lost Cause disguised. Studying it not only shows the genesis of these myths but also contributes to the rich historiography on the Confederacy and the ways Confederates saw their world.

CHAPTER 1

Iconography of the Confederate Government

At last we are,
A nation among nations; and the world,
Shall soon behold in many a distant port,
Another flag unfurled!
—HENRY TIMROD, "Ethnogenesis"

The instruments and structures of a government help build a sense of national unity. These systems and articles capture not only a nation's laws, borders, economy, and duties but also its shared myths, oppositional models, and things of public culture that suggest a people's commonality.[1] By 1861 many nation-states and their institutions used iconography such as a national flag, military uniform, stamps, seals, and currency to brand, express, and legitimize their authority. In its attempt to establish political authority, the Confederate government developed and used a variety of these forms.[2] Examining each of these visual representations provides insight not only into how the Confederate government presented ideas current within their developing republic but also about the nation's tensions and weaknesses.

The creation of the Confederate States' official iconography began as Southerners, disillusioned by Washington politics, fearful of the impact of antislavery Republicans and President Abraham Lincoln, and steeped in decades of Southern Nationalist rhetoric, sought the sanctuary of their own government.[3] In early February 1861, within three months of Lincoln's election, seven slave states across the South seceded, and their representatives met in Montgomery, Alabama. From secessionists' initial efforts to constitute a permanent national government, Confederate politicians and officials enlisted imagery to make their nation appear more substantial. The development, final form, and usage of these markers contained intentional and implied meanings about the nation.

The actions of the state representatives who assembled at Montgomery suggested that the fledging nation's politicians grasped the role imagery could play in nation building. A week before they adopted a constitution, they had already agreed upon a national flag. Over the next months, distinctive Treasury bonds and notes, military fashion, seals for arms of the government, and postage stamps joined the national colors to mark the presence and authority of the Confederate nation. The resulting imagery and iconography contained American themes of progress, republican values, and a mythic present. The subsequent history of the government's attempt to represent itself showed not only these ideas transformed into distinctly Confederate iconography, but also the complexity of the task.

A NATIONAL FLAG

The effort and intricacies involved in the Confederate government creating lasting iconography are evident in the story of their three successive national flags. The most constructed and considered of all the Confederacy's official imagery, each successive design derived from a degree of collaboration between the people and their politicians (fig. 1.1). Their development and the use of these national colors in the Civil War South captured the differences between sections, the people, their representatives, and the various imaginings of their nation.[4]

The range of ways Southerners conceived the Confederacy became clear as the Provisional Congress met in early February 1861. There representatives tabled and discussed a steady stream of flag proposals. Attachment to what they called the "Old Union" came to the fore in Mississippi representative Walker Brooke's call to adopt a flag "as similar as possible to the flag of the United States."[5] His speech stirred the emotions of some present. As one representative wrote, "I felt for a while like some few people used to feel at a Fourth of July celebration after the champagne had freely circulated."[6] However, straightaway William Porcher Miles, the chair of the Flag and Seal Committee, "chased away" Brooke's "Yankee Doodleism." He did so by recollecting the shift in loyalties from England to America that the Revolution's generation had experienced. He also reminded members of the greater attachment he felt to his state than to the United States.[7] Whereas men like Miles steered Congress away from the United States flag, references to it continued to recur in flag designs and discussions. They indicate that Brooke expressed a connection shared by many Southerners.[8] Although in the flag committee's official report Miles stated that they had rejected any designs like the "Stars and Stripes," this was not the case. Later he admitted its similarity and the difficulty in tearing "people away from some reminiscence of the 'old flag.'"[9] Although similar, the chosen design, as Robert Bonner has

FIG. 1.1. Flags of the Confederates States of America. *Left to right:* First national flag, March 6, 1861–May 1, 1863; second national flag, May 1, 1863–March 4, 1865; third national flag, March 4, 1865. Drawings created by the author.

explained, used the positive associations of the United States flag to refocus Southern passions on their new government rather than express a loyalty to the former Union.[10]

Adopted on March 4, 1861, the first national flag, or "Stars and Bars," became but one of many flags the Southerners used. Over the previous months, the states of South Carolina, Mississippi, Louisiana, and Florida all instituted individual state flags, and by the end of 1861, each Confederate state had its own flag.[11] These flags not only flew in each respective state but also appeared across the Confederacy as troops carried them outside their borders. Furthermore, North Carolina and Virginia's initial decision to issue regimental flags aided the visibility of some states' flags until at least the middle of 1862. Carried across the South, these flags visually reminded Confederates of their people's multiple loyalties.

Other flags came into use that further provided visual evidence of Southerners' diverse allegiances. Besides national and state colors, other designs appeared in late 1861 as Confederate armies adopted distinctive "battle flags."[12] In November 1861, the earliest appeared as generals in both the Eastern and Western armies worried that the similarity of Union and Rebel flags made it difficult to differentiate each side's troops on the battlefield. In the West, General William Hardee adopted a blue flag edged in white that bore a white disc in its center for his corps. Meanwhile, in the East, the chair of the Flag and Seal Committee, W. Porcher Miles, and Generals P.G.T. Beauregard and J. E. Johnston worked to introduce their own: a red flag crossed with diagonal blue bars and white edge and stars that soon became known as the Battle Flag. Miles developed the basic design in early 1861. Although Congress rejected it, Miles stayed alert for another opportunity to see it used in the Confederacy.[13] During the July 21, 1861, battle of First Manassas, Confederates experienced problems distinguishing their flag from that of the enemy. Miles brought his design to Confederate generals Beauregard and Johnston. But the flag committee rejected their attempt to have it adopted as a "war-flag." In the fall of 1861, the thwarted generals bypassed all official channels and instead arranged for 120 of the flags to be made and issued independent of any government body.[14] In similar fashion, generals in other Confederate armies instituted distinctive divisional and corps flags that bore little similarity to the national flag. The red battle flag supplanted many of these as Johnston and Beauregard took the design with them as they transferred to Western commands. As a result, by 1863, most Confederate army units carried banners based on Miles's design. On balance, Southerners developed affections for many flags: state, army, and national. They represented visibly the complex intersecting and contending loyalties that make up a nation. In the Confederacy, these attachments proved fluid.

Newspaper accounts indicated that war loosened Southern attachment to their first national flag. "We believe we speak for three-fourths of the Confederate people," wrote one critic from Louisiana in late July 1861, "when we state that the Confederate Flag has not only failed to satisfy them but has greatly disappointed them." It looked, they explained, an amalgam of two despotic national banners, "the Union and *three* stripes of Lincoln's abolition banner" and the white and red bars of the Austrian flag.[15] In late August 1861, a group of Fredericksburg, Virginia, women sent a resolution to Congress that stated that the "stars and bars fail to meet the objects of a flag."[16] Both called on the nation to adopt the "Southern Cross." This design, while similar in color and motifs to the Battle Flag, featured a perpendicular rather than diagonal cross. Although a variety of contending designs emerged over the following nineteen months, events would show where the majority of Southern opinion about flags lay.[17]

As public disfavor with the Stars and Bars grew, the Confederate Congress and its Flag and Seal Committee moved slowly to develop a replacement. While between winter 1861 and spring 1863, Congress devoted time to dealing with pressing matters, such as ensuring that the nation's armies had enough men and supplies, some politicians also filled days with hours of stump speeches.[18] Amid this activity, the designs tabled over 1862 lacked any momentum in Congress. Despite growing criticism from the press, it took until May 1, 1863, for the nation's representatives to determine to act. At the end of two days of what one congressman described as a "whirl of business" that was more than he could remember, both houses agreed on and adopted the second national flag—the Battle Flag as the union on a field of white.[19] The design maintained the tricolor palette of the first flag symbolizing valor, truth, and purity. It also reflected the popular wish for a distinctive national color. However, the actions of some Confederates suggested an uncertain grasp of its significance.

The manner in which Congress unfurled this flag over the capitol building said much about politicians' appreciation of iconography. On May 6, 1863, an "accidentally assembled" group saw a small version of the second flag appear atop the capitol.[20] Soon after, Richmond's *Examiner* welcomed news that officials had set the Clothing Bureau to preparing a large official flag to fly permanently over the congressional building. To the *Examiner,* the significance of its unfurling required a "representative of the civil or military power appointed for the purpose."[21] The paper predicted that when hoisted above the capitol, the Armory Band and other "demonstrations" would help celebrate the occasion.[22] It would be disappointed. On May 14, 1863, without official fuss or notice they lowered the old flag, and the new one appeared in its stead at the southern end of the capitol. Although contemporary newspapers welcomed its appearance, Congress failed to mark the event. Richmond's *Enquirer* lamented:

> The operation was unattended by any appropriate demonstration, as anticipated and should have been the case; and it is to be regretted that there was not, since we may have, some day, to number amongst the incidents of our history the hoisting of that flag, for the first time, over the capitol of the Confederacy, and it will read very prosily that it was drawn up and let loose when nobody was looking at or even dreaming about it.—It just slipped quietly into the place of the other old flag! It was not an EVENT as it should have been; not a cannon bade it welcome, not a voice said "hurra," not a drum beat. Only the little birds that twittered among the trees of the Square beheld the beautiful rag as fluttered in the breeze. And there it floats like a cloud dyed in one corner with the gorgeous coloring of the red sunshine, without the prestige of a "bravo" of welcome in its infancy; or the recollection of a brass band to hang around its folds in the great days of its futurity.[23]

Politicians' lack of consideration or awareness of this moment's significance to the people, press, and posterity is at first surprising. However, as Paul Escott has stated, the Confederate Congress was composed of a "group of wealthy but self-interested people."[24] And this incident seems evidence of their limited vision. Congress passed the flag bill on the last day of sitting before a seven-month recess. It appears that none in government could wait around long enough to be present and ensure that the flag's official unfurling over the seat of government was appropriately endorsed by a ceremony. The raising of the Confederacy's 1863 flag suggests that officialdom did not appreciate the event's significance. Their absence suggested either a lack of interest in joining the "thousands" of people who came to see and commend the new flag or desire to court popularity.[25]

Confederates embraced the new emblem. Its first official use, on May 12, 1863, when it appeared draped over the coffin of dead Confederate hero General T. J. "Stonewall" Jackson, as his body processed through Richmond's streets, started the process. Although some found associations with religion and race in it, the Battle Flag and its use over Jackson's coffin acknowledged the fundamental relationship between their military and their nation. The second national flag's subsequent use by the army cemented this association.[26] Until late 1864, Congress and the people remained largely silent about the flag. When one congressman suggested adding a blue border, the *Southern Punch* derided the move. It wanted no "ginger bread" added to the banner. It was "simple, beautiful, and imposing," according to the magazine, which concluded, "Let the flag alone."[27] Not all Confederates agreed with the *Punch*.

In December 1864, artillery major Arthur L. Rogers sought to improve the flag by adding a red bar to the fly. His attempt to make it look less like a surrender flag met with a mixture of approval and criticism. For example, Richmond's *Whig* considered it "childishness" to change the flag for the third time during the war. Pointedly, an army officer considered it "foolishness" when the "question really is, are we to have a nationality at all?"[28] Regardless of these opinions, the proposal stirred a dozen or so Southerners to put forward their own ideas over January and February 1865.[29] However, none of these other individuals possessed Rogers's desire to see their proposal succeed. Not only did Rogers seek support from leading Confederate senior officers, including Generals Joseph E. Johnston and Fitzhugh Lee, but in December 1864, he contracted printers Hoyer and Ludwig to print up his design in color. Rogers used these prints to promote his concept around Richmond. He pasted copies on walls and windows, and circulated them among congressmen. He even induced the doctors at one of the Confederate hospitals to make and fly a model over their institution.[30] By the second week of February 1865, it became well-known in Richmond, and on March 4, 1865, Congress crowned Rogers's campaign by instituting the design.[31]

The story of Confederate flags reflected more than a nation distancing itself from its parent nation. It suggested a government struggling with the complexity of the task. In formulating each version, it showed itself reactive, developing each design through a process of accretion and response. Furthermore, the impermanence of each model showed the difficulty of creating a consistent, encompassing, and popular flag for the new nation. For Congress's part, when it tried, it appeared strangely distant and struggled to read or capture a prevalent public mood. Moreover, though many Southerners hoped for more open governance, Miles's and Rogers's success in bypassing the political process and Rogers's ability to co-opt public opinion show that Confederates had not escaped the scheming of prewar politics.[32] Away from the politics of the House of Representatives and Senate, other sections of the government worked to obtain official emblems.

THE CONFEDERATE GOVERNMENT'S SEALS

Flags provided totemic foci for enacting patriotism and imagining a nation. But the machinery of government also required the concrete visual marker provided by seals to authenticate documents. Their use added to the government's sense of permanence and substance. Soon after a government formed in Montgomery, Alabama, on February 4, 1861, politicians launched a committee to establish a seal. But they moved too slowly, and in the vacuum this created, the Confederate government adopted an interim device (fig. 1.2). This design and the seals adopted by its various departments trace themes and ideas current in the embryonic government.

Reflecting the preeminence of finance and legislation in government, the provisional government and Treasury adopted and used the earliest Confederate seals. Ringed with oak leaves, the seal of the provisional government declared in emphatic serif capitals, CONFEDERATE STATES OF AMERICA and PROVISIONAL GOVERNMENT. These words circle an image of a scroll bearing the word *Constitutional* in sans serif capitals curved like a rainbow over the word *Liberty* in a classic Gothic typeface. The arrangement of components suggested the Constitution provided a new beginning or covenant. In addition, its oak leaves suggest stability, success, and protection and the scroll knowledge. The serif and sans serif typefaces, used in the Roman Empire, conveyed both longevity and Republican values. The angular swashes of black-letter glyphs evoked a knightly past. Impressed onto documents

FIG. 1.2. Seals of the Confederate States of America. *Clockwise:* Provisional Government; War Department; First Treasury Department, 1861–64; Second Treasury Department, 1864–65; Great Seal of the Confederate States of America, May 1863–65; Post Office Department. Drawings created by the author.

from 1861, this seal pictured a Confederate vision of the nation as inheritor and guardian of democracy.

The seal of the Confederate Department of the Treasury does not show such a clear national scope. Made in New York by George Lovett during March 1861, the Treasury used the fundamentals of this design until the war's close.[33] Its typeface and design repeated the circular and some stylistic aspects of the provisional government's seal (such as the circular format) but substituted the words *Treasury Department* ("Tre^{s} Dep^{t}")and a lone palmetto. In March 1864, worn down by use, the Treasury replaced the seal with an almost identical one. The tree in both devices acknowledged South Carolina's driving role in secession and the first treasurer's home state. Furthermore, its parochial overtones reflected the nation as a Confederacy of independent states.

The seals employed by other branches of government conveyed fewer political ideas. In Julius Baumgarten's design for the War Department seal, a twelve-star Stars and Bars flies over a cannon, tents, and a bearded soldier. Combining the new Confederate flag with a figure dressed in uniform from the War of 1812 and Revolutionary War cannon makes its imagery an odd mix of past and present. However, their grouping also connected America's military past with a Confederate present. Similarly, other departmental seals essayed themes close to their area of focus. Baumgarten also designed the Post Office Department seal, probably after May 1861. In it, he expressed more contemporary and contiguous ideas of connection through forms of transport: a paddleboat, stagecoach, and steam train. In contrast to the sense of modernity in the Post Office seal, the Department of Justice's use of Themis, the Greek titaness of justice, linked that branch of government to classical times. Other departmental seals, like that of the Patent Office, which featured the Confederate president Jefferson Davis, or the Department of State, which featured the Battle Flag, took imagery from contemporary experience. These devices made the Confederate government seem more authoritative, substantial, and present.

While government departments procured seals with little delay, the committee working on the great seal and flag appeared to be a most sluggish group. In February 1861, its members worked feverishly and released a flag to an eager nation within a month. But a great seal took longer. With secession's flush gone, the committee's activity slowed. Congress rejected the designs they submitted, and a year later the government still used the temporary seal. Reflecting on the situation, one newspaper bemoaned, in March 1862, that a design "could be done in a morning by capable individuals."[34] Then, as Lee's army advanced into Maryland in September 1862 and weeks after the second session's start, Congress rejected another flurry of ideas presented by the committee. As a result, as 1862 drew to a close, the Confederacy still had no great seal.

January 1863's third session proved more productive. The committee worked with energy and, alongside prototypes for the second national flag, developed a series of designs. The wreath's evolution suggested the scope of the congressmen's concerns. Consisting of wealthy planters, the committee initially chose only images of the slave-raised cash crops that brought them riches: sugarcane, rice, cotton, and tobacco. However, in a clear nod to the South's majority of non-slaveholding farmers, they later added staples of wheat and corn in the final design. An attempt by slaveholders to install a cavalier as its central image led to the choice of the equestrian statue of George Washington displayed on the grounds of the Confederate capitol. While this spoke to their American past and referenced war and independence, Washington's Southern blood and slave-based wealth linked him more to the ruling class than to common Southerners. Finally, their choice of motto, "Deo Vindice" (meaning "God [our] Defender/Protector), the product of intense last-minute debate and various translations, proclaimed God as an active force in the nation. In late April 1863, the committee published its description of "The Great Seal of the Confederate States of America." Its later history showed both the growth and limitations of Confederate identity.

In June 1863, the newly commissioned captain of the CSS *Alabama*, Raphael Semmes, decorated his commission with a version of the seal. Fashioned from donated boxwood, using penknives and surgical tools, its use marked a rare appearance of the great seal on an official document.[35] Although engravers existed within Confederate borders, the government believed none possessed the skill or machinery needed to create a work befitting the nation. The government's choice of a premier manufacturer of state regalia in the United Kingdom doomed the enterprise. Completed in late June 1864, the silver seal arrived in Richmond in early August 1864. However, a strengthening Union blockade kept the large press needed for it to work in Bermuda. The great seal's story and its imagery captured the Confederate story: a nation with grand ideas and patriotic citizens but lacking the capacity to realize them due to internal weakness and a Union intent on its subjugation.

Still, the image of the great seal entered the Confederate visual milieu. Between 1863 and 1865, three Confederate periodicals—the *Record of New, History and Literature, Southern Field and Fireside,* and the *Mercury*—adopted it as their masthead. Publishers' decision to use the Confederate seal reflected a wish to associate their magazines with the Southern nation.[36] Additionally, it appeared on 130,000 6 percent Treasury bonds (Types 157, 158, and 159) and on over 150,000 five hundred–dollar Confederates notes (T-64) issued from April 1864. Yet no evidence exists to prove that their inclusion expressed any more than the printer's whim. The copies of the great seal joined other more widely used iconography to make the Confederate government visible.

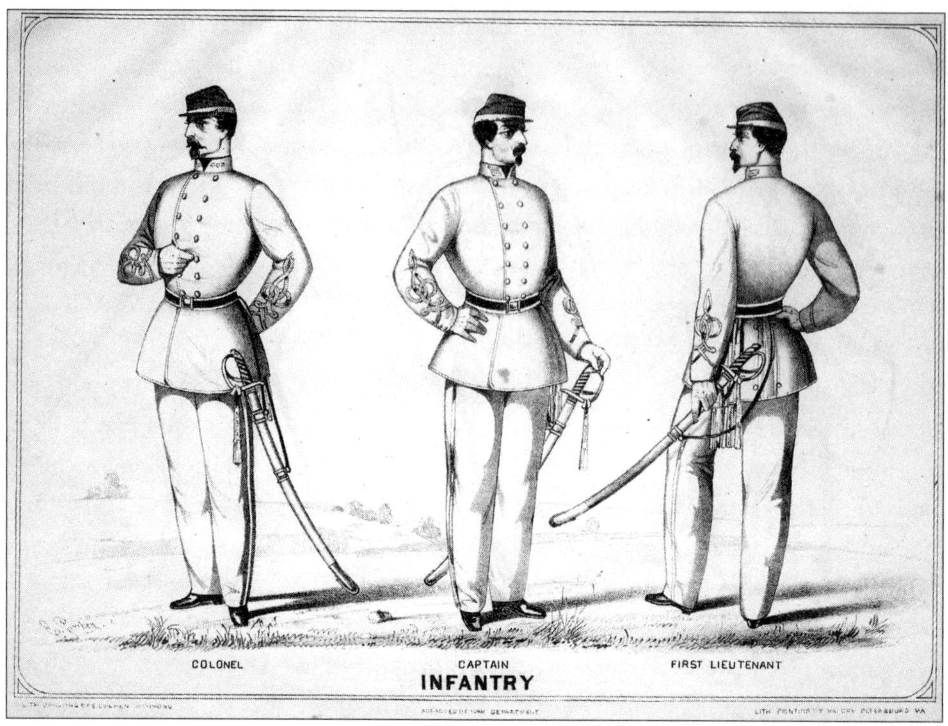

FIG. 1.3. Infantry officers' uniforms, by Eugene Crehen, *Uniform and Dress of the Army of the Confederate States* (Richmond, Va.: Charles H. Wynne, 1861). Courtesy of the National Archives and Records Administration.

AN ARMY UNIFORM

In the design of the army's uniform, the War Department created a national marker that consciously projected a modern nation. Over May 1861, enthusiastic amateur and professional soldiers, together with a tailor, met in Montgomery, Alabama, to draw up this outfit.[37] On May 4, 1861, Francis S. Bartow, congressional military affairs committee member and captain of a Savannah, Georgia, showpiece volunteer company, determined gray for the coat's color.[38] Two days later, Quartermaster General Myer requested that merchant tailor Henry Hamburger come from New Orleans to Montgomery. Hamburger was unavailable, however, and the authorities in New Orleans sent Edward Cain (1834–71) in his stead.[39] Meanwhile, on May 15, 1861, Myers's request for samples of gray cloth from six major Southern woolen mills confirmed this choice as the shade of the uniform.[40] With Cain's "experience and judgment" and the input of Lieutenant Colonel George Deas of the Adjutant General's Department, the quartermaster developed details of the Confederate uniform.[41] By

May 23, 1861, they had established the cadet-gray double-breasted tunic with sky-blue trousers as the regular army's basic livery. The color of cuff and collar facings showed the wearer's branch of service—sky-blue for infantry, yellow for cavalry, red for artillery, and buff for staff and general officers.[42]

The design of their military's uniform displayed more than military fancy. Contemporary military science rejected formfitting and showy uniforms in favor of more practical and austere clothing that allowed greater ease of movement.[43] The Confederate regulation's "loose-cut" trousers, its tunic's lack of epaulettes and lacing, full-cut sleeves, and collar to be made low enough to "permit the chin to turn freely" embodied these ideas.[44] Its thigh-length tunic, adopted within a decade by the United States Army, showed more similarities with European than American military dress. Additionally, the use of the kepi as headgear and the Austrian knots prescribed for officers' sleeves showed the influence of the preeminent Western military nation of the time—France (fig. 1.3).[45] The Confederate uniform not only differentiated its forces from those of the United States but also presented their nation as forward-looking.[46]

After creating such a dynamic design, the military showed little awareness of its symbolic importance. With little notice, the Adjutant General's Department released the full dress regulations on June 6, 1861. Even a week later, Quartermaster General Myers wrote to an officer that "no uniform has been proscribed for the Confederate States Army."[47] Ultimately, it took more than two months before the outfit received publicity. At that time, the War Department went into partnership with printer Blanton Duncan to produce an illustrated edition of the orders for distribution.[48] While antebellum military suppliers produced illustrated catalogs of the United States Army dress, the Confederate government's sponsorship of this publication broke new ground. With "superb" illustrations prepared by Eugene Crehen, Blanton Duncan published colored and uncolored editions between September 1, 1861, and June 1, 1862.[49] Duncan printed an extra one thousand black-and-white copies and later offered full-color editions for private sale. The most novel aspect of the work was the cutting plate, designed to offer "full guidance to tailors."[50] It showed that despite a slow start, the Confederate War Department had determined to use innovative methods to ensure the public and military knew the proper appearance of their regular army.

The Confederate War Department never mandated or issued regulation dress for its enlisted men, and only toward the end of the war did it provide uniforms for officers unable to afford them. As will be seen in later chapters, circumstance or choice more than anything determined what Confederate soldiers wore. Unlike military clothing, the nature of currency and postage stamps meant that Confederates had greater need for the central government to provide a regular and reliable supply of both. However, this effort strained Southerners' trust in their government.

A NATIONAL CURRENCY

Governments, like people, need money to survive. While nations now appreciate currency's iconographic power in conveying national narratives, and so closely manage their designs, the Confederate government did not take this approach. Treasurer C. G. Memminger performed his role with what Douglas Ball described as "a strange amalgam of laxity and severity."[51] It is clear in Memminger's response to a request from a New Orleans engraver for plates and paper for a bond on February 27, 1861. Notably, his only instructions as to the design were that it be "handsome and difficult to counterfeit."[52] And a little more than a week later, he asked another New Orleans engraver to merely alter an existing United States bond rather than create an original design.[53] Shortly thereafter, any mention of design disappeared from Memminger's correspondence, and his subsequent record showed him to be more pragmatist than idealist. The nation required money, and the treasurer gave more attention to the paper needed to print the first forty-one different Treasury notes than to the designs that appeared on them.

Congress authorized the issue of interest-bearing Treasury bonds on February 28, 1861, and notes a little over a week later. These made it possible for the Confederacy to begin paying for itself. It did so in a setting that emerged from antebellum America's complicated monetary system. Before the war, Americans had conducted business using a mixture of species, paper money, and promissory notes. Although the Union produced coinage, its supply varied, and necessity forced entities such as banks, townships, and railroad companies to issue their own notes to meet the shortfall. Memminger's actions in early 1861 indicated that he intended to continue this pattern. The three mints that existed in seceding states added $1.3 million in silver and gold coins, using United States dies, to Confederate coffers. But, although Memminger intended to produce distinctively designed Confederate specie, ultimately war intervened before he finalized any Confederate coinage.[54] Later, Memminger determined it too expensive to keep the mints running and decided bullion and paper notes would be more useful than coinage. On May 14, 1861, following the treasurer's advice, Congress approved an act abolishing the mints after June 1, 1861. Although in 1862 the Senate twice attempted to introduce Confederate coinage, paper notes became the major form of Confederate currency.[55]

Confederate paper currency's history began on March 9, 1861, when Congress authorized the Treasury to issue notes to pay sums for "such exigencies as public need may require."[56] However, with no suitable engravers in the South, Southerners faced the indignity of seeing a Yankee company's name under their nation's title on their first Treasury notes.[57] Production quickly slipped South of the Mason-Dixon Line when, on April 25, 1861, Union authorities seized the plates for the Confederacy's bonds and banknotes.[58]

Although the Confederate constitution placed severe restrictions on its government's ability to promote or protect industries, the needs of the central government trumped these restrictions.[59] The Treasury sent agents throughout the South and North for men and materials, and later it helped businesses by importing skilled laborers and protecting civilians from conscription. Because of these efforts, by the end of 1861, the government's help and patronage helped growth-minded men to set up five separate printing companies (including three newly formed enterprises) to design and produce Confederate currency. The money they created tied citizens to a national economy.

Americans had experienced national paper currency before, but the Confederate's use of these notes surprised Memminger. In March 1862, he admitted that "the Treasury notes of this Government perform some function that was not foreseen, and that function is probably their agency in providing domestic exchange."[60]

The imagery used on these notes has recently attracted some historians' attention. They have postulated the meanings that Treasury note vignettes conveyed to Confederate audiences. John Majewski sees clues concerning Confederates' attempts to modernize their economy.[61] In the mixture of pictures, Ian Binnington finds evidence of a developing "Confederate Americanism" that embraced slavery, American heritage, and government.[62] More recently, Christian M. Lengyel has recognized the predominance of white heroes and officials and the increased use of tangible subjects that conveyed a sense of permanence and trustworthiness.[63] It is not so clear if Confederates themselves shared these understandings. Indeed, Confederate documents show that practicality rather than concerns about meanings or messages determined the appearance of most Confederate Treasury notes.[64]

Initially, rather than conscious and directed constructions, Secretary Memminger left the choice of vignettes to the notes' five printers.[65] Until the latter part of 1862, a request to Southern banks to borrow their printing plates was the Treasurer's sole contribution to the imagery used on Confederate notes.[66] In August 1862, this led one insider to write that up to that time, "every item of ornament was a specimen from an existing engraving."[67] Studying prewar banknotes shows that at least two-thirds of Confederate notes used recycled imagery (see appendix). Besides these, Memminger's printers turned to any other suitable and readily available pictures. This approach brought Confederate currency festooned with allegorical imagery. Around half of the notes related to law, industry, and commerce, and almost as many portrayed American personalities and characters. As the war progressed, portraits of a handful of Confederate leaders joined the secondhand vignettes. Collectively, the notes' familiar style and imagery, interspersed with an occasional original vignette, presented a continuity of antebellum ideas and made Confederate banknotes incidental rather than intentional nationalist iconography.

While Confederates may not have intended that imagery used on their notes conveyed distinctive messages about their nation, the quality of the notes did, creating concerns about the competence of the government. At their best, Confederates viewed their banknotes with pride. Charleston's *Mercury* praised the Southern Bank Note Company's five dollar bill (Type-31), describing it as "one of the most perfect specimens of workmanship we have ever seen."[68] Presented the proof for Hoyer and Ludwig's issue, an optimistic Memminger wrote across its back: "When the money changers become more familiar with these uncanny bills, it will be as difficult to pass a counterfeit as if they had been engraved on steel by an expert—maybe more so."[69] But they did not impress others. For example, in August 1861, when the Richmond *Whig*'s editor saw the first notes, he said they were "printed on flimsy paper" and "engraved with more expedition than care."[70] Initially, the notes that entered the Confederate economy reflected not only the disparate assortment of printers but also the government's disorganization. This resulted in problems that further compromised the government's standing.

The staggering thirty-odd designs used on eight denominations issued up to December 1862 created financial uncertainty and compromised the government in the public eye. Issued often with little public notice, the notes' unfamiliarity and variable quality led some financial institutions to declare genuine notes counterfeits.[71] Additionally, the lithographic printing technique added to confusion because it resulted in subtle differences between notes bearing the same design. The *Augusta Chronicle and Sentinel* reported in September 1862, for instance, that it discerned 11 variations in a packet of 150 Confederate twenty-dollar notes. The newspaper wondered: "How can it be expected counterfeiting can be guarded against when every engraver is allowed to choose his own design and mode of executing his work . . . We are sometimes inclined to think that the Government itself does not know its own issues."[72]

The mediocre quality of Confederate notes stung the editor of the *Tuscaloosa Observer*. The notes were, he observed wryly, "so badly executed that the Yankee cannot attempt to counterfeit them without the display of superior artistic skill which betrays the fraud."[73] Ultimately, at one point in August 1862, Memminger recalled hundreds of thousands of dollars of notes printed by Hoyer and Ludwig because of uncertainty about whether they were genuine.

The poor and inconsistent printing quality of these notes as much as the plethora of designs fueled the manic fear of counterfeiting that grew between September 1861 and August 1862. Northern facsimiles and Southern fakes appeared with startling regularity. "Money," Josh Lauer wrote recently, "is fundamentally a measure of social trust," and the amount of sham Confederate money in circulation eroded public confidence in the currency.[74] In response to the crisis, Congress made counterfeiting and forgery a capital offense and pressured the Treasury to act.[75] The solution delivered a more standardized set of banknote designs. The arrival of Scottish engraver George Dunn and his team of skilled craftsmen became fundamental in this initiative. Contracted by the Confederate government in early 1862, Dunn and five other English engravers arrived in July 1862. In time, their experience, expertise, and awareness of all facets of banknote and pictorial engraving impacted many parts of wartime print imagery.[76] In short order, Dunn advocated that Confederates "adopt a style of our own" and engaged with Irish-born Edward Charles Keatinge (1825/6–82) to develop a set of unique and standardized designs.[77]

Unlike earlier notes, Memminger and his staff took a more active role in the development of these notes. Treasury officials kept him informed about the intended designs and the alterations they made to Keatinge's designs. Memminger himself sourced images of subjects and specified that the image of C. C. Clay replace that of W. L. Yancey on the one-dollar note.[78] Furthermore, he checked and approved the proofs of each note.[79] Although the Treasury intended to issue a five hundred–dollar note in this series, the department deferred its release after the one hundred–dollar note as the five hundred–dollar note's plate's complex designs slowed production.[80] From December 1862, the results of Memminger's collaboration with his staff and artists Dunn and Keatinge, the notes of the fifth series, entered circulation from lowest to highest denomination.

Released between December 1862 and April 1863, this set of notes represented a vast improvement over the department's earlier issues. While Memminger's Treasury acted as pragmatists rather than nationalists, their efforts served both objectives to some extent. The notes' use of symmetry and original vignettes featuring contemporary national figures, locations, and scenes rendered using high-quality engraving represented a distinct departure from the previous series.[81] Predominantly depicting government identities or state capitols, they presented the nation as primarily a political entity. The single martial scene, the only sign of the war, downplayed the military's importance in the nation's survival. Although their imagery made them uniquely Confederate in proportion and design, they shared more similarity to U.S. greenbacks than to any other note issued in the Western hemisphere.

Discussing these notes, the press found much other than the vignettes for comment. In early January 1863, a Raleigh newspaper described the new issue one-dollar note as "handsomely printed . . . the engraving finely executed on steel." It stated that the bills represented "a great improvement on the old notes."[82] However, the quality was not consistent. Viewing a fifth series ten-dollar bill, Richmond's *Enquirer* praised Keatinge's engraving but described the Blanton Duncan's printing as "execrable."[83] Despite these reservations, the influential *Charleston Mercury* greeted the improvement. At last, wrote the editor, the government had "permanent" and "extremely beautiful" banknotes "honorable to us as a nation."[84] Confederate editors took pride not only in each bill's appearance but also in the process used to create them. Before the war, one informed observer wrote, "shrewd Yankees" monopolized all engraving and printing. Now, "despite the blockade," the Treasury had five separate establishments working on government bills whose quality defied "the ingenuity of Northern counterfeiters."[85] The improved quality met with the approval of many Confederates and reduced their nervousness about fakes.

Original portraits and scenes became the main feature of these notes and the main obstacle in their production. Their selection and development offer insights into the Treasury's priorities. Each portrait depicted a Confederate personality of some note, and the scenes featured Confederate state capitols or the military. In the present day, currency designers commonly use depictions of internal assets such as these to promote national identity.[86] While superficially the Treasury's choice of imagery appeared to signal this intention, the evidence shows that it was merely a by-product of Memminger's battle against counterfeiting.[87] This is seen in the portrait of deposed secretary of war George W. Randolph used on the one-hundred-dollar bill (fig. 1.4). Although Memminger suggested replacing it with the image of the current secretary, James A. Seddon, they could find no suitable likeness, and Randolph head remained on the issued note.[88] But such a choice probably made little impact on the populace. Indeed, the identity of those portrayed on Treasury notes mystified some Confederates. Even a year after their introduction, Wilmington's *Journal* was uncertain if the portrait on the twenty-dollar note represented Vice President Stephens. Additionally, it believed that the portrait on the ten-dollar bill represented Secretary of Navy Mallory, rather than R.M.T. Hunter, despite Hunter's portrait's appearance on six earlier Confederate notes.[89] What was clear was the imagery's "Confederateness." And thanks to these pictures and other security measures (such as tinting the paper pink and intricately colored back designs), counterfeiters now faced more hurdles.

While the improvements decreased the number of counterfeit notes in circulation, the fake bills did not disappear. In late 1863, detectives uncovered a circle of counterfeiters that included a printer from the Treasury's Note Bureau. In response, the Treasury ordered printers to add further safeguards to each note's design. To meet this demand, Keatinge and Ball requested the transfer of artist Henry Hunton (1840–1921) from his position in the Topographical Engineers to the Note Bureau.[90] Hunton probably designed the new vignette of Confederate artillery in action that

FIG. 1.4. $100 Confederate Treasury note (front and back). Type-49, fifth series issue, Apr. 1863, including portraits of Mrs. Lucy Pickens, wife of the South Carolina governor (*center*), and George W. Randolph, former Confederate secretary of war (*right*). Courtesy of Pierre Fricke, https://www.buyvintagemoney.com.

appeared on the 1864 ten-dollar bill (Type-68). This replaced the picture of South Carolina's proposed state capitol that appeared on the previous issue. Reporting on the new vignette, Richmond's *Enquirer* hoped that the issue notes would be "something beautiful, tangible, and worth keeping."[91] Released as the seventh series, these alterations entailed reworking each notes' blue back device and adding a red linear pattern to the face.[92]

Released in April 1864, the notes of the seventh series issue met with a mixed reception. "Though rapidly got up," wrote the *Macon Telegraph*, "the new issue is an improvement on the old."[93] Their Confederate nickname—"Blue Backs"—showed that some felt more than a monetary attachment to these slips of paper.[94] None mentioned, however, that the imagery on all notes now related directly to the Confederate nation or that a third now featured military scenes. Rather, it was the quality of design and production that provoked comment. The *Richmond Enquirer* feared that the currency suggested to the world "that we are barbarians in all that pertains to the fine arts."[95] Later Richmond's *Examiner* presented the "tinkering and scratching" with the notes' designs as evidence of "haste and confusion."[96] A writer for *Smith and Barrow's Monthly Magazine* went further in criticizing the design: "To all the absurdities of design which disfigured the old, we have superadded, in the notes of the new issue, a tawdry system of tinting, strongly suggestive of the cheap style 'popular' colored prints."[97] More significant than the imagery was the shortfall in the amount issued and the apparent favoritism shown in its distribution. "Whether such conduct is to be entitled as autocratic indifference or as reckless stupidity, we do not care to inquire," wrote the *Richmond Examiner.* It concluded that the problem lay with Memminger. Despite "nearly two months wherein to manufacture his new money . . . he has done little more than walk the streets with his head wrapped up in a red comforter and indulge his other little eccentricities."[98] These voices used Treasury notes as a vehicle to attack an arm of a government that faced falling popularity and charges of despotism.

The Treasury notes Southerners carried with them reminded them of their shared Confederate nationality. Confidence in these slips of paper, as one newspaper reported in 1862, "is a pretty good thermometer by which to test the ardor of . . . patriotism."[99] Like flags, however, Confederate money did not enjoy a monopoly. The accounts of robberies in Confederate Richmond allow an insight into the diverse currencies Confederates carried with them. In August 1863, a thief stole from a Mrs. Murphy "$1 in Yankee money, $20 from the Bank of Georgia, and $50 in State money."[100] In April 1864, an unknown individual reported having lost a pocketbook containing "$15 in old issue 5's, $5 counterfeit—face green with a piece of paper pasted across the back, $1.30 in 10 cent stamps, 30 cent Richmond note and 25 cent Washington County note."[101] A review of court cases and reports of lost or stolen pocketbooks shows that while most Confederates carried Treasury notes, they also carried a mix of prewar specie, state and local banknotes, checks and promissory notes, and mementos in their pockets. Such reports indicate that, like flags, Confederate pockets expressed multiple and, occasionally, contending associations.

The variety of currencies Confederates needed also reflected a continuity of the prewar situation in which various shinplasters filled the need created by the frequent shortages of fractional species.[102] The Treasury's decision not to print denominations less than five dollars until 1862 worsened the situation. Across the South, cities, banks, and other organizations issued paper notes for amounts up to one dollar. By mid-July 1861, Richmond's *Enquirer* noted that the small notes had driven coins out of circulation.[103] Yet, like antebellum America's less-regulated economy, counterfeits abounded, and merchants became wary. In February 1862, when shinplasters from Atlanta, Montgomery, and Mobile "flooded" Selma, Alabama, the local newspaper suggested "a word to the wise" that they only use the change bills issued by the Tennessee and Mississippi Railroad.[104] In North Carolina during March 1863, newspapers warned that criminals had produced shinplasters for two bogus North Carolina manufacturers. The editor of Asheville's *News* stated, "The country is flooded with trash of this description and the people cannot be too careful."[105] However, caution generated other issues. Around the same time, spurious notes like these caused traders in states neighboring North Carolina to be selective in the money they accepted. This move stung the pride of the editor of Raleigh's *Weekly Standard*. "Our negroes," he wrote, "are quite as valuable, and are held by as secure a tenure as those of South Carolina . . . we have more white men, and consequently more labor and intelligence than that State . . . we have more and better minerals . . . more and better timber . . . more and better manufacturing establishments of all kinds . . . our currency is as good as that of any State on the continent [and] we have more troops in the field."[106] In this context, one writer worried, "If this is the confidence which is to exist between the States of the Confederacy, I predict that it will be short-lived."[107] While confidence in North Carolina's currency returned, the situation arose because the monetary systems struggled to deal with wartime stresses.

The variety of monies Confederates carried in their pockets reflected not only the fractured but also the fragile nature of their economy. Insecurity and inflation ensured that metal currency did not disappear from the economy. In May 1862, Richmond vendors reacted to uncertainty about the worth of shinplasters by demanding payment only in specie. Richmond's *Enquirer* lamented that payments required "two or three Yankee made, and Union emblemed copper cents."[108] The newspaper noted, in March 1864, that buyers parted with "hoarded species" to take advantage of merchants who sold goods for silver or gold at a fraction of what they cost in currency.[109] However, shortage of specie, as much as anything else, guaranteed that Confederate currency circulated more than any other money in the Civil War South.

Confederate Treasury notes contributed to the story of the Confederate government in a variety of ways beyond their monetary worth. Like the diverse loyalties and associations at play within the Confederate borders, the notes existed as one form of money among many and a visually unstable one at that. The treasurer's loose management of the design and production of Confederate currency and the need to produce Confederate notes in quantity led to expedience. Produced using substandard materials by printers of varying skills, they made a physical statement of the South's unpreparedness to be a self-sufficient nation. Additionally, the variety of designs used on the first issues led to confusion that affected the economy and provided an avenue for attacking the Davis administration. From late 1862, the issues of notes presented a more coherent and standardized appearance. Focused on combatting counterfeiting, the designers settled on images that would foil criminals ahead of those aimed at unifying the people. However, even after these efforts Confederate notes still embarrassed some. In March 1864, Richmond's *Enquirer* wrote of the notes that "no one of taste" could help but "blush every time he handled one."[110] While the Treasury's notes enabled the Confederate economy to function, their production showed an arm of the Confederate government with little appreciation of their capacity to reinforce or build national ideas.

POSTAGE STAMPS

Smaller visual articles afforded the government another avenue to create a visual presence. At first, under its dutiful secretary, John Reagan, the Post Office initially enjoyed popular acclamation. At its best, Reagan's Postal Department contributed subtly to nation building. Its services linked families but also ferried Confederate printed matter and ideas across the South. Like many other arms of the administration, however, aspects of its operation compromised public opinion of the Richmond government. The availability of stamps joined rising postal rates, delivery delays, and failures as channels for public condemnation and dissatisfaction.

In April 1861, Reagan began arrangements to procure stamps. But as the Treasury and anxious Confederates found, a lack of Southern expertise slowed the process.[111] Without postage stamps, Confederates created alternatives to show that the post office had received the fee for mailing an article. In New Orleans, Postmaster Riddle printed stamps for use in his locale. Other postmasters simply stamped or marked envelopes as "paid." These stopgaps wore on Confederate patience. In September 1861, Nashville's *Republican Banner* agreed with Richmond's *Examiner* in calling the delay in supplying stamps "curious, if not inexcusable." The lack of facilities for engraving, the *Examiner* maintained, was no reason for delay. "Stamps," its editor wrote, "have been prepared and used in New Orleans and Memphis. Almost any design or execution might answer temporary purposes, and avoid the serious inconvenience of mailing letters only during office hours."[112] When a month later the *New Orleans Picayune*'s Richmond correspondent announced the imminent issuing of the first stamps, he reported that the delay was a "serious subject of complaint" among people.[113] Having waited so long, the *Charleston Mercury*'s "Hermes" was skeptical. In mid-October 1861, he wrote: "There are no such things as Confederate Postage

Stamps and never can be. They are myths, spectres, ghosts, hobgoblins, phantoms, sheeted dead, and the like."[114] New Orleans's *Delta* took a more philosophical view. "Our people," the paper concluded, "must learn to bear and forbear in the peculiar circumstances in which we are placed."[115]

The first stamps appeared across the Confederacy over the last months of 1861. Although welcomed for their convenience in mailing envelopes and as small change, the new stamps brought more reasons to criticize the government.[116] The quality of printing, from lithograph rather than the traditional engraved steel plates, worried people. As one observer noted, the results were little better than if printed from "an ordinary brass stamp."[117] The ten-cent blue, bearing Thomas Jefferson's portrait, exhibited such low quality that in November 1861, one correspondent mistook Jefferson for George Washington. He described it as "a hideous attempt" and thought it "will be laughed at."[118] A little later, another newspaper reported the stamps' only weakness was "that they have a bad habit of seceding from the letter on which they are placed . . . they need a little adhesiveness."[119] Moreover, Reagan underestimated the number of stamps needed. The post office in Montgomery, Alabama, ran short within days, and the postmaster in Savannah, Georgia, reported that by the end of November 1861, they were still waiting to receive any stamps.[120] In January 1862, the *Memphis Appeal* concluded that the stamps were "poor quality, high priced and not enough in number to supply the wants of our people."[121]

As the war progressed, criticisms of Reagan and his department abated.[122] While the first stamps were being distributed across the South, Richmond's *Dispatch* reported that Reagan had contracted with a steel plate engraver. This, they reported, would enable the production of stamps "in the best style of the art," bearing the "likenesses of different statesmen of the South."[123] Reagan also made sure that supply matched demand. In April 1863, the Post Office Department supplied the new ten-cent stamp in such amounts that newspapers reported that they quickly became a "popular currency . . . as much sought for change . . . as for posting mail matter."[124] This pattern only grew, and the next year the *Macon Telegraph* reported that individuals were paying debts worth over one hundred dollars using stamps alone.[125] When, in May 1863, the Post Office Department's annual report showed a profit, the *Richmond Sentinel* called it "a most gratifying result" compared to the department's performance in the previous year. The *Sentinel* predicted that the report for 1862–63 was "one that the country will contemplate with pleasure." Furthermore, the *Sentinel* called the new twenty-cent stamp not only "very handsome" and its likeness of George Washington "very excellent" but also a most convenient way of paying postage on double letters and packages.[126] The postmaster general's reports for the period July 1, 1862, to June 30, 1864, show that his department supplied the Confederacy with over 44 million two-cent, 74 million five-cent, 335 million ten-cent, and 9 million twenty-cent stamps.[127] By the end of the war, a critic of Confederate currency designs viewed the nation's postage stamps as superior to any nation's and a point of pride.[128] But problems in supply arose when postage stamp production moved from Richmond to Columbia, South Carolina. In response, Confederate postmasters, in places such as Salisbury, North Carolina, prepared and sold envelopes stamped PAID for citizens to use.[129] Even as Federal forces took back more of the South and the Confederate transportation failed, criticism of the Post Office remained muted.

The same could not be said for Southerners' opinion of all the "Southern statesmen" featured on the stamps. Though the choice of portraits of Washington on the twenty-cent, Jefferson for the ten-cent, and Jackson on the two-cent drew no comment and reinforced notions of Southerners' historic fitness to rule, some found President Jefferson Davis's likeness problematic. The first living American to have his portrait appear on a stamp, the choice reflected the popularity Davis enjoyed. But when the *Charleston Courier*'s Richmond correspondent, "Sumter," learned in late September 1861 that Davis's portrait would appear on the five-cent stamp, he worried that it "savors too much of monarchism."[130] The writer's observation anticipated the increased criticisms the president faced as his government encroached on Confederate lives.[131] However, few newspapers made any comment that Davis's portrait appeared on more stamp designs than any other figure. A rare and widely published exception appeared during spring 1863. "Hermes," the Richmond correspondent of the bitterly anti-Davis *Charleston Mercury*, reported an anecdote. In it, a drunken soldier "accosted" the president near the capitol. The infantryman identified "Mr. Davis" because he "looked like a postage stamp."[132] The tale belittled Davis as his government's impact on Confederate lives grew. Conscription and greater government control of agriculture, manufacturing, and Southerners' lives drove Confederates from Davis and his nation.[133] Nevertheless, the only suggestion of disrespect or distance visible in Confederates' use of stamps bearing Davis's likeness was the occasional stamp turned sideways or upside down on the envelope. The need or desire to communicate drew Southerners to post offices and the use and dissemination of iconography that reinforced Confederate identity.

Circumstance as much as intention played its part in the way government shaped its official iconography. In the nation's first peaceful months, the Provisional Congress and various departments worked proactively, but in an ad hoc manner, to create iconography. In March 1861, the convention established a flag but did not ratify it. The Treasury issued national currency but in a plethora of designs that shook Confederate's trust in their currency. Likewise, the War Department adopted a uniform but failed to correct erroneous reports about it or publish the correct dress regulations for months. Then, from the second half of 1861, the Confederate government slowed its response to the nation's need for imagery. As Southern politicians debated matters of necessity, such as the impact of increased martial law or conscription, matters of national symbology took a back seat to necessity.[134] To one newspaperman, it seemed the Flag and Seal Committee only leapt into action when "stimulated."[135] Certainly, it moved in fits and starts between 1861 and May 1863, when it delivered designs for the new flag and great seal. Similarly, Memminger's Treasury instituted a standard currency only when counterfeiting threatened the financial system. Additionally, concurrent to the Confederate government's creation of iconography, states created their own flags, seals, and currencies that competed with the central government. However, regardless of these flaws, many Southerners embraced both the government and its symbols.

The Confederate government intentionally and incidentally established its insignia. Part of the trappings of the nineteenth-century nation-state, these emblems projected a sense of the government as an entity throughout the nation's borders. Some contributed to an impression of solidity and substance and provided symbolic glue for the new nation. The subjective iconography of individual pieces expressed ideas of progressiveness, continuity of American nationalism, and sui generis "Confederateness." But collective imagery told of more than an embryonic nation struggling to present itself with a coherent nationalism. It presented evidence of political self-interest, a government learning its business, and not only the diversity of public opinion but also people's increasing disenchantment with both Congress and the administration.

Besides the government, other sources provided Confederates with artifacts that allowed them to see their nation and the ideas that bound them together. Of these racism was fundamental. While often cloaked in the government's iconography, a less restrained Confederate mass culture also drew on these emotions and ideologies. In their representations of race these producers shaped and presented these ideas in a variety of ways as they sought a share of their nation's marketplace.

CHAPTER 2

Nativism and Depictions of Race

The Constitution of the Confederate States of America is based on the acknowledged inequality of the races.
—ALEXANDER HAMILTON STEPHENS, Atlanta, March 13, 1861

They have given another stunning and dishonoring blow to the villainous invaders of our soul and have illustrated afresh, in the eyes of the world, the mastery of the Southern race over the bastard hordes of the North.
—*Richmond Whig*, October 25, 1861

Division formed an inherent part of the Confederate national fabric. The systems and iconography developed by the Confederate government in 1861 may have helped Southerners to imagine a collective unity, but to do so ignored their diversity. Drawn together by mass paranoia and a determination to protect racial slavery, the nation lacked the emotive unifying narratives common to contemporary European nationalist movements. Compared to the deep-rooted national narratives, distinct languages, and rich cultural heritage of Europe's nations, Southerners' justifications for separation from the North seemed slight. In the quest for a raison d'être, Confederates cast around for grounds other than fear and self-interest. Some, like Vice President Alexander Stephens, looked to race.

Using race to create a sense of national unity made some sense. With around 87 percent of white Southerners having been born in America, it afforded a sense of homogeneity. Other sections of antebellum America also used race to foster a common identity. As David Roediger has shown, white workers in Northern states manufactured a sense of commonality through language, humor, song, and folklore that created a sense of racial distinctiveness.[1] Additionally, writers used the spurious pseudoscience surrounding race and ethnicity to imagine a hierarchy of humanity.[2] Southerners drew on notions of racial superiority to defend black people's servitude and imagine a national role as mentoring guardians for any people they considered inferior.[3] They also used race to explain Southern exceptionalism and the North's antagonism to slavery, and to demonize their enemy.[4] Building a nation on race also came with powerful political and scientific precedents. Casting the South's attempt to safeguard their political and economic power as a "racial struggle" fit into the ideas of romantic nationalists.[5] Writers such as Sir Walter Scott and Johann Gottlieb constructed mythic pasts to claim a national identity among particular European groups. Drawing on ideas like these, Southern nationalists, and their Confederate inheritors, sought to define themselves as a separate people. However, writes Stephen J. Gould, "errors" pervade racial pseudoscience that are both "deep and insidious."[6] Manipulated by social attitudes, these theories confused subjective considerations such as race, ethnic background, values, and personalities with scientific certainties.[7] Confederates pictured these ambiguities and issues as they attempted to represent race.

The Confederacy's primary national symbol—its flags—showed the reach and impact of these ideas. Of the over 110 designs submitted by Southerners to the Flag and Seal Committee, only five designs referred to race, which suggests that few Southerners believed race deserved acknowledgment in their national colors. However, it figured in the committee's decision making. In rejecting the popular call to adopt the U.S. flag's red and white stripes, the accompanying report stated that the committee did so to free the design from any associations with races they believed inferior.[8] In similar fashion, the committee avoided any overt depiction of race in its design of the Second National colors. Despite the committee's intentions, one Confederate commentator called it "the white man's flag," and another stated that it represented "a superior race and higher civilization."[9] For these individuals, the flag symbolized a belief in white people's preeminence.

NATIVE AND FOREIGN-BORN NORTHERNERS

Confederate ideology also revealed different shades of white in imaginings of race. Antebellum Southern nationalists had already embroidered differences between North and South, and in wartime Confederates built on these ideas. Newspapers portrayed Northerners as their people's counter die and the "Yankee" their absolute opposite: Yankees were a people morally weak, pretentious, and prey to fanatical obsessions with radical moral philosophies. They imagined Yankees as a rapacious people whose selfish desire for material things extended to acquiring nations.[10] Identifying this opposite helped Confederates conjure who they were and created a psychological distance between themselves and their former countrymen. However, while making race the cause of these differences enabled Confederates to justify their pursuit of nationhood, it also showed the limitations of using such a plastic concept.

Uncertainty surrounded whether birth, behavior, or merely where they lived made a person a Yankee or Confederate. Those who believed in lineage's role claimed Confederates descended from aristocratic Norman cavaliers or Scots-Irish and Anglo-Saxons. Northerners, they thought, derived from Puritans of either Anglo-Saxon or undetermined blood.[11] Other Southerners rejected these concepts and reasoned that the differences between Northern and Southern peoples lay elsewhere.[12] In 1853, a member of the South's ruling class, James Chesnut, found a people's "character and condition" more important than ethnic heritage.[13] Confederate visual culture reflected this uncertainty in its representations of Yankees.

Physiognomy provided Confederates with a visual vocabulary capable of depicting Yankees as a race. Sources such as Eden Warwick's *Nasology: or, Hints toward Classification of Noses* identified noses by nationality.[14] *The Yankee and the Dutchman,* a series of six cartoons published in May 1863 by arch-secessionist Blanton Duncan in *Fun for the Camp—A Comic Medley,* used noses to show ethnicity. The fourth scene showed Jonathan "the Yankee" and Hans "the Dutchman" and a brutish-looking recruit learning to drill (fig. 2.1).[15] Jonathan's triangular nose conformed to Warwick's "Anglo-American" nose: "thin and sharp . . . as a national nose, the most unthinking of any of the Gothic stock." Its owner acted on "animal impulse and not sage reflection."[16] The series presented Jonathan as an archetypal Yankee, encouraging Hans to enlist to gain his enlistment bounty. In camp, he relishes playing soldier but leaves the sturdy Hans and his comrades to fight. Being a Yankee, his own desires, rather than higher matters, govern his actions.

The Yankee and the Dutchman shows that Confederates possessed the capacity to depict the Yankee as a racial type.[17] However, they rarely used it. More often, they used other methods to show the differences between people. This is clear across the thirty-three scenes of *Pictures of the Great American Fight,* also contained in *Fun for the Camp.* This illustrated story presented the war as a boxing match between North and South. In it, the contestants' actions, rather than altered facial features, identify them. The Confederate is nimbler, more resilient, and his blows more telling. In scenes 18 and 19, the South's withdrawal from Manassas allows him to dodge a Northern jab and then administer a passing rap on his slow-moving opponent (fig. 2.2). Other works used behavior instead of physiognomy to show the differences between people.

The vignette used on the 1862 two-dollar note presented this on the nation's currency. Described by its printer, Blanton Duncan, as depicting the South prevailing over the North, the artist showed no obvious differences in either figure's appear-

FIG. 2.1. "Jonathan, and Hans Drill," from *The Yankee and the Dutchman.* This appears to have been a Confederate version of a work of the same name originally published by Christopher, Morse and Skippon, New York, 1862. From *Fun for the Camp—A Comic Medley* (Columbia, S.C.: Blanton Duncan, ca. 1862–63). Courtesy of the Boston Athenaeum.

FIG. 2.2. Scenes 18–19 of *A Full Report of the Great American Fight.* From *Fun for the Camp—A Comic Medley* (Columbia, S.C.: Blanton Duncan, ca. 1862–63). Courtesy of the Boston Athenaeum.

ance (fig. 2.3).[18] Dressed and coifed alike and with almost identical facial features, only their poses and relationship to the eagle differentiate the two individuals. They appear more like biblical brothers than racial others. In the same way, Armistead Hurdle's (1834–65) illustration *Now Mars Walter* (fig. 2.4), created for Mary Jane

FIG. 2.3. *The South Rising in Its Might and Striking Down the North and Crippling the Eagle,* May 1862 (Types-38, 42, and 43). Central vignette of third series two-dollar note (1.7 million issued). Printed by Blanton Duncan, Columbia, S.C. Courtesy of Pierre Fricke, https://www.buyvintagemoney.com.

FIG. 2.4. "Now Mars Walter," by Armistead Uriah Hurdle, 1864. From Mary Jane Haw, *The Rivals: A Chickahominy Story, Southern Illustrated News,* Apr. 23, 1864.

Haw's novel *The Rivals,* pictured no obvious difference. Although the character and life of Walter and Charley led one to fight for the Confederacy and the other for the Union, Hurdle drew them with similar features. Duncan's and Hurdle's pictures envisaged the war as a battle between different aspects of the same people rather than races at war.

Such images encouraged Confederates to imagine Yankees as other than a race. They sidestepped differing racial backgrounds and reflected what Robert Bonner describes as Confederates' diminishing "insistence on racial difference" between Northerner and Southerner.[19] In July 1863, the *Richmond Enquirer* told its readers, "All the talk about race is dubious and spurious."[20] Discerning historic racial differences between Americans became less important when the conduct and ethnic makeup of the Northern army offered Confederates clearer targets for racism.[21]

Foreign-born Americans made up around a quarter of the Union army. While their presence expressed their gratitude for the blessings of American freedom and provided another avenue for political integration, Confederate propagandists concluded otherwise.[22] Drawing parallels between their war and the Revolution, they called these men "Hessians": "hirelings" fighting for the promise of spoils.[23] The series of cartoons titled *The Yankee and the Dutchman* contained representations of this group. In the fourth frame, "Jonathan and Hans drill," another figure joins them whose profile echoed that of the stereotypical Irishman of the period. Both Hans and the new figure's bulbous, turned-up noses were what Eden Warwick called "snub," or "celestial," noses. Such noses showed "natural weakness, mean, disagreeable disposition . . . petty insolence." The shape and greater length of the Dutchman Hans's nose, according to Warwick's theory, showed he possessed greater shrewdness and intellectual power than his snub-nosed comrade.[24] Besides the clues to their character their faces provided, other physiognomical traits, like heavy brows and full lips, hinted at both men's sensuality and indolence.[25] Men with these facial forms, works such as Warwick's suggested, lacked the intellectual capacity to appreciate the Confederate cause.

Confederate audiences also saw the Union army's ethnic diversity and relationships performed onstage. In J. J. Delchamps's *Love's Ambuscade,* the heroes converse with three enemy prisoners—a Yankee, Dutchman, and an Irishman, all captured because of the Yankee's cowardice. Each told why they had enlisted. The Irishman wanted his whiskey, the Dutchman his sleep, and the Yankee is afraid of getting cold. All want to go South for profit. The Confederate hero asks them, "Think you the brave soldiers who have defeated your plunder seeking hordes will bear to see you enjoy the wealth producing labor they have shed their blood to save?"[26] Delchamps made his audience consider a Confederate future, but Union armies brought issues of race into their midst in the present.

Hans's sensual nature also suggested darker threats to the Southern nation's future. In James D. McCabe's *The Guerrillas,* the married heroine Rose has to repel the ardent advances of two Yankee leaders. In this and other plays, Yankees' inability to resist Southern women's allure raised the specter of mixed-race offspring.[27] Contemplating the possibility in April 1863, the *Richmond Whig* wrote that once it had won peace, the South should pass "stringent laws to restrain immigration of Yankees and other foreigners." Citing "ethnologists'" warnings of mongrelization, this would, they stated, keep the "superior . . . Southern breed pure."[28]

FOREIGN-BORN SOUTHERNERS

Depicting the enemy as base, urban, and ethnically mixed hirelings made some Confederates feel more racially homogeneous.[29] However, doing so overlooked the fact that almost 5 percent of Confederates were born outside of the South. These individuals, such as English-born Confederate Francis W. Dawson, experienced bigotry from native Southerners. In 1861, Dawson ran the Federal blockade and served dutifully for two years as a captain on the staff of Confederate lieutenant general James Longstreet. Despite that service, in 1863, fellow staff member Major Walton told him, "When the Confederacy had its independence he did not intend having any 'damned' foreigners in the county."[30] Although some Confederate writers reminded readers that gallant immigrant soldiers served in defense of the South, strident nativist voices appealed to the xenophobic. These bigoted Confederates fanned episodes of racial intolerance in the Civil War South.[31]

From April 1863, Confederate newspapers and Congress subjected the nation's foreign-born population to growing distrust and other nativist sentiments. Propaganda and rhetoric regarding the Union army's "Hessians," profiteering, and some nonnative Southerners' defection tainted other Confederates' opinion of these relative newcomers. Men such as Senator Clay of Alabama moved to withdraw naturalization from any man who did not serve in the military. In July 1863, the State of Georgia ordered any foreigner who had not volunteered for state service to leave the state. This growing hostility made some nonnative Confederates doubt their place in the Southern nation.[32] Feeling unwelcome and facing trying times, growing numbers crossed into Union lines. Making up a disproportionate number of the Confederacy's expert craftsmen, their departure robbed the South of their valuable skills.

Of all the groups, the South's twenty-five thousand Jewish people found themselves singled out. Over the two decades before the war, people of the Judaic faith had emigrated from European nations and assimilated into all levels of American social, economic, and political life. Although their numbers were small, they entered the Confederate struggle as ardently as any group within the South. While antebellum pseudoscience designated Jews as members of the white race, that did not mean Confederates considered them equals.[33] The anti-Semitism they faced was mild compared to what they had experienced in Europe, but nevertheless, Confederate Jews encountered increased bigotry as the war progressed.[34]

FIG. 2.5. *Pages from the Unpublished History of a Celebrated Financier*, ca. 1863. Courtesy of the American Civil War Museum.

Confederate Jews faced prejudices regardless of their position. Jefferson Davis's administration contained three men whose Jewish faith fueled scorn and criticism from Confederate newspapers—Judah P. Benjamin, Abram C. Myers, and Christopher G. Memminger.[35] The likenesses of two, Benjamin and Memminger, appeared on Confederate currency. The portraits affirmed each man's place within the nation and helped counter the anti-Semitism directed at them by others. However, a series of cartoons satirizing Memminger represented a visual attempt to tarnish the positive image of Jews in government.

Produced around 1863, the anonymous leaflet criticized Memminger's selfishness, power, and his handling of his department (fig. 2.5). Similar in style to Blanton Duncan's works (see fig. 2.2), it may have been part of the publicity campaign Duncan waged after the Treasurer ended his contract in late 1862. The first frame shows shoeless soldiers in the snow ignored by citizens scrambling to make money. In the second, Memminger is a poor young immigrant receiving charity. Next, fifty years later, Memminger denies soldiers the same charity once shown him. In the final scene, a bull with Memminger's face turns on the public that once feted him. To Confederate audiences ignorant of the events, it represented a foreign-born Confederate government leader putting his needs before those of the nation and its people.

As this image circulated, Jewish people within the Confederacy's borders experienced greater intolerance. In late May 1863, Richmond's *Examiner* wrote, "One of the essential differences on which the Confederacy may pride itself, in making us a distinct people from the Yankee nation, is the complete absence of religious intolerance." However, such was not the case.[36] Jewish businessman Moses Jacob Ezekiel recalled that Jew and Gentile mixed like "oil and water" in Richmond society.[37] In January 1863, congressman and master of prejudice Henry S. Foote railed in the House of Representatives against an imagined Jewish monopoly over trade.

Confederate image makers contributed to this stereotype. Published in John W. Overall's *Southern Punch* in early 1864, "Exodus of Israelites" used imagery and text to disparage Jews (fig. 2.6). The title and the enlarged hooked, or "Jewish," noses of several of the men suggest their racial background. The accompanying poem explains that these men left the Confederacy because their love of money trumped their love of country.[38]

> We're coming, Father Abraham,
> The Promised Land! The Promised Land!
> Full many thousands more,
> It flows with milk and honey
> To kneel before thy mighty throne,
> And better, Father Abraham,
> And wait upon thy door.
> 'Tis said it flows with *money!*
> Our tribe in Dixie sore oppress'd
> By all the Conscript Band,
> A second Red Sea crosseth now
> To view the Promised Land.

To the "nasologist," the men's noses showed individuals with "good, useful" skills and intelligence suited to the commercial world but unable to "reach the peaks of intellectuality."[39] The poem's lack of dialect suggested the author's intention to criticize race rather than place of birth. Through cartoons like these, the *Southern Illustrated News*, *Southern Punch*, and other graphic media spread this divisive stereotype across the Confederacy.[40]

FIG. 2.6. "Exodus of Israelites." From *Southern Punch*, Feb. 27, 1864. Courtesy of the Library of Virginia.

BLACK AMERICANS

Nativist Confederates and the confusion over depictions of race undermined notions of a uniform and unified white race. Instead, racial bigotry alienated groups of white Confederates from each other. This disunity concerned Confederates, such as the editor of Richmond's *Enquirer*. On July 11, 1863, he reminded Confederates that they fought not for the "fancied superiority" of one white race over another but to set up a nation built on black people's inferiority.[41]

Racial theorists and slavery advocates dreamed up differing self-serving and mistaken theories about black people's origins and personality types to imagine their racial deficiencies. Polygenesists, such as American Samuel G. Morton (1799–1851), believed in the separate evolution of black and white people and that nature determined a race's hierarchy.[42] Monogenesists, such as South Carolinians John Bachman and Thomas Smyth, held that God created and ordered races in a scale of perfection. Regardless of their differences, both polygenesists and monogenesists believed black people to be lazy, dishonest, childlike, and inferior. Within the black race imagined by proslavery rhetoric, Confederates fancied distinct personality types. John Blassingame found that slave owners identified three types of black person, which he termed "Jack," "Nat," and "Sambo."[43] Jack represented the type whom slave owners believed, with fair treatment, worked well and predominated among the enslaved.

FIG. 2.7. Vignette of slave picking cotton. Detail from Bank of Lexington (N.C.), five-dollar note. Printed by American Bank Note Company ca. 1860–61. This vignette also appears on a Bank of Charleston (S.C.) twenty-dollar note printed between 1851 and 1857, by Toppan, Carpenter, and Co., Philadelphia and New York. Courtesy of Pierre Fricke, https://www.buyvintagemoney.com.

FIG. 2.8. Vignette of slave picking cotton, from Blanton Duncan, Sept. 2, 1861, ten-dollar note (Type-29). Printing began in Mar. 1862. Records show that the Treasury received 286,629 of these notes. Courtesy of Pierre Fricke, https://www.buyvintagemoney.com.

Conversely, the Nat character exhibited a sober yet surly intelligence and a rebellious streak. Finally, there was the Sambo type, who was thriftless, slow working, and joking, but a loyal slave.[44] Through ideas like these, planters found convenient "evidence" that ancestry and character suited black people for little else than being chattel in the Western world.

Racial theories fostered stereotypes and psychological distance between whites and blacks. Confederate depictions of black people that exaggerated their features to suit their expectations of the race aided this divide. This is seen in the way a Confederate printer used a prewar banknote vignette of a slave picking cotton. The original image showed a slave dutifully working in the field. However, rather than following common practice of making an exact copy, the artist who created the version on the Type-29 Confederate ten-dollar note made subtle alterations to the figure's proportions. The legs and body are shorter and thickened, the hands enlarged, head rounded, lips extended, and forehead shortened. Moreover, the artist changed the figure's expression to make him look more absented-minded and apelike. These physical characteristics, prominent racist writer Julien-Joseph Virey stated, made black people "less inclined to think" and readier to abandon themselves "to sensual pleasures."[45] Issued from March 1862 and carried on 286,629 Treasury notes, the vignette confirmed Confederates' belief that race fitted African people for subjection (figs. 2.7 and 2.8).

While these physical characteristics reoccurred in Confederate images of black people, depictions of slaves at work appeared irregularly. Rather, Confederate artists commonly depicted black men as harmless, personifications of what Blassingame termed the Sambo stereotype. This figure predominated as ever more unexpected slave behaviors, such as supposedly "loyal" slaves who joined the 800,000 other black people who fled bondage, raised Confederates' anxieties.[46] Additionally, the rumors and incidents of slave resistance and aggression displayed by other slaves surprised and unsettled Confederates. Amid this disturbing environment, the comic, bumbling, and inoffensive Sambo character represented a calming psychological oasis.

Confederates freely created and disseminated the Sambo stereotype through a variety of media. Minstrel shows were the most common among them. Popular across nineteenth-century America, these shows offered a dynamic, palatable, and escapist vehicle. The white actors who mimicked slaves enabled each show's producers to make "black" people act and speak exactly as Confederates wanted. Despite exaggerated dialect and mannerisms, the Confederate need for reassurance made them consider blackface actors' representations as truthful.[47] Seeing Sambo's harmless joke cracking and bumbling helped sustain blackface minstrel shows' popularity. Moreover, live theater's transportive capacity to reshape reality enhanced the distraction these performances provided.[48]

The number of minstrel shows swelled in the Confederacy and included both professional and amateur troupes.[49] Professional groups such as the "Ironclads" and "Confederate Nightingales" regularly toured the larger cities.[50] Military units formed

FIG. 2.9. "Jem Wells, of the New Richmond Theatre," by "Cave," 1864. Wells performed in blackface in both light and serious entertainments. From *The Punch Songster: A Collection of Familiar and Original Songs and Ballads* (Richmond, Va.: Punch Office, 1864). Courtesy of the Library of Virginia.

groups to entertain their comrades in winter quarters, and in towns, people created amateur shows to raise funds for the war effort.[51] Regardless of their contrived nature, Confederates accepted these shows as honest depictions of black people's character and behaviors.[52] Studying them provides an insight into how Confederates pictured the race they ruled.

Two rare images show how Confederate performers represented black people in minstrel shows. The Confederate soldiers in a small John Omenhauser watercolor smudged their faces with carbon and donned black curly wigs and black costumes. Experienced and successful blackface performer James Wells made a more polished appearance (fig. 2.9). An 1864 engraving showed him ready for stage: charcoal covered his face, and his outsized hat and upper garments made his head appear smaller and his legs shorter. In combination, his costume gave Wells a more apelike look. Such artifice made these actors conform to match Confederates' racist imaginings.

Apart from a few songs, little detailed documentary evidence about the staging or content of Confederate minstrel performances survives. Omenhauser provided a rare insight in a watercolor he produced while a prisoner of war at Point Lookout, Maryland.[53] The artist presented the action before a backdrop suggestive of the

FIG. 2.10. *Confederate Variety's*, by John Jacob Omenhauser (or Omenhausser), 1864–65. This work shows a blackface act performing to a predominantly Confederate audience. From John Jacob Omenhausser, Civil War sketchbook, 1864–65, Maryland Manuscripts Collection, #5213. Courtesy of Special Collections, University of Maryland Libraries.

mythic "Old Virginny" (fig. 2.10).[54] The performers' dress and the arrangement suggest that Omenhauser had drawn the first act of the traditional minstrel show. At this point, the more genteel "interlocutor" sits in the middle of a line of players, and the "endmen," or "cornermen"—Bones and Tambo—sit at either end.[55] In Omenhauser's picture, Bones and Tambo's poses suggest animation. While the interlocutor was normally well-spoken, Bones and Tambo were usually represented as ignorant, rowdy, and gullible. Their animated poses suggest that, like other minstrel shows, these "delineators" used exaggerated plantation dialects, vocal modulations, and overblown gesticulations in their act.[56] Besides hawking racial stereotypes, minstrel shows helped blind Confederates to slaves' humanity.

Although highbrow critics derided "burnt-cork opera," its popularity and resilience were undeniable. It survived negative criticism and the ravages of conscription that forced companies to replace male with female minstrels.[57] Low prices and predictability attracted both blacks and whites to the shows until the war's end. The black presence added to each entertainment's air of authenticity even as events challenged Confederates' views on race.

FIG. 2.11. "Illustration of the New Yankee Doctrine about the Darkey," by unknown artist, engraving by S. Casey. From *Southern Illustrated News*, June 11, 1864.

Minstrel shows joined a body of representations that highlighted black people's harmless and childlike natures. This view provided reassurance as external events added to plantation owners' fears of slave insurrection. It sustained a sense of white superiority and control over black people even as events challenged their assumptions and illusions.

Confederate ideas of race led white Southerners to believe that only whites possessed the qualities that suited them to be soldiers. When the United States' Congress allowed black enlistment in July 1862, the Confederate belief that black men lacked the mental or moral capacities to fight meant that many underestimated its impact. These assumptions proved resistant, despite being challenged by the disciplined and courageous performance of black Union soldiers in battle. Race, many Confederates thought, fixed the character of peoples in perpetuity, and only white men possessed the "higher" attributes that soldiering required. Conversely, it made slavery the "natural" condition of the black man. These views prompted unusual Confederate responses when black troops fought. In May 1863, a Confederate correspondent added to a report about the bloody repulse of black regiments near Vicksburg, Mississippi: "How cruel and beastly to put negroes [*sic*] who he [the Yankee] had seduced from their happy homes, and under the delusion of liberty and freedom, or by force, induced to become soldiers and then put them in front of the battle to be mercilessly shot down by their former mentors and protectors and then leave them in their first hour of trial to die, as so many beasts."[58] Confederates could not imagine black men fighting of their own accord, and Confederate visual culture echoed the denial and minimization of black men's martial ability conveyed in the print media.

The June 1864 cartoon "Illustration of the New Yankee Doctrine about the Darkey" depicted for its audience this belief that black men were not naturally fit for war (fig. 2.11). The woodcut shows an unarmed black Federal corporal running away after a distant shell burst as an officer attempts to stop him. They are the only figures visible, and the trees in the background suggest a protective cover. Following a similar pattern, the artist exaggerated the proportions of the black corporal's head and hands. Set alongside the Yankee officer, the exaggerated features emphasized the difference between the two men. Although he is a noncommissioned officer, the black figure—presented as childlike in appearance, word, and action—cannot control his fear. Drawn despite almost two years of evidence to the contrary, images like this sustained Confederates' belief in black inferiority and scoffed at Northerners' trust in their abilities.

Captured black troops presented more practical issues. Confederates turned most black prisoners over to state authorities, who returned them to slavery.[59] However, some black Federal soldiers found themselves in Confederate prisoner of war camps. Over the course of 1863, their status assumed importance as it related to the question of parole. This exchange system assigned each rank from private upward a relative value. To give African American troops prisoner of war status meant that they were being equated with white soldiers, And because of their racist logic, Confederate authorities rebuffed every attempt by the United States to include them in the system. The cartoon "Personification of the Yankee Proposition for the New Cartel of Exchange" illustrated Confederate logic about the scheme (fig. 2.12). Published in the October 3, 1863, edition of the *Southern Punch*, it showed a prisoner exchange. On the left, a nattily uniformed Confederate officer brings a barefoot black man, with exaggerated features and dressed in field clothes, for exchange. A caricatured Yankee officer and wounded Confederate soldier face them. The stark

FIG. 2.12. "Personification of the Yankee Proposition for the New Cartel of Exchange," by unknown artist. From *Southern Punch,* Oct. 3, 1863. Courtesy of the Library of Virginia.

contrast mocked the proposed system. Likewise, in September 1863, an article in the *Montgomery Weekly Mail* posed the question "Is a black soldier worth equal to a White [*sic*] soldier?"[60] Images like this reflected and affirmed Confederate opinion that they were not.

Despite their prejudices, a growing number of Confederates considered using slaves as soldiers. Writing to his wife in July 1862, General Richard Ewell explained, "The Yankees are fighting low foreigners against the best part of our people, whereas if we were to fight with Negroes [against them] they would be far offset."[61] The serious consideration of arming slaves took another thirty months. The debates not only exposed how little the war had altered the beliefs of many Confederates but also reflected their contradictory attitudes.[62] On one hand, Confederates stated that the black race's laziness, flightiness, and weak intellect suggested that they would make poor soldiers. On the other, however, Confederates spoke of their slaves' physical strength, natural loyalty, and obedience to a master's rule—qualities that suggested black men would follow orders and provide the manpower to help offset Lincoln's hirelings.[63]

The movement to enlist black Confederate troops gained momentum over the winter of 1864–65. Faced with military and social collapse, the debate came into full public view. Yet even in the face of looming defeat, some Confederates' vision of the "cornerstone" brooked no compromise. Speaking in February 1865, Georgia's governor, Joseph Brown, told his state's houses, "Whenever we establish the fact that they are a military race, we destroy our whole theory that they are unfit to be free . . . when we arm the slaves we abandon slavery."[64] As Governor Brown spoke, every Confederate port lay under Federal control and the Union had reclaimed swathes of the South and outnumbered the Confederacy's armies by five to one. Facing defeat, desperation to sustain their nation overcame ideology.[65]

On March 13, 1865, with the support of General Robert E. Lee, Congress passed a bill to enlist 300,000 black troops. But the military situation made it possible only to organize a few hundred black troops in the immediate vicinity of Richmond, Virginia.[66] Observing them marching in a parade, the *Richmond Whig* opined, "Sambo could be taught to handle a gun as well as the hoe."[67] Several weeks later, the show *Recruiting Unbleached Citizens of Virginia for the Confederate States Army* brought its efforts to defend white Confederates to Richmond audiences. Mere days before their capital fell, "packed houses" greeted the "laughable burlesque" that spoofed the black soldiers' medical examination, their drill, and their behavior in battle with "shouts of applause."[68] The audience's inability or unwillingness to take these black men's efforts on their behalf seriously showed the resilience of the Confederate belief in black people's limited capacities.

Their derision also masked fears created by their racist theories. Antebellum proslavery writers pronounced the black race as unstable. This, stated self-proclaimed "Negro" expert Dr. Samuel Cartwright, made them either the "slave of man or the slave of Satan."[69] Through such thinking, white Southerners felt a manic dread of their slaves' sexual nature and the threat of racial hybridity.[70] Influenced by the primitive and spurious studies of eugenics, the fear of racial contamination led some, like Northerner Sidney George Fisher, to advocate for the total segregation of black and white people.[71] Over the winter of 1860–61, South Carolina's ambassadors of secession played on this fear. They warned of a bleak and stormy future with their pure white race destroyed by social disintegration and rapine unless Southern states seceded.[72] From antebellum times, these expectations contributed to a system that resulted in the legal or summary execution of black men for crimes on white women.[73] In July 1864, this context led observers to praise soldiers in Meridian, Mississippi, who lynched a slave they believed intended to rape a white woman.[74] The execution fitted the Southern pattern of white men as defenders of white women's virtue. Similar beliefs led Confederate captain Thomas Key to confide in his diary that Confederate loss meant giving his womenfolk "up to the embraces of their present 'dusky male servitors.'"[75] Over the same period in 1864, Governor Zebulon Vance used fears of race wars to counter antiwar feeling in his successful reelection campaign.[76] As a result, many Confederates believed a Union victory would unleash a rampage of Northern black and white troops as well as slaves on the South.

Within this context, in late 1864, William Washington painted and exhibited his work, *The Burial of Latané*. The work depicted the May 1862 burial of Confederate cavalry captain William D. Latané. The sole Confederate casualty of a notable Confederate cavalry raid on Union forces threatening Richmond, Latané's comrades left his body for local women to bury. Newspaper accounts, official reports, and a poem written by John R. Thompson popularized the incident and inspired Washington to produce the work. For the female models, Washington posed members of Miss Mary Pegram's "fashionable" girls' school in Richmond.[77] It is unknown on whom he based the figures of the enslaved men and women. The artist's thirty-six- by forty-six-inch painting of the event, now in the Johnson Collection, pictured the ideas of manly sacrifice and the dutiful care of the fallen by those "behind the lines" contained in these accounts.[78] Unveiled in late October 1864 at the Minnis Photographic Gallery in Richmond, it drew crowds and won great popularity.[79] What helped it gain such acclaim reveals how well Washington understood Confederate audiences. Through the bowed heads of most of the black figures, Washington conveyed messages of slave loyalty and contentment.[80] However, the artist did more than regurgitate ideas of black loyalty.

The Burial of Latané carried other allusions. Richmond's *Enquirer* reported that Washington "grouped his figures with a mastery that tells the story at a glance."[81] And indeed, in his tableaux, the trained artist selected and posed his models to create a composition that presents a rich narrative. It showed what the *Richmond Whig* described as a group gathered around the "new made grave . . . [and] body of the dead Cavalier."[82] Richmond's *Enquirer* stated that any one of the white women, "isolated and alone," who take up around two-thirds of the picture, "could never be pronounced anything but a *Southern lady* [*sic*]." Almost lost in the shadowy foliage, most of the black players in the scene are squeezed into the remaining third. Washington posed most of the black and white figures in what the *Whig* described as "pensive attitudes." However, four of them are looking elsewhere. The central woman looks up with an expression that the *Enquirer* described as a blend of "sorrow and hope."[83] Two children and a black man leaning on a shovel gaze toward the right. This black man stands in contrast to the others in the scene. His lips are larger than those of the other black people and his forehead more slanted. While other adult figures either close their eyes in respect or look to heaven, Washington chose to paint this man with open eyes, his line of sight across the grave. A few simple strokes, and Washington could have painted the man's eyes closed like the other enslaved figures. However, by choosing to paint him with eyes open, the artist created a variety of meanings, both benign and darker. His attitude could be read as staring off lost in thought or, like the children, looking away from the somber scene. But his sight line creates a psychic line that connects him to the group of women on the opposite side of the grave. Moreover, written in the figure's physiognomy are messages: the full lips denote lasciviousness and the slanting profile an animal nature.[84] Viewed through this lens, Washington's black male carried messages of the duality of the black psyche, the defenselessness of Confederate white women, and the racial consequences of defeat.[85]

Washington's work intimates the fears Confederates had around racial amalgamation. These fears crystallized in the idea of "miscegenation" coined in a Northern pamphlet. Published during late 1863, this propaganda work advocated the intermarriage of whites and blacks.[86] When Richmond's *Examiner* learned of its publication in April 1864, it branded the concept as lewdness and rejoiced that the South was "happily separated by a belt of fire" from the North. The paper stated that the "reality" that prominent abolitionists "enjoyed" this "doctrine" showed the degraded state of the Northern race.[87] Furthermore, it provided evidence to Confederates, such as officer Thomas J. Key, that Northerners were a "base and amorous race of puritans."[88] A small cartoon that appeared in the May 1864 edition of the *Confederate Spirit,* "Miscegenation; or, The 'Free American of African Descent' Enjoying His Long-Lost Freedom," represented a Confederate vision of this idea (fig. 2.13). The artist staged the scene in an ambiguous but open public space. Two modishly attired white women pay attention to a well-dressed man with spindly limbs and large head.[89] With two blank circles for eyes and a large mouth and lips, his face bears a slight human resemblance. Regardless of his appearance, the ladies appear to fawn. The physiognomy of the woman on the left reveals a sharp, "acquisitive," "Anglo-American" nose. Her heavy-lidded eyes convey sensuality and her receding chin suggests a weak mind.[90] The other woman's round face, large eyes, small full mouth, and tiny flat nose show a lustful, slow, and materialistic nature. It is at once a critique of Northern society and the imagined impact of abolition. Underneath the image is a story from a "Yankee Newspaper" that reported how single Massachusetts women who set up schools for free black children had long practiced miscegenation. It was not the only work to capitalize on and critique this idea. The short career of an 1864 play affords insights into Confederate opinion on interracial relations.

In April 1864, the sensational aspects of miscegenation prompted New Richmond Theater owner and actor Richard D'Orsay Ogden to bring a version to the stage. At a benefit for the actress Miss Eloise Bridges, he introduced the play *Miscegenation; or, Life of a Virginia Negro in Washington.* Written by a "gentleman of this city," it played

FIG. 2.13. "Miscegenation; or, The 'Free American of African Descent' Enjoying His Long-Lost 'Freedom,'" by unknown artist. From *Confederate Spirit and Knapsack of Fun,* May 1864. Courtesy of Princeton University.

to a "tremendous crowd." Ogden played Sam, the "Virginia Negro" and "beau and beau idéal of all lewd Northern damsels of pale complexion."[91] In playing the role, a critic stated that Ogden "brought up every piece containing a negro character" by his "great tumblings" and "sassy" expressions. Some reviewers complained that the "Southern version" of "Northern miscegenation" did not convey the "horrible" aspects they imagined Yankees practiced. Others feared a "surfeit of negro for weeks to come."[92] When its run closed after a few days, the *Illustrated News* rejoiced at its withdrawal. Such ideas, the *News* stated, could and should "exist only in Yankeedom."[93] Despite the satirizing of Yankees, it is interesting that Confederates struggled with ideas such as miscegenation. In their concerns about it, Confederates conveniently ignored the over 400,000 mixed-heritage Southerners in their midst, individuals who indicated that racial amalgamation already existed in their new nation. However, in a country built with racism as its cornerstone and fighting a foe who so clearly challenged their ideas, dealing with such knowledge seemed beyond Confederate visual culture.

In their battle to protect white Southern women from the supposed carnal desires of an inferior race, Confederates looked to General Robert E. Lee and his army as the greatest guardians. John Adam Elder pictured these ideas in his now lost painting *The Battle of the Crater, Morning after the Explosion.*[94] It depicted the final moments of the sad engagement of July 30, 1864, when Lee's army recaptured earthworks blasted by a mine and invested by fifteen thousand black and white Federal troops. Poorly planned and led, the assault proved a bloody disaster for Union forces. Confederate news presented it as "unscrupulous and brutal Yankees" using "cunning lies" and "strong potations of whiskey" to stir "Yankee negroes and their white co-adjudicators" to action.[95]

Written accounts of the lost original painting portrayed its subject as a battle between and about races. Amid a broken landscape and over the body of a rebel who has fallen on a dead black soldier, a lone Confederate opposes Union forces. (A reporter for the *Richmond Whig* described these troops as black and the white soldier as not "Yankee" or "Northerner" but "evidently a German.") Meanwhile, a wave of Confederate soldiers bearing a tattered scarlet flag advance to support him.[96] Despite being outnumbered, the Southerner holds his own against a multiracial enemy. Confederates who viewed the original *Battle of the Crater* saw a racial struggle between unequal populations: a conflict of the North's foreign hirelings and weak-minded black men tricked into fighting for them against a Southern people unified by race and purpose.

Race initially appeared to offer Confederates a ready way of rationalizing or explaining Northern antagonism and creating a divide between the North and the South. However, Southern imaginings of differences between themselves and other Americans were fluid. Robert Bonner's study of Confederate ideas of race found a "waning of the Norman/Saxon theme" over the course of the war.[97] Visual culture captured some of this variance, picturing the Yankee both as racial type and character. Xenophobic Confederates found greater ease in picturing foreigners as racially different. The material they produced added a pictorial element to rhetoric that alienated foreign-born Confederates. But like the concepts of racial difference between North and South, not all Southerners shared these prejudices.

Confederate ideas of race became less problematic when applied to the enslaved. While racist thinking left white Southerners unprepared and unwilling to adapt, it helped them to justify slavery. After studying Southern soldiers' thought, Chandra Manning concludes that "slavery could not be separated from race." Indeed, Confederates could not imagine one without the other, and Confederate depictions of black people shared one common quality—it showed them enslaved.[98] While Confederate images of black people reinforced concepts of their intellectual and moral inferiority to white people and their underlying animal natures, they also justified their enslavement. These depictions supported Confederate beliefs that black people were not naturally constructive members of their society. Moreover, they reinforced convictions that, morally and spiritually, black people required caretakers. Ultimately, it bolstered the conclusion that slavery provided the ethical, social, and economic answer to these needs. In doing so, pictures of black Southerners also conveyed white illusions about slave life and labor. With black bondage forming such a fundamental part of their nation, these images joined with racist ideas to become part of the Confederate defense of slavery.

CHAPTER 3

The Southern Defense of Slavery

In James D. McCabe's play *The Guerrillas: An Original Domestic Drama,* Jerry, an enslaved black man, is offered his freedom as a reward for protecting his master's wife from being insulted by a Union colonel:

> JERRY. (*Starting back in surprise.*) Marse Arthur, you'se a jokin'.
>
> ARTHUR. (*His master.*) No, Jerry, I am serious. You are free.
>
> JERRY. (*Indignantly.*) A free nigger? I don't want to be free.
>
> ARTHUR. But, Jerry, you can go North if you wish to do so, and be as good as the white people there.
>
> JERRY. De Norf! Ain't dat whar de Abulishuners live?
>
> ARTHUR. Yes.
>
> JERRY. (*Indignantly.*) Marse Arthur, I'se s'prised at you, 'deed I is. (*Drawing himself up proudly.*) I tank he [*sic*] good Lord I 'siders myself heap better dan any abulishuner dat eber libed. What I want to be free for? (*With feeling.*) Marse Arthur, I bin in your family eber since I bin born. If you'se tired of old Jerry, jus' take him out in de field and shoot him, but don't send him away from you; don't set him free. Please don't, Marse Arthur.

Contemporary reviews described McCabe's play as a "spirit stirring drama, abounding in startling events," and received it "enthusiastically." The playwright achieved the mix of themes that delighted Confederate audiences, and it enjoyed weeklong runs across the Confederacy from December 1862 to December 1864.[1] Set within this melodramatic tale of heroic Confederates battling against a variety of Yankee blackguards, the scene that contained Jerry's refusal of freedom fit neatly into Southern slavery fantasies.

McCabe's choice to depict a slave rejecting freedom fit Confederate expectations. Jerry's refusal carried with it fanciful racial theories and other misperceptions. It also reflected the many stories of slavery's positive good that Southerners digested in the decades leading up to the war. These counterpunches to the abolitionist rhetoric told them that an enslaved black labor force delivered moral and economic benefits to all segments of society. They related a master's benevolence to a slave's loyalty. It represented slavery advocates' misinterpretations of the enslaveds' culture and planters' belief in slavery's superiority over other social systems. It characterized the ideas that Confederates expounded in their proslavery bubble, and made audiences not only receptive to but hungry for confirmation of their erroneous beliefs.

Southerners used every available medium to spread and confirm their views of slavery. Written sources provide great resources for us to understand Southern and Confederate opinions about slavery.[2] They show that Confederates not only continued to peddle prewar myths about slavery but also responded to the pressures exerted on the institution. From pulpits, church leaders called on slave owners to make slavery conform more to Christian morality. Politicians and ideologues developed theories to explain their enslaved population's behaviors. Alongside these efforts, Confederate literature reinforced notions of slavery's good in the popular imagination.[3] Confederate visual culture provides another lens through which to study how Confederates pictured the world of those they enslaved.[4] Moreover, cartoons and the dynamic realm of the stage allowed Confederates to put words in the mouths of black figures that made "slaves" appear as proslavery advocates.

Confederates had good reason to want to defend chattel servitude. In 1860, the toil and value as property of generations of bonded black men and women made slave states the wealthiest in the Union. The roughly 5 percent of the South's population who owned slaves relied on their sweat to keep farms, factories, and households running and themselves at the top of the social order.[5] For though slave owners made up only around 1 percent of the United States' population, their slaves' labor let them acquire 20 percent of the nation's private wealth. Whether, like most of America's 316,000 slaveholders, they possessed only one or two enslaved people or, like a handful, had 500 or more, this group relied on their bonded labor force to maintain their lifestyles.[6] Further, slave owners expected that this living inheritance would sustain and grow their families' fortunes into the future. For this group, proslavery's use of sources such as science, literature, philosophy, and the Bible provided reasons beyond purely economics for embracing the institution.

Even though most of the South's white population of nearly nine million were non–slave owners, many supported the system. The possibility of owning slaves promised greater productivity, a pathway for asset and wealth building, and therefore, movement up the social ladder. For these millions, however, theirs was an outsider's view of slavery, one influenced more by proslavery ideology than experience.[7] Their physical and psychological distance from slavery hid the threats and violence that kept black men and women at work. Few situations that could have challenged their prejudices brought them into contact with the system. Maybe they saw a trustworthy slave whose compliance earned him or her brief liberty to visit town. Perhaps they saw an occasional group of enslaved people as slave dealers led them to auction. Possibly they caught sight of sheriffs leading a recaptured runaway, or maybe they belonged to a slave patrol.[8] Apart from instances like these, more often theirs was an imagined view of slavery, one that enabled them to ignore, downplay, or dismiss the extent to which enslaved people suffered.

Despite the slave population's growth and the financial rewards the system provided, the South's addiction to slavery faced greater challenges in the years leading up to the Civil War. Western nations, including Britain and France, had abolished slavery, and within the United States, the weight of opposition grew steadily. Confronted by these objections, Southerners became sensitive and even paranoid to any perceived threat to their "right." Voices emerged to defend what became termed the "peculiar institution." In 1837, former vice president and then state senator John C. Calhoun's landmark speech in support of slavery proclaimed the slave owners' position. Slavery, he stated, was a "positive good." Calhoun based his claims of the system's benefits on flawed theories of race and the convenient notion that slavery's paternalism advanced every level of society. In addition, others intertwined theories of race and religion to make slavery a "Divine institution" established by God to civilize and improve black and white people.[9] Proslavery ideologues also used social theory. On the eve of the war, James Henry Hammond, another man whose wealth depended on slave labor, declared that a slave underclass sped up civilization and stabilized society.

Secession from the Union and the Confederacy's creation represented an extreme attempt to maintain black servitude. However, in early 1861, Confederates dissembled or feigned other reasons than protecting slavery for leaving the Union. In the "Declarations of Causes," Mississippi, Georgia, Texas, and South Carolina cited reasons such as exploitative Northern manufacturers, President Lincoln's election, or the failings in the U.S. Constitution.[10] Other Confederates constructed their own theories. Some found reasons in pseudoscience, notably the supposed racial differences between "Puritan" Northerners and "Cavalier" Southerners. Yet others used more simple ideas to justify secession. In July 1861, for instance, two Alabamians wrote that those who believed slavery had anything to do with war were wrong. "It was jealousy of the prosperity of the South accruing from great staple," they concluded, "which fueled the North's aggression towards the South."[11]

Other Southerners enjoyed no such doubts. In July 1859, a writer concluded that "negro slavery is the South and the South is negro slavery."[12] Across the South, many shared his conviction. An attack on one meant an attack on the other. Lincoln's election presented such a threat and triggered slave states to form their own government and to write a constitution.[13] Markedly, the constitution that secessionists wrote shielded "negro property" and gave the nation the right to introduce slavery into any territory it gained. Speaking in early 1861, statesman Robert H. Smith told Alabamians: "We have now placed our domestic institution, and secured its rights unmistakably, in the [Confederate] Constitution."[14] Its drafters believed it addressed imperfections within the United States' document. Furthermore, some even hoped theirs would supplant the parent document and draw other states from the Union into their nation.[15]

However, the framers of the Confederate Constitution did not present slavery as a dominant part of their nation. Instead, through clauses that protected slavery from political tampering, they ensured that as long as their nation existed, so too would their peculiar institution. Their nation was, as an Alabama newspaper described in June 1861, a "great Southern conservative slave republic."[16]

Confederate visual culture presented Confederates' views of slavery in a variety of ways. Despite enslaved people making up a third of the population and the opportunity to represent slavery onstage and in imagery, it appears from surviving examples that slavery appeared in less that 6 percent of Confederate theatrical and visual works. Yet slavery's economic, social, and political importance and decades of proslavery rhetoric meant that it could never be totally absent. Rather, its presence is inferred through imagery such as the wreath of slave-produced crops in the nation's great seal or the portraits on its postage stamps of Southern leaders who were slave owners.[17]

Explicit representations of slavery in the Confederacy presented slaves at work and at rest. Within the vignettes of enslaved people working dutifully that appeared on some early war Confederate banknotes, Ian Binnington identified the trope of the "silent slave."[18] This idea of the enslaved as a voiceless partner in the Confederate struggle is also present in photography and fine art. Of known wartime artists who depicted black Southerners, Conrad Wise Chapman (1842–1910) was the Confederacy's most productive.[19] Chapman brought his allegiance and an artist's eye to the Confederacy. In the fall of 1861, the native Virginian left his family and studio in Rome, Italy. Slipping through the Federal blockade, he enlisted in the Confederate army. Over the next two years, he sketched and painted the world he witnessed, some of it exhibited at Richmond's Ordnance Bureau.[20] From a non-slaveholding background, he captured an outsider's view of the system. His depictions presented slavery in a variety of ways. In his versions of *Camp, 59th Virginia Infantry at Diascund*

FIG. 3.1. *Camp, 59th Virginia Infantry at Diascund Bridge,* by Conrad Wise Chapman, 1863. Oil on board. Courtesy of The Valentine.

FIG. 3.2. *The Fifty-Ninth Virginia Infantry—Wise's Brigade,* by Conrad Wise Chapman, ca. 1864. Probably oil on canvas. Size and present location unknown. Courtesy of The Valentine.

Bridge, a Confederate camp scene becomes the stage on which Chapman exhibited each of them (figs. 3.1, 3.2, and 3.3).

The original oil sketch from midway through the war presented a scene of energy and purpose (see fig. 3.1). The loose brushstrokes, dragged paint, and indistinct

FIG. 3.3. *The Fifty-Ninth Virginia—Wise's Brigade,* by John Gadsby Chapman, ca. 1864. Etching. Courtesy of the Boston Athenaeum.

delineation of texture and form suggest that Chapman captured or composed the image from snippets he saw: a record of moments. The action culminates in the mid-foreground. On one side, a blur of shapes suggests armed and equipped soldiers moving hastily toward an undetermined location, and on the other, a slave struggles with an unsettled horse. The movement links soldier and enslaved. In works like this, Chapman showed both free and bonded men engaged in pursuits. This image reflected Confederate beliefs in the equal engagement of both blacks and whites in the defense of the South.[21]

On his return to Rome during 1864, Chapman used the sketch's pastiche of hectic glimpses to prepare a more polished version of this work (see fig. 3.2). He kept the spectator's point but refined depictions of the scene's structures and geographic features, even keeping the washing on the line. However, he worked many changes that altered the composition, mood, and messages of the painting. The most noticeable difference between this work and its oil sketch is its lack of action. Instead of the black man fighting to control an agitated horse and hurrying soldiers, Chapman substituted casual infantrymen. He removed the black figure in the foreground; instead, he adds several black figures in the distant camp.[22] The rifles the soldiers carry suggest recent or impending military activity. These changes alter it from a scene of black and white activity to one of order and white ease.

Following the pattern of his European contemporaries, Chapman, back in Italy, turned several of his 1864 works, including this piece, into prints (see fig. 3.3). With the aid of his talented father, John Gadsby Chapman, he created reproductions for the public. The etching's composition is, at first glance, identical to its parent work. However, on the work's extreme left foreground, he added the figure of a sleeping black man—a resting slave. In this and other scenes by Chapman, the enslavement is visible but is cast as a relaxed lifestyle.[23]

Consciously or not, in each work, Chapman depicted slavery as one of three different situations: as clearly involving work, as embedded in the landscape, or as an idyllic existence. These were concepts from antebellum proslavery ideology carried into the Confederacy.[24] Of Confederate depictions of enslaved people, those showing them at work appeared the least. Nevertheless, studying these representations helps us understand how Confederates saw the condition of slavery.

ENSLAVED AT WORK

During 1861, George S. Cook (1819–1902) photographed one of the earliest Confederate depictions of black servitude. The Connecticut-born artist took his camera to the camp of a Confederate battery on James Island, near Charleston, South Carolina (fig. 3.4). Because of long exposure time required by photographic technology, formal poses and conscious composition are common in Civil War photographs. And such is the case in this work. In the left foreground, three black men are around a fire; one carries an ax, and the others prepare a meal. Behind them, a knot of soldiers reads, plays cards, and lounges at their leisure, seemingly unaware of the figures on their right. Cook portrayed a Confederate fantasy of dutiful slaves engaged in work that freed white men for other pursuits.

Cook's photograph conformed to the Confederate idea of the slave as foundation for the nation.[25] Loyal servants released their white owners from onerous labor so they could defend the Southern nation. Masters rewarded the enslaved who exhibited the greatest loyalty with roles such as personal servants. As manservants, the enslaved in this photograph likely experienced better conditions and a greater variety of experiences than the enslaved who remained on plantations.[26] However, good service did not translate into loyalty, and many black Southerners felt conflicting emotions about their association with the Confederate army. Seven decades after the war, former slave Martin Jackson, who spoke frankly of the cruelty of slavery, still could not reconcile his war experience. The ninety-year-old explained to an unidentified interviewer: "Just what my feelings was about the War, I have never been able to figure out myself. I knew the Yanks were going to win, from the beginning.

FIG. 3.4. *A Confederate Picket Post near Charleston, S.C.*, by George Smith Cook, 1861–62. Half-stereograph albumen mounted on board. These men are identified as members of the Palmetto Battery in a photograph that shows them gathered around a cannon (see LC-B8184-4389). Courtesy of the Library of Congress, LC-B8184-4390.

I wanted them to win and lick us Southerners, but I hoped they was going to do so without wiping out our company."[27] Jackson's memories offer an insight into the complex emotions that may have existed behind the "black masks" used by the men in Cook's photographs.

The feelings or opinions of the enslaved men in this photograph are unclear. When set before Cook's camera, they performed as loyal hardworking servants. Their attitudes showed no obvious sign of what they thought of their situation. Other media provided greater capacity for artists to use context, expression, or pose to create a clearer depiction of slaves at work.

In July 1861, George Fitzhugh accused the North of "poisoning the minds of the people against Southern institutions." Fitzhugh referred to prewar Northern publications that carried increased amounts of antislavery imagery and text.[28] To safeguard the South's system of slavery, he called for a ban on all Northern print media.[29] Secession and the Union blockade achieved Fitzhugh's hoped-for separation. Freed from the "pestiferous" contamination of Northern pictorial print culture, Confederates created proslavery versions in their place. Through them, they circulated images of slavery full of figures who responded to bondage in ways more suited to their palate.

The power of Confederate depictions of slavery, framed and fashioned to suit and convey proslavery ideas, increased because they enjoyed a monopoly in the Con-

FIG. 3.5. "Slavery in the North—Slavery in the South." From *Southern Punch*, Sept. 19, 1863. Courtesy of the Library of Virginia.

federate marketplace. John Overall's *Southern Punch* was one of the South's illustrated periodicals that sprang up in this environment. In "Slavery in the North—Slavery in the South," published in September 1863, the artist used stance, countenance, and setting to compare a free and a slave society (fig. 3.5).[30] In both kitchens, a servant and mistress interact. In the Northern kitchen stands a cook whose low forehead, square face, broad mouth, and pug nose reveal her brutish nature. (They reused this figure to represent an Irishwoman in a later cartoon.) Additionally, her employee's expression and stance convey her ill temper and the lack of harmony in her relationship with her servant. Conversely, the Southern kitchen is a place of plenty and light. The sight of the well-provisioned Southern kitchen is ironic given the extreme shortage of food in the South by this time. In this place, happy slave and mistress chat over a baked item just brought from the oven. Such images conformed with and confirmed white Confederates' conception that slavery benefited both the enslaved and their owners. Further, the artist's choice of setting reinforced the sense of harmonious relationships between black and white.[31]

Advocates believed slavery was the black person's happiest and healthiest situation. Evidence came not only from their warped science and ideology but also from celebrated exceptions to the norm.[32] On the eve of the war, Harrison Berry published a twenty-five-cent pamphlet entitled *Slavery and Abolitionism, as Viewed by a Georgia Slave*. The forty-year-old Georgian shoemaker had returned to slavery after a sour experience of freedom. Giving his full support to the system that held him in bondage, he warned potential runaways that "subordination of the poor colored man [in the] North, is greater than that of the slave South."[33] In Southern minds, when owners

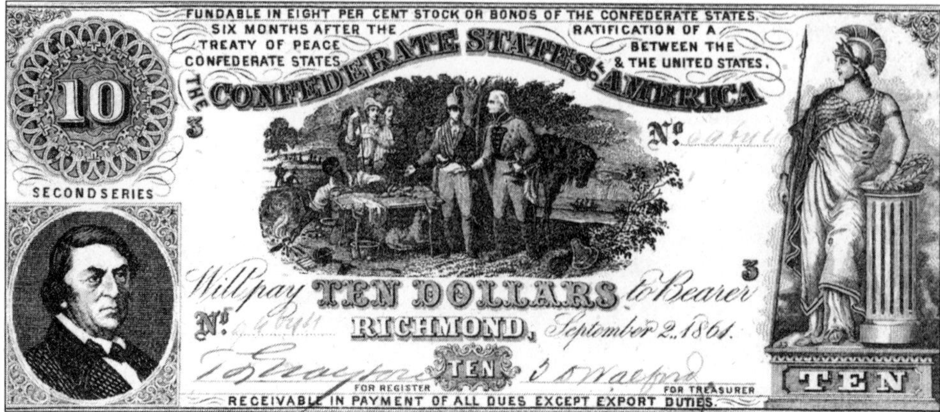

FIG. 3.6. *September 2, 1861, Confederate Ten Dollar Note* (Type-30). Featured are Robert M. Hunter, then Confederate secretary of state; Revolutionary War hero Francis Marion, in the "Sweet Potato" incident; and the allegorical figure of Minerva, goddess of wisdom. Courtesy of Pierre Fricke, https://www.buyvintagemoney.com.

treated and cared well for their slaves, the enslaved not only thrived but returned their labor and loyalty.

This idea of reciprocity proved popular in the South. In response, prewar banknote producers began to create and use images of slaves loyally working.[34] Early in the war, producers of Confederate Treasury notes, such as Blanton Duncan, reused these images on the nation's currency. On May 21, 1862, in a report of work undertaken during the preceding days, Duncan added information regarding a new note design. He stated: "I enclose to you the proof of my new $10 note. Mr. [Robert] Hunter's likeness is to be inserted in the oval and the vignette is to be Marion and the British officer. I shall have some plates prepared in a few days of that denomination."[35] Soon after printed on almost two million Confederate banknotes, the vignettes on this note conveyed an idea of enslaved people's loyalty and labor across the South (fig. 3.6). The scene's subject came from a Revolutionary War incident in which a captured British officer responded to South Carolina guerrilla Francis Marion's offer of a sweet potato meal by asking, "How can we defeat a people who live on forest roots?" In the decades before the war, John Blake White (1781–1859) painted the event in a piece entitled *General Marion Inviting a British Officer to Share His Meal.* Its popularity led White to produce an engraving and two slightly different vignette versions for the American Bank Note Company.[36] Duncan used the version of the scene in which White added a dog and repositioned the horse, hound, and slave so that all look toward Marion. Doing so established Marion as the figure in control. It

FIG. 3.7. *Cotton Field*, after James D. Smillie, from fourth series Confederate $100 note (Type-41). Courtesy of Pierre Fricke, https://www.buyvintagemoney.com.

also drew allusions of subservience and faithfulness between the enslaved and the beasts.[37] Duncan's use of this image alongside a portrait of prominent Confederate cabinet member Robert Hunter and the allegorical figure of Minerva, goddess of wisdom, art, and war, related the Confederate project to history, the government, and the relationship between blacks and whites.

While this image conveyed ideas of slave loyalty, other imagery on Confederate currency depicted the more physical side of slavery. In late 1860, aspiring artist James D. Smillie produced *Cotton Field* for New York's National Bank Note Company (fig. 3.7). The New Yorker's vignette imagined three industrious slaves weeding around cotton plants. They are the only humans in an otherwise empty field. The only suggestion of their owners is a white double-story verandaed home in the distance.[38] In common with Confederate depictions of slavery, the men work without an overseer or suggestion of coercion. Although it was first used on a Bank of Savannah two-dollar note (Haxby 325-Ga8), dated January 1, 1861, its subsequent usage on 1,600 fifty-dollar (Type-4) and 670,400 one-hundred-dollar (Type-41) Confederate Treasury notes issued in 1861 and 1862 made it more widely known. The printers, Keatinge and Ball, added a portrait of slavery promoter John C. Calhoun and the allegorical figure of Columbia to the one hundred–dollar note. This design associated *Cotton Field* with Calhoun's concepts of slavery's benefits to America. Idyllic pictures of plantation owners' wealth makers laboring loyally spurred confidence in the system and the note's value.[39] Furthermore, it encapsulated beliefs in the profitability and white ease that slavery promised, expectations that kept demand and prices for slaves high until the Confederacy collapsed.[40]

For all the proslavery messages about the value of slavery, two-dimensional works depicting black men or women engaged in work for their masters on banknotes or other graphic print media are rare.[41] Only six out of seventy-two Confederate banknotes unambiguously show black men or women working.[42] Even fewer scenes appear on Treasury bonds or the currency issued by individual Confederate states.[43] Explicit portrayals are even less common in commercial or private imagery. Ultimately, despite slavery forming a significant part of the nation's economy and rationale, images of working slaves appeared infrequently in the Confederacy's graphic or fine art form. Its rarity helped minimize awareness of black people's labor.

IMAGINING SLAVE LOYALTY

There is little shame or embarrassment about chattel slavery in depictions by Confederate artists and designers. Rather, they presented slavery as what Alice Fahs terms "Confederate fantasies."[44] The idyllic and lazy world of slavery that white people imagined bore little relationship to the hardships that black people endured or what they felt about the situation. Slave owners considered those they enslaved as extensions of their white families and subject to the same concepts of deference, affection, and reciprocity.[45] Confident that they understood enslaved people's psychology, defenders of slavery, such as James H. Hammond, repeatedly expressed a firm belief in their slaves' loyalty.[46] African Americans, Confederates thought, appreciated and preferred bondage. By extension, slaves did not run away. Rather, Yankees kidnapped and exploited them and then subjected them to a more inhumane form of labor or made them fight.[47]

The illusions of slavery presented in imagery presented those held in servitude as silent partners. Like popular literature, they provided a vehicle to disseminate notions surrounding slave loyalty. Unlike popular literature, however, they did not rely on literacy for access. Other visual forms, theater and cartoons, existed that enabled Confederates to put words into the mouths of their slaves showing that they identified with the masters' values and endorsed slavery for the less literate. The words and actions white authors and artists ascribed to slaves contributed to the genre Drew Gilpin Faust has identified as the "faithful slave."[48]

The study of original Confederate dramas showed that many, like McCabe's *The Guerrillas,* included a loyal black servant among its cast of characters.[49] From its

FIG. 3.8. "Aunt Abby." From *Southern Illustrated News*, Nov. 1, 1862.

creation toward the end of 1862 until the end of the war, *The Guerrillas* was a staple of theater companies throughout the South.[50] The drama reached its climax with both hero and heroine captured by a dastardly Yankee colonel. In a moment, Jerry, "the faithful old slave," engineers their escape. Subsequently, the hero and Jerry join local guerrillas and, with them, foil the plans of the Yankees.[51] The age of the Jerry character was important. He represented a slave with long experience. He embodied acceptance of and attachment to the peculiar institution. Alongside McCabe's Jerry, other faux-slaves appeared onstage, acting and speaking out to support slavery. John H. Hewitt's *The Scouts* included "Uncle Abe—a Faithful Negro," who closed act 1, scene 2, with the song "Agin de law to rob a hen roost on dis plantashun."[52] Captain George W. Alexander made "Joe, the Faithful" a significant player in his work *Virginia Cavalier:* protecting family, tracking the villain, and leading the hero to do his duty.[53] In *Great Expectations*, "Aunt Sarah—a negro servant," while never directly questioning her mistress's judgment, amplifies her mistress's friend Mrs. Stubbs's concerns by adding, "Dat what I say agin."[54] Confederates used plays like these to tell and show audiences that slaves returned loyalty for good treatment. They complemented the image of happy, if occasionally mischievous, slaves conveyed by minstrel shows and added a "slave's" partisan proslavery voice to the power of the stage's transformative narratives. These qualities made theater a compelling medium for proclaiming the positive good of black bondage to the soldiers who commonly filled the audiences.[55]

Characters like Jerry and Uncle Abe also fed Confederate audiences another sweet untruth: that having worked for the master, the enslaved enjoyed their master's benevolence into old age. It was also present in the images that accompanied fictional tales. In November 1862, the *Southern Illustrated News* pictured this idea in an engraving that appeared in the story "Getting Married." The character of Aunt

Abby features in a tale of an "artist's" journey to his beloved's plantation. There he meets Aunt Abby, a slave woman, "aged and near death." The artist takes it upon himself to inform her that a horse has just killed her husband, Uncle Phil. He goes to Aunt Abby's cabin, where he finds her sitting on a turned wood chair before a stone fireplace (fig. 3.8). Her clothing, the tiled or timber floor, tableware on the mantelpiece, and lantern convey an image of a woman living a comfortable life. Although she is aged, infirm, and no longer productive, her owners still care for her. Her character, like Jerry, helped Southerners imagine a paternalistic world of slavery. Additionally, it allowed white Southerners to believe black people thrived because of this "benign" institution.[56] Such representations also fed the Confederates' delusions about reciprocity between the enslaved and their masters that fostered loyalty.[57]

Fictional accounts onstage and in print, like the story of Aunt Abby, made slave life appear a bucolic existence. A Confederate image maker for *Southern Punch* drew on recent events to advance this and other ideas in "Lo! The Poor, Unhappy Slave!" (fig. 3.9). It is a scene of domestic tranquility in which black children play on the floor and a woman stands by a large cooking pot as a black man and a white youth sit at a table. The relaxed interactions of white and black, as the white boy directs the black man's attention to the object he is holding, suggest harmony. Furthermore, its identification as "engraved from a photograph" stamped this depiction with a photograph's truthful authority.[58] The peaceful domesticity of this scene reinforced proslavery ideology of benevolent masters and contented slaves. It is, however, an idyllic image of life before the Yankees' arrival destroyed it. Whereas Southerners, the image told its viewers, were interested in the welfare of their slaves, cruel Yankees' mismanagement exploited black people and led to disorder.[59]

Imagery of contented slaves served other purposes. In November 1864, Richmond's *Whig* told readers that "servitude is a divinely appointed condition for the highest good of the slave."[60] Certainly, many Confederates shared the *Whig*'s opinion concerning the relationship between their religion and enslavement. Sensitivity to any tampering with the "institution" stifled calls from antebellum Southern churchmen to use slavery to improve the spiritual and moral life of slave and master. Once freed from the fear of Northern interference, however, Confederate clergy accelerated their calls for slave owners to use their control over black people to do God's work.[61] As the war progressed, church leaders pressed Confederates to reform slavery to gain God's favor.[62] Images of harmonious scenes suggested slavery's moral rectitude and helped ease the consciences of those concerned about the system's morality.

Even as Confederates consumed these comforting delusions, a growing number of slaves ran away, enlisted to fight the Confederacy, or resisted their bondage.[63] In this environment, masters welcomed any evidence that slaves consented to their en-

FIG. 3.9. "Lo! The Poor, Unhappy Slave!" "Our engraving is from a photograph of the interior of a negro cabin on the MILLAUDIN [*sic*] plantation, near New Orleans, taken just before the war. The bloody tragedies that have been enacted on the said plantation, since its going into Yankee possession, as detailed by the New Orleans press, furnish a sad and striking contrast." The accompanying text referred to a story, barely covered by the Confederate press, of violence and difficulties on the plantation owned by Laurent Millaudon. Through another party Millaudon hired former slaves. The system worked until Millaudon tried to take control of the workers' labor, and in the resulting upheaval two workers killed an overseer. In the Confederate imagining, it was Northerners and not slave owners at fault. From *Southern Punch*, Sept. 5, 1863. Courtesy of the Library of Virginia.

slavement.[64] Confederates' visual culture joined other sources to provide it, presenting stories that helped them believe that blacks understood and willingly defended white Southerners' way of life. These sources enabled Confederates to frame the war as a struggle for Southern independence, rather than one to defend the system of slavery, thereby easing the consciences of those worried by the ethics of slavery. These fantasies also appeared in less serious forms of visual culture.

PICTURING SLAVE DISQUIET

With their humor delivered through text and images, cartoons provided another tool for Confederates to depict their view of slavery. Published in April 1864, "Slaves Apprehend a Colored Correspondent of the New York Tribune" showed enslaved men and women bringing a black journalist from an arch-abolitionist newspaper to their master for judgment (fig. 3.10).[65] The artist has added deeper messages by differentiating the head profiles, and therefore the characters, of the black people. While both black men's foreheads slope at the same angle, the reporter's forehead is lower, compared to the dutiful slave's. This physiognomy suggested that the *Tribune*'s correspondent had a weaker intellect,[66] and his large lips displayed his lustful passions. Unintelligent and animalistic, the *New York Tribune*'s correspondent, the artist told Confederates, was an unreliable source. The form of the master's face conveyed a strong, dominant, serious personality. The upper lip protruding over the lower made his face a noble one, and the almost total absence of a lower lip showed a personality free of sensuality.[67] It presented the slave owner as a man of high character, free of passion, and wise when dispensing justice. Overall, these figures personify George Fitzhugh's belief in the benefit of slavery on both slave and master.[68] They reassured Confederates that whatever they saw or experienced, the prewar status quo remained essentially unchanged. Moreover, they upheld the idea that only slaves who lacked the intelligence to appreciate slavery's advantages sought to attack or undermine it.

This idea pervaded the cartoon "What's Master's," from April 1863 (fig. 3.11). It

FIG. 3.10. "Slaves Apprehend a Colored Correspondent of the New York Tribune." From *Southern Punch*, Apr. 23, 1864. Courtesy of the Library of Virginia.

FIG. 3.11. "What's Master's." From *Southern Illustrated News*, Apr. 18, 1863.

showed two slaves, Sambo and Jeff, in a rainstorm. In contrast to Jeff, the round-faced Sambo has removed and shelters his hat under his coat. He does so, the text makes clear, because he prefers to soak what the master owns rather than the hat he owns. By ridiculing Sambo's small act of rebellion, the artist minimized societal concerns about growing examples of slave disobedience and insubordination.[69]

Such reading, though, required sensitivity to their slaves' situation and is not discernible across Confederate depictions of enslavement. In Confederates' benign imagining of slavery, such behavior was inconceivable: slaves respected their masters, lived in comfortable homes, and were allowed their own possessions. More than this, cartoons showed a degree of Confederate awareness that slaves valued their possessions. Ownership gave control, and acts such as Sambo's provided some self-determination in an existence in which enslaved people enjoyed little.[70] The artist's acknowledgment of this reality represents awareness of slave psychology unusual in Confederate visual culture. Anything more, however, would be anathema to Confederates: a critique of slavery.

For slave owners, Sambo's appearance and name in "What's Master's" had another reading. Instead of seeing subversion in his actions, they saw the shiftless and untrustworthy slave. Additionally, the hatless slave's name, apelike stance, sheepish expression, and moon-faced physiognomy all suggested his harmlessness to readers. Making another slave, Jeff, ridicule Sambo told Confederates that only unintelligent slaves did not appreciate that masters cared for them. The cartoon revealed many white Southerners' belief that not every slave understood the logic of reciprocity.

The need for the harmless Sambo persona became more pressing as the war progressed. Despite proslavery rhetoric, the actions of bonded men, such as the hatless slave, displayed little of the loyalty that writers like Hammond and Fitzhugh promised. Further, such acts exposed Confederates to growing evidence that slave-master relations were not as seamless as they imagined.[71] Almost a year earlier, Mrs. Clement C. Clay of Alabama wrote: "The faithful slave is about played out. They are the most treacherous, brutal and ungrateful race on the globe." Writers such as Emory Thomas have used her words to illustrate the psychological blow that slaveholders felt when they realized "loyal" slaves only acted in their own interests, rather than those of their "paternalist" owners.[72] Furthermore, reports of violent acts committed by slaves, such as the 1864 murder of Mrs. Ann Copelia in Mobile, provided further evidence that proslavery ideologues had seriously misread the system. Examples like these presented Confederates with more evidence of slaves acting with agency and in ways contrary to proslavery rhetoric.[73]

The testimony of former slaves about their lives as enslaved people showed they disliked bondage and wanted to be free.[74] The disjuncture of war made it possible for between 500,000 and 700,000 of the South's 3.5 million slaves to leave family and friends and become what people during the Civil War termed "contraband."[75] Slaves who left the Confederacy challenged the proslavery ideas of slave loyalty to master and system. Conversely, for Confederates, the greatest sign that slaves appreciated Southern slavery were the few among hundreds of thousands of runaway slaves who, having escaped slavery and tasted freedom, returned to bondage.[76] Ex-slaves had many reasons for leaving the North. Some left because of the appalling and inhumane conditions they endured in Federal camps, the coercive practices of the Union military, or because they missed home.[77] Southerners convinced themselves that scheming Federals snared weak-minded slaves to rob Southerners of their wealth. On the other hand, they interpreted a slave's return as a conscious and physical endorsement of their system and evidence of the slave's awareness of its positive good.[78]

On at least two occasions, Confederate creatives used the instances of individuals who returned to slavery to refute abolitionists' critiques of the institution. The sketchy details of Richard Ogden's play *Miscegenation* indicate that Sam, a contraband, rejected freedom in the North to return to Virginia. The *Southern Punch* cartoon "The Returned Prodigal" provides a clearer instance of why a black man would return to slavery (fig. 3.12). Barefooted and with ragged clothing, Sambo comes back home. His dress and attitude contrast with that of his well-dressed and happy wife, Dinah, and child. The figures' faces, rendered in profile to heighten their physi-

FIG. 3.12. "The Returned Prodigal." From *Southern Punch*, Jan. 1, 1864. Courtesy of the Library of Virginia.

ognomical traits, suggested their personality. While similar, the "prodigal's" sloped forehead emphasized his slow wits. It implied that he had insufficient intellect to know, without experiencing both systems, that enslavement was preferable.[79] Additionally, the title alludes to the biblical story of the impecunious prodigal child who returns home to a forgiving father and also reminded viewers of concepts of paternalism. In the accompanying text, the prodigal told viewers he returned to escape the unremitting labor he had experienced in the North.

The belief that black people enjoyed a better lifestyle in the South was a key theme in Confederate imaginings of slavery. In early 1861, J. G. Richards wrote the lyrics for "I'm Coming to My Dixie Home" for the George Christy Minstrels.[80] When in January 1862, Blanton Duncan published a Confederate version, he added the phrase "Lincoln's Intelligent Contrabands"—a term used by Northern newspapers to identify escaped slaves whom they considered reliable informants—and added an illustration to the work's cover.[81] Created by Jacques Wissler (1803/6–87), it allowed Confederates to visualize a returned slave (fig. 3.13). Wissler depicted a cheerful slave in worn clothes, carrying a banjo under one arm and his belongings over his shoulder. He leaves behind a large building, reminiscent of a courthouse, and moves toward a palmetto tree, representing the South.[82] Additionally, Wissler gave the figure a face that looks less animal-like than many other images of slaves. His features suggested that while any slave might run away, those with sense enough returned to the South. The image complements the song's lyrics:

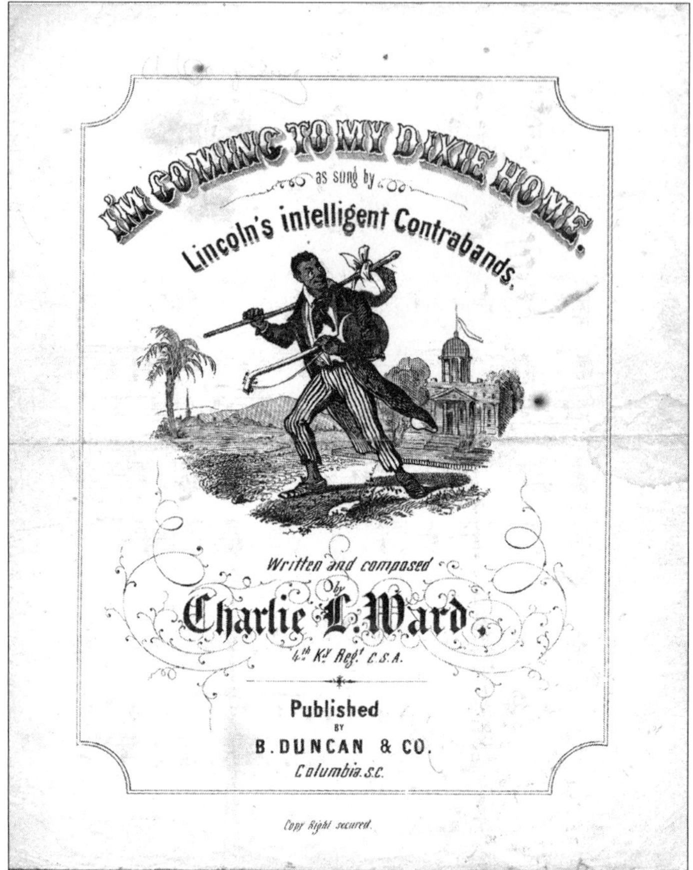

FIG. 3.13. Cover of Charles L. Ward's "I'm Coming to My Dixie Home," by Jacques Wissler (Columbia, S.C.: Blanton Duncan, 1862). Courtesy of Lincoln Sheet Music, John Hay Library, Brown University.

> I'd rather work de cotton patch
> And die on corn and bacon
> Dan lib up Norf on good white bread
> Ob abolition makin'.

With Wissler's image in mind, Confederates sang of black people preferring the system of slavery over freedom.

Images of happy slaves onstage or in artwork helped comfort Confederates. They conformed to and affirmed their belief that the enslaved appreciated the system's value, and helped counteract worrying evidence to the contrary.[83] Furthermore, in these fantasies of Yankee exploitation and mistreatment of slaves, they found confirmation of their enemy's inhuman greed. Contrasted with benign images of Southern slavery, it contributed to many Southerners' trust in the institution's permanence.[84]

FIG. 3.14. Masthead of *Southern Illustrated News,* by William Ludwell Sheppard, 1865. This design was used from Jan. 14 to Feb. 2, 1865 (last issue?) and shows two important events in the Confederacy's "life's struggle." On the left is the 1861 bombardment of Fort Sumter, and on the right the "splendid victory" in 1862 of the CSS *Virginia* in Hampton Roads. From *Southern Illustrated News,* Jan. 21, 1865. Courtesy of Emory University.

One of the last pieces of imagery created in the Confederacy conveyed this optimism. On January 14, 1865, the *Southern Illustrated News* unveiled its new masthead (fig. 3.14). Designed by William Ludwell Sheppard (1833–1912), Captain John W. Torsch (1834–89) engraved it "upon the picket line—within musket shot of the enemy."[85] The central vignette featured four figures, two black and two white.[86] Sheppard intended the drawing to show African Americans in "their happiest sphere"—working for white people among sugarcane, tobacco leaves, and cotton bloom and sheltered under the shade of Southern palmetto and pine. The black woman proffers a basket of cotton to a black man who carries a harvesting basket on his shoulder. Their lack of physiognomic distortion lent the figures dignity and added to the idea of intelligent and contented enslaved Southerners, ready to work. Although divided by space and gaze, the composition acknowledges both free and slave in the Confederate nation. Despite almost four years of evidence to contradict the proslavery rhetoric, Sheppard's illustration presented Confederates with little change in ideology. It is a harmonious world where slave and free exist on the same plane but in their separate spheres.

By altering and manipulating presentations of slaves and enslavement, Confederate visual culture contributed to white Southerners' blindness to the institution's inhuman aspects. Whether presented silently or with dialogue, it joined sources, such as proslavery literature, to help Confederates imagine the slavery they fought to maintain and refute its critics.[87] This material helped create psychological distance for Confederate whites, cloaked slavery's problematic aspects with the fallacies of benevolent paternalism, and helped lessen anxieties about an enslaved people's loyalty.[88] Yet while wartime evidence proved these were illusions, their reemergence after the war, as part of the myths of the Lost Cause, showed the resilience and attraction of these ideas.[89]

Many Confederates believed slavery was not only peaceful and morally beneficial but also the best method to fully realize the potential of the South's agricultural wealth. However, slavery's presence did more than provide a reason for their struggle. It sharpened Southerners' sensitivity to notions of dependence and independence. This awareness deepened as it became clear that they were engaged in a protracted war and that independence would require more than agricultural production. Without radical shifts in the South's economy it would be impossible to protect the cornerstone from outside interference, and subjugation by the North.

CHAPTER 4

Manufacturing and Southern Autonomy

> All the forges and machine shops of our Confederacy are busy with engines of war, and can spare but little time for those of peace.
> —"The Manufacturing Enterprises of the South," *Charleston Mercury*, January 22, 1862

War found the Confederate manufacturing woefully ill prepared to meet the nation's needs. On June 1, 1860, though almost 30 percent of the United States' population lived in the South, the region possessed just 17 percent of the nation's manufacturing capacity.[1] President Lincoln's closure of the borders in April 1861 further emphasized Southern reliance on Northern factories for the largest to smallest machine-made item. In response, from spring 1861, Southerners built and expanded manufacturing to meet demands and needs. Historians such as Emory Thomas, Raimondo Luraghi, and Harold Wilson have recognized and documented the phenomenal rate of industrialization Confederates achieved.[2] More recently, Michael Bonner has detailed the corporatist nature of the Confederacy through a study of both the Tredegar munitions complex and Alabama's Shelby Ironworks.[3] Bonner concludes that "Confederate industrial policy was one of the essential ingredients in southern nationalism."[4] However, what increased domestic production meant to Confederates or how they understood the social, economic, and political changes that took place is less well-known. Confederates found that industrialization affected not only how they saw themselves but also their relationship with the government and each other.

MANUFACTURING AS AN ECONOMIC WEAPON

At the war's outset, manufacturing figured into Confederates' notions of what differentiated them from the North.[5] Northerners' natural insatiable greed, they believed, suited them for manufacturing and moneymaking pursuits.[6] Indeed, their avarice swept aside their morality. As Macon's *Georgia Weekly Telegraph* told readers, Yankee dishonesty suited them for production, for "they are a manufacturing people—they appear to delight in fabrications generally."[7] Moreover, to Southern ideologues, the North's need for a free labor force attracted European immigrants. In some partisan Southerners' minds, these immigrants imported and enabled the development of dangerous radical movements that threatened social order.[8] For some planters, a *Southern Monthly* writer explained, introducing industry meant bringing in a Northern "population unfriendly to our institutions."[9] Yankees in the midst of the South, they held, could not resist destabilizing and agitating against slavery.[10]

Such thinking reflected Southern prejudices against manufacturing and contributed to its comparative weakness.[11] It was present in Confederate leader Louis T. Wigfall's statement to *London Times* reporter William Russell: "We are an agricultural people . . . we want no manufactures."[12] Wigfall was not alone in this belief.[13] At the outset of the war, many Confederates envisioned an agrarian South.[14] The Confederate Constitution reinforced this concept by limiting government's ability to "promote or foster" manufacturing and Congress's capacity to "facilitate commerce."[15] This attitude was not realistic, for as one editor stated in 1861, the South depended on Europe and the North for "everything save meat and bread." Prejudices against manufacturing did not augur well for Confederate industry.[16]

In the prewar period, some Southerners had called for more manufacturing. However, this was not always for independence alone. By 1861, a number saw manufacturing as a weapon against the North.[17] They imagined avarice as the Yankees' Achilles heel. As the editor of the *Columbus (Ga.) Daily Sun* told his readers in November 1860, the "change of purchase from North to South is affecting punishment for enemies of our institutions."[18] Attempting to keep their cash from Northerners led many prewar military companies to purchase Southern-made material for their uniforms. Newspapers and manufacturing advocates heralded each undertaking as practical and symbolic acts of independence and encouraged others to do the same.[19] When Professor Joseph Jones addressed a cotton planters' convention in Macon, he told them: "The fire and sword with which our Northern enemies threaten us, will be our ultimate good and their final injury" because of the loss to Northerners of Southern markets.[20]

When the "fire and sword" came, only the South's textile industry proved ready to contribute meaningfully to the struggle. In 1860, the South ranked fourth in the world for the number of pounds of cotton its mills consumed. The industry enjoyed the proximity of raw materials, the plantation economy's demands, profits, and the promotion of Southern control of Southern produce.[21] As one North Carolina editor told readers in May 1861, while they lacked armaments "in the matter of uniforms we can help ourselves and we should."[22] This situation went to the core of their struggle for independence. Without manufacturing, the South could not sustain its separation. In May 1861, the *Augusta Chronicle and Sentinel*, reprinted an article from Huntsville, Alabama's *Advocate* that warned: "Whatever can be made at the South now should be. The war may be upon us for years and our people should prepare to endure privations and provide for its necessities. The time for arrogance is over. We should husband our resources so as to be independent."[23] The outbreak of war transformed industrialization from a symbolic weapon for Southern nationalists into a part of the quest for Confederate autonomy.

Linking manufacturing to ideas of national profit and self-reliance made its expansion more palatable.[24] Establishing textile, button, and munitions factories, rather than relying on Europe or the North, Baton Rouge's *Daily Advocate* told readers, would create a deep "foundation wall for the establishment of a solid fabric of Southern Independence."[25] Further, the *Southern Monthly* told readers, international law required a nation to have a self-sustaining economy as a prerequisite for recognition by the world's governments.[26] These articles linked the need to expand industry with the Confederacy's wider political aims and encouraged the formation and expansion of Southern manufacturing.

The idea of self-reliance resonated deeply with Southerners. Slavery sensitized them to concepts of dependence and independence, and allusions to it emerged in Southern discussions of industrialization.[27] In late 1861, for instance, a Mississippi soldier correspondent hoped to never "wander again into the disgusting field of dependence, which has shamefully characterized us all along."[28] Southerners advanced a variety of reasons for their reliance on others, such as Northerners shaping self-serving legislation, Southerners' implicit trusting natures, or even their own prejudice against manufacturing.[29] Each added impetus to increase manufacturing while changing the way Southerners imagined themselves.

Factors other than war and political independence motivated Southerners to value manufacturing. As prewar stocks disappeared from shops, Southern manufacturers attempted to fill the vacuum. Demand and the positive reception of domestically made goods prompted other Southern manufactures to launch ventures. Gradually, Confederate-made versions of produce, from beer to fans made from wheat, appeared in the marketplace.[30] The everyday nature of these objects highlighted the South's reliance on the North but also gained other meanings in Confederate rhetoric.[31]

By the first winter of the war, Confederate newspapers turned these items into emblems of Southerners' skills, their desire for independence, and evidence of their improvement as a people. From being unready and ill prepared, Confederates read that Southern ingenuity and goods enabled Southern armies to win victories against a better-supplied enemy.[32] Even the smallest items, such as buttons, indicated to the *Savannah Republican* that the South was "becoming a free and independent people."[33]

Confederates enlisted these artifacts as indicators of the success of their national project. For example, describing how Samuel Griswold had altered his cotton gin factory to one that built Colt-style revolvers, a Georgia newspaper called it "a strong illustration of the power of the South to supply her wants."[34] Griswold's story provides a model of Confederate industrialization. Georgia's secession in January 1861 brought the seventy-year-old, Connecticut-born manufacturer out of retirement. In 1835, Griswold established his own community, modestly named "Griswoldville," and began making the cotton gins that brought success to his business. By the time Georgia seceded, his various mills and factories employed over one hundred enslaved and white workers. After a Union incursion on Georgia's coast prompted a call for arms, Griswold turned his factories to making weapons. Beginning in March 1862, he converted his machinery first to create pikes and then revolvers (fig. 4.1).[35] By July 1862, twenty-four hands (all but two of whom were enslaved) worked twenty-two machines, producing between fifty and sixty revolvers a week.[36] Lack of arms making expertise and the use of iron rather than steel compromised the revolvers' quality. Under testing by Confederate ordnance officers in October 1862, three of their first twenty-two revolvers burst.[37]

The quality improved from July 1862, until Union cavalry destroyed the township by November 22, 1864. Over that period, the business delivered over thirty-five hundred serviceable revolvers to Confederate forces. Griswold's revolvers show that the factory used alternatives, such as recycled scrap and donated brass or bronze, to overcome shortages. Additionally, it developed hardening techniques to create the springs required for each revolver's mechanism and also used unseasoned walnut for the grips. However, though most of the pistols appear to have been soundly made and finished, inclusions and variations in the ironwork suggested inconsistent foundry techniques.[38]

Enterprises such as Griswold's provided Southerners with evidence of their nation's growing industrial independence and character. The comparison with non-Southern products also showed their success. The *New Orleans Bee*, for example, reported that Cook Brothers' Enfield pattern rifles bore barrels and intentions "truer" than either English or Belgian rifles.[39] Memphis's *Daily Appeal* reported Schneider and Glassick's revolvers as "a beautiful weapon, not inferior to the Colt's make in any particular."[40] Altogether, articles like these framed Confederate-made goods as tokens of independence and also bolstered Confederate confidence in their ultimate success.

Manufactures also provided Confederates with yet another avenue through which to critique the North. Long before the war, many Southerners believed that Yan-

FIG. 4.1. Griswold and Gunnison Revolver #1321. Although Griswold's mechanics copied the form of the Colt 1851 navy revolver, the frames were made from brass and the cylinders from twisted iron due to the shortage of steel in the South. Photo courtesy of the National Rifle Association Museums.

kee-made items instanced Northern trickery and sharp business practices.[41] For example, a writer in Richmond's *Dispatch* explained, "Examine all the fabrics of Yankee industry and invention, and those practices which hide defects and impose cheats upon the world are multifarious and ever apparent."[42] In similar fashion, a visitor to the Crenshaw Woolen Mill, then engaged in making cloth for the Confederate army, noted that while their fabric lacked "the high finish," it was heavier and stronger, with more "honest coloring," than "Yankee cloth."[43] Such reports encouraged Confederates to embrace industry as part of their struggle for political independence and to see their products as tokens of difference between North and South.[44]

Other Confederates drew meaning from the speed with which the South industrialized itself.[45] In September 1861, George Fitzhugh suggested evidence of a miraculous hand in the "harmonious and efficient movement" between the people and the state and Confederate governments.[46] Two months later, President Jefferson Davis saw God's influence in the South's "new branches of manufacturing."[47] Similarly, just over a year later, one writer viewed the war as "God ordained instrumentality." Through war industrialization, the Almighty revealed the "respectability of labor" and their "native genius and constructive habits" to Southerners.[48] Such associations lent industrialization both patriotic and spiritual significance.

The relationship of entrepreneurial capitalism and independence led Confederate ideologues to sanction investment in manufacturing. "Every good citizen," intoned the *Southern Field and Fireside,* by contributing work or wealth, "will do his best to supply some public want in this emergency."[49] In the same fashion, from early in the war Confederate newspapers encouraged investment in industry.[50] For example, writing from the Black Belt township of Holly Springs, Mississippi, the editor rejoiced at the rapid advancement of "Messrs. Jones, McElwane & Co['s]" plans to expand and retool its manufactory to produce small arms because it would not only aid the South in achieving "national independence" but also attract capital that would "add greatly to the prosperity of our happy city of flowers."[51] Confederates' embrace of manufacturing enabled entrepreneurs to consider themselves patriots and provided previously unimagined levels of encouragement for investors.

While Confederate print idealized the South's manufacturing, experiencing these articles tested the hype. "Confederate," wrote Louisiana teenager Sarah Morgan, "means anything that is rough, unfinished, unfashionable or poor." Here she referred to a mule-drawn four-seat wagon termed "Confederate carriage," in which Morgan "gladly" accepted a ride, "partly for the ride and sight, [and] partly to show we were not ashamed" of the vehicle.[52] Driven by necessity to use substandard Confederate versions, people like Sarah Morgan turned them into patriotic tokens.[53] However, few news sources came close to Morgan's critique of Confederate goods. When the government issued these articles to its armies, it influenced the nation's visibility and political profile.

MANUFACTURING AND THE WAR EFFORT

Records show that over 350,000 individuals or businesses supplied the Confederate government with the services and goods required to conduct the war.[54] Their contracts bound these enterprises to the Confederate government and the fate of the nation. This mutual reliance helped define the government and provide it with greater substance. Produced for the government and distributed to Confederate citizen soldiers, the manufacturing standards and supply of these goods provided physical evidence that an independent Confederacy existed. However, issues such as the variable quality and quantity of these goods undermined Confederate soldiers' and citizens' opinion of both Confederate manufacturers and the government for which they worked.

Armies need arms and ammunition, and in 1861, the South lacked both. In response to this need, munitions factories sprang up across the South. The Confederate army's Ordnance Department and the Nitre and Mining Bureau assumed responsibility for providing the arms, ammunition, and accouterments required to keep Southern soldiers ready for combat. Historian Richard Goff explained that "faced initially with few shops or skilled workmen or mines on which to build an ordnance complex," these efforts formed "one of the most impressive chapters in Confederate history."[55] Likewise, others believed that the Confederacy's efforts to centralize control of industry presented a rare example of success by the nation.[56] Regardless of such positive reports, studying what they made and how Confederates received it reveals greater complexity.

Although the former head of the Ordnance Department, Josiah Gorgas, reflected that the South never lost a battle for want of arms or ammunition, few civilian Confederates knew of the efforts of the Ordnance Department to achieve this feat. A dearth of newspaper reports meant that the department's work made little bearing on Confederate civilian morale and ideology.[57] However, Gorgas's department made greater impact in the field. The quality of Confederate-made ammunition and equipment affected the military's morale and efficiency.

Civil War period soldiers mainly used leather and/or fabric accouterments. Leather housed ammunition, encased feet in boots and shoes, fastened knapsacks and haversacks, and was used for cap visors. But the South possessed limited stocks of this valuable material and lacked the infrastructure to produce it in meaningful quantities. The attempts to satisfy this want led Southern manufacturers to use a variety of stopgap or makeshift measures. For example, New Orleans saddlers Magee and George produced an abundance of leather infantry and artillery equipment during the first year of the war. A study of this firm's output by Thomas Czekanski reveals that it responded to shortages by using expedients, such as thinner leather.[58] Later companies, including N. Crown and Company and Williams, Brands and Company, both of Columbus, Georgia, produced sets made of tarred canvas cartridge and cap boxes. Unlike many Confederate producers, these companies proudly stamped each piece with their company name on goods they made for Gorgas's Ordnance Department between October 1863 and February 1864.[59] Whether leather or canvas, however, Confederates such as Ephraim Anderson and his Missouri comrades considered their leather gear inferior to that of the Federals. Despite "C.S." patriotically decorating the new accoutrement, they kept their U.S. gear because they considered it "better than those they were drawing."[60] Practical Confederates, like these, chose quality over a show of allegiance. Other artifacts also showed the Confederate government's inability to supply military equipment equal in standard to their enemy's.

In the 1890s, Josiah Gorgas recalled President Davis's logic in the ordering of Confederate supply: "Men must first be fed, next armed, and even clothing must follow these; for if they are fed and have arms and ammunition they can fight."[61] Regardless of this intention, a study of the arms and ammunition issued to Confederate soldiers reveals an Ordnance Department not always able to deliver on Davis's second intention.

Confederates regarded the Tredegar complex in Richmond as their premier armory. After a tour of the facilities in 1861, one enthusiastic correspondent wrote, "I hazard nothing in affirming that the work turned out from the Tredegar shops will compare favorably with any in the world." To the writer, the reasons were obvious. "It has all the advantages of the best iron, the most consummate skill, and its machinery is driven by water power—the cheapest force at our command."[62] Almost three years later, another observer reported that its 480 hands produced muskets "pronounced by military men fully equal to any made by the enemy, and as a general thing, preferable to them."[63] Despite such a glowing report, the quality of the arms produced in Tredegar's Richmond Armory did not match these superlatives.

The Richmond armory produced some of the forty thousand versions of the U.S. M1855 Rifle made in the Confederacy.[64] A study of a sample of these weapons by E. Larry Jackson found that all bore inspection marks indicating that the Confederate Ordnance Department believed them to be serviceable. While functional, however, the Richmond armory firearms compared poorly to the United States–made versions. Their barrels are made of metal that shows inclusions, the weld lines are visible, and their bores are uneven. In addition, their overall finish is much rougher than the United States product (fig. 4.2).[65] These factors led Confederate soldiers to prefer English-made Enfield or the U.S. Springfield Rifles over their local version.

The quality and supply of other Confederate armaments and ammunition also varied. An adequate inspection system ensured that most Confederate-made ordnance performed its job to some extent. However, substandard gunpowder fouled guns after six or seven rounds, shell fuses exploded prematurely, bullets arrived at the front line unable to fit muskets, cannon carriages broke in combat after a few shots, and especially in the early part of the war, large guns blew up.[66] After a battle in 1862, one frustrated general wrote his commanding general that he believed "that there was treachery in the Ordnance Department."[67] As the war progressed, former Confederate general of artillery Edward Porter Alexander recollected that though "we gradually made great improvements, the enemy were always far ahead of us."[68] Faulty arms and ammunition further decreased the effectiveness of already outnumbered Confederate soldiers in battle. Nevertheless, knowledge of these deficiencies remained largely within the army and War Department. Confederate newspapers fed the belief in the quality of Southern-made arms and ammunition with reports such as one written in November 1862 concerning a Confederate States–made Sharps rifle. On inspecting it, the *Richmond Enquirer* puffed, even a Yankee would have to "acknowledge our own ability to soon compete with them in everything."[69]

While lower on Davis's scale of importance for soldiers, Confederate government–issued clothing received greater public attention. Over its existence, the Con-

FIG. 4.2. *Muzzles of M1855 Muskets.* The example on the left was produced by the United States' arsenal at Springfield, Ill., the three others at the Confederate States' arsenal at Richmond, Va. Note the varying thickness of the Confederate versions. Photo courtesy of *North South Trader* 18, no. 3; "Whistling Dixie," by E. Larry Jackson, photo by Allan Ruprecht.

federate quartermaster harnessed the production of the South's factories and built an enormous department capable of clothing every Confederate soldier. One South Carolina editor stated, "There is as much patriotism in manufacturing and making a suit of clothes for a soldier, as in fighting for independence."[70] However, the behavior of government officials in marshaling and organizing manufacturing injured the cause and eroded popular support for the Davis government.[71]

The Quartermaster's Department became a visible arm of government in people's lives. This began when the quartermaster took greater responsibility for supplying the armies with clothing and shoes. In late 1861, Charleston's *Mercury* told its readers that being in front of the world, the government had an obligation to clothe its troops.[72] In response to practical and public pressure, in October 1862, Congress eventually authorized the Quartermaster's Department to supply all soldiers.[73] Charged with gathering the raw materials required to supply the army quartermaster, impressment officers often became the point of contact between the central government and the people.[74] From April 1863, this became formalized in the "tax-in-kind" system, in which citizens paid tax using produce rather than money. Although successful in practical terms, tax-in-kind put one more strain on the relationship between the public and Confederate officialdom.[75] In the public's perception, the state and the Quartermaster's Department blurred into a single entity.

Beginning in May 1861, Southern mills produced gray woolen cloth for the Quartermaster's Department.[76] Until April 1863, most mills wove wool purchased in the marketplace by the quartermaster, but tax-in-kind made it possible for quartermasters to purchase the South's scant supply of wool at three dollars a pound when the marketplace paid five dollars a pound.[77] By the middle of 1864, the over 178,600 yards of fabric that the mills produced for the government helped make over 600,000 suits a year.[78] This amount, Quartermaster General A. R. Lawton estimated, provided two-thirds of the material used to make Southern uniforms.[79]

Surviving examples of central-issue clothing show the plain but generally substantial nature of uniforms made by the Quartermaster's Department. Cut by teams of tailors from either imported English wool cloth or Southern-made jeans (wool woven on cotton warp), according to patterns peculiar to each clothing depot, women sewed the pieces together with undyed cotton thread and lined each garment with Southern-made cotton, and inspectors checked the batches before shipping them to the front. Once in the field, brigade or regimental officers again inspected and rejected substandard articles.[80] Sometime the issued clothing even drew favorable comment from the other side.[81] In late January 1863, "an individual direct from the South," who traveled extensively around the Confederacy, reported that the Confederate government dressed its troops in "stout serviceable uniforms of coarse gray jeans."[82] In May 1864, an Ohio officer even wrote, "I had the pleasure of seeing 4,000 prisoners . . . they were all clad in neat gray jackets and pantaloons with entire seats. In contrast, we were in rags."[83] By providing this clothing, the Confederate government went some way toward meeting its responsibility to its troops.

The provision of what soldiers often termed "government clothing" impacted army morale.[84] Army clothing freed families and communities from the cost of making their soldiers' apparel.[85] Moreover, some soldiers, like Floridian Seton Fleming, saw it as evidence of their nation's independence. In late 1863, looking at his well-clothed, shod, and equipped comrades, he wrote with pride that the Confederacy was now "dependent for nothing upon those who used to furnish us everything."[86] Overall such garments acted as physical tokens of the government for which they fought and its ultimate responsibility for the business of clothing the troops.[87]

MANUFACTURING'S SOCIAL IMPACT

When the quality or quantity of government clothing varied, it prompted dissatisfaction among the soldiers. While nineteenth-century men rarely complained about clothing, comments about rough material, poor-quality construction, and the cost of government articles sometimes appeared in newspapers and letters.[88] According to one well-supplied Texan soldier in early 1865, "too much speculation on the part of the authorities" led to the poor-quality of the clothes they received.[89] Markedly, in late 1862, a correspondent for the *Mobile (Ala.) Weekly Advertiser and Register* explained that "a planter who would take as little care of the health of his slaves as the Government does of its soldiers would soon have none to care for." Moreover, "he would be driven out of the community by his indignant neighbors."[90] Such reports further damaged quartermasters' standing and, by extension, the government that had appointed them.

Perceived favoritism in the way the government issued clothing also led to concern. "The conscript is the prodigal son," an Alabama officer wrote to his local newspaper during May 1864; "he was lost and is found; for him a house is built, good clothes and shoes are plentiful."[91] In a similar vein, one disgruntled soldier wrote to a Richmond newspaper in November 1863: "We made requisition for uniforms and never get them. The best clothing provided to the army is distributed to the soldiers and 2nd Class militia about Richmond, whilst the inferior and refuse clothing is sent to the Army."[92] The sight of well-dressed garrison troops while soldiers in the field went poorly clad created resentment among soldiers and led to charges of partiality.

For other Confederates, when the government failed to provide enough clothig for the army, it threatened the nation's special relationship with the Almighty. For example, when calling attention to the army's inadequate clothing in November 1862, Richmond's *Whig* warned, "God will not prosper the cause of such people."[93] Inspection reports of Confederate forces surviving from the last year and a half of the war show the difficulty the government faced in keeping units supplied with clothing.[94] In addition, they also revealed how much clothing the nation's soldiers could represent an Achilles' heel for the relationship between the people, the army, and the government.

When the Quartermaster's Department, the government's arm for supplying clothing, failed to procure sufficient supplies for the army, it damaged the standing of both in civilian eyes. By the midpoint of the war, government officials involved in supplying army clothes suffered from a declining reputation in the Confederate South. Additionally, the visibility that their buff-faced uniforms gave quartermasters stationed in towns and their contrast with poorly dressed frontline soldiers reinforced public prejudices.[95] In a widely republished article from mid-1864, one Confederate grumbled, "Let a private come in from the army and apply for clothing and shoes, and the probability is that he be told there are none to give him, while at the very same time officers of that bureau are strutting the streets in their suits of Confederate gray."[96] Further, an 1863 editorial regarding commissaries and quartermasters called attention to the "selfishness" that had "usurped the place of patriotism and public duty in too many." Nevertheless, they quickly added that, bad as they were, Confederate quartermasters were still much better than the "corrupt set of men who are ravaging our territory."[97]

By late 1863, such instances poisoned public opinion. The *Savannah Daily News* wrote of the "general suspicion in the public mind, that speculation and plunder, and misuse of authority for private purpose, have often been put before public duty and public service" by members of the Commissary and Quartermaster's Departments.[98] In like manner, the *Richmond Examiner* reported, "Quartermasters sometimes get rich—they ought never get rich."[99] One joke held that AQMCSA, the acronym for "Assistant Quartermaster Confederate States Army," actually stood for "A Quartermaster Can Steal Anything."[100] Articles like this further spread public disenchantment with this branch of the Confederate government.

On November 5, 1863, the selfishness and greed of Confederate quartermasters appeared onstage at the New Richmond Theatre, through the farce *Great Expectations; or Getting Promoted.*[101] Set in Richmond, the play told the story of "Captain Singleton, AQM." Returned from a "devilish rough time," tending wagons during the early stages of the Gettysburg campaign, the self-absorbed Singleton is intent on getting a position as "Post Quartermaster, with the rank of Major." According to Singleton, speculation is "perfectly legitimate" when costs are so high and his pay so "very small." After listening to him, Singleton's friend Robinson reads this poem from a slip of paper:

Of all the officers I know,
    I'd rather be a Quartermaster,
Unless to me some man you show,
    Who makes his money faster,
I'd wear my uniform always,
    Unless it was on battle days,
And then, I'd wear my duster:
    For I decline the battle line,
Or any other muster.

To this, Singleton replies, "Pretty hard on us, but in the main true." Despite a letter of recommendation bearing the signatures of influential men, along with "a seventy-five dollar hat and a bottle of whiskey" in this morality tale, his application failed.[102] The play showed that many Confederates shared a low regard for quartermasters.

Great Expectations joined stories that poisoned the reputation of all quartermasters, from leaders to the lower ranks.[103] Incessant rumors of financial and moral improprieties led common Confederates to treat quartermasters with disdain. In a letter to the *Columbus (Ga.) Sun,* published in late January 1864, an unknown quartermaster complained, "It has become the custom, throughout the Confederacy, to abuse, indiscriminately, the officers serving in the Quartermaster Department."[104] Indeed, in early 1864, such pressure compelled former West Point graduate and regular army officer Harry J. Raphael to resign. The principal reason he offered was "that the Quartermaster's Department has become so disreputable and odious to the Army and Public at large that I am ashamed to acknowledge that I am a member of that institution."[105] Despite the appointment of a new department head in August 1863 and a number of reforms, inefficiencies persisted; overall, the government's efforts to clothe its soldiers marred the Quartermaster's Department's public standing.[106]

Textile manufacturers who supplied the materials shared a similarly poor reputation. From early in the war, demand drove up prices. In late 1861, William Holden of the *Raleigh Semi-Weekly Standard* asked, "How is it" that factories paid between eight and ten cents for cotton but demanded nearly a 100 percent increase over former prices? He concluded that they are "taking advantage of necessity."[107] The *Dallas Herald* asked in May 1862, "Will the manufacturer explain, and, if he can, relieve us from the necessity of setting him down as an extortioner, and denouncing him as such?"[108] By the last year of the war, legislation meant that the Quartermaster's Department claimed two-thirds of the fabric issuing from mills at government prices. The mills could charge whatever price suited them for the remaining one-third of their product. To Confederates, the price of the material bore little relationship to the costs of the labor and raw materials. Considering reports like these, it seemed a spirit of greed was developing across the South (fig. 4.3).

Mill owners and their supporters used newspapers to try to improve their reputation. They reported not only information on production but also acts of generosity and any steps factory owners had taken to improve the living standard of their workers.[109] In late October 1862, the *Savannah Republican* reminded readers who blamed the factories for high prices that they had "saved the country from Yankee domination." Further, without them, "the Southern Confederacy would, by this time, have been forced into subjection, or like the ancients, been 'clothed in sheep skins and goats skin, being destitute, afflicted, tormented.'"[110] In June 1864, managers and owners of twenty-seven factories from North Carolina and Georgia reported that they felt "misunderstood and misrepresented" and sought to clear up matters. They laid blame on high prices and shortages of materials and on the slow payments of debts by the government and its control of factory supplies. Rather than blame

FIG. 4.3. "In Favor of the Prosecution of the War." This cartoon linked the "patriotism" of government contractors to personal profit rather than the Southern cause. The contractors form a circle, with their hands reaching into each other's pockets or holding cudgels or moneybags. They appear arrogantly unified in defense of their own endeavors. From *Confederate Spirit and Knapsack of Fun*, May 1864. Courtesy of Princeton University.

mill owners, Confederates should thank them. The fault, stated the manufacturers' group, lay with the "Confederate Government" and not them.[111]

As Confederates increasingly struggled to clothe themselves, the results of high-priced fabrics became visible in the streets. Touring the Confederacy in November and December 1862, Englishman W. C. Corsan frequently noted the cost and shortage of dry goods. In Jackson, Mississippi, he found empty stores and owners unable to obtain new stock. In Mobile, Alabama, he discovered stores "dribbling" out goods "for cash, at enormous profit." Charleston, South Carolina, stores offered blockade goods for sale at high prices, and he heard whispers of profiteering.[112] On May 2, 1863, Richmond War Department clerk John B. Jones wrote, "A portion of the people look like vagabonds," and only "speculators, and thieving quartermasters and commissaries" appear "sleek and comfortable."[113] Although most people wore make-do, the wealth of some Southerners showed in the luxury blockade-run goods they wore. Their appearance divided the population. It indicated that not all Confederates suffered equally, and this knowledge demoralized Confederates.[114] Rather than unifying the South, textiles showed a fractured nation.

Factors such as these contributed to the frustrations that fired a spate of civil disorders across the South from June 1862 to the fall of 1863. Starting in Bartow, Georgia, and affecting both small and large communities, women agitated for greater access to materials. Sometimes these actions extended to riots and looting.[115] To some Confederates, the fault lay not with the manufacturers but elsewhere. "Our press," the *Countryman*'s Joseph Addison Turner wrote in April 1863, "have sown dragon's teeth in their ceaseless, inane ravings about speculation and extortion."[116] No doubt, high prices and empty shelves in stores also played a part. Even as social disturbances petered out by the winter of 1863–64, the South's industrialization created other concerns.

For some, manufacturing risked the very soul of the Confederacy. With dread, they watched as some countrymen adopted behaviors reminiscent of Northerners.[117] In April 1862, the *Charleston Mercury* wondered, "Do manufactures invariably turn men into Yankees?"[118] In late 1862, visiting English manufacturer William Corsan observed: "Whether they consider it a complement or not, it is a fact that there is enough of the Yankee about them to invent and make machines, and look uncommonly sharp after making them pay."[119] Manufacturing revealed the uncomfortable truth of the small distance between the Confederate "us" and Yankee "them."

As the war closed, some Confederates' faith in the capacity of manufacturing to gain economic independence reflected their capacity for self-deception.[120] In September 1864, the *Macon Daily Telegraph and Confederate* thanked God for the war as it had awoken Southerners' heart, genius, and skill and swept away "Yankee ideas and systems."[121] Even in January 1865, though the South was "hermetically sealed" from the outside world and organizations like the Quartermaster's Department operated by eking out limited materials, Richmond's *Whig* believed that the Confederacy could still achieve great things if the government adopted a "properly organized system" for its industries.[122] Given the poor standing of both the government and manufacturing and the Union forces moving with impunity across the Southern states, this was delusion on a grand scale.

Newspaper articles, such as these, revealed a disjuncture between Confederate rhetoric about manufacturing and reality. The reality, represented by the Confederate Quartermaster's Department, showed that as the government increased its control over materials and production, the public became more aware and critical of its inefficiency and self-interest. Moreover, Confederate-made goods appeared makeshift; they lacked the same quality and workmanship when compared to goods made elsewhere. And the ways Southern manufacturers acted suggested that differences between "Yankee systems and ideas" and those in the South were not so great as imagined.

Ultimately, historians' assessment of the South's rapid wartime industrialization is accurate, but it masks the stresses the process brought to bear on the people. The government managed to sustain the army, but in doing so, it compromised the Constitution and its reputation.[123] In garnering necessary resources, Confederate civilians suffered from shortages. The process of supplying the army brought people into closer contact with government officials with varying degrees of competence and honesty. The experience, whether personal or perceived through print media, disillusioned many Confederates about the quality of their government. Southern manufacturing failed to deliver either the goods or icons required to defend, rally, or unite the nation. Fostered at least as much by the government, graphic print businesses offered another industry with the potential to help Confederates imagine their nation.

CHAPTER 5

The Photographic and Graphic Print Industries

Though we're exempt, we're not the *metal*
To *keep* in doors when duty calls:
But onward will we *press,* to settle
This knotty *case* with *lead*-en *balls.*

. . . .

And when, in after years to come,
Our history's read by youth and sage,
They'll make a *side-note* of "well done,"
On this, our *volume's* brightest *page!*

—HARRY C. TREAKLE, "The Printers of Virginia to 'Old Abe,'" *Confederate Spirit, and Knapsack of Fun,* February 1864

In March 1864, the *Richmond Whig* reported on the recently published *Southern Literary Messenger.* "The great attraction to the ladies," the paper announced, "is the colored lithographic plate of the latest Paris fashions." "The picture," it continued, "is quite a novelty in the South, where such things were wholly unknown even in the palmiest days of peace."[1] Produced by newcomer to the Confederate print marketplace, George Dunn (1816–83), the plate was not only the first colored image to appear in the *Messenger* but also the first ever featured entirely engraved and printed in the South. Both the publication of this tinted print and the *Whig*'s notice show the growth of Confederate domestic reprographic industries.

A study of the Confederacy's photographic and print industry indicates the extent and impact of its development within the Civil War South. The potential for growth was great. Across the Western hemisphere, reprographic technologies flourished to feed the contemporary taste for visual stimuli. This imagery encompassed the ephemeral to the treasured and represented the ideas current in each respective parent society.[2] In a society like that of the South, with low literacy levels and a social gap between those who did or did not own slaves, a flourishing reprographic industry promised a vehicle through which to pictorially deliver unifying ideology throughout the classes. Furthermore, a study of this industry as material culture reflects the efforts Southerners applied to meet their reprographic needs and desires.

From stereoscopic photographs to postage stamps, nineteenth-century Americans purchased and used a range of reproduced imagery. In 1861, however, the Confederacy lacked the infrastructure and manpower required to maintain supply close to prewar levels. As in so many other industries, the North's reprographic industries dwarfed those in the prewar South. In 1860, the U.S. Census reported that 1,400 printing houses operated in northern states, while only 151 similar businesses existed in the South. Moreover, none of the Southern enterprises identified themselves as offering engraving or lithographic services. Instead, a handful of individual lithographers and engravers dotted across the South, such as Nashville's John F. Wagner, provided a local source producing small-run jobs.[3] Journals produced south of the Potomac River, such as *De Bow's Review*, rarely featured plates. Similarly, besides around three hundred itinerant photographers, only thirteen photographic establishments, employing a total of twenty-four men, existed across the future Confederate States.[4] Southern publishers, including sometime Nashville music publishers C. D. Benson, who contracted lithographers in Louisville, Kentucky, to produce the illustrations for their more ornate covers, often looked northward. In January 1862, Richmond's *Daily Dispatch* found in the South's graphic print industry evidence of the "beaten path of listlessness and inactivity" that generally surrounded Southern industry. The newspaper added that the South's readiness to pour "the products of their fertile fields into the lap of Yankee avarice," instead of supporting its own printing establishments, had hindered printing's development in the region.[5]

In addition to the preexisting factors, the war created other trials. Commercial enterprises dealt with a difficult economic context. Inflation and wages rose steadily but unequally throughout the war. The cost of living increased by around 9 percent a month, while wages rose by just over half that amount.[6] Similarly, the Confederate dollar was progressively devalued throughout the war until its purchasing power became insignificant. Moreover, prices for overseas goods soared as the Union naval blockade captured a greater proportion of incoming ships.[7]

The blockade also revealed the South's industrial limitations in every aspect of printing, from paper to type, and forced greater self-reliance. Paper, what one newspaper column described in mid-1863 as a "necessity of government and the press," mostly came from the Confederacy's twenty-nine mills.[8] This output wrapped each round of ammunition, recorded every transaction, and was fundamental to the nation's continuance. While establishments such as the Rock Island Paper Mills developed expedients to replace materials—the felts required to press the paper, for example—a shortage of imported bleach affected every mill and meant that Confederate printers received paper in a range of earthen hues.[9] While those print houses engaged in government work used the highest-quality paper available, commercial enterprises worked within a difficult marketplace. Demand for paper led to an almost tenfold price increase in its cost and forced publishing and printing businesses to close or economize.[10] Those that survived or established themselves during the war dealt with variable quality and supplies of newsprint.[11] Printers also contended with shortage of type, plates, and other printing media.[12] Finally while some praised domestic alternatives, printers and their customers endured stopgaps, like inks that smudged.[13] As Wilmington, North Carolina's *Daily Journal* confessed in August 1864, "The people of the Confederate States have not succeeded in the manufacturer of printing ink."[14] For high-quality products and specialist equipment, Confederate photographers and printers relied on materials snuck past Union warships.

The industry required more than materials for it to run. Nineteenth-century reprography needed specialist labor- and time-intensive technologies. These techniques encompassed intaglio, relief, and lithography. In each process, skilled journeymen produced plates using different methods. Intaglio, used by those who engraved on steel, produced the sharpest and most detailed images and hardest-wearing plates. Relief, used to create woodcuts, lacked the detail or subtlety of intaglio. The plates also wore down more quickly than intaglio unless stereographed in metal. Lithographers drew the image onto prepared stone and used chemical processes to produce the plate. Although quicker than the other two processes and with the capacity of replicating painted or drawn pictures, the plates degraded quickly and required frequent remaking. Meanwhile, Confederate photographers worked with a variety of positive and negative techniques—the wet plate collodion process (for ambrotypes, tintypes, and as negatives for albumen prints); calotype, or salt prints; and occasionally daguerreotypes. Each photographic process required a specific range of skills and knowledge. Larger establishments, such as Minnis and Cowell, employed not only camera specialists but also workmen to prepare materials and artists to color images. Overall, in early 1861, the Confederate reprographic industry faced a shortage of the skilled practitioners necessary to supply the nation's demand for imagery. How the Confederate government fostered these industries to provide the imagery they required and how Confederates received and responded to them reveals more about the story of the Confederacy.

PRINTING MONEY FOR THE GOVERNMENT

Currency became the most visible of the government's efforts and also highlighted the South's weakness in every area of printing. In 1864, besides describing the specialist materials required to manufacture banknotes, Keatinge and Ball identified seven different skilled professionals, from designer to printer, required to produce a plate for a note. Each step and each feature required distinct areas of expertise—from the designing through to the person who transferred the final design to the plate. Furthermore, the company stated, while some individuals performed more than one role, there was "no recorded instance of any one man possessing sufficient knowledge to successfully produce a set of duplicate plates" of the standard required by financial institutions.[15] Only the final step, the pressing of the inked plate, required little or no skill.[16]

The Confederacy's paucity of skilled craftsmen was clear in the contract awarded to New Orleans's Southern Bank Note Company in late May 1861 for a set of notes worth twenty million dollars. Originally a branch of the National Bank Note Company, many of its workers left after Louisiana seceded. Unable to find replacements, its manager, Solomon "Samuel" Schmidt (1806–76), attempted to do all parts of the job himself. But illness and difficulty in buying enough quality paper meant that four months later, only two of four plates were complete. Frustrated, Confederate treasurer Christopher Memminger looked for alternatives. But as Schmidt possessed the only banknote engraving equipment in the South, Memminger was forced to resort to lower-quality lithographed expedients. Soon after, Memminger seized all Schmidt's materials. "With these tools in our possession," he wrote to a New Orleans banker, "we need not have been embarrassed about our engravings, and Schmidt's retaining them is a great public injury."[17] Now, with Schmidt's skills lost, the treasurer needed to find men able to use the seized equipment.

Similar to other war needs, the government sidestepped the Confederate Constitution's limitations on its ability to promote or foster industry. Recognizing the nation's straits, Memminger determined to import quality materials and skilled workers from the North.[18] Because of his efforts, by the end of 1861, five separate printing companies (including three new enterprises) produced Confederate currency. These actions offset the impact on Confederate pictorial printing of the fall of New Orleans in April 1862.

A diverse group of men gathered at Memminger's urging to make Confederate money. Initially, they included skilled engravers living within the South, like John Douglas (1825–1900) and John V. Childs (1817–72). However, Northern imports such as Edward Keatinge, John Halpin (1806–70), and John Archer later entered the Treasury's employ. The number also included less experienced men, like former dentist James Thompson Paterson (1831–68), Blanton Duncan (a firebrand secessionist and soldier), and the firm of jeweler-turned-printer Ludwig Hoyer (1818–68) and lithographer Charles L. Ludwig (1829–75).[19] For workers, these businesses scoured the South. Soldiers such as lithographer George W. Elam (1840–97) found themselves transferred from the army to Blanton Duncan's employ.[20] To keep their workers, printing firms also arranged exemptions from military service and poached each other's workers.[21] By these steps, the Confederacy began to print its bonds and notes.

Newcomer or experienced printer, each company used like processes to produce Treasury notes. This began with the domestic and internationally sourced equipment and materials they used. In their 1864 book on banknote production, printers Edward Keatinge and Thomas Ball wrote: "The manufacture of machinery and presses gives employment to mechanisms of the most novel character in the South; in fact, to establishments of this kind, necessity has added to the machine shop the laboratory of the chemist."[22] Although examples of what the authors described as "improvised" measures do not appear to have survived, written reports provide some indication of what they included. Captured sawmill blades and recycled plates provided a source for steel on which to engrave.[23] As for ink, with a nationalist flourish, Keatinge and Ball reported that their company made its ink from carbon from "the swamps of South Carolina" and oil from "the hills of North Carolina and Virginia." Regarding paper, Blanton Duncan recalled that after running out of his first supply, his company printed notes on a version made from cornhusks produced by D. Froneberger's Buffalo Paper Mills in North Carolina.[24] These articles supplemented the many items such as ink, stone, paper, and acid for etching that came from overseas. Indeed, from the individual tools used to produce the plates' imagery, lettering, and tracery up to presses, the highest-quality materials and equipment came through the blockade. Lithographic stone was one of the most fundamental of the items needed to print Confederate banknotes. Even though sources in Alabama and Tennessee promised domestic alternatives, printers used blocks of Bavarian stone. These stones, ten by fourteen inches and at least two and a half inches thick, not only delivered the highest-quality prints but, with refinishing, could be reused multiple times.[25]

Lithographers used both imported and domestic printing presses. At least one lithographic press, used by Hoyer and Ludwig and known as "Number 3," survived the war. The machine is about four feet high and five feet long and weighs around one thousand pounds. Although now aged, its curved legs and fluted frame still lend the desk-sized machine a rustic elegance. With no maker's name visible, it may have been locally produced. According to one of the firm's wartime workers, Frank Baptist, a soldier detailed to the firm, it was used to print notes and stamps. After the war, it passed through several print shops before being made a part of the museum of the Dietz Printing Shop.[26] The quality of the work Hoyer and Ludwig produced matched the finish of this machine.

New firms such as Hoyer and Ludwig, which formed in 1860, found that government contracts brought both potential benefits and disadvantages. Exemptions from military service, for example, guaranteed that businesses had the skilled printers and journeymen needed to operate the machinery.[27] Additionally, government contracts allowed companies to grow. Blanton Duncan's establishment doubled the number of presses it operated from twelve to twenty-four between January and August 1862 and imported at least fourteen engravers "selected from the best shops of the Old World."[28] Conversely, when banknote printers ran afoul of the Treasury, they suffered. Memminger showed great patience with Hoyer and Ludwig's work initially because, in 1861, the company's notes had relieved the government's need when it experienced the "utmost difficulty for Treasury notes."[29] However, in May 1862 Memminger ordered printing moved to Columbia, South Carolina. When Hoyer and Ludwig refused, he forced the firm to sell its equipment and materials to another government contractor, and its business shrank.[30] Similarly, Duncan found much of his materials and equipment confiscated in April 1863, after an acrimonious and very public falling out with Secretary Memminger.[31] These businesses' association with the Treasury provided a cautionary tale for firms engaged in fulfilling government contracts.

The Treasury may have dealt more generously with these companies if they had produced quality banknotes. The poor and inconsistent quality of both Duncan's and Hoyer and Ludwig's banknotes and the plethora of their designs fueled the manic fear of counterfeiting that gripped the nation between September 1861 and August 1862. In September 1861, for example, one observer concluded that "the work of the lithographer in the counterfeit bill is better than the original" (figs. 5.1 and 5.2).[32] Comparing the engraved portraits of the Confederate secretary of state, Judah P. Benjamin, that appeared on a banknote produced by Duncan with one by another printer shows the difference in quality. Duncan's line work and tonal range is cruder, and the details create an image with less finesse. When the Treasury delivered a more standardized set of banknote designs, it influenced not only government but also private graphic printing.

Between 1861 and the war's midpoint, Confederate commercial reprographic

FIG. 5.1. *Portrait of Judah P. Benjamin.* Detail from fourth series, June 2, 1862, two-dollar note. Types-42 and 43. Lithographed and printed by Blanton Duncan, Columbia, S.C. Courtesy of Pierre Fricke, https://www.buyvintagemoney.com.

FIG. 5.2. *Portrait of Judah P. Benjamin,* by Edward Keatinge. Detail from fifth series, Dec. 2, 1862, two-dollar note. Type-54. Engraved and printed by Keatinge and Ball, Columbia, S.C. Courtesy of Pierre Fricke, https://www.buyvintagemoney.com.

print industry products generally lacked a quality finish. In 1861, volunteering, government work, or defections stripped the South's few print houses of many of their skilled engravers and lithographers. From this period, only eleven pictorial prints of Confederate scenes or personalities are known, and four of them featured in the Confederacy's first illustrated journal, the *Southern Monthly.*[33] For the first twelve months of the war, less-skilled artisans supplied the Confederacy with printed patriotic imagery.

From small presses across the Confederacy came stationery decorated with pictures of Confederate flags, soldiers, cannon, portraits of President Davis and (more rarely) General Beauregard, and a few vignettes.[34] This printed ephemera afforded Southerners a visual way to signal their support for the cause. However, Confederates intent on purchasing patriotic covers or decorated letter paper often faced slim pickings. The shortage of trained craftsmen meant that rudimentary imprints outnumbered more finely wrought designs in any stationer's inventory, and few printers left their names on their products. James L. Gow provided one exception. During March 1861, this Augusta, Georgia, printer turned his hand to engraving and produced envelopes bearing a "very neat" colored image of the Confederate flag.[35] However, the skills of some other engravers did not satisfy the more discerning customer. In April 1862, when the *Richmond Examiner* tried to produce a simple woodcut to show the design of a new Confederate flag, it was "unable to find an 'Albrecht Durer.'" The paper gave the job to Julius Baumgarten (1835–1915), who titled himself as "J. Baumgarten, C.S. Engraver."[36] But even though the *Examiner* described Baumgarten as the "best engraver in the Confederacy," he proved incapable of successfully transferring the design onto wood. The result, the newspaper concluded, showed the "very moderate standard of the art of wood engraving in Richmond."[37] Until the Confederacy enlarged and improved the standard of its reprographic print industry, its citizens' access to homegrown print imagery of any quality remained limited.

PHOTOGRAPHY

At the same time that engravers festooned Confederate currency with recycled images or decorated letters and envelopes with often poorly produced motifs, Southern photographers experienced their heyday. With a promptness that surpassed their Northern cousins, Confederate cameramen across the South recognized and responded to public demand for images of contemporary incidents. From February 1861, when A. C. McIntyre used his camera to capture President Davis's inauguration, Confederate photographers recorded points of interest. Besides topicality, the common belief in the absolute truthfulness of photographs gave their works a power and popularity unavailable to other reprographic forms. Reports of these products captured their impact.[38] On April 15, 1861, Charleston's *Tri-Weekly Courier* described the images that Alma A. Pelot took around Fort Sumter as "full and perfect representations."[39] Confederate appetite can be judged from the case of New Orleans photographer Jay Dearborn Edwards's series of photographs of the Confederate defense of Pensacola, Florida. Even though the public focus shifted to other theaters of operation, demand enabled him to continue to sell the set of over sixty ten-by-eight albumen prints for a dollar each for over three months.[40] For a similar fee, less adventurous artists took studio portraits of soldiers. As the war began, photographs became the most common form of commercial print imagery available to Confederates.

After the initial surge in demand for likenesses, Confederate photographers continued to work until the last months of the war.[41] Apart from portraiture of clients, friends, family, or the famous, they also worked for the Confederate government. Artists such as Daniel T. Cowell and George S. Cook duplicated maps, recorded objects, and produced portraits to identify people.[42] For Cook, his military work provided access to hard-to-get chemicals.[43] A handful of artists also took their cameras into the outdoors after 1861. Better-known artists such as George S. Cook of Charleston, South Carolina, and Charles Rees of Richmond, Virginia, photographed the war around their respective localities. Meanwhile, less well-known photographers, like Texan Solomon "Tom" Blessing (ca. 1832–97), made views closer to the war zone. Blessing had moved from New Orleans to Galveston, Texas, before the war. He worked there until enlisting in a company that became part of the First Texas Infantry Regiment. In early April 1862, one of his comrades, William Schadt, wrote home that while in winter camp over 1861–62, Blessing had his "fixings" sent to him and photographed many of the company's messes posed before their winter cabins. Subsequently, businesses such as Water's and F. Hitchcock's in Galveston made these photographs available for people to copy.[44] However, as the prewar supplies used by photographers like Blessing ran out, many lacked an avenue to replace them.

Regardless of these difficulties, several photographers continued to find sufficient materials to keep working. Daniel T. Cowell and his partner, George W. Minnis, for example, advertised large and small portraits that Cowell produced of Stonewall Jackson in late 1863 for ten dollars and five dollars, respectively. In April and July 1864, this firm released a first and second series of "very delicate and expensive and highly creditable" military medallions featuring Confederate generals.[45] Additionally, domestic expedients supplemented the materials that made it through the blockade. In 1864, for example, newspapers shared the story of Virginia artist and "daguerran" David L. Clark, who had developed a process for making silver nitrate "equal, if not superior to, any ever bought in the North."[46] Expedients and demand enabled a handful of photographers to continue to operate until the Confederacy fell.

Although photography remained popular for creating portraiture and reproducing artworks, the industry struggled amid a difficult economic environment. In early 1862, carte de visite portraits of General Beauregard sold for as little as fifty cents apiece.[47] But the price increased. Photographer George S. Cook's account books up to March 8, 1864, show that even as his business boomed, inflation rose faster than his prices.[48] The tenfold increase in the price of photographs between 1861 and 1864 made them luxury items. Other reprographic forms provided much cheaper, if less accurate, copies.[49]

The Confederacy's few commercial print shops mainly used lithography to produce images. This technique provided images at a tenth of the price of photographs. Sensing an opportunity even before Confederate notes issued from their presses, companies including Hoyer and Ludwig as well as Blanton Duncan set a section of their workforce to commercial production.[50] The Confederacy's lithographers included individuals like Frenchman Eugene Crehen (1833–95) and Hesse Cassel native Frederick W. Bornemann (1828–65), who worked alongside or independently of the larger concerns to produce lithographic prints over the course of 1862.[51] These individuals made modest contributions. As the Confederate graphic print industry developed through late 1862, some entrepreneurs attempted more ambitious projects to supply Southern demand for imagery.

ILLUSTRATED JOURNALS

Antebellum Southern nationalists like James D. B. De Bow and John R. Thompson resented illustrated periodicals such as *Frank Leslie's Illustrated News* and *Harper' Weekly Magazine of Civilization*.[52] Like the Trojan horse, alongside the countless engravings of topical and emotive scenes that attracted Southerners, they carried abolitionist ideas into Southern homes. As the secession fever flared in New Orleans, *Harper's* became a symbol of Yankee repression, and Southerners dealt with it accordingly. In November 1860, a Texas correspondent from New Orleans wrote that *Harper's Weekly*, "the hitherto most popular newspaper in the South," burned on bonfires in principal streets like "the stamped paper in the days of our colonial existence," and vendors were "threatened with a hempen neck-tie" if they continued to sell it or "other such obnoxious publication."[53] However, such acts only held Northern pictorial journals at bay. In June 1860, the *Southern Literary Messenger* stated, "As the Devil must be fought with fire, so must the Northern papers and periodicals be fought with pictures."[54] For the next twelve months, until June 1861, the *Messenger*'s pictorial weapons consisted of an average of eight New York–made images each issue. When the war closed access to the Northern illustrators and engravers who provided the antebellum *Messenger*'s imagery, Southern magazines had an opportunity to produce fully Southern counters to the North's illustrated papers.

History showed that establishing an illustrated magazine faced difficulties. Since the 1850s, several publishers attempted to launch American versions of the *Illustrated London News* and *Le Monde*. When in September 1861, Memphis publishers Hutton and Freligh launched the first Confederate illustrated journal, the *Southern Monthly*, it enjoyed success. They advertised it as an illustrated magazine, and true to the advertising, the first issue featured three lithographs—portraits of President Davis, General P.G.T. Beauregard, and a map of the battle of First Manassas. Contemporaries praised the magazine and its map and two pictorial portraits. They approved not only of its articles' contribution to Southern intellectual independence but also its typographical execution, elegant paper, neat binding, and "excellent lithographic illustrations."[55] Although "not so profusely illustrated" as popular Northern weeklies, Little Rock's *Arkansas True Democrat* hoped that as a "southern enterprise," once people knew of it, they would "prefer it to the gilded but trashy publications of the North."[56]

FIG. 5.3. *Portrait of General Simon B. Buckner*, ca. 1860. Detail from "Cadets' March" sheet music. Courtesy of Johns Hopkins University, Sheridan Library, Lester S. Levy Sheet Music Collection.

FIG. 5.4. *Maj. Gen. S. B. Buckner*, by Otto Lederle. From *Southern Monthly*, Dec. 1861. Courtesy of the Library of Virginia.

Despite its intentions, the next three issues appeared with no illustrations. This forced the editors in December 1861 to confess that while artists abounded, a lack of engravers or materials meant that "a well illustrated magazine *cannot* yet be produced in the South." They added that like the government's inability to "get up a good engraving" on its currency, it afforded evidence of "the evils inflicted on us by our laziness in the Union."[57] However, their admission did not signify capitulation.

By February 1862, they "closed an arrangement" with "Colonel" David H. Huyett (1832–73), a former employee of some of the North's illustrated papers. In partnership with Otto Lederle (1827–91), Huyett guaranteed to present one or two lithographs each month.[58] Working from photographs, he furnished portraits of Confederate generals William Hardee and Simon Buckner for the *Monthly*'s February issue.[59] The result drew little praise. "Caricatures," "dreadful pictures," and "two *horrors*" were a few of the terms leveled at the portraits.[60]

Comparing the prints with the original photographs on which Huyett based them allows insight into what had offended their audience (figs. 5.3 and 5.4). Technically, the rough grain of the image of Buckner suggests the artist worked on either a poor-quality or poorly prepared stone that made it impossible to achieve the level of detail seen on higher-quality lithographs. Additionally, Huyett's choice of less than flattering images of both generals made the task more difficult. Finally, the artist's decision not to add evocative embellishments ensured faithful but ultimately pedestrian prints.[61] Overall, the effort created illustrations unable to meet the expectations of an audience raised on higher-quality images.

The editors bowed to pressure and informed the readership that "in regard to Illustrations, our publishers have decided that such as they can give (and at present they can do no better) meet with such general condemnation, in regard to execution, that it is best to discontinue giving 'more of the same sort.'" They admitted that illustrating the magazine "must wait upon opportunity."[62] In June 1862, however, the advance of Federal forces into their region denied the *Monthly*'s publishers the "opportunity" to do so.[63]

The history of the *Monthly* showed that for success an illustrated magazine needed not only a steady stream of imagery but also the artists, engravers, and materials necessary to deliver them. With every lithographer and engraver of any merit either engaged filling government contracts or in the army, any publisher intent on publishing an illustrated journal needed a reprographic process other than lithography.

Hutton and Freligh's attempt at a journal failed because the Union war effort created an environment that made it impossible for it to survive. Their effort to make it illustrated miscarried because they proved incapable of consistently including pictures. When Virginians E. W. Ayres and William H. Wade planned the *Southern Illustrated News*, it is clear they had learned these lessons.[64] Setting up their establishment within the relative safety of the Confederate capital, in the fall of 1862, they engaged the services of an artist and engraver. Armed with these individuals, they promised subscribers a "handsomely embellished literary journal" every week with engravings "acceptable to all" at a cost of fifteen cents an issue or seven dollars per annum.

"The courage," wrote the experienced editor of the *Augusta Chronicle and Sentinel*, on learning of Ayres and Wade's venture in late August 1862, "that would lead any one to start an illustrated paper in these times is sublime."[65] Certainly, the omens were not good. America's earliest illustrated weekly, produced by showman Phineas Barnum in 1852, sank before the end of the next year.[66] Its list of 50,000 subscribers proved insufficient to fund the staff of specialists required to publish a product of substance. Achieving the correct balance between circulation, size, and scale was essential. In 1860, readerships of over 100,000 enabled leading illustrated weekly journals, including *Leslie's* and the *Illustrated London News*, to each employ between 130 and 160 men to write, typeset, draw, engrave, print, and collate each edition. Their scale provided these establishments with impressive capacity. Each week, they produced a sixteen-page issue festooned with an average of twenty-five woodcuts varying in size from full to an eighth of a page. Moreover, when needs demanded, *Leslie's* artisans could transform an image into a woodcut within forty-eight hours.[67] Even during peacetime, no Southern publisher had managed such a feat. To attempt it with a single artist and engraver during wartime was brave indeed.

Initially, the task of making the *Southern Illustrated News* illustrated fell to artist James W. King (1832–77) and engraver John W. Torsch (1834–98).[68] King, an able miniature portraitist and former employee of George Minnis's photographic studio, began the time-consuming process by transferring an image onto a hard, close-grained boxwood block. Thereafter, Torsch, an experienced engraver from Baltimore whose previous employers included both *Leslie's* and *Harper's Weekly,* worked for a week or more with a magnifying glass, bright light source, and small sharp cutting tool to incise areas to be left unprinted.[69] The contoured hatching required to create the greater tonal range on faces took the longest. While magazines outside of the South sped up the process by dividing large images among a team of engravers, the *News* did not have that luxury. The initials *SC* (the abbreviation of the Latin *sculpsit,* or "carved") or *Eng* (meaning "engraver") alongside the names printed on woodcuts showed the craftsman labored alone. Short time frames, a shortage of trained staff, and limited income were but a few of the obstacles that those who were engaged in producing the Confederacy's first illustrated journal faced.

Torsch's elaborate banner and his original portrait of Confederate hero Thomas J. "Stonewall" Jackson on the first issue's front page were most promising. However, as with most of the next five issues, pictures appeared only on the first page. Moreover, contributors delivered more cartoons than their artists "could engrave in a year."[70] Noting an early issue, Charleston's *Mercury* erred on the side of generosity and described its appearance as "thrifty."[71] In contrast, Columbia's *South Carolinian* described its engravings as "rough specimens of art, though they may be likenesses."[72] Even the owners later admitted the first issue's shortcomings. Printed on material little better than "wrapping paper," with ink that smudged and illustrations "not of a character to please us," the first issues did not augur well for the venture.[73]

Even with its flaws, twenty thousand people quickly subscribed to the *Southern Illustrated News,* and the publishers moved to provide more illustrations. Posting advertisements for two more engravers, they obtained the services of William B. Campbell, artist William L. Sheppard, and then artist and apprentice engraver Armistead Hurdle.[74] With their appointment, the number of engravings increased, and the next eight issues featured an average of six engravings in each.[75] Applauding the November 8, 1862, issue of the *News*'s "seven fine engravings," Richmond's *Enquirer* described it as the "best number yet."[76] By the middle of March 1863, with a readership approaching 100,000, W. W. Daniels, editor of Atlanta's *Southern Confederacy,* noted the "great improvement of late in pictures."[77] But not all in the Confederacy agreed. In late March 1863, during the Richmond Theatre's production of *Pocahontas,* when offered a choice of death, Captain Smith responded:

> I have a plan I'm sure you can't refuse—
> Just put my picture in *The Illustrated News.*
> No hero bold has e'er been pictured there,
> But has been murdered foully, I declare.

The *News*'s supporters hissed, but the soldiers who filled the house affirmed the speaker's sentiments "with a roar of laughter that shook the building."[78]

Quality was but one challenge that confronted the *News.* A shortage of boxwood led to a fall in the number of illustrations, and the cost of a subscription rose to ten dollars per annum. Additionally, the pool of engravers fell as William Campbell departed and Torsch's appointment as an officer in the Second Maryland Infantry diverted his attention. In late June 1863, Mobile's *Register* requested that critics be kind, explaining that "the establishment of such a paper at these times was an undertaking few would have attempted" and adding that the owners had "sent abroad for engravers, box-wood, and other necessary things, and when they arrive the paper will be greatly improved."[79] Until that time, toward the end of July 1863, only one issue appeared with more than a single illustration.

Despite Torsch's duties as an officer and Campbell's departure, the *News* recovered. Torsch continued to work, and advertisements added the services of one S. Casey. From August 1863, Ayres and Wade increased the number of engravings in each issue to two or three. By then, the publishers also added the services of Eugene Crehen to produce the illustrations.[80] Even the death of engraver James D. Lonergan in mid-March 1864 did not result in any decrease.[81] Furthermore, until the end of September 1864, every issue featured multiple engravings. Even those produced in October 1864 included at least one picture. From this point until March 1865, the weekly's banner provided the *Illustrated News* with its only picture.

An examination of the work of John Torsch shows the difficulties attendant in creating an illustrated weekly in the Confederate South. From September 1862 until January 1865, Torsch, the paper's principal engraver, performed this role while he served as a frontline officer in the Confederate army. During June 1863, for instance, he sent a package of woodcuts "engraved within sight of the Yankee pickets." In publishing his engraving of Major General Gustavus W. Smith, the editors revealed that being deprived of tools, Torsch had engraved the picture with the tip of his sword.[82] Richmond's *Whig* complemented the "practised hand" of an "accomplished artist"

FIG. 5.5. *Lieut. Gen. Richard S. Ewell*, by John W. Torsch. From *Southern Illustrated News*, July 4, 1863.

FIG. 5.6. *Richard Stoddert Ewell*. Courtesy of the National Archives and Records Administration, LC-B813-6585 B.

presented in Torsch's likeness of General Ewell.[83] The *Illustrated News*'s accompanying article described Ewell, who succeeded Stonewall Jackson, as "the true Elisha to that military Elijah" and "to the Yankees an object of unbounded terror."[84] A comparison with the photograph he based the portrait on indicates that though he created a recognizable likeness, Torsch's treatment roughened the forty-six-year-old's appearance, thickened his beard, and changed his eye shade (figs. 5.5 and 5.6). Perhaps this is the evidence of an "accomplished artist" to which the *Whig* referred. Although the campaigns of 1864 reduced Torsch's output, they did not stop it.[85]

In October 1862, George Bagby, editor of the decades-old *Southern Literary Messenger*, looked at the *News*'s success with a mixture of envy and admiration. He acknowledged the importance of engravings in the *News*'s success. "The obvious inference," he concluded, "is that we ought to go to making pictures."[86] While unable to make this happen, other publishers who reached the same conclusion enjoyed more success.

In August 1863, with the loss of Vicksburg and retreat from Gettysburg still fresh in Southern minds, five additional illustrated periodicals emerged across the South. From August 1, 1863, the new editor of the *Southern Field and Fireside* introduced engravings to each week's issue. Furthermore, new humorous magazines, including the weekly *Southern Punch* and monthlies the *Confederate Spirit, and Knapsack of Fun:*

A Humorous Monthly, Devoted to Wit, Humor, and the Spirit of the Times and the *Bugle Horn of Liberty,* entered the marketplace. Additionally, Ayres and Wade introduced the substantial and finely illustrated *Confederate States Medical and Surgical Journal.* Introducing their first issue to feature engravings, S. A. Atkinson, the editor of the *Field and Fireside,* stated, "We do not promise our readers an illustrated paper . . . for it is impossible, in the present state of the country." However, he added hopefully, "should our efforts in this new field be successful, we shall increase the number of engravings, as we can secure additional competent artists."[87] Atkinson was unaware that his and the other periodicals formed part of the apex of the Confederate graphic print industry.

GRAPHIC PRINTING'S MODEST HIGH-WATER MARK

Michael Bernath described this period as the "high-water mark" of Confederate publishing.[88] Something of this growth is also clear in commercial graphic print culture. Over the month of July 1863, Confederate presses produced only six engravings. In the following month, they produced at least thirty. That number continued to rise to more than forty-four in October 1863, reaching almost sixty in February 1864. While the modest scale of this growth is evident when compared to the hundreds of images produced in the North during the same period, it was more significant within the Confederacy's borders. For example, the eight pictures in the May 1864 edition of the *Confederate Spirit, and Knapsack of Fun* exceeded the number of images featured in many of the *Southern Literary Messenger*'s prewar illustrated issues. And unlike the *Messenger,* every image in monthlies like the *Confederate Spirit* was Southern made.

While each new monthly was made in the Confederacy, native Southerners produced few of the images they contained. Many of the artisans who contributed to this growth worked in other fields or other locales when the war began. Most shared a gypsy lifestyle and a foreign nationality that kept them out of reach of conscript officers. They included individuals such as the wealthy English adventurer Alfred Maurice, who worked for the *Field and Fireside;* mercenary William Campbell of the *Illustrated News* and the *Southern Punch;* and the inexperienced Canadian Charles Van Felson of the *Southern Punch.*[89] However, their backgrounds affected their reliability. Over the winter of 1863–64, the opportunistic artists Campbell and Maurice departed from the South. As a result, the number of engravings in the *Punch* dwindled, and the *Field and Fireside*'s attempt to produce an illustrated journal ended. Despite their transience and differing degrees of skill and loyalty to the Confederacy, these men joined a diverse range of foreign-born individuals who contributed to the highpoint of Confederate image making.

FIG. 5.7. *Battle-Field of Fredericksburg, from General Lee's Head Quarters on the Field*, by John Ross Key, 1863, engraved by William Gellatly (Richmond, Va.: George Dunn, 1863). Courtesy of the American Civil War Museum.

Although the world outside their borders often frustrated Confederates, foreigners rather than Southern-born craftsmen produced most of their imagery. The government played a significant role in increasing the number, and overall skill level, of these imports. In late 1861, it authorized Major Benjamin Ficklin to travel to England to find skilled artists, engravers, and printers.[90] In June 1862, he made a contract with George Dunn that secured a group of skilled engravers and artists for the Confederacy.[91] This group formed the elite of Confederate engravers. Donald Ball described Dunn as "without doubt the best engraver with the Confederacy."[92] From July 1862 to mid-1863, the Treasury absorbed Dunn and his men's attention. Their efforts removed from Confederate currency what, according to the *Richmond Whig*, people "honestly called their 'native ugliness.'"[93] When they finished their Treasury contract, in early May 1863, they moved to Richmond and opened their own printing shop. The quality of their work was so fine that the *Whig* described it as "scientific."[94] One of the first engravings to come from Dunn's shop, William Gellatly's version of John Ross Key's *Battle-Field of Fredericksburg*, shows an example of this skill (fig. 5.7).[95]

John Ross Key's sketch recorded the unfortunate Virginia town of Fredericksburg and its surroundings from the site where General Robert E. Lee led Confederates to victory on December 17, 1862. It is probable that Gellatly produced the small work (approximately 9¼ by 2¾ inches) around the middle of 1863. Although Key's drawing is lost, it is difficult to imagine that it shared the finish of Gellatly's version. The engraver re-created Key's drawing using intricate carvings that captured the smallest details and rendered the scene in a broad range of tones and textures. Albeit equal to much produced from George Dunn's shop, only the engraving on later series of Treasury notes and bonds by other producers, such as Keatinge and Ball, approached this standard.

The increase in print imagery resulted from the interplay of factors, including public demand for pictorial matter, the government's actions, and blockade-runners' success in slipping through the Union blockade. For example, despite a Constitution that precluded the government promoting any industry, such restrictions were impossible to sustain given the necessities of running a nation and a war. This meant that the government played a significant role in creating this environment. Between 1861 and 1863, the Confederate Treasury brought more than seventy-five skilled engravers, lithographers, and printers into the Confederacy from abroad.[96] Additionally, by September 1864, Treasury contractors in Columbia, South Carolina, employed fifty men detailed from the army.[97] This effort released Dunn's engravers and afforded men like Augustus Grinevald, Eugene Crehen, and Jacques Wissler, who worked for Blanton Duncan and his successor's firm, Gray and Valory, the opportunity to produce commercial work. Besides these factors, discharges, details, and the conscription laws released skilled or suitable men from the army—in this way, men like Armistead Hurdle could contribute to Confederate imagery. Their collective work presented an illusion of progress even as Confederate fortunes waned.

The growth of graphic print media did not mean it all found favor with critics. Some commentators disparaged the technical quality and originality of the Confederacy's printmakers. While Mobile's *Register* considered the *Confederate Spirit, and Knapsack of Fun* "decidedly above the average," the paper considered its engravings showed the impact of the blockade.[98] Faced with a shortage of original artworks, producers appropriated images printed in the North.[99] The *Illustrated News* reproduced and retitled several woodcuts from Northern pictorials. These adjustments were so obvious to the editor of the *Bugle Horn of Liberty* that for the October 1863 issue, he created a pictorial "burlesque" of the *Illustrated News*'s "slender efforts" by illustrating a comic article using only common stock newspaper advertising cuts.[100] Around the same time, others worried what Europe thought of their national imagery. Observing the latest issues of the *Southern Field and Fireside, Punch,* and *Illustrated News*, the *Mobile Register* hoped "these specimens of art do not reach foreign countries, or, they will take our progress on level with China or Japan."[101] Even the Fifth and Sixth Treasury note issues, high points of Confederate engraving and printing, concerned Richmond's *Daily Enquirer.* In early 1864, its editor likened the portraits of "several distinguished gentlemen" to "botanical" or "geological illustrations."[102] Even the multiple and intricate notes of the seventh issue did not impress Columbus, Georgia's *Daily Enquirer.* The paper's editor complained that these notes failed to "look any more like money than the old."[103] Such comments not only betrayed Confederate sensitivity to international opinion but also showed that with printed imagery, loyalty to the Confederacy did not equate to myopia about the limitations of his graphic print media.

The war created more pressing considerations than the quality of printed imagery. Confederate armies were shrinking, and officials sought men to replace those lost during the campaigns of 1864. Besides conscript officers, the Adjutant and Inspector General's Office sent officers like Captain Walter Bowie, across the South with the purpose of finding men for the army. In Columbia, South Carolina, Bowie soon rejected returning detailed printers or engravers to the army because their expertise was irreplaceable.[104] Even though Bowie kept Treasury contractors working, other officers stripped publishers of the workforce required to sustain the production achieved over the winter of 1863 and 1864. In late April 1864, the *Southern Confederacy*'s editor, W. W. Daniels, launched a new pictorial humor magazine, the *Hardtack.* When Macon's *Daily Telegraph* examined the first issue, it noted that its humor and illustrations were "such as the times will admit." This was certainly the case. Because of the "unavoidable absence of our 'Special Artist,'" it turned to recycled stock newspaper cuts to provide a vignette for the masthead and all of its illustrations.[105] In early July 1864, a lack of printers forced Ayres and Wade to suspend the *Southern Illustrated News*, and by November, women typeset the *Southern Punch*. When in late 1864, William B. Smith attempted to publish his magazine, the *Illustrated Mercury*, he resorted to a mixture of crude, recycled, and original engravings. By March 1865, Ayres's office had one employee—a one-armed soldier. When Dr. Middleton Michel arrived to print a copy of his report on the yellow fever epidemic in Wilmington, North Carolina, for the Surgeon General's Office, he had to learn to set type and print his own essay.[106] As the Confederacy died, so too did many parts of its graphic print industry.

Despite this downward trend among illustrated journals, some media proved resilient. In late 1864, Charles Ludwig lithographed "in the highest style" dozens of illustrations soldier-artist William Sheppard had produced for seven children's books, which publisher George L. Bidgood was offering for sale as Christmas presents.[107] Although well within the age for conscription and no longer working for the government, Ludwig's status as a foreign national allowed him to continue to work. In Augusta, during late February 1865, John C. Schreiner released new music, including "Flag of the Sunny South," which featured the Battle Flag as its frontispiece.[108] Another foreigner produced probably the last pieces of Confederate print imagery. On February 14, 1865, John W. Davies and Son advertised, among a list of "New Popular Songs and Music," a new edition of "Just before the Battle Mother" (fig. 5.8).

The cover of "Just before the Battle Mother" was, according to Richmond's *Dispatch*, "exceedingly well-illustrated" by Eugene Crehen.[109] Despite nearly every major city in the South being back under Federal control and the total collapse of the Confederacy's military only weeks away, Crehen created a vignette of relaxed confidence. The lithograph captured the artist's skill in using this medium to render the various forms and materials within the scene. The Frenchman's illustration showed that regardless of the failure of illustrated Confederate periodicals to sustain their pictorial content, some areas of the Confederate print industry remained capable of addressing the demand for illustrations.

Crehen's work on "Just before the Battle Mother" also hinted at a factor that limited the Confederate graphic print industry. While pictorial matter formed a part of most engravers' and lithographers' work, most of what they printed was sheet music of popular song titles. In 1863, Confederate teacher Catherine C. Hopley said of her female students' appetite for new music, "Nothing could satisfy them . . . [new songs] were caught up as soon as they were printed."[110] Conscious of the profits this promised, Confederate publishers satisfied this appetite with over sixteen hundred

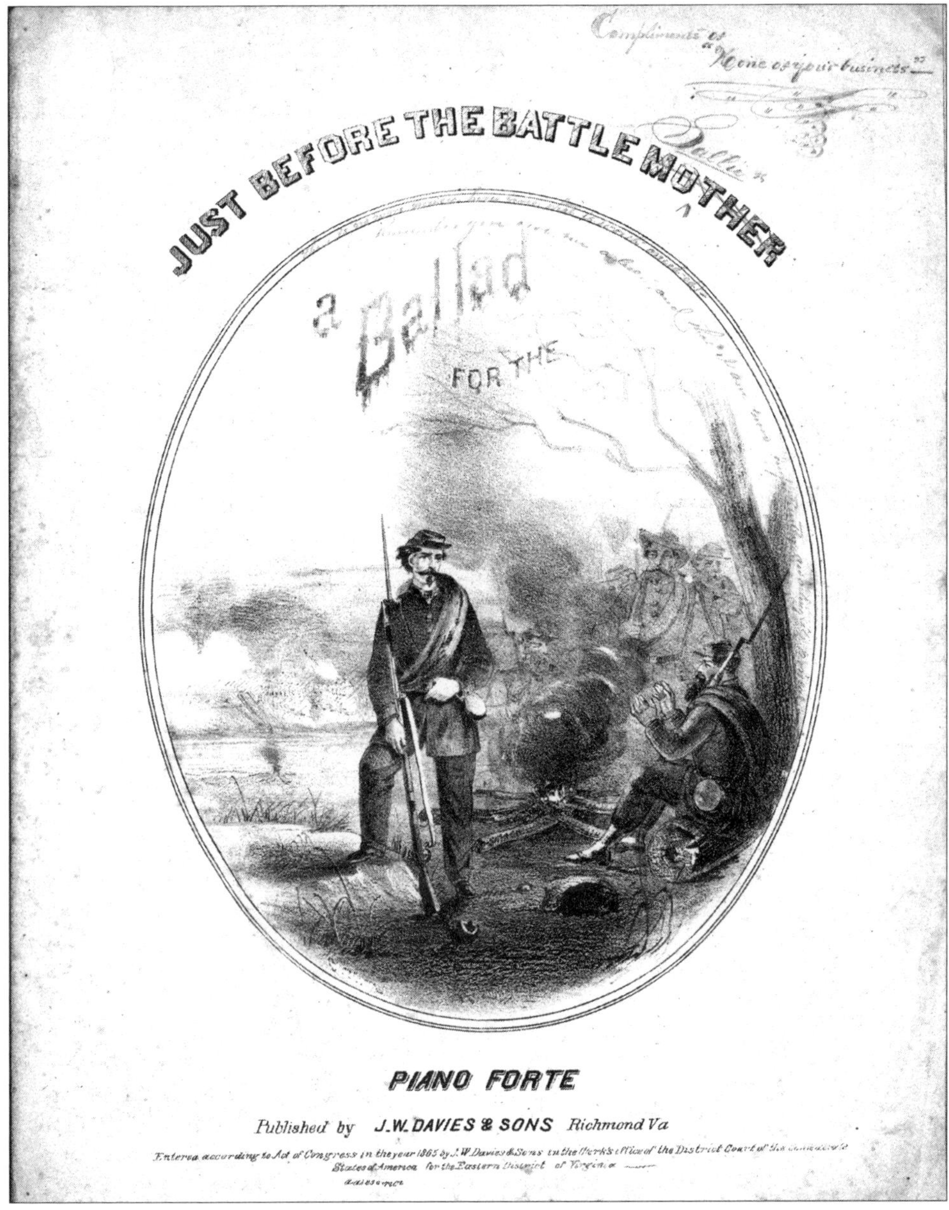

FIG. 5.8. Cover by Eugene Crehen to "Just before the Battle Mother" (Richmond, Va.: John W. Davies, 1865). Courtesy of the Historic American Sheet Music, Duke University.

titles.[111] These often featured attractive covers, occasionally beautified with expensive and time-intensive colored tinting. Studying Confederate newspaper advertisements shows that besides smaller concerns, each of the main publishers—Blackmar and Brothers, P. P. Werlein and Halsey (early in the war), Blanton Duncan and Company (and its successor Gray and Valory), John C. Schreiner and Son, J. W. Davies and, later, George Dunn and Company—released an average of three titles each month. On March 18, 1865, this production made it possible for Raleigh's Branson and Farrar to advertise eleven new titles recently released by Richmond and Augusta publishers.[112] The number of song titles produced within the rebellious states reflects the popularity of parlor music. It also shows the marketplace's effects on where the limited number of skilled artisans and materials used their skills.

In 1987, one study incorrectly described the Confederacy's print imagery industry as "moribund."[113] Such an assessment is severe. While print and photography never matched the North in output and only infrequently approached its quality or consistency, it did not simply decline. The story is more complex. Certainly, the production of patriotic covers that ballooned in 1861 dwindled by 1863.[114] However, the number of illustrated magazines grew from almost nothing to dwarf the prewar offering of similar Southern publications before their pictures disappeared during late 1864. And some forms, as one historian observed, "quietly flourished" into 1865.[115] Printing houses continued to produce the image-laden notes, stamps, and bonds required to sustain the Confederate government until it was overtaken by Federal forces. Similarly, despite facing shortages, a few commercial lithographers supplied imagery suited to Confederate tastes for as long as they could. Photographers continued to capture and reproduce likenesses of the famous and little known. These artists, artisans, and businessmen generated print imagery that circulated ideas mirroring and supporting those expressed by Confederate intellectuals through the printed word.

Commercial graphic printing formed a slender volume when set alongside the tens of thousands of pages of text produced by Confederate publishers. However, the growth of this industry and its contributions contradicts the idea of a nation that existed only in its military and government institutions. Pressures such as waning popular support for the cause, military reverses, and shortages of suitable personnel did not stop Confederate printers' efforts to feed Confederate demand for imagery. Despite its contribution to the cause, and unlike the loyal slave or other trope of the Lost Cause mythology, neither printing nor manufacturing became icons of the nation they supported. Rather, Confederate reprography provided vehicles for copying and disseminating ideas in visible form and helped create a sense of Confederateness.

CHAPTER 6

The Meanings of Confederate Military Clothing

> Then fold it up carefully, lay it aside,
> Tender touch it, look on it with pride!
> For dear must it be to our hearts evermore,
> The Jacket of Grey our loved soldier boy wore.
> —MRS. C. A. BALL, Charleston, S.C., 1866

Confederates' sense of national identity drew on ideas of economic and intellectual independence and misguided ideas about race and slavery. They also projected more concrete signifiers of their nationhood: banknotes, stamps, flags, government seals, and a livery for their military. Through these tangible objects, the government sought to give the nation an iconographic legitimacy. Of all the Confederacy's official trappings, the regulations for the Confederate army's modish cadet-gray tunic changed least on paper over the course of the war. Although adopted by many officers, authorities only retained its shade when they began clothing their armies. This was part of a broader and more revealing story about the Confederate military and its clothing.

Uniforms, Nathan Joseph writes, are "social artefacts," with meaning derived from social contexts.[1] Putting one on layers a body with social signals, marking not only one's nationality but also the transition from civilian into military life.[2] Adding insignia expresses rank, field of service, and other signifiers.[3] In the modern day, soldiers exchange the individuality of citizen dress for a systematized military outfit that expresses a collective national and organizational identity. The messages that these uniforms send are, likewise, regular and coordinated. The situation, however, is not as straightforward when studying the clothing of Confederate armies. Confederate soldiers' dress and its production expressed many things—from their varying loyalties to their values or the pressures within their nation.

GOING TO WAR

In 1861, soldiers went to war dressed in what some contemporary observers regularly termed an "endless" variety of styles and designs of apparel.[4] As the war developed, variable supply and hygiene meant Confederates often wore dirty and worn clothing. Overlaying this, individualistic Southerners used clothing to express group and individual identities. The diversity of apparel has led some to consider the term "Confederate uniform" an oxymoron.[5] But as Nathan Joseph reminds us, because of its symbolic qualities, "uniformity is not essential to the uniform."[6] Despite its range of cuts and colors, Confederate military dress also possessed qualities that unified and divided. As is clear in examining manufacturing, Confederates saw indications of economic independence in the making and issuing of government clothing. Moreover, despite the variety of sources, gray emerged to become a national color and jackets as the iconic outfit of Confederate soldiers. Through military clothing, Confederates showed their relationship to soldiering, their home, and their nation.

The variety of dress observers noted in early 1861 is understandable. No national uniform existed when President Davis first called on the states for volunteers. When in late April 1861, Floridian John Parker sought advice from the War Department about what his company should wear, he received the reply, "The uniform [is] not established save that normally worn by our soldiers—viz. a brave heart and a deadly arm."[7] Beyond rhetoric, this response acknowledged that the government's "Volunteers Bill," which provided twenty-one dollars, and later twenty-five dollars, every six months for troops to reimburse them for clothing purchased, meant that the choice of dress rested with each unit.[8] As companies formed, groups, individuals, or communities took responsibility for providing many of their uniforms.[9] Their dress ranged from the finery of companies such as Mississippi's "Prairie Guards," so splendid that President Davis mistook a private for an officer, to the visual anarchy of the "Texas Polk Rifles."[10] These Texans, after spending fruitless hours in determining an outfit, decided that each man should "get just what suited his fancy and have it made up in any style, jes' so long as it was a uniform."[11] Despite the lack of governmental guidance, a degree of uniformity often existed when ten separate companies formed a regiment.

The costumes of the companies that gathered in Augusta, Georgia, between April 28 and May 3, 1861, to form the Third and Fourth Georgia Infantry Regiments showed some of the patterns of soldiers' dress common across the South. Around a third wore the service uniforms of their respective volunteer companies.[12] Clad in blue, red, buff, or green, their garb mirrored prewar social influences. The number of uniformed companies not only reflected America's volunteer military culture and contemporary Western males' fascination with war but also the significant Southern response to John Brown's Harpers Ferry raid in October 1859.[13] Amid the paranoia that accompanied the failed uprising, the number of volunteer units ballooned across the South.[14] As Virginian Selina Powell wrote her family, "There is a perfect furore on the subject of uniforms, a plain coat is nowhere to be seen—that John Brown has certainly raised the military spirit in Virginia."[15] Drilled and trained more regularly and thoroughly than the militia, these units represented an elite civilian force. Among regiments like those that gathered in Augusta, well-tailored uniforms showed the wearers' experience and status as early responders to the perceived threats to the South.

The attire of other units visually linked them with their state. Before hostilities started, states such as Georgia introduced regulation uniforms for their new regular armies. Georgia's adjutant general sent copies of the regulations to captains, including John A. Strother of Columbus, who wrote, "We are anxious to get into 'State Livery,' please send a copy of the regulations, examples of cloth, etc."[16] Among the units gathering in Augusta, gray uniforms trimmed with black worn by nine companies of the twenty companies showed the units chose dress that indicated they were Georgians.[17] Besides Georgia, the states of Alabama, Mississippi, North Carolina, and Virginia also instituted dress regulations that enabled companies to show the state to which they belonged.[18] In June 1861, for example, after dressing themselves in the gray coats trimmed with red and tri-corns that the state of Mississippi proscribed for its soldiers, Captain Bassett G. Lawrence of the "Samuel Benton Relief Rifles" reported with satisfaction to his governor, "We are uniformed as Mississippians."[19] By selecting the state uniform, these units expressed their desire to be seen as citizens of a state rather than a community or a nation.

Among all the South's states, the dress of North Carolina's soldiers made the greatest collective statement of affiliation. Of its first twenty-eight regiments, over half wore full North Carolina regulation uniforms.[20] For the rest of 1861, North Carolina's active state Quartermaster's Department and its substantial woolen mills helped put many more of its men into state uniforms. Likewise, but not so extensively, over 1861 the states of Tennessee, Alabama, and South Carolina also issued uniforms to some of their units.[21] Through regulations and clothing issues, dress alone became sufficient to identify some soldiers' home states early in the war.[22] For instance, a member of the Seventh Texas Infantry proudly wrote home in November 1861: "I notice the Texas troops are better uniformed than any State. I have seen the Tennessee and Mississippi troops, and also the Kentucky troops. Texas is in no way behind these people."[23] This clothing not only showed state identity but also became a measure of each state's commitment to its soldiers.[24]

Other Confederates selected costumes or elements of their uniform based on outfits worn by armies involved in struggles for independence. Headgear such as kepis, feather-adorned slouches ("Liberty" hats), and nightcap-like "Sicilian" hats worn by many soldiers all carried associations with European nationalist struggles over the previous thirty years.[25] Hunting shirts, worn by units like the First Kentucky Battalion or Virginia's "Culpeper Minute Men," evoked links between the current struggle and the War of Independence.[26] Furthermore, even the gray or brown everyday flannel shirts (sometimes decorated with trim and gilt buttons to appear more military) popular among Arkansas, Louisiana, and Virginia troops possessed meanings.[27] During the German revolution of 1848 and Giuseppe Garibaldi's war of Italian Unification, many troops wore these garments as a conspicuous part of their outfit.[28] While comparatively easy to create, such dress overlaid uniformity of appearance with concepts of independence and a common people's struggle for liberty.

THE USE OF GRAY CLOTHING

Despite a lack of guidance from any central authority, most companies adopted gray clothing. Its widespread selection revealed ideas of continuity, realities of supply, and contemporary military thought. In antebellum America, gray commonly identified a unit as being a volunteer company. Moreover, while not as cheap or available as hues of brown, it was a relatively economic shade produced by most Southern woolen mills.

There is no evidence, however, of the media advocating gray for any of these reasons. Rather, newspapers and magazines advanced gray as the dress for soldiers because of contemporary military science. In late April 1861, Richmond's *Whig* called the blue shirts with red trim worn by several recently mustered companies "inappropriate for the field" and authoritatively cited gray as best.[29] Sources stated that the adoption of the rifle, with its longer ranges, made a soldier's visibility in battle a liability. Sixteen years before the war, an English officer stated that the gray clothing worn by British troops serving in Canada prevented them from being "good as object[s] for American or Canadian Riflemen." In 1860, such thinking led Great Britain to dress its volunteer corps in this shade.[30] Newspapers helped spread this idea by publishing reports on the matter. The *Raleigh Standard* identified experiments carried out by the "French Emperor" as the source for the empirical data that showed gray the best hue for uniforms.[31] Additionally, a widely reprinted article from April 1861 informed readers that on the smoky battlefield of the nineteenth century, "all colours which make the wearer a clearly defined spot in the landscape puts his life in instant peril." Of all colors, gray (followed by light blue) offered the least visibility and, therefore, was the best for volunteer uniforms.[32] Over the following year, the shade became so associated with the Southern nation that Richmond's *Examiner* earnestly promoted a flag design based upon it.[33]

Initially, however, the Confederate War Department did not adopt a gray uniform. Rather, on April 19, 1861, the secretary of war approved the use of blue single- or double-breasted blouse-like like flannel shirts and gray pants as an interim uniform for recruits in the Confederate States regular service.[34] While quartermasters arranged contracts for these articles, such news escaped Confederate editors and reporters.[35] Out of public awareness, even troops such as those under Colonel W. J. Hardee that were issued the initial Confederate uniform of coarse gray pants and "butcher's gown"–like blouse seemed unaware of their outfit's source.[36] Among the tens of thousands of different uniforms, however, the five thousand of these suits issued to regular troops in places like Baton Rouge, Louisiana; Mount Vernon, Alabama; and Charleston, South Carolina, made little visual impact.[37]

As the war progressed, some units, and many officers, adopted Confederate regulation dress. On May 23, 1861, the Quartermaster's Department sought to make contracts to produce ten thousand regulation suits of tunic and trousers. If they made any more of these outfits is unknown. On June 3, however, three days before the Adjutant General and Inspector's Office published the regulations, Quartermaster Myers issued orders to his officials to make contracts for another five thousand suits of clothing and specified "grey jackets" rather than tunics.[38] Short-waisted, single-breasted, and with full sleeves, jackets required less material than tunics or frock coats. By the end of August 1861, the *Raleigh Standard* reported that Richmond's Clothing Bureau had well over seventy-five thousand of these suits on hand.[39] Over the next year, jackets entered usage in a variety of ways, commonly by units using their commutation money to purchase them from the Quartermaster's Department.[40]

Myers's move to gray as the predominant color of Confederate uniforms reflected the trend across Southern states. By the end of 1861, the states of Tennessee, Louisiana, Georgia, Alabama, Virginia, and North Carolina had manufactured and issued jackets of this shade to their troops.[41] In July 1861, the *New Orleans Bee* applauded Louisiana's effort to put its state's troops in gray jackets that conformed to the "established standard of our War Department," rather than the state's blue livery.[42] The War Department's August 1861 request for families and communities to furnish volunteers with gray (or brown) jackets as winter clothing further assisted the process.[43]

The state's and the War Department's efforts to uniform soldiers did not result in every Confederate wearing gray or even similarly designed clothing. Richmond's *Examiner* complained in early January 1862 that the commutation system led soldiers to array themselves in "all sorts of toggery and color."[44] Sometimes this variety existed within a single article of clothing. One Louisianan, for example, described a regiment as looking like "harlequins" after its soldiers received costumes made from pieces of different shades of gray material.[45] Other Confederates expressed graver concerns that the lack of specific orders from the War Department allowed troops to dress in any color. In the *New Orleans Daily Crescent*, a Richmond correspondent worried about cases of mistaken identity after seeing two regiments dressed top to toe in uniforms identical to those worn by Yankees.[46] As Richmond's *Daily Dispatch* wrote in December 1861: "Our enemies are of the same race with ourselves—of the same color and even shade of complexion—they speak the same language, wear like clothing, and are of like form and stature. (The more shame that they should make war upon us!) Our general appearance being the same, we must rely solely upon symbols for distinction. The danger of mistake is great after all possible precautions have been taken. Sufficient attention has never been paid to this important matter, involving life or death—victory or defeat. Our badges, uniforms, flags, should be perfectly distinguishable from those of the enemy."[47] The increased number of jackets made of gray fabric manufactured by various state, community, or government bodies, rather than coats or tunics made in other shades, aided distinguishing them more clearly from their foes. Using gray also made the wearer appear to be more of a Confederate soldier than one from a particular area of the South.

Although each state and Confederate clothing depot produced distinctly styled jackets in a range of grays, most shared similarities in construction. Comparing Confederate jackets to the ubiquitous Federal fatigue or sack coat makes this clear. Federal sack coats consisted of five pieces, while Confederate depots made issue jackets from ten differently shaped pieces. Southerners' jackets employed the "Wellington" style of tailoring used by the French and English to make their armies' uniform jackets.[48] The fitted appearance that this method produced differentiated these articles from the baggier United States military dress.[49] However, it came at a cost. A Confederate jacket required more fabric and sophisticated tailoring than the much looser and comparatively formless Federal sack coat. In contrast to the Federal garment pattern's use of easy to cut and sew straight edges and one-piece sleeves, the Confederates' used curves and sleeves constructed from two pieces. Additionally, the jacket's tailoring made it necessary for the seamstress to fit all the six body pieces to each sleeve. For some, however, the jacket's final appearance justified the effort. While the Federal sack coat gave its wearer what former Confederate J.F.J. Caldwell called a "massive appearance," it lacked what another contemporary writer described as "panache." The Confederate jacket made waists appear narrower, legs longer, and shoulders broader (fig. 6.1).[50] Beyond their shade, these factors lent the garments a distinctive appearance that contrasted decidedly with the attire of Federal troops.

FIG. 6.1. A Confederate soldier (*left foreground*) with Union troops in front of Appomattox Court House, after Apr. 1865. Notice the lack of buttons on the Confederate soldier's jacket. Beginning in May 1865, Federal regulations required Confederate soldiers to remove all insignia. Courtesy of the Library of Congress, Prints and Photographs Division, Washington, D.C., HABS VA,6-APPO,6-2.

GOVERNMENT-ISSUED CLOTHING

By the spring of 1862, Confederate soldiers still wore a mixture of jackets, coats, and other garments in many hues. In Virginia, the 1862 spring and summer campaigns wore out clothes and took soldiers away from sources of resupply. Further, the loss of the key manufacturing centers of Nashville and New Orleans denied authorities significant sources of supply. These factors increased the number of poorly clad Confederate soldiers. On October 8, as disaster loomed, the Confederate government assumed responsibility for clothing all its troops.

For the remaining two and half years of the war, Confederate clothing depots manufactured around 1.3 million suits of military clothing for the Confederacy's approximately 450,000 soldiers.[51] During the last autumn and winter of the war, the Confederate Quartermaster's Department delivered over 215,000 complete uniforms to its troops. General Lee's 70,000 odd–strong Army of Northern Virginia had received over 104,000 of them. By Christmas of 1864, General Hood's 30,000-strong Army of Tennessee had received pants for over 38,000 men, shoes for over 42,000, and jackets for over 45,000.[52] The overall success of this supply can be judged from photographs of dead Confederate soldiers taken in the trenches of Petersburg in early April 1865: less than a fortnight before the surrender of Lee's army, they are universally dressed in central-issue jackets.

Factors other than the amount of government clothing produced by the dozen large depots spread throughout the South led to Confederates wearing central-issue garments. Not only its increased availability, quality, and durability led soldiers to wear army-issued clothing; its cost also assumed importance for some. Alabama state quartermaster W. R. Pickens reported that many soldiers purchased Confederate clothing rather than state clothing because it was cheaper.[53] While the amount issued often did not meet the needs of Confederate soldiers, it afforded Confederate soldiers a greater degree of uniformity.[54]

As gray uniforms became more common, some Confederate soldiers' disdain for issued clothing of other shades emerged. When in March 1862 a Missouri brigade appeared in outfits made of undyed woolen fabric, their comrades assailed them with choruses of "baa."[55] A year later, members of General Richard Taylor's Army of Western Louisiana required punitive measures before they agreed to don uniforms of a similar shade because by that time volunteer soldiers associated uncolored clothing with conscripts.[56] By contrast, incidents of charivari, or disobedience, like these are unknown when the clothing was gray, which suggests that Confederates came to consider gray as a badge of service in defense of the nation.

Popular culture helped cement the association between Confederate soldiers and gray jackets. For example, in early 1864 John Archer used a jacket-clad figure on an 1864 bond (fig. 6.2). Later that year, Blackmar Brothers pictured a similar figure on the front cover of Carrie B. Sinclair and E. Clarke Ilsley's *The Soldier's Suit of Grey* (fig. 6.3).[57] Although the details and tailoring varied, both images convey the artist's idea of how a Confederate soldier should appear. Sinclair's lyrics contrast the "simple suit of grey" with showy dress:

FIG. 6.2. *Vignette of Confederate Soldier,* by John Archer (?), detail from Feb. 17, 1864, 6 percent $100 bond, printed by Archer and Halpin. Courtesy of Richie Self, American Coins and Collectibles, www.amercoins.com.

FIG. 6.3. *The Soldier's Suit of Grey* (Augusta, Ga.: J. T. Paterson, 1864). Confederate Sheet Music Collection. Courtesy of Warren D. Allen Music Library, Florida State University.

I've seen some handsome uniforms,
Deck'd off with buttons bright.
And some that are so very gay,
They almost blind the sight.
But of those handsome uniforms
I will not sing today
My song is to each soldier lad,
Who wears a suit of grey.[58]

Additionally, *Southern Illustrated News* and *Southern Punch* contributed by consistently presenting engravings of serving soldiers wearing army issue–style jackets. However, while pictures of soldiers dressed in this uniform encouraged conformity, the dress of some Southern soldiers expressed their sense of democratic individualism.[59]

CONFEDERATE SOLDIERS' USE OF CLOTHING

In response to more standardized dress, some soldiers personalized uniforms to convey ideas such as individual identity, values, or a hardihood that drew on religion and culture. In the war's first year, Mississippian Robert Moore recorded in his diary that while nearly every soldier in his company got measured for a new outfit, "some of the boys will not have a uniform."[60] Members of the Sixth Georgia Infantry's "Sidney Brown Infantry" rejected efforts to have them dress in regimental attire.[61] In a petition to their state governor, they told him, "We want no other uniform" than their present one, "least of all one merging us into the Sixth—destroying our company identity."[62] But as the war progressed and distinctive company uniforms became impossible to get, Confederate soldiers found other ways to convey messages through what they wore (fig. 6.4).[63] Military suppliers or the soldiers themselves provided a variety of badges and pins. In early 1862, Virginian Kate Sperry recorded, "There goes another [soldier] with the whole alphabet on top of his cap—these soldiers have the greatest delight in putting letters on their caps—they wish everyone to know where they are from."[64] Other soldiers decorated their uniforms for reasons other than to advertise their state affiliation. One Texan recalled that in 1861 he added a star to his to hat to make himself appear more "fierce and military."[65] Others sewed "fancy" hearts, lozenges, and animal shapes cut from scarlet cloth onto their clothing to express more personal meanings.[66] While a fatalistic concern for identifying their body if they fell in battle may have prompted some of them, others used badges for other purposes.[67] In February 1862, a member of the Fifteenth Georgia Infantry wrote, "We all wear blue [secession] cockades here and as we had at one time a

FIG. 6.4. *Camp Scene, Belle Plain, Virginia, May 16 or 17, 1864.* A group of prisoners from the Confederate Army of Northern Virginia. Five of the seven Alabama soldiers wear clothing of government-issue style. The figure in the center left has adorned his hat with "AL 4" to denote his membership in the Fourth Alabama Infantry Regiment. Courtesy of the National Archives and Records Administration, 111-B-5219 529323.

fondly [*sic*] for that peculiar headdress."[68] While these men's pins drew associations with the past, Sergeant Thomas J. Lyon of the First Georgia Regular Infantry wore a silver device on his cap inscribed with *God and Our Rights* to advertise what he was fighting for.[69] Choices like these made it possible for a Southern soldier to present himself as both an individual and a member of his nation and other groups. Meanwhile, other soldiers fashioned their uniforms to transmit different ideologies.

Regardless of the amount of clothing made by and issued to Confederate soldiers, the term *ragged* firmly attached itself to *Rebel* early in the war. Undoubtedly, despite the efforts of the central authorities, many soldiers endured discomfort and hardship due to the condition of their dress.[70] Since the war, popular imagination has cast the Confederate soldier as victim. But the evidence shows that the soldiers' struggles over dress went beyond supply shortages. Indeed, some soldiers fashioned their rough appearance.

Practical and personal reasons led to the motley appearance of some Confederate soldiers. Members of a congressional special committee into soldier pay and clothing laid the blame on the lack of "energy or promptness" displayed by officers in meeting soldiers' needs. Others blamed the men themselves. Writing around 1896, when most authors promoted the idea of rebel soldiers enduring "chronic starvation and nakedness," former staff officer W. W. Blackford observed that soldiers' "thriftlessness" caused most of their raggedness.[71] Soldiers' records from wartime support his contention. Several soldiers and observers of the army believed that "improvidence and wastefulness of soldiers" occasioned their "suffering."[72] But it was more than wastefulness that led to their ragged appearance. Some soldiers associated neat and clean uniforms with the militia, and as one Confederate recalled, those wearing them were "unmercifully ridiculed."[73] Some troops, such as the members of the Twenty-Seventh North Carolina, who in October 1863 received new gray jackets and blue trousers, continued to wear their old worn clothing to safeguard their newly issued articles.[74] This practice may have contributed to what one newspaper correspondent saw and reported. Describing a parade by the Army of Tennessee in October 1863, the *Knoxville Daily Register* wrote: "The troops presented a most gratifying appearance. They had laid aside the rough and crude, ragged appearance which so many of them seem to take a pride in, as a contrast to the gaily-dressed and well supplied Yankees they have so often whipped."[75] Soldiers like these purposely fashioned themselves as "ragged rebels."[76]

They did so for varied reasons. An anecdote from the second year of the war tells of an exchange between opposing pickets—a shabbily dressed Confederate and a smartly dressed Federal. It reveals how one Confederate made sense of the situation. Responding to the mocking taunts of the Union soldier, the Southerner caustically replies, "Do you think I would put on my best clothes to kill hogs?" Others, like the author of the January 1864 poem "Peace," associated Confederate soldiers' suffering from having to wear "tattered" clothing to that endured by their stoic Revolutionary forebears.[77] Such thinking dovetailed into the ideology of sacrifice and suffering that developed in the South.[78] It is evident in Augusta Evans's popular novel *Macaria; or, Altars of Sacrifice* (1864), in which Evans describes the attire of one of its heroes. His "faded and worn uniform," she writes, "showed an acquaintance with the positive hardships and exposure of active campaigning."[79] To Evans, a rough, frayed, and weather-beaten uniform showed a veteran soldier—one who had suffered and sacrificed for the cause. For some, the ability of tattered Southerners to prevail against better-appointed Yankees showed God favoring their national project.[80] Such rationalizations provided powerful incentives for Confederates to "take a pride in" their raggedness.

CONFEDERATE OFFICERS' CLOTHING

Officers faced their own issues. Initially, their dress exhibited the same variety as that of enlisted men. In early May 1861, most Louisiana officers ordered a version of their state's uniform. However, the publication of an erroneous report of the Confederate army's regulation dress on May 24, 1861, caused issues. Writing the following day from Camp Moore (Louisiana's large army training post), Lieutenant William D. Foley of Wheat's Battalion told his father: "I am glad that I did not purchase a uniform. The uniform adopted by the Confederate Government leaves all the Officers who have purchased theirs, so much out of pocket, as the new one, changes the old one entirely."[81] Widely published across the South, these regulations, brought from the Confederate capital by merchant tailor Edward Cain, had officers wear dark blue and also used a system of small and large stars to denote rank. Despite the expense and with no obligation to purchase them (holding state rather than regular army commissions), newly made officers across Texas, Louisiana, Georgia, and especially Tennessee adopted the uniform described in this account. Unfortunately, Cain got it wrong. On July 1, 1861, Myers wrote Cain to correct him, adding, "I cannot conceive where you got the idea of 'dark blue' for Generals and Staff from."[82] The willingness of officers to wear this uniform shows their wish to be associated with the central, rather than their state, government. Further, it suggested that the pool of nationalism that existed within the officer class developed early in the war.[83] But with two contending sets of regulations, it set the stage for greater diversity of officer dress, even as more enlisted men dressed in gray.

More than misinformation led Confederate officers to modify, or even reject, the army's uniform. Former Confederate officer G. Moxley Sorrel recalled that while officers accepted most aspects of the regulations, nearly all ignored the unconventional mid-thigh-length tunic in favor of the knee-length frock coat.[84] Other commentators criticized the "incomprehensible labyrinths" of gold lace that designated rank.[85] In March 1862, the editor of New Orleans's *Picayune* felt the need to publish details of the correct uniform because he saw officers using so many styles and combinations of badges to indicate rank. "We think it is wrong," he told its readers; Southern "officers ought to adopt exclusively our Southern badge."[86] In July 1862, Richmond's *Enquirer* warned officers that not wearing the proper uniform and insignia threatened army discipline and effectiveness. "We have never known," it argued "a slovenly, careless brigadier or colonel whose regiment or brigade was not indifferent." It concluded that despite any reservations, "we have a uniform and it should be worn."[87] However, whether for reasons of nationalism, military discipline, or a desire for military show, the photographic evidence indicates that many officers went to the expense of purchasing regulation dress. Seeing officers dressed in a uniform styled after Confederate regulations not only created some continuity across the normally plain and varied dress of Confederate armies but also indicated the wearers' willingness to present themselves as Confederates rather than representatives of their state.

Even as the media advocated its adoption, the uniform's showiness led officials to provide an alternative. In a June 1862 circular, aimed at dissuading officers from

FIG. 6.5. *Captain Alexander Dixon Payne, Company H, 4th Virginia Cavalry Regiment,* 1863–64[?]. Payne was appointed captain on Sept. 4, 1863. He wears an army-issue jacket typical of the style made later in the war by the quartermaster general's Richmond Clothing Bureau. The three gold bars on his collar are the only indication of his rank. Courtesy of the Library of Congress, LC-DIG-ppmsca-33343.

"unnecessary exposure," the Adjutant and Inspector General's Office permitted them to adopt plain caps, either the regulation coat or "gray jacket" without embroidery, and rank shown only on the collar (fig. 6.5).[88] The abundant gold lace and buttons on the regulation uniform made it not only a dangerously visible but also an expensive outfit. Additionally, officers found that rampant inflation forced them into less costly garb. As officers of a brigade from the Army of Tennessee explained in late 1863, it was impossible for a lieutenant earning eighty dollars a month to dress in regulation attire, when a hat alone cost that much and a tailored coat over four times that amount.[89] The Confederate Congress therefore acted and ordered that the quartermaster general draft an order to ensure that officers be clothed.[90] When the quartermaster general enacted this law on March 4, 1864, it added a proviso that allowed officers to draw clothes once the needs of all the men had been supplied or purchase privates' clothing from any quartermaster at cost.[91] The effect of these moves solved problems; however, they brought new ones in their stead.

The situation the Army of the Tennessee found itself in during the Siege of Atlanta over July–August 1864 illustrated not only the weaknesses of the system for clothing officers but also its broader impact. A lack of sufficient supplies to clothe privates compelled officers to find other sources. An inspecting officer explained that, being unable to get to clothing stores due to the proximity of the enemy and cut off from home sources, privates dressed better than officers. In August 1864, an inspector concluded that due to such factors, officers found it "difficult to keep up a *decent* military appearance."[92] The inspector of another brigade worried that the army's effectiveness would be lessened because the officers' rough dress threatened their ability to perform their responsibilities. The condition of officers' dress, he feared, "compromises their influence with the men and [is] altogether incompatible with dignity of the positions they occupy."[93] By October 1864, an observer of this army drew a link between the lack of distinction between officers' and men's apparel and lax discipline. Dressed alike, privates commented "on the commands of their immediate superiors with an unction and broadness of diction common to the lower order of the South."[94] As Confederate military effectiveness failed, it seemed that improving the dress of its officers might rectify the decline.

In late 1864, the Confederate Congress responded by forming a special committee to look into officers' clothing. As a result, Quartermaster General A. R. Lawton ordered the manufacture of a thousand "affordable" officers' uniforms befitting their rank. By war's end, these measures did not make an appreciable difference. A witness of Lee's army surrendering at Appomattox Court House reported that it was "hard to distinguish betwixt the officers and the privates as they are all dressed alike."[95] Although some newspapers feared that supplying their need for better clothing might tempt some officers to speculation, the nation had greater concerns.[96] The desertions that wracked the army over the last month of the war showed the erosion of morale and military order. In Confederate minds, and maybe in reality, the similarity of dress between the ranks contributed to this decay. It suggested that those soldiers who remained under arms did so because of a desire to continue the struggle rather than because of military discipline.

CIVILIAN USE OF CONFEDERATE GRAY CLOTHING

Shortages and factors conspired to put not only the army but also civilians into Confederate gray. Drawn into contracts with the Quartermaster's Department, Southern textile mills produced millions of yards of gray material, a third of which passed into the marketplace. Additionally, from early 1862, soldiers' families and government employees purchased or received Confederate gray cloth or clothing from govern-

FIG. 6.6. "Child's Cloak made of Confederate gray cloth, trimmed in braid and velvet buttons." From *Southern Illustrated News*, Jan. 17, 1863.

ment stores.[97] A rare Confederate fashion plate from January 1863 that specified this fabric acknowledged its impact in the civilian world (fig. 6.6).[98] Used in articles like these, "Confederate gray" expanded from the color of the military to the color of the Confederacy. However, while this plate represented a unifying aspect of Confederate gray in the marketplace, in other instances, civilian use of gray army cloth was problematic.

As prices for cloth soared out of reach of most Confederates, well-dressed Confederate civilians became the exception rather than the rule. Civilians dressed in newly made outfits of Confederate gray indicated the use of contacts, influence, or government position for personal benefits.[99] Additionally, soldiers took advantage of the demand to sell excess government-issued clothing. Even though, in the fall 1863, Congress made it an offense for any person to purchase soldier clothing or material, the regulation made little impact.[100] Around this time, Confederate cavalryman James L. Wilson told his sister that while his new overcoat cost twenty-five dollars, he was certain he could sell it for one hundred dollars.[101] By the autumn of 1864, the use of Confederate gray clothing in towns such as Richmond reached such proportions that the Quartermaster's Department instigated investigations to discover the extent of and processes that sustained these illegal activities.[102] The knowledge that both patriotic and unpatriotic Southerners wore Confederate gray compromised its positive association with the nation.

The Confederate gray that clothed Southerners conveyed many meanings. Similar to Confederate flag culture, the centralized manufacture and distribution of uniforms removed links to local community or state and helped foster a stronger sense of Confederate identity.[103] Confederate gray also represented the presence of Southern industry. Used to make central-issue jackets, Confederate gray combined the height of military science with continental military tailoring. It made the relationship between a citizen army and its government visible. In a dilapidated state, these garments showed a soldier's veteran status and faithful devotion, despite difficulties and shortages. In the postbellum South, these jackets transformed into venerated relics. However, while the rough gray jacket became an icon of Confederate military endurance and determination, it did not enable Confederates to picture military success. The creators of Confederate visual culture attempted that task. While Confederate uniforms signified the military presence, Confederate images conveyed their gallant soldiers in action.

CHAPTER 7

Visualizing the War for the People

Stand, nobly stand in unity!
Our armies' triumphs brilliant are—
Our heroes weapon's brightly glare—
Our navy shall resplendent burn,
Be glitt'ring as the polished sun!
—R. LYNDEN COWPER, "Poem: Confederate America," 1864

Home front and front line, "they are all one in reality," General Robert E. Lee explained to President Jefferson Davis in 1864.[1] Neither army nor nation could survive without the other's support. The August 20, 1864, cartoon "The Peace Movement North" put Lee's contention into pictorial terms (fig. 7.1). Under a battle-scarred flag, animated weapons with their arms entwined carry a scroll labeled "$500,000,000 levy" as they advance into a territory sparsely inhabited by doll-like figures. The scene linked civilian contributions made because of Congress's authorization of 6.5 percent bonds in February 1864 to raise funds for the army to a recent military success: General Jubal Early's recent raid to the gates of Washington, D.C. It represented the relationship between the people and their army, Confederate confidence that their military would prevail, and the attempt of a Confederate creative to picture the struggle.[2]

Of all the ideas that bound people to the Confederacy, the strongest stemmed from or related to the war.[3] Practically, the fate of the nation rested on their ability to defend it until they achieved independence. Psychologically, warfare generated national myths for them to celebrate. It transformed men into idols and turned places across the landscape into fabled stages on which these heroes strode. Its casualties consecrated the countryside and helped define their country as a geographical reality

FIG. 7.1. "The Peace Movement North," by unknown artist. Engraved by S. Casey. From *Southern Illustrated News*, Aug. 20, 1864.

in their minds. In addition, serving menfolk linked households to the fates of armies. Confederate creators of visual culture contributed to, pictured, and influenced the construction of these ideas.

Confederate image makers enabled Southerners to picture their soldiers' experiences, their leaders' faces, their armies' triumphs, and the land they all sought to defend. Additionally, depictions of the armed contest strengthened psychological links to their relatives in the field and added substance to the nation. Furthermore, the narratives they presented reinforced ideas of Confederate superiority. Collectively, they functioned as antidotes against the uncertainties they faced in their struggle.

OPENING SHOTS

Some Confederates drew connections between the civic and military realms before hostilities started. On February 18, 1861, in Montgomery, Alabama, as Jefferson Davis prepared for his inauguration, photographer Archibald C. McIntyre (1832–1890) set up his camera to capture the "momentous event." Working quickly, McIntyre captured Davis ascending the podium, the entire crowd rising from prayer, the delivering of the inaugural address, and finally, Davis taking his oath of office. The advertisement promoting the photographs' sale used fonts of varying type and size similar to those of a breaking news story. Moreover, it specified that they were pictures for "patriots" who desired more than "merely the memory" of the "most momentous event." Indeed, McIntyre's description of the images as "four discharges from the ten-inch Photographic Columbiad [heavy cannon]" identified them as weapons in the establishment of the new nation.[4] McIntyre became the first Confederate who used patriotism to peddle imagery. In later Southern image makers' works, real armaments replaced McIntyre's metaphorical ones.

Through early 1861, Southern saber rattlers promised a bloodless revolution. However, holdout Federal garrisons at Fort Pickens, Florida, and Fort Sumter, South Carolina, troubled the more cautious. Their presence scorned and threatened the South's independence. Also, Fort Sumter's strategic position in Charleston Harbor and formidable bastions caused the apprehension. To batter its walls down seemed nearly impossible, and an assault on the fort from across the harbor threatened enormous casualties. When Southern gunners opened fire on April 12, 1861, the South held its breath. As the two sides exchanged fire across Charleston Harbor, in Richmond, Virginia, *Tarrant's Chemical and Mechanical Exhibition of the Crimean War* introduced "eyewitness" paintings of Fort Sumter. On April 14, 1861, amid the euphoria that accompanied the Union surrender of the fortress, Tarrant's artist altered the flag flying over Sumter from the Stars and Stripes to the Stars and Bars.[5] In Charleston, on the following day, photographers descended on the fortress. They captured more than fifty single and stereoscopic "full and perfect representations" of the location. "Ideal presents," advertisements said, for "distant and anxious friends," they provided Confederates with evidence and experience of their victory.[6] Collectively, the pictures operated as palm-sized, indelible proofs of Southern troops' success and, as significantly, Northern defeat. Entrepreneurs soon offered other forms of depictions to satisfy those who wished to experience the war through more immersive visual experiences.

On April 22, 1861, in Memphis, Tennessee, theater manager John D. Fitz premiered his *Panopticon of the South.*[7] His show, a large circular painting viewed from the inside, combined automata with paintings to create a forceful depiction of the bombardment and surrender of Sumter. "No mere pictures" of the battle, the *Memphis Daily Appeal* reported, Fitz's work depicted figures, forts, "rolling waters, blazing shells, dashing lightening, rolling thunder, [and] rattling artillery" that made a "life-like series of scenes."[8] The scenes "enraptured" and "disarmed" audiences.[9] The final tableau, which showed the lowering of the Stars and Stripes and raising of the Stars and Bars, brought the greatest ovations.[10]

Fitz's show developed from the panoramic shows that started in Europe a century earlier and had become popular diversions in the Western world. Their dynamic nature made them compelling entertainments. Alan Wallace used the phrase the *panoptic sublime* to describe the overwhelming sensations created as the imagery flooded the viewer's eye.[11] As a Georgia reverend explained in early 1862, while paintings and prints were to "be studied at leisure, panoramic views came crowding upon my mind."[12] These presentations came in a variety of formats—from those that simply used a long canvas that passed before the audience to shows that featured animated figures, with light and sound effects. Regardless of type, all enjoyed great popularity among "blue collar" audiences. They embraced these shows' narrative form and their mixture of biblical accounts and travel to exotic places with contemporary events and national stories.[13]

Fitz pioneered not only Confederate panoramas but also their pattern: evening exhibitions for ladies and gentlemen and Saturday matinees for children, with the proceeds frequently advertised as being donated to soldiers' aid societies or military hospitals. Within months, J. B. Nixon recognized the demand for panoramic shows and toured Augustus Grinevald's twenty-six-scene exhibition of paintings of Fort Sumter through the upper South.[14] Presentations like these enabled Confederates to picture their capacity to prevail and contributed to the developing myth of Yankee inferiority. The coming summer propelled Southern hopes and belief in their soldiers' superiority to greater heights.

VICTORY ON LAND

The battle of First Manassas, Virginia, fought on July 21, 1861, provided a rich and enduring source for Confederate mythmakers. At the campaign's outset, bellicose Northern newspapers and politicians made their army's intentions clear: to defeat Confederate forces and capture their capital. The battle became a contest between two sides of almost equal size and inexperience. The Confederates won after reinforcements hit and routed exhausted and outnumbered Federal troops. Southerners reveled accordingly. They celebrated their troops' courage, rejoiced at the defeat of vaunted Yankee units, and attempted to comprehend the number of arms and equipment their army had captured. From this, they developed the main tenets of the myths of Manassas. From pulpits, print, or chambers of government, the Confederates learned that they had won against a larger and better-appointed enemy due to the help of a pro-Confederate God, their brave soldiers, their brilliant generals, and the inferior character of their enemy.

Manassas promised success despite the South's comparative weakness in manpower and materiel, and imagery related to it helped lift optimism. Graphic print media provided the first visual formats that pictured these positive feelings. Two of the earliest depictions appeared in Confederate publications on August 6, 1861. Each captured a different Southern mood. The first appeared in Mobile's normally

FIG. 7.2. "Great Victory—Taken on the Spot by Our Own Artist." From *Mobile Daily Tribune*, Aug. 6, 1861. Courtesy of the Alabama Department of Archives and History.

staid *Daily Tribune.* Created from an array of stock advertising woodcuts, it spoofed the style of Northern illustrated periodicals by claiming to have been drawn "on the spot by our own artist" (fig. 7.2). At the top and bottom, images of a rooster, representing Mexican War hero and Union commander General Winfield Scott, bracket the arrangement. At the top, the cock crows, while at the bottom, it is crestfallen.[15] In between these images, tiny stock cuts trace the Federal army as a powerful force motivated by a desire for the South's food, wine, and women and ultimately routed. The only Confederate is a small slave, ironically depicted using a woodcut usually featured in runaway slave ads, who drives a captive Yankee. Overall, the composition captured Confederates' buoyant feelings about the victory.

At the same time, New Orleans's *Daily Delta* published a more sober depiction in the form of a map. Engraved by John V. Childs (1812—72) and accompanied by text that compared Manassas to the great ancient battles of Marathon and Plataea, it presented, "at a glance," ground "consecrated to the cause of Southern independence."[16] Using military cartography's conventions, Childs showed forty-two Federal rectangles outnumbering and pushing back the Confederates' twenty-nine units. Furthermore, the names of notable locales, leaders, and units dot the field. This information helped Confederates to visualize the battlefield.

However, both images stretched the relationship between reality and imagination. The *Tribune* portrayed the Union forces as a well-appointed cowardly piratical band, easily dealt with by Southerners, whereas Childs's map depicted it as an orderly battle in which a small group of Confederates resisted and overcame

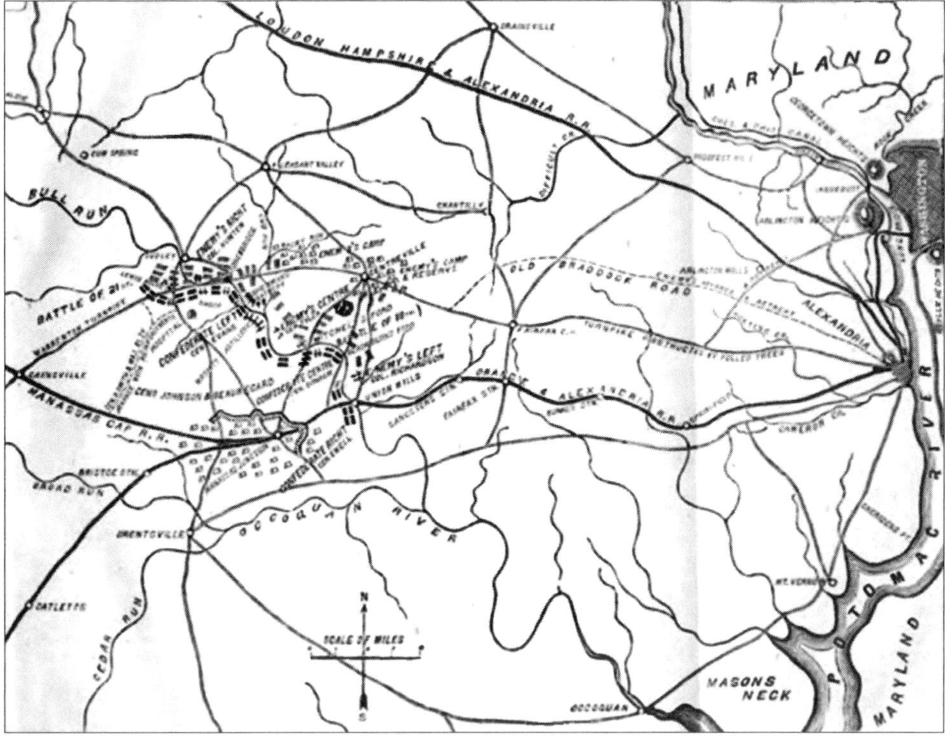

FIG. 7.3. *A Revised Map of Manassas*, by F. T. Hampton, engraved by Ellis and Moffett. From *Southern Monthly*, Sept. 1861. Courtesy of the Library of Virginia.

a numerically larger Federal force. Of the two depictions, Childs's enjoyed much greater reach.

Maps help build national identity, and Childs's helped embed Manassas in Confederate mythology.[17] Its path to the mainstream started when New Orleans man P. T. Eaton "struck off a large number" of broadside copies of the map and its description.[18] Later, Nashville, Tennessee's *Daily Patriot* reprinted the diagram, alongside an account of the battle and the Confederate Constitution on its front page. Childs's map, reprinted in each of the *Patriot*'s next forty-eight issues, told its readers that in this David and Goliath struggle, "Heaven smiled and the God of battles crowned our banners with laurels and glory."[19] The combination of Constitution and the battle's description reminded readers that God supported their nation. Belief in his blessing eased Christian Confederates' consciences about warfare and slavery. In short, Manassas provided early proof to Confederates that God rewarded piety with victory and chastised sinful behaviors with suffering and defeat.[20] Finally, the *Southern Monthly* incorporated Childs's version of the battle in a map it commissioned Memphis draftsman F. T. Hampton to produce (fig. 7.3). Thanks to these efforts, Childs's depiction of the engagement reached across the Confederate states. Its view of how Southern forces won against the odds met Confederate expectations and is seen in other maps of the battle produced in the South during 1861.[21]

For some Confederates, being a holy nation, though, brought with it burdens and obligations. With the Bible the measure of behavior, human emotions, such as greed, gloating, or anger, assumed national significance, and Confederates used them to differentiate themselves from Northerners. Whereas godless Yankees could revel in their forces' successes, faithful Confederates needed to praise Heaven for either triumphs or failures.[22] Static, silent, and neatly fashioned, maps became ideal instruments for depicting a godly nation's battles. However, Confederates published comparatively few battle maps.[23] Rather, the success of panoramic depictions across the South showed that rather than seemly still imagery, many desired more spectacular and sensational ways of connecting to their young country's achievements on the battlefield.

A little over three weeks after night fell on the field of Bull Run, J. D. Fitz introduced three "splendid" and "life-like and thrilling" exhibitions of scenes from Manassas: the battle, the rout, and its aftermath.[24] For the next four months, as Fitz toured his show across Southern towns, he used this series to close each season. However, while local press lavished attention on the rest of the show, the Manassas scenes received little attention. As he departed the Confederacy in late November 1861, artist impresarios Lee Mallory (1830–66) in New Orleans and William J. Burton (1814–1900) in Memphis completed more enduring and popular Manassas shows. Separated by almost four hundred miles, each premiered his show to acclaim within days of each other.

Although different in format, both exhibitions climaxed with the Federal army's Manassas flight. Mallory included it as part of a narrative that primarily traced New Orleans's Washington Artillery's journey to the front and its troops' part in the battle. Described by the *Daily Delta* as the most "perfect mechanical entertainment ever witnessed in New Orleans," Mallory's *Pantechoptomon* used thousands of moving figures, sound, and light effects to contrast the steady disciplined movements of Confederate troops with the "Yankees' furious run."[25] Meanwhile, Burton painted his *Panic at Manassas* on a scroll of canvas eight feet high and three hundred feet long. One of three separate scenes, he used lighting to enhance its drama. Experts applauded Burton's faithful and beautiful rendering of the field: the blood, gunfire, and "belching cannon"; the "terrified . . . expressions" of brightly uniformed Yankees in "their craven despairing flight" over their discarded equipment; and "stricken" comrades before "deadly" Confederate forces.[26] For at least the next two years, these showmen continued to tour these presentations. In a world in which restraint and control mattered, the battle was more than a Confederate victory. The rout of the Northern army showed Yankees' lack of self-control. However, more than Southern victory and Union humiliation emerged when other forms of visual representation drew on this battle.

On the stage, the Bull Run engagement became both setting and agent in the drama. At least two plays featured the battle: John Davis's *Roll of the Drum* and John Hill Hewitt's *The Scout: or, The Plains of Manassas.* Of the two, Davis's work, described as a "very amusing drama," enjoyed greater popularity. In it, the combat reunited Northern-born girl Catherine—a vivandière—with her Southern lover, Herbert Dickinson.[27] In Hewitt's play, Edward Ashwood's death in the battle not only resolved a love triangle, but his sacrifice also lets an unhorsed General Beauregard remount and win the engagement.[28] Through works like these, Confederates humanized and celebrated the victory.[29] These two playwrights, along with other creatives, found victories through which to relish Southern success.

VICTORY ON WATER

Confederates pounced on almost any opportunity to depict Confederate triumphs and Union defeat. William J. Burton chose to introduce a little-known naval action, the battle of the Head Passes, which took place below New Orleans, as one of his diorama's scenes. In the bloodless and blundering engagement on October 12, 1861, a small Confederate flotilla, which included the small ironclad CSS *Manassas,* drove off the Union blockading fleet. Burton focused on the small turtle-like gunship *Manassas* destroying the enemy's wooden ships, rather than the Union fleet's flight. Burton intended his work, *Glorious Turtle Ram Fight,* to show the North's folly in "lying in waters when our friend Turtle sails."[30] It made the clash one between a dated North and an advanced Confederacy. As Burton continued to feature this battle as part of his presentations over the following years, subsequent events reinforced the idea of an innovative Confederate States (CS) Navy beating its opponents.

As the Northern navy blockaded Southern ports, the CS Navy grew in significance. If it could drive off Union ships, contemporary international law made the blockade illegal. The resurrected remains of the USS *Merrimac* offered the navy an opportunity to achieve this feat. Confederates repaired the six-year-old vessel, mounting new guns and encasing the deck with oak clad with railroad iron. In early 1862, they relaunched the *Merrimac* as the armored steam ram CSS *Virginia.* On March 8, 1862, the powerful vessel sailed into the Union fleet blockading in Hampton Roads and set about sinking, burning, or driving off three of the Federals' strongest ships. The following day, the CSS *Virginia* and the United States' revolutionary ironclad the USS *Monitor* pummeled each other in an inconclusive contest. Despite this, Southerners considered the battle of Hampton Roads a victory for the CSS *Virginia*. It promised the end of the blockade, raised spirits bruised by recent reverses, and prompted nationwide "gunboat fever." One anonymous young artist captured the optimism in a cartoon that depicted one hundred two-legged gunboats carrying carpetbags necessary for a quick journey, "climbing furiously" from the Richmond's shipyard on the Rockett's Landing.[31] However, as the work was only exhibited among the artist's friends, the drawing experienced limited reach. Public interest prompted businesses to create images that enabled people across the South to picture the vessel.

On Sunday, April 20, 1862, Mobile's *Advertiser and Register* provided its readers with a rarity—an illustration. While there are no known editions of this issue, thankfully the *Register* shared the plate with its competitor, the *Mobile Evening News* (fig. 7.4). Based on an eyewitness drawing by Sergeant J. K. Hoyt of the Third Alabama, the engraving represented the steamer as it appeared returning from the engagements on March 8 and 9. The engraver was careful to render the damage inflicted by the *Monitor*'s big guns "fired at a distance of not over fifty feet" captured in Hoyt's original drawing and kept the small waving figures lining the deck and the large flag.[32] However, he also idealized aspects of the scene. With its low waterline, the real vessel would have struggled with the rough waters the engraver's version steams through. Also, the smokestack shows none of the damage inflicted by the countless missiles that peppered it. While this image gave Mobilians a fairly accurate depiction of the ship, it had limited reach. Soon after, other depictions appeared that allowed more Confederates to see the gunboat and to relive its victory.[33]

Panoramists created the most widely seen images of the battle. The first such depiction featured as the final of the seventy-two scenes created by Augusta, Georgia's luckless and inexperienced theatrical artist Monti de Rosecruz.[34] Advertisements suggested a compelling evening. Styled as the "Great Southern Scenic Magician," Rosecruz intended a "magnificent spectacle." As the show's highlight, he promised a tableau vivant of the "great victory of the *Virginia* in Hampton Roads," depicting the "*Cumberland* sinking; *Congress* burning; *Minnesota* riddled" and the CSS *Virginia* "Triumphant."[35] Despite the promotion, Rosecruz presented a ponderous and poorly made show. On opening night, the audience grew restless before the show's halfway point. Growing cries of "humbug" arose among onlookers as only the occasional scene related to the war appeared sandwiched between several pedestrian fantasy and juvenile tableaux. Finally, Rosecruz fled the auditorium, followed by a horde of small boys, and disappeared into the night.[36] His exhibition showed the limits of Confederates' appetite for patriotic entertainment and left room for more experienced and audience-aware showmen.

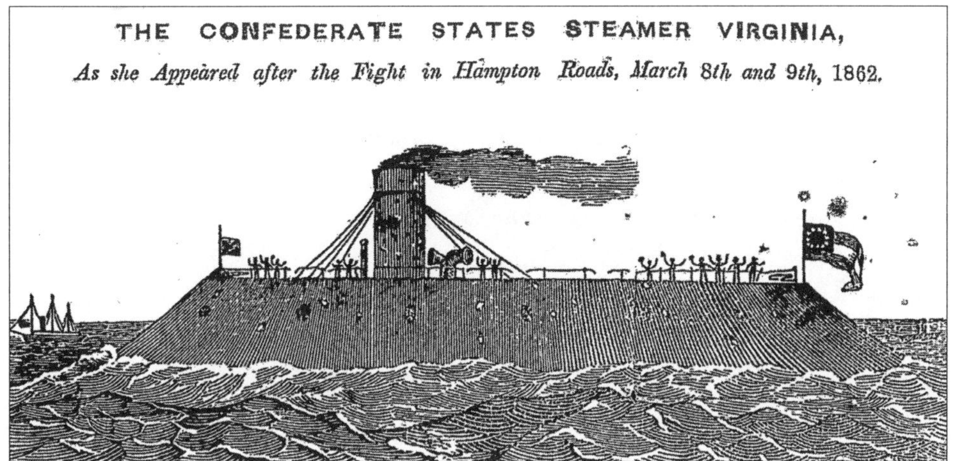

FIG. 7.4. "The Confederate States Steamer Virginia," by John K. Hoyt, engraved by William R. Robertson. From *Mobile Evening News*, Apr. 21, 1862, reprinted from *Mobile Register*. Courtesy of the Alabama Department of Archives and History.

Lee Mallory was the man, and by the second week of April 1862, the artist-impresario had started work on the *Great Southern Naval Victory in Hampton Roads.*[37] However, the war moved faster than Mallory, and on May 11, 1862, five days before the show opened at Richmond's Metropolitan Hall, Confederates scuttled the CSS *Virginia.* If the warship's combat "electrified the South," its destruction produced frustration and a profound and lasting sadness among Confederates. Even a year and a half later, one editor noted that "the grief of our people when this catastrophe was made known was unbounded, and to this day they refuse to be comforted."[38]

Opening his show so close to the destruction of a craft bearing so many Confederate hopes seemed unwise. The subject of Mallory's presentation promised to irritate audience members still sensitive about the loss, and no doubt some stayed away. The show's history suggests, however, that many enjoyed the solace the performance offered their collective sorrow.

Based on sketches made upon the spot by Louisiana captain Robert W. Armistead (1830–62), Mallory's use of scenic trickery created an "air of reality" that made spectators believe they were gazing "upon a genuine sea of water." "The auditor," reported Richmond's *Dispatch,* enjoyed "views of Old Point Comfort, Fortress Monroe, Rip Raps, Sewell's Point, Newport News," and the Federal ships destroyed by the "gallant *Virginia.*" In this "perfect miniature Naval Battle," the "strange looking *Virginia*" moved among "correct models" of the vessels engaged. However, unlike the lumbering original, Mallory's *Virginia* darted "upon her victims."[39] The show drew and thrilled audiences for the next year.[40] It let audiences believe that the *Virginia* still steamed and also promised similar results from the ironclads under construction.

It is unsurprising that other impresarios capitalized on Confederates' gunboat passions. Even as Mallory moved southward, other entrepreneurs sought to profit from Confederates' appetite for seeing their armored steamer either alone or in action. In Richmond, during October 1862, an individual offered viewings of a brass model of the ship and "lying Yankee" illustrations of the battle.[41] At around the same time, in Mobile, Alabama, an almost unknown pair, scenic artist John T. Budd and machinist Thomas Wheelen, premiered their version of the *Virginia*'s destruction of the USS *Congress* and its duel with the USS *Monitor* in their *Dioramic Pantomorph.*[42] Despite being well received, Budd's obligations to a touring theater company put a halt to the show until April 1863. On his return, Mobilians saw an improved portrayal that featured novel effects, ingenious mechanism, and illuminated moving pictures.[43] Like Mallory, Budd's show found receptive and eager audiences who provided full houses for nearly a two-week run.

On March 17, 1863, Mallory returned to Richmond and relaunched a modified version of the Hampton Roads duel. However, he now faced competition. On the same evening, two blocks away at the African Church, former soldier and experienced scenic artist George W. Grain (1827–[?]), with the financial backing of merchant and novice theatrical producer Zorah H. H. Cropper (1818–69) and technical support of carpenter mechanic Richard P. Mundin (1820–67), opened the *Panoramic Mirror.* Narrated by veteran actor Walter Keeble, the range and quality of the extensive show, "all in miniature," displayed the significant time and money devoted to its production. Whereas Mallory's shows told stories, Grain crowded each presentation with an abundance of shorter "instructive" and "beautiful painted" scenes depicting highlights from the war that climaxed with the battle of the ironclads.[44] Within days, hinting at the *Mirror*'s nomadic future, Grain moved his performance first to the Trinity Church and then to the Richmond Varieties Theatre, which lay almost diagonal to Mallory's Metropolitan Hall. As Grain departed for the South in early May, Mallory paused the advertising for his show in Richmond newspapers.

The image of the CSS *Virginia*, however, remained in the Confederate visual environment. For instance, on January 27, 1864, the Virginia Library exhibited a large "truthful representation" watercolor of the vessel in action.[45] Within a few months, a similar scene became officially enshrined in iconography as the vignette on a series of Confederate Treasury bonds (fig. 7.5). There it reminded Confederates of more than their navy's ability to safeguard them and their nation on one occasion. The artist made the CSS *Virginia* seem larger than the ill-fated USS *Cumberland* and truncated its fore and aft casemate. Doing so not only enhanced its power, but it also

FIG. 7.5. *Vignette,* by George Dunn (Richmond: George Dunn, 1864). Four percent registered bond, under the act of Feb. 17, 1864. Courtesy of Richie Self, American Coins and Collectibles, www.amercoins.com.

made the vessel look more like the armored steam rams that then guarded cities like Richmond, Charleston, and Mobile and a number of waterways. In January 1863, off Charleston Harbor, two of these, the CSS *Palmetto State* and CSS *Chicora,* damaged two Federal warships, drove off the Union fleet, and lifted the blockade for a period. Images of Southern ironclads in print or onstage reminded Confederates of the real vessels that defended their ports. Furthermore, whether represented visually or physically posted on Southern waterways, the ships also promised that victories such as those at Hampton Roads or before Charleston still lay within the realm of the possible.

In 1865, W. L. Sheppard revisited and updated the image of a Confederate ironclad ram destroying a Union vessel for a vignette designed for the masthead of the *Southern Illustrated News.* In his version, a Rebel gunboat flying the current national colors is silhouetted against the smoke that shrouds the Union ship it attacks. As three major seaports remained open, thanks to armored Confederate vessels, Sheppard's illustration reminded Southerners not only of their past but also of their present and possible future (fig. 7.6). Additionally, bracketed by this vignette and one that showed Fort Sumter under attack are four central figures. Protected by these scenes, their relaxed poses project confidence. The scene of Fort Sumter being bombarded evoked other ideas prevalent in Confederate ideology and its depictions of war—endurance and resilience.

Engaged in a losing war nearly every month threw up new disappointments. Con-

FIG. 7.6. *Southern Illustrated News Banner* (detail), by William Ludwell Sheppard, engraved by John W. Torsch. From *Southern Illustrated News*, Jan. 21, 1865. Courtesy of Emory University.

federate visual culture reflected a people not only rejoicing triumphs but also dealing with misfortunes. Although image producers continued to include pictures of Union defeat, images of resilience increasingly joined the South's conceptual and visual topography.[46]

CONFEDERATE DETERMINATION

Wishful Confederates, like their President Jefferson Davis, believed in white Southerners' fortitude. In a December 1863 speech, Davis described the "resolute spirit" displayed by the populace in the face of disappointments and proclaimed that history taught the indomitable qualities of "people fighting for home, liberty and independence."[47] Before Davis spoke these words, Confederate artists were already weaving similar notions into their work.

By late June 1862, New Orleans, Nashville, and Memphis lay in Union hands as a Federal fleet steamed toward Vicksburg, Mississippi. The loss of the first three cities, some Southerners believed, had occurred too easily. "In a war like this," stated a writer in November 1862, no city should submit without a fight "when the least advantage can be gained by endurance of bombardment."[48] Vicksburg, the last point of access between the Confederate Gulf and the far Western states, would not fall as easily. On June 28, 1862, Union naval attacks began on the city, and Confederates started to address its suffering in terms of sacrifice and unflinching heroism.[49] To acknowledge the town and its people's significance, the *Illustrated News*'s ninth issue replaced the usual portrait of a general with an engraving of the town. The city, with church and courthouse outlined against the sky and paddle steamers in the foreground,

FIG. 7.7. *Southern Illustrated News Banners*, 1862–1865 (details), by various artists. First masthead (Sept. 19, 1862–July 4, 1863): Charleston Harbor with steamer in foreground. Second masthead (illustration by Eugene Crehen, engraved by Armistead Uriah Hurdle, July 11, 1863–Jan. 7, 1865): Steamer, similar in form to commerce raiders, in front of fort, no city visible. Third masthead (Jan. 14–Feb. 2, 1865). Courtesy of Emory University.

is a peaceful picture of faith, law, and trade in harmony. Even though Vicksburg's continued resistance "established the fact that iron-clad gunboats are not invulnerable," it is a peaceful scene.[50] By contrast, masters of more sensational visual forms, John T. Budd and George W. Grain, introduced scenes full of aggressive Union gunboats engaging and being repelled by Vicksburg's pugnacious Confederate batteries.[51]

After Vicksburg's eventual surrender on July 4, 1863, the city remained a symbol. At the start of that August, Confederate newspapers announced the preparation of a lithograph entitled *The June 28, 1862, Bombardment of Vicksburg*.[52] The print showed a line of Federal ships strung across the page, silhouetted against the smoke issuing forth from cannons. Explosions over the city showed that Union forces had aimed their guns at civilian targets rather than the town's soldier defenders. The church, central to the composition and its narrative, is placed in the middle of the piece, with the courthouse moved closer to it. The design not only depicted the people's endurance but also the Union's disregard for civil or sacred order, a message that continued to affect Confederates after Vicksburg's fall.[53]

Charleston, South Carolina, and its forts resisted Union forces longer than Vicksburg. Despite Federal attempts to close it, Charleston's defenses, led by Fort Sumter, helped it remain open to the world. Charleston was considered an "object of Confederate pride," and Southerners regarded Federal efforts to retake it as marks "of Yankee spite and desire for revenge."[54] Confederates acclaimed the "sublime fortitude and heroic endurance" of Charleston's people and devoted considerable resources to keeping the city and its harbor in Southern hands.[55] The *Southern Illustrated News*'s decision to include successively more prominent images of Fort Sumter in its masthead echoed the fort's military and symbolic importance (fig. 7.7).

As Federal forces toiled to wrest control of the port from the South, image makers crafted pictures of the city's stout defense for Confederate consumption. From April 1863, both Lee Mallory and George Grain added "instructive" panoramic presentations of the harbor to their repertoires. Their use of "pyrotechnics," as they depicted the Yankee bombardment, increased each show's reality effect and further emphasized the port city's resilience. Directed by a narrator, entranced audiences watched a pack of small-scale model monitors assault Fort Sumter through rolling seas and thrilled as simulated Southern shot and shell repelled the small craft.[56] These showmen were not alone in tapping into this subject matter.

Sidelined to Charleston during 1862, General P.G.T. Beauregard employed civilian and military artists in an effort that matched the showmen's efforts. After taking unofficial leave, the early war hero memorialized his gallant defense of the city.[57] His endeavors increased the number of practicing artists in Charleston to nearly the same as worked in Richmond. A few of the works these painters, draftsmen, and photographers produced entered the public sphere.

Lieutenant John Ross Key (1832–1920) and Conrad Wise Chapman and civilians Augustus Grinevald and George S. Cook all enjoyed the distinction of having their images of Charleston and its defenses exhibited and publicized during the war.[58] Grinevald created at least three paintings of the engagements around Charleston's harbor, with what one witness described as "great faithfulness of detail" (fig. 7.8). As a panoramic artist, the painting teacher aimed to make pictures rich in grand history. However, his depiction (currently in a private collection) of the April 1863 engagement between the armored ships of the United States fleet and the fort is dry and the action remote. Sometime after the painting's completion in August 1863, Grinevald produced a print of the painting. The work depicted the black log-like USS *New Ironsides* and small monitors with oversized turrets emitting puffs of smoke reminiscent of cotton wool as they assault a two-tiered Fort Sumter. The stronghold's walls look seemingly unscathed by two years of war.[59] Grinevald rendered Fort Sumter as impervious and under Confederate control. Other images drew attention to other aspects of the fort's defense.

Conversely, Lieutenant Key created a documentary record of the shell-hammered fort. His views make the structure seem claustrophobic as its soldiers move purposely through ruins strengthened by Key's fellow engineer's efforts. In 1864, citizens of Richmond viewed a selection of his pictures of dueling batteries and bombarding monitors.[60] These depictions underscored Southern intransigence in the face of the ferocious and relentless Union attack.

On the other hand, Chapman approached the topic more artistically. In early 1864, a number of the "patriotic" artist's views went on public display at the Ordnance Bureau in Richmond, Virginia.[61] The clarity of color and subject matter of these "beauti-

FIG. 7.8. *The Attack on Charleston by the Yankee Iron Clad Fleet, April 7th, 1863,* by Augustus Grinevald (Columbia, S.C.: B. Duncan, 1863). Courtesy of the John Johnson Papers at the South Carolina Historical Society. (The image has been digitally enhanced for clarity.)

ful" scenes not only reflected well on his skills but also conveyed strong nationalistic messages. Spirited depictions of staunch Fort Sumter's battered interior spoke to the resolution of its defenders. His sketch of imported powerful cannons suggested the Union blockade's ineffectiveness. The painting of the small Confederate torpedo steamer CSS *David,* which drove off the heavily armored USS *New Ironsides* in October 1863, recalled David and Goliath's struggle. Unlike Grinevald and Keys, however, Chapman used palette and technique to romanticize and aestheticize his nation's efforts to keep Charleston open. Like them, he also repeated themes of resistance.

Another artist, George S. Cook, used more modern technology to capture images of the defense that conveyed similar ideas.[62] Like Key, his photographs attempt to record scenes accurately. In late July 1863, the Confederate States Engineer Department employed him to produce and duplicate documentary photographs: images of Union "Devils" (rafts attached to monitors to clear mines), Fort Sumter, and monitors.[63] While these earlier works are now apparently lost, a later effort received greater notice and distribution. In early September 1863, Beauregard's loyal brigadier general, Thomas Jordan, approached Cook and J. M. Osborne. Desiring "faithful delineations of Fort Sumter to show future generations what Southern troops can endure in battle," he requested they obtain a "faithful likeness" of the Union fleet. The two photographers volunteered and, according to a contemporary newspaper,

FIG. 7.9. *View from Fort Sumter parapet showing Union monitors and USS New Ironside* (detail), by George S. Cook, 1863. Courtesy of the Cook Collection, The Valentine.

Fig. 7.10. *Interior view of Fort Sumter,* by George S. Cook, 1863. Courtesy of Library of Congress, LC-DIG-ppmsca-35435.

thereby preserved "a valuable memorial of the defense almost unequaled in its obstinacy."[64] On September 8, 1863, they took their cameras and equipment into a war zone and produced an exceptional series of images (figs. 7.9 and 7.10). The shots of monitors firing at Fort Sumter and soldiers among the rubble of its interior are early examples of combat photography. For Confederates, the photographs delivered truthful depictions not only of the soldier's endurance but also of the bravery of Confederate artists.

Beauregard's determination to make a thorough official record of the siege enabled a variety of artists to convey their individual perspectives to their fellow Confederates. Whether idealist, patriot, pragmatist, or fearless artist, the scope of approaches provided Southerners with a more extensive idea of Charleston's defenses whether they desired factual or more poetic imagery. The works celebrated the defense more objectively than panoramic performances. Furthermore, they showed Beauregard's desire to ensure a national profile as defender of the country.

CONFEDERATE HEROES

Two incidents related to imagery show that Beauregard's efforts at self-publicity achieved only partial success. In Columbia, South Carolina, a fund-raising bazaar held in mid-January 1865 featured a painting of the State's palmetto tree with the names *Beauregard* above and *Sumter* below.[65] Two months later, with Charleston lost and the Confederate collapse weeks away, Georgians in Augusta attended a fund-raising auction for the local soldiers' aid society. At the conclusion of the event, portraits of President Davis and Beauregard remained among the handful of unsold lots. The reporter bemoaned that despite these two men's efforts on behalf of their nation, likenesses of them "could not be sold at any price." On the other hand, a photograph of Generals Joseph E. Johnston or Robert E. Lee would be snapped up for fifty dollars.[66]

These stories say something of the fickleness of Confederate celebrity. In 1861, at the height of their popularity and hero status, Davis's and Beauregard's visages flooded the Confederacy in print, paint, photograph, and stone. It may be that the inability to sell their images in March 1865 related to their standing in popular opinion. In President Davis's case, Confederates idealized him until their nation's fortunes declined and debate about his leadership increased. By contrast Beauregard retained the fame he had earned in 1861 for most of the war. However, as Sherman pushed forces under his command out of Georgia and then South Carolina, Beauregard's star may have waned for some Southerners. Notwithstanding these reasons, it is possible that the auctioneer attempted to sell images of Davis and Beauregard in a marketplace already saturated over the past four years with their likenesses.[67]

Confederates displayed an endless fascination and curiosity about their generals' appearance. Just as image makers used a variety of media and ways to satisfy Confederates' demand to see Southerners victorious in battles, they did so too, when they pictured those who led their armed forces. For instance, in 1861 painter Annie Perdue Sebring (1833–1913) produced a noted portrait of Sterling Price.[68] In New Orleans during 1861, porcelain artist R. T. Lux reproduced Beauregard's likeness on a vase and tea set.[69] In Virginia, sculptor Alexander Galt crafted a bust "as true to nature as nature itself" of General Benjamin Huger.[70] Yet some producers attempted to create a more comprehensive visual record of their military leaders.

On October 17, 1862, Knoxville portraitist Samuel M. Shaver (1816–78) hosted a meeting of local luminaries at his Art Room Gallery. Wishing to preserve "correct statements of events" and to "familiarize this people and their children with the faces and deeds of the heroes of this war," the group formed the East Tennessee Art Association. Although the set of portraits first commissioned by the association included paintings of President Davis and Vice President Stephens, only military leaders are mentioned in subsequent reports.[71] Of all the series, only two stiffly formal portraits of lieutenant generals survive: Shaver's original painting of E. Kirby Smith (fig. 7.11) and a carte de visite copy of his portrait of Leonidas Polk dressed and posed similarly in the American Civil War Museum's collection. Picked out with crisp contours and a bright light source, both men dominate their portraits. Each man's uniform bears only hints—Smith's double row of Confederate staff buttons arranged in groups and the suggestion of a wreath around the stars on Polk's collar—that they are generals. While the background is indistinct in Polk's portrait, Shaver sets Smith under a gloomy clouded evening sky and amid a mountainous landscape. A hatless and determined-looking Smith grasps his sword. Behind him, an orderly struggles to settle a horse. In the distance, and under a fiery sunset, three rows of troops—cavalry, infantry, and artillery, respectively—advance westward toward an enemy hidden by gun smoke. It insinuates that Smith, then in command of troops in East Tennessee, would drive out Union forces. However, the reverse happened, and the Confederate evacuation of Knoxville forced Shaver to carry the portraits to Augusta, Georgia. There the works moved audiences, who viewed them at Perkins Photographic, and in response, the studio created and sold copies of the likenesses.[72]

Even though portraits like Shaver's were popular, their presence concerned some. They hinted at idol worship. While to be expected in Yankees, some Confederates warned their fellows against such behavior. Confederate ideologues worried that the people's adulation of heroes transferred their hopes for success from the Almighty to men.[73] Confederates must strive to maintain moral superiority over their enemy.[74] Charleston's *Mercury*, in August 1863, told readers that the primary cause of their national misfortune lay with the people's "credulous and unreasoning man-worship."[75] In this context, the simple act of collecting a hero's image carried spiritual and national consequences.

While this thinking may have dampened some people's enthusiasm, many Confederates not only consumed but were also encouraged to purchase famous generals' photographs. For those willing to tread the fine line between their Christian faith and patriotic fervor, photographic galleries in cities such as Richmond, Wilmington, Augusta, and Charleston offered a host of their heroes' portraits.[76] Moreover, journals such as the *Illustrated News* sent conflicting messages. In August 1863, the *Illustrated*

FIG. 7.11. *Gen'l E. Kirby Smith,* by Samuel Shaver, 1862–63. Oil on canvas. Courtesy of the East Tennessee Historical Society, Knoxville.

News justified the purchase of generals' portraits, adding, "What country on the face of the habitable globe, save the Confederacy, can boast such illustrious heroes?" Two months later, it warned against "hero worship."[77] Regardless, many people collected and coveted pictures of important military men. Pictorial journals—the *Punch, Field and Fireside,* and the *Illustrated News*—picked up on this interest and attempted to entice readers by including likenesses in their pages. The *Field and Fireside* chose Lieutenant General Thomas J. "Stonewall" Jackson as the subject of the first of its "occasional portraits of distinguished military and civic officials." Although based loosely on a prewar portrait, its selection acknowledged both Jackson's fame and the public's desire to see images, even if inaccurate, of its military leaders (fig. 7.12).[78] These images allowed people to carry the image of their armies' leaders into their homes. Their popularity may have been the catalyst that prompted one showman to significantly change his presentation.

In late 1863, with his patronage dwindling, Lee Mallory looked for a presentation to replace his mechanical show. Ready in early March 1864, his new show featured the "Stereoscopticon," a powerful calcium light imported from France. He used this apparatus to project life-size stereoscopic portraits of generals onto screens. Carefully arranged ahead of time, the hour-long presentation featured likenesses, accom-

FIG. 7.12. "Lt. Gen. Thomas J. Jackson," by Alfred Maurice, 1863. Engraving. *Southern Field and Fireside,* Aug. 1, 1863. Courtesy of David M. Rubenstein Rare Book & Manuscript Library, Duke University.

panied by biographic narratives and an orchestra's music. In addition, Mallory sold or distributed copies of the likeness of each personality featured in the show and handed out lists of where patrons could purchase images of other generals.[79]

Confederate audiences responded so warmly to Mallory's new show that he had to put measures in place to control the crowd's response.[80] Innovative and entrepreneurial, when he reached Mobile, Alabama, in May 1864, Mallory introduced "interviews" with each general and added dissolving views of parts of the world, colorful "chromotropes," and Chinese fireworks.[81] But on his return to Mobile later that year, he reverted to the less sensational original format. Of all the generals, Robert E. Lee and Stonewall Jackson were his headliners.[82]

The apogee of Confederate heroes, Lee and Jackson featured prominently not only in Mallory's exhibition but also in Southern hearts. Robert E. Lee's successes, after he took command of the Army of Northern Virginia in 1862, earned him the optimistic affection of the South. In 1863, Mallory and Grain both included panoramic scenes of Lee's army.[83] For those within the South keen to know what Lee looked like, artists, illustrators, and photographers obliged. Artists John A. Elder, James W. King, Edward C. Bruce (1825–1909), Louis Guilliame (1816–92), and soldier-artist William E. Trahern (1838–1927) painted portraits. Photographers produced eleven wartime portraits of Lee. These were reproduced not only by the *Illustrated News'* engravers but also by Grinevald (as a lithograph) and by other photographers. Additionally, in early February 1865, photographs of Edward Valentine's statuette of Lee began to circulate in Richmond.[84] Posed seated or standing; viewed from the front, three-quarters, or the sides; armed or unarmed—these images presented many versions of Lee: relaxed, authoritative, or akin to a figure from imperial Rome.

Stonewall Jackson's performance at Manassas and in Virginia's Shenandoah Valley propelled him into the Confederate pantheon of heroes. Visual culture made his face the best known of all Southern military leaders. Painters such as John A. Elder and Edward C. Bruce painted large-scale fine art pieces.[85] Mechanical representations toured the South showing Jackson's division arriving on a battlefield or advancing across the Potomac River. Furthermore, lithographic prints, photographs, and engravings in the *Southern Illustrated News* and *Southern Field and Fireside* and a bust by renowned sculptor Alexander Galt (1827–63) distributed his visage.[86] Days before a volley of friendly fire sealed Jackson's doom and scotched Confederate hopes, photographer David Cowell captured his best-known portrait. Additionally, sculptor Andrew Frederick Volck (1833–91), Maryland Confederate propagandist Adalbert J. Volck's brother, gained permission to make a death mask of the general in preparation for a proposed statue. Endorsing the movement, Richmond's *Enquirer* stated, "Every heart craves a life-like *eidolon* which may be a national memento to his glory." Confederates donated forty-five hundred dollars to Volck's project, and by the end of August 1863, he patented, displayed, and arranged the mass production of a three-quarter-size bust of "Stonewall."[87] Meanwhile, across the South, enterprising individuals such as "Mr. Hutton" of Keatinge and Ball and publishers Ayres and Wade reproduced and sold printed copies of Cowell's portrait.[88] Although many never saw Volck's *eidolon*, by April 1864, Confederate creatives satisfied the people's desire to see Jackson. When that month the Confederate Treasury placed Jackson's name under his portrait on the new five hundred–dollar note, one observer scoffed, the familiarity of his "mien" to Confederates made it as redundant as an artist labeling a painting of a steed, "This is a horse."[89]

Image creators provided Confederates with opportunities to see and experience vicariously the war's heroes and morale-building victories and to appreciate their soldier's fortitude. In doing so, they also afforded civilians with links to the military world. When most Confederates' nation consisted primarily of family and friends, this connected civilians to their soldiers.[90] In late 1861, painter Benjamin Franklin Reinhart (1829–85) provided a rare Confederate artist's depiction of the relationship between home and the soldier at the front. Reinhart produced a painting, now lost, that New Orleans's *Crescent* described as "a family group; the old father of the family, specs on nose, is leaning back in his easy chair, reading a newspaper; he is reading aloud to the family the first news of the battle of Manassas; the daughters stand or crouch around in various attitudes of silence, their faces expressive of the liveliest anxiety; a portrait on the wall, in the background, representing two soldiers in full uniform is the key to the piece; the anxiety of the listeners is at once explained. The most lively as well as lovely figure in the group is that of a young lady on her knees on the carpet, leaning across the old man's lap, holding the lower part of the paper, and reading in advance of him whilst listening to him."[91]

The apprehension and interest expressed in this work captured the mood in many homes throughout America. In the early months of the war, photographers from the North and South counted on these feelings when they ventured to parades, camps, and near the front lines to capture images of soldier life. Through staged scenes of soldiers drilling, cooking, and relaxing around camp, the composed narratives aimed at showing the men's confidence, strength, hardihood, and natural soldiering abilities. As photographers became more studio bound, panoramic exhibitions that showed soldiers in the field increased.

MILITARY LIFE

From 1861, Fitz's *Southern Panopticon,* Lee Mallory's *Pantechoptomon,* and Burton's *Southern Diorama* all featured idealized depictions of military life. At the same time that disease ravaged Confederates camps, civilians watched images of neatly drilling soldiers, orderly campsites, and amusing scenes of soldier life. However, regardless of their regular claims to "truthfulness," these shows packaged and presented a sanitized version of not just camp life but also the more violent aspects of war. The Confederacy's creatives rendered their fighters' combat experiences for audiences in a variety of ways.

"Who wants to see a battle?" the *Memphis Daily Appeal* asked in December 1861 as it promoted Burton's Manassas diorama.[92] To judge by the success of panoramas of battle, the answer was "many." Descriptions of these shows hint at what audiences saw. According to critics, Burton's work gave "an idea of what a battle is that printed descriptions can never impart." In "vivid and natural hues," his scene showed Yankee casualties and their fleeing comrades before a wall of Confederate flags and troops.[93] In Mallory's *Pantechnoptomon,* Confederate figures moved "with astonishing precision," stopping, loading, and discharging weapons "full of reality as can come within the scope of art."[94] However, the basis of this "reality" was slender. Only one artist-impresario, the former artilleryman George W. Grain, had firsthand knowledge of battle. Nevertheless, until at least late 1864, when records of panoramic shows touring ceased, most continued to offer at least one scene of soldiers in battle. These were not the only opportunity for home front Confederates to see their soldiers fighting.[95]

Mapped and choreographed in theatrical performance, Confederate stages afforded civilians another avenue through which to see soldiers in combat.[96] Sometimes necessity made this incidental. In Mobile, the theater company used soldiers in uniform as extras. "It was no unusual sight," recalled actor Theodore Hamilton, to see "a company of swash-bucklers in a Roman party armed with rifles instead of swords."[97] Contemporary original war dramas provided more intentional depictions of Confederate soldiers in combat. The surviving scripts of three plays each presented different ideas of battle. In *Love's Ambuscade,* justice of the peace and sometime playwright J. J. Delchamps placed the fighting offstage and used narration to create it in the mind's eye.[98] While James D. McCabe included movement and mock gunfire in the battles he created for *The Guerrillas,* text is still central to the action.[99] The third, Joseph Hodgson's *The Confederate Vivandiere,* is more balletic and melodramatic. Accompanied by music, drums, shouting, and the rattle of musketry, hero and villain struck poses before the "battle" concluded, with the entire stage illuminated.[100] Reporting on John Hewitt's *Jayhawkers* in mid-May 1863, Savannah's *Morning News* wrote, "We are glad to see drama of this kind put up on the stage; they give the people a pleasing history of the war, and, if not too much exaggerated, instruct the masses, and, as it were, daguerreotype scenes that, otherwise, they would live in ignorance of."[101] Such stylized scenes not only softened battle's brutality and added to national morale but also helped people cope with the most tragic result of war—death.

SOLDIER MORTALITY

Death in wartime wrenched apart antebellum understandings concerning the end of life. Individuals died suddenly in hospitals or on the battlefield alone or among strangers, their bodies buried in places often unknown to those dear to them. Family members craved insight into their soldier's death, and Confederate image makers responded. In Delchamps's *Love's Ambuscade,* the critically wounded Edward Delafield told audiences, "I have done my duty and am ready to die." Delafield's fatalistic approach to dying embodied the concept and rituals of the "good death." Death demanded reverent acceptance as it provided a direct portal to Christ's presence and the previously departed.[102] Such performances helped viewers believe that their loved ones had faced death with noble resignation.[103]

Artists' attempts to depict the dreadful aspects of war met with varying responses. In August 1861, panoramist John D. Fitz attempted one approach in the "Aftermath" scene from his *Battle of Manassas* series. The *Delta* described it as "a very impressive picture; the field appears covered with the dead, and the slow movement of the hospital wagons, and their attendants picking up the wounded, impresses one with the terrible horrors of war"[104] Despite a four-month tour, however, this was the sole description. Perhaps its depiction of "terrible horrors" repelled Confederates and limited its success. Significantly, the next panoramic artist to venture into this area used a different approach and achieved greater note.

Lee Mallory's "The Wounded Officer and His Steed," a scene within his *Pantechoptomon of War Illustrations,* presented soldiers' death in a more stylized and personal manner. It premiered on January 12, 1862, in New Orleans's Academy of Music. Repeated for over a year and replicated in Mobile, Alabama, by John T. Budd, its realism affected crowds.[105] Indeed, during one performance, as the rider's mount died, a correspondent reported hearing a child ask, "Pa, why don't they fetch a doctor for the poor horse?"[106] Responses to the show included not only applause and tears but also poetry. So moved was Mrs. V.E.W. (McCord) Vernon that she penned a 120-line poem, "The Warrior's Steed," after seeing one of Mallory's first Richmond exhibitions. It provides an insight into what touched the crowds so deeply.

A horse and rider galloping into battle are struck down by a shell. Initially, the rider is unaware of their mortal wounds; however, the deep gash in his horse's panting side and his weakness prompts the realization that both are dying, and he prepares for death. He laments:

> Ah, faithful friend, upon my breast
> Thy aching head may'st lie,
> Since thou alone art left to hear
> My last, sad parting sigh.

Although saddened that his horse would be unable to comfort his family, the knowledge that no Yankee will ever possess the animal consoles him. Finally, no longer capable of speech, the rider falls silent, and the horse, struck by gunfire, reels and dies. As the sun sets and a breeze is seen sweeping over the "uncomplaining dead," the soldier breathes his last.[107]

A similar image of the good death is contained in the song "The Drummer Boy of Shiloh" and the image Augustus Grinevald created for Blanton Duncan's edition of the sheet music's frontispiece (fig. 7.13). Among his comrades, the dying boy first calmly prays for God's forgiveness for the carnage and then to his dead mother. Scenes such as these enabled people to believe that, while unnatural, battlefield death could still conform to their ideals for dying.

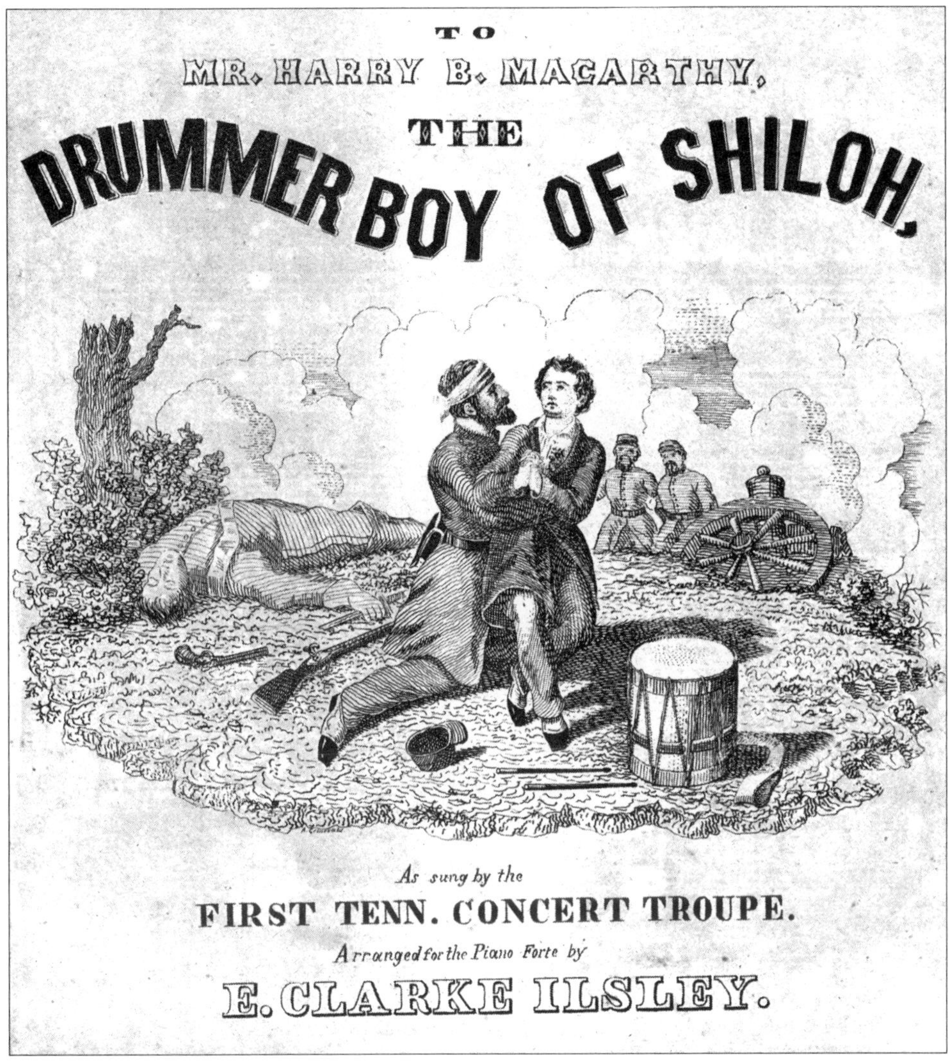

FIG. 7.13. "The Drummer Boy of Shiloh," by Augustus Grinevald, 1863 (Augusta, Ga.: Blackmar, 1863). Confederate Sheet Music Collection, courtesy of Warren D. Allen Music Library, Florida State University.

Faced with battles' dead, the military abandoned good death's observances and adopted pragmatic efficiency. Regardless, Confederate popular culture attempted to paint a more orderly and caring process. In Fitz's "most admirable" *Panopticon* and Mallory's *War Illustrations*, automated figures collected and carried the dead from the battleground.[108] Similarly, in late 1863, the *Southern Illustrated News* conveyed the idea that soldiers treated battlefield dead with care and respect. The front and

FIG. 7.14. "Louisianans of Hays' Brigade Burying the Dead on Malvern Hill." From *Southern Illustrated News*, Dec. 12, 1863.

back pages of its December 12, 1863, issue featured images related to the July 1, 1862, battle of Malvern Hill. A depiction of the battleground as it appeared months after the fight was featured on the front page. The back page carried an engraving that showed Louisiana soldiers burying their dead after the engagement (fig. 7.14). The Louisianans, reputedly the roughest and hardest of Confederate soldiers, outnumber the bodies they carefully move. In stark contrast to the reality of the dead being dragged, the deceased are carried on stretchers as if they are wounded. One man in the background, smoking a pipe, is the sole indicator of any casualness about the operation. W. D. Washington's *Burial of Latané* repeated the idea of strangers caring for the dead. For those who grieved, visual culture provided comforting images.[109]

Artists and theater companies continued to present their patriotic depictions of the war to an audience keen to consume these shows until the war's finish. A map of known panoramic shows in the Civil War South indicates that this imagery reached repeatedly into many areas of the Confederacy (fig. 7.15). Each delivered a different experience. Gazing at still images stimulated thoughts of imagined victories, while live performances provided the illusion of experiencing them. In April 1863, commenting on one of Lee Mallory's depictions of war, Richmond's *Enquirer* wrote, "The lessons of the war, its realities and recollections cannot be more pleasantly studied."[110] Their treatments repackaged and amplified Confederate narratives of military

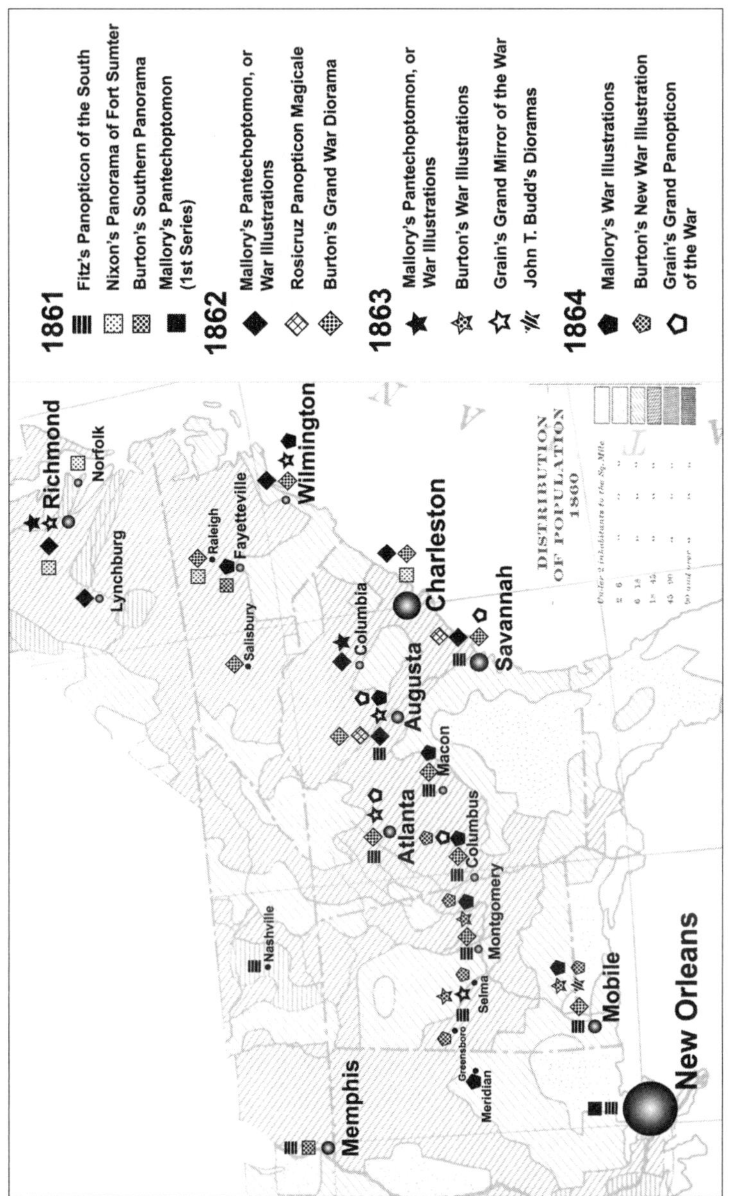

FIG. 7.15. Panoramic Performances in the Confederacy, 1861–1865. The symbols plot recorded panoramic performances. The base map shows population density in 1860, and the size of a city's symbol and name relate to its population. Image created by the author.

superiority and linked citizens to the army, counteracting the growing estrangement between soldiers and civilians.[111] They allowed audiences to see historic events, heroic personalities, and the traits they imagined separated them from Northerners. Additionally, showmen contributed thousands of dollars to the war effort. "In this Revolution," the introduction of Ayres and Wade's *War and Its Heroes* explained, "all are heroes."[112] While visual culture helped Confederates imagine this claim as a reality, like other aspects of visual and material culture, it also faced limitations.

A lack of new victories on which to base their work restricted the pool of material and impacted all visual forms. After May 1864, George Grain added just one new scene to his show, the minor but bloody April 1864 engagement at Fort Pillow, Tennessee. Here Confederates, under former slave auctioneer General Nathan B. Forrest, slaughtered black and white garrisoning troops.[113] There were few other victories to celebrate. In the Eastern theater, the war descended into an unrelenting and murderous slugfest. In the West, only the September 1863 battle of Chickamauga presented an opportunity for celebration or commemoration. By January 1864, an "Alabama lady's" play premiered in Montgomery.[114] Finally, in early 1865, John A. Elder exhibited his *Battle of the Crater.* Apart from these works, in the last year of the war visual culture offered Confederates few other opportunities to experience recent victories.[115]

The media of panoramic exhibitions suffered from its own particular weakness: These shows benefited from the novelty of the experience. To achieve it, stated Richmond's *Examiner* in September 1863, impresario Lee Mallory was willing "to go to any lengths to please the public."[116] Since the start of the war, these shows proved the most widely viewed and long-lasting art form to depict the struggle. However, Richmond audiences dwindled. From early April 1863, Mallory and Grain added magicians, bands, a variety of performers, and even a "Trip to Fairy Land" to draw crowds to their shows.[117] Despite these efforts, by Christmas, Grain had departed, and critics wrote that "an overdose of Mallory's 'War Illustrations' had killed the Metropolitan Hall as dead as the 'first bald Caesar.'"[118] By September 1863, panoramic showmen had abandoned Richmond and expanded their circuits to bring their shows to new audiences.[119] Set adrift on the Confederacy's diminishing rail network and progressively hemmed in by the Union armies, Mallory, Grain, and Burton staged their final performances for those who still dreamed of Confederate victory.

Although the air of defeatism that hung over the South in 1865 dampened many Southerners' spirits, not all had lost hope.[120] The response of some Confederates to the news of Lee's surrender showed the resilience of Confederate confidence. In Griffin, Georgia, nurse Kate Cummings recorded that in her hospital stunned silence, followed by gales of disbelieving laughter, met the report. A week later, they still considered the surrender "mythical."[121] The existence and resilience of these beliefs were complex and individual. Alongside other Confederate media, visual culture helped Confederates sustain these hopes. Studying Confederate soldiers, Jason Phillips finds that newspapers fostered a culture of invincibility within Southern armies. Instances of civilian disbelief that Lee's army could surrender show that some behind the lines shared similar convictions.[122] While Confederate news sources undoubtedly contributed to civilian trust in the military, Confederate visual culture aided the effort in its own way. Images of the military—its heroic leaders, victories, and experiences—complemented the information carried by the Confederate press. They also provided a way for families to picture their menfolk's experiences, strengthening the bonds between the home and the front. Collectively, these images nurtured Confederates' comforting delusions of superiority and added another layer that helped insulate them from the reality of their military losses. Victories enjoyed importance beyond their worth, and through these sources, defeats were downplayed, ignored, or denied.[123] Such misconceptions about the war's progress did little to assist Confederates in maintaining an objective view of the war. Although this misinformation increased optimism and helped bolster nationalism, it also made it difficult for Confederates to accurately understand the war's trajectory and respond appropriately.[124]

Ultimately, after the war, as the bitterness of defeat abated in the memories of former Confederates, aspects of the military struggle present in Confederate visual culture reemerged within the mythology of the Lost Cause.[125] While facets such as the Manassas mania abated, some ideas remained. The private soldier's resolute service became mingled with the gray jacket. Others, like the generals who became revered figures, formed significant parts of the mythology. They joined two mainstays of the fiction: loyal, happy slaves and a glorified concept of Confederate womanhood.[126] The inclusion of these two groups among those related to the military indicated the importance allotted to them by former Confederates. Regarding the enslaved population, wartime visual culture conveyed a skewed and simple view of their part. The public representations of women in the Civil War South show Confederates responding to and conveying a more complex range of ideas.

CHAPTER 8

Representations of Womanhood

MRS. DELAFIELD: Ah! Olivia, what can weak woman do to aid in repelling the myriads which our foes are marshalling against us.
MRS. WALTON: Do, mother! Much, if nerved by a proper spirit. They can toil and endure; do as we are doing, spin, weave and knit, that their brave defenders may be provided against the winter's frost and the summer's sun. They can teach their infants that "resistance to tyrants is obedience to God!" And imbue their tender minds with an unquenchable hatred of the Puritan race, that would enslave their fathers and their mothers.
—J. J. DELCHAMPS, *Love's Ambuscade; or, The Sergeant's Stratagem*, 1863

The Civil War disrupted and transformed Southern women's lives.[1] State and central governments demanded more of their families and resources, inflation weakened the buying power of their money, and the conflict disrupted the social order. It also stimulated greater visibility for women.[2] "Patriotic expectations" led women out of their homes to contribute to the war effort and gave them a physical presence in the army and in city life.[3] Early in the war, they volunteered their services to make clothing. Later large townships such as Richmond saw "battalions" of women carrying "bundles of soldier's apparel" to and from the quartermaster's clothing depots as piecework.[4] Women featured prominently in concerts and plays on the Confederate stage. At the same time, some developed a new collective political identity and even worked to oppose the Confederacy.[5] Depictions of women in illustrated journals captured Confederate men's responses to their labors.[6] Collectively, these works helped make manifest women's presence in the Confederate States.

Male artists usually pictured women and their lives in the Civil War South.[7] However, nineteenth-century men were not well placed to do so. They distanced themselves from real women and treated them as abstractions.[8] Most commonly, they imagined and produced nonspecific or allegorical images of women rather than individual portrayals. The value of these depictions of Confederate women lies in showing another way Southern men imagined and attempted to control the white female population.

WOMEN AND WAR WORK

In neat prewar theories, men bestrode the public world while the kitchen, garden, bedroom, and parlor constituted a woman's domain. God and nature, the press and pulpit regularly proclaimed, suited genders for specific separate realms.[9] An antebellum visitor to the South described his host's wife as almost invisible, appearing only at supper, after which she "retired immediately."[10] However, Christian faith and a belief in women's nurturing qualities also enabled a few women to move out of the home. Under men's control, prewar women worked anonymously for philanthropic organizations in cities such as Mobile, Alabama, and Savannah, Georgia, and involved themselves in benevolent groups.[11] Such orderly notions of how women operated in the world proved inapt for a society in tumult and forced men to change the scope of the women's sphere.[12]

Southern men built their view of manhood on the control of women and the black enslaved population. From 1861, however, soldiers' collective need for military clothing broadened women's rights and privileges, providing what Catherine Clinton termed a "permissible excuse."[13] In thanking the women who sewed his company's uniform, former lawyer and new captain Andrew S. Herron explained that though it was "right and proper" for men and women to give their energies for the cause, each should do so from their "respective spheres." "That," he explained to the women, "is what you are doing, and what the women of the south all over the country are doing."[14] His surroundings and print media supported Herron's opinion.

The South's transport network carried men dressed in uniforms made by women through its towns, and newspapers reported stories from farther afield.[15] Reading news exchanges from Mississippi in late February 1861, the editor of Atlanta's *Gate City Guardian* concluded that the "ladies throughout Mississippi are engaged in making uniforms" and "raising money for arms" for their volunteers.[16] Such reports created similar expectations for women across the South and helped create the idea that women in the South shared a collective identity.

The responsibility for making clothing assumed a variety of meanings. Some recipients cast it as part of an almost contractual obligation. Observing a company of Georgians dressed in "brown country jeans" passing through his town, an editor in Columbus wrote that "their dress showed that they were going to fight for the right sort of women."[17] Others, like one group of Arkansans, conceived it in more knightly terms. They promised "deeds of bravery and chivalry on the battlefield" dressed in these "souvenirs" made by "fair hands."[18] Reports like these reflect early instances of the reciprocity some Confederates imagined existed between the sexes.[19] Other reports showed alternate consequences of these efforts. The scale of the effort required to make a soldier's clothing did more than make patriotism visible. It provided women with an environment in which to share news, gossip, and anxieties.[20] It also loosened conventions. Although late in the war an editor wrote that women's "modest delicacy" meant she "naturally shrinks from public praise," patriotic ladies' names appeared with increased regularity in newsprint.[21] Listed as donors, organizers, or participants, women became public individuals and experienced public profiles that would have been unimaginable in the prewar South.

Even after the South's early war *rage militaire,* homemade clothing continued to make women's support of the Confederacy visible. By the end of 1861, soldiers' relief and aid groups formed across the South. Sometimes coordinated by states, they made articles of clothing by the thousands. In late 1862, after traveling for two months in the Confederacy, one visitor observed that Southern women spent "their time and wear out their fingers in making clothing" for their soldiers.[22] Even before the war's second winter, the Ladies' Volunteer Aid Association of Augusta, Georgia, reported making eight thousand garments.[23] By the end of February 1863, it had enough clothing on hand to halt work for two months.[24] Groups of this kind produced millions of dollars' worth of garments. Their work improved soldiers' comfort and morale and eased the burden on the Confederate government.[25] It also brought other positive effects.

For many Confederate soldiers this clothing afforded more than mere covering. It provided a tangible link to the home front. South Carolinian private J. W. Reid explained that he felt "as big as a dog in a meat house" when he donned homemade clothes.[26] Arkansas captain J. P. Andrews thanked the women of Decatur, Georgia, "doubly" for their "liberal contribution of clothing" and the "patriotism" it represented.[27] In studying Civil War soldiers, James McPherson found that morale crumbled without a "firm base of support in the homes and communities" in which they lived.[28] The reception of articles from home countered the growing belief among some soldiers of wavering civilian support.[29] The officers and men of the First Confederate Battalion summed up their feelings in early 1863: "By such acts you not only give substantial aid and comfort but inspire the soldier with feelings also, of yet more determined purpose to 'do or die' in his country's cause."[30] Simple articles of clothing offered proof of women's support and produced an emotional impact that government clothing could never match.[31]

Sometimes clothing provided other forms of connection between the frontline and home front. Some women attached notes with their names or sentiments to the garments they made. These personal touches sometimes prompted thank-you letters from soldier recipients. In early 1864, the Prattsville, Alabama, Soldiers' Aid Society received letters from two Alabama privates—Evander J. Wiggins, age twenty-three, and Henry T. Stringfellow, age eighteen—addressed to Miss Julia Smith. From separate regiments, both thanked her for the shirts she had made and described their war service. Stringfellow added that since receiving the garments he and his comrades were now "determine [*sic*] to fight for the ladies" and had reenlisted for the war. These shirts carried other meanings. In Wiggin's letter, for example, he hoped that he "may be permitted to carry in the pocket a letter from you before the shirt wears out."[32] These young soldiers viewed the pieces of apparel as opportunities for building personal relationships. As the Confederacy approached total war, the opportunities for connections between soldiers and the home front decreased.

The need for a more efficient and uniform system of clothing soldiers disrupted these connections. From October 1862, soldiers' aid societies felt the impact of the Quartermaster's Department's increased monopoly of the South's textile production. Over the third quarter of 1863, "very great scarcity" of material meant that the Soldiers' Relief Association of Charleston produced five thousand dollars' worth of clothing for nineteen units and 281 individuals.[33] A year earlier, an expenditure of fourteen hundred dollars enabled them to produce at least three times the amount of clothing.[34] In October 1863, Alabama's quartermaster reported that the state's people would have forwarded more than the seventy thousand articles but the Confederate States clothed "soldiers more cheaply."[35] By the end of 1863, Confederate and state bodies laid claim to most of the textiles produced by Southern factories for the army. As the government provided more clothing, soldiers made their own choices.

Not all rebel soldiers embraced government clothing. In June 1863, English officer Arthur Fremantle recorded that "within a week" of receiving new government uniforms, one army division resumed wearing the "coarse home-spun jackets and trousers made by their mothers and sisters at home."[36] In April 1864, the inspector of Kershaw's South Carolina Brigade noted that its "decidedly inferior" appearance stemmed from the troops' "home production" clothes.[37] Gray clothes came from the government, and clothing made of brown jeans, according to one Confederate soldier, meant the wearer came from a community of caring "friends."[38] Clothing supplied from family or community provided a mark of individuality and manifested a soldier's link to home.

The nature of the household a soldier came from affected how clothing he received from home was made. Enslaved Southerners commonly spun, wove, and made the clothing sent from plantations. Troops from towns wore garments sewn by women but cut from fabric purchased from manufactories. Sometimes, as an April 1861 letter reported, "white, soft hands, unused to toil" made military garments.[39] However, most Confederate troops came from farms and their clothing reflected their rural background. War brought family looms and spinning wheels out of the barns to which ready-made clothing had consigned them.[40] When, for example, in the early 1900s, the Tennessee State archivist asked fifteen hundred of its Confederate veterans who had made their clothing, almost 74 percent of them recalled that their womenfolk had spun, wove, and sewed their clothing.[41] It is highly likely, given the widespread descriptions of Southern troops wearing butternut-dyed non-uniform clothing, that this pattern extended throughout the Confederacy.[42]

Women who made soldiers' clothing enjoyed the praise of the Confederate nation. Mary Cronin observed that most Southern editors both recognized the necessity and "frequently encouraged and applauded such actions."[43] Editors drew many allusions, linking philanthropy and patriotism, soldiers' bayonets and women's needles, and the women of the first and second wars of independence.[44] Choosing to devote column space to these accounts, male editors complimented the clothing women made in affirming and promoting a place for Confederate women on the outer edges of the domestic sphere that provided greater visibility.

Newspapers' readiness to celebrate women's work did not extend to every collective effort. After the CSS *Virginia*'s battle in March 1862, women across the South led a popular movement to raise public monies for ironclad rams. Predominantly through March to May 1862, newspapers published the names of many of the thousands of donors. Their efforts helped add four armored vessels of war, commonly known as "Ladies' Gunboats," to the Confederacy's naval force. On January 31, 1863, two boats funded in part by donations, the CSS *Palmetto State* and the CSS *Chicora*, steamed out of Charleston Harbor, attacked, and drove off the blockading Union fleet. The following day, a Columbia, South Carolina, newspaper added to its report of the action: "God bless the ladies! All will say."[45] However, it provided a solitary voice. Instead of acknowledging the women's role, editors focused their praise on the fighting men. Confederates readily acknowledged the effort to raise funds but found it harder to recognize the results of their contributions.[46] Machines of war were part of the men's world. Men, not women, gained most of the public notice and glory when the vessels women caused to be made went into action.

More than their patriotic benevolence made women's support of the cause visible. Recruiting for the army created jobs across the South for women and slaves. Women worked farms and businesses, stitched army clothing, made munitions, and performed various clerical jobs for the government. Government and newspapers alike acknowledged that victory required the active involvement of the entire Southern population.[47] Employing women freed more men for service in the army. It also prompted the reconfiguring of gender roles, especially when some Southern men were shown wanting.

ENTERING THE MALE SPHERE

Clothing, flags, munitions, and signatures on currency provided concrete examples of Confederate women's support of the struggle. Confederate visual culture presented little evidence, however, of their significant contributions to the war effort. While women appeared regularly in graphic culture, few images showed them working either for pay or patriotism. "Exeunt—Entrée" is a rare example (fig. 8.1). The scene depicts a well-dressed man with swept fringe and goatee and two women in an office. His prominent nose runs in a line into his sloping forehead. While physiognomists considered this beautiful in a woman, in the "wee-man" it denoted affectation and a shallow mind. Leaning against a large writing desk, he gazes dismissively toward its hidden counter. The women's foreheads show intelligence, their noses reflect an even temperament, and their dress is modest. The word *exeunt* in the title echoes the change in spheres represented in the scene. Yet despite the man's shortcomings, it requires two women to take his place.

In the Confederate imagination, women's presence and their voice became forces in restoring manhood. For example, John Hill Hewitt's farce *The Veteran '76 and '62*, a tale of five generations of the Mayfield family, featured Marion, the great-granddaughter of a centenarian and veteran of the American Revolution. When Hector Homespun tells her that a dislocated trigger finger prevents him from volunteering, she chides him, "It's your courage that's out of joint."[48] Two years later, the *Southern Punch*'s engraving "The Last Call" reconfigured a similar tale (fig. 8.2). A small woman dressed in hoopskirts and a slouched military-style hat, armed with a sword-like parasol, confronts a character in a large hat and shirtsleeves, with a receding chin. The cartoon appeared ten days after Miss Fannie King, of Henrico County, apprehended Joshua West, a Confederate deserter.[49] Richmond's *Daily Examiner* cast King's actions as typical of Confederate women's heroism and suggested that Congress award a badge for such behavior.[50] Unimaginable only years earlier, female service to country made even greater assertiveness excusable.

Studying Southern women, Catherine Clinton described women who defied gender norms as "impermissible patriots."[51] With military service the most ultramasculine of domains, women who ventured into this arena placed themselves in an uncertain territory.[52] The South's treatment of individuals who crossed this most pro-

FIG. 8.1. "Exeunt—Entrée." From *Southern Punch*, Feb. 6, 1864. Courtesy of the Library of Virginia.

nounced gender boundary varied greatly. Invariably treated in the press as novelties, some women experienced acclaim, while others faced incarceration.[53] Representations of martial women showed the extent and conditions under which Southern men could allow women into their field of honor.

The character of the vivandière became the most common and recognizable heroic Confederate female role on the Confederate stage. Vivandières, women attached to regiments as sutlers or canteen keepers, developed in the French army and reached the height of popularity 1861. At the beginning of the war, vivandières accompanied some units, especially those from Louisiana, to the war. In New Orleans during 1861, images of vivandières appeared in a variety of media. Photographer J. D. Edwards sold copies of photographs of them on parade with CS Zouave Battalion at Pensacola, Florida; the sheet music for A. Waldauer's "Zouave Mazourka" featured actor Mrs. Clementine de Bar dressed as a cantinière on its cover; and later in the year, at the New Orleans Opera House, one stood out among serving soldiers who formed the tableau vivant *A Camp Scene*.[54] While they played only a bit part in the war, onstage they assumed greater prominence.

After the vivandière appeared in the opera house tableau vivant, at least another five original Confederate plays emerged that included this figure. The descriptions, notes, or scripts for four of them survive.[55] In Hewitt's 1863 operetta *The Vivandiere*, young Louise, whose cheery personality inspires her regiment, sings, "At my country's call I come, with cheerful lips and eyes." Critics who question her virtue and purity because of the pantaloons she wears and revolver she carries are chastised because her actions, including converting a long lost brother to "Southern Rights," exhibit the highest principles.[56] Act 3 closes with "Be Ever Lov'd as Now," a song that includes the lines "and wildly beats my heart twixt love and duty." Ultimately, Louise chooses love.[57] In a piece written by John Davis entitled *The Roll of the Drum*,

FIG. 8.2. "The Last Call: Amazonian Detective on Duty Makes an Arrest." From *Southern Punch,* June 18, 1864. Courtesy of the Library of Virginia.

Emma Cameron "a Northern girl with Southern principles," disguises herself as "Catharine," a vivandière, and enlists in hopes of slipping through the lines to be with her captive Yankee husband. After a love triangle develops, she falls for a brave Confederate private. Her husband's death in battle resolves the issue, and the "adventurous female" marries her Confederate swain.[58] In Joseph Hodgson's drama *The Confederate Vivandiere,* the dumb and orphaned Clara Brandon, the title role, possessed a "devotion to the cause" that prompted her to join the war after nursing wounded soldiers at Manassas. When faced with the choice of saving "her lover or her country," she chooses the latter.[59] In *The Scouts; or, The Plains of Manassas,* John Hewitt's Alice, the ward of a wealthy planter, is determined to show "the lords of creation" that women can fight. Adopting military dress, she enlists with some friends, and they capture a Yankee picket. Returning to Confederate lines, to the strains of "Dixie," their captive, a "big Yankee" officer, laments, "It is a pity that you're a rebel." To this, Alice replies: "A 'rebel' as you interpret it, I would always be. If to love our home institutions—to cherish our rights—to have respect for the constitution and the laws—to despise canting hypocrisy, and to oppose lawless invasion, constitutes rebellion, then I am proud of being a 'rebel'; for I have the example of the immortal Washington."[60] Through their words and deeds, these characters presented the image of women as vigorous agents and partners in the Confederate struggle.

Audiences saw four different types of Confederate woman in these plays: northern born, disabled, privileged, and commoner. All joined the cause for different reasons, but each character shared qualities of youth, activeness, and a transition from single to married by each play's conclusion. These plays repeated stories printed in the Confederate press that women could have amazonian adventures so long as they eventually married and retreated to the domestic sphere.[61]

The Confederate stage and press sent mixed messages about those women who stepped beyond domesticity's bounds. When in April 1864, Confederate forces captured Union doctor Mary E. Walker, her captors noted the costume and behavior

FIG. 8.3. "Miss Mary E. Walker, M.D.," by S. Casey. From *Southern Illustrated News,* May 14, 1864. Courtesy of the Boston Athenaeum.

of the future Medal of Honor winner with a mixture of outrage and fascination. Not only did she dress in the "latest miscegenation style," a stylized blue uniform that featured "pantalettes" under a skirt that reached "mid-way between the ankle and thigh," but when captured, she rode "a male saddle with *one foot in each stirrup.*" Dressed and riding like a man, Walker demonstrated the North's moral decay.[62] Described by a contemporary newspaper as a "disgusting production of Yankeeland," she became the subject of one of three portraits of real women published in the *Southern Illustrated News.*[63] The simple engraving is not benign. To heighten her "unsexed" nature, the artist flattened her chest and raised her coat's skirt length from mid-calf to above the knee, making it look like a man's frock coat. Her hair is shown worn up in a net (fig. 8.3). The illustrator made Walker's form appear more masculine to indicate the degree to which Northern women's femininity had eroded.

Confederate women in uniform received more mixed treatment. Although some found themselves detained by officials, others were celebrated. For example, in May 1863, when a seventeen-year-old Mississippi girl appeared dressed in military apparel (because she could get no other clothes), the reporter proclaimed that if Southern girls did "take to britches and guns woe betide old Uncle Abraham."[64] Likewise, in his work *The Guerrillas,* playwright James D. McCabe expressed similar sentiments. Rose Mayleigh boasts to the evil Yankee general Frémont: "You may kill every man and boy in our land but you will then have to meet the women and woe to you when that day comes!"[65] In late 1864, a widely republished article even suggested conscripting women into a "Corps of Industry."[66] However, despite this proposal, the popularity of vivandières in theaters, and the newspaper reports that publicized Confederate women in the army, the time when Rose Mayleigh's avowal would become reality seemed distant. Most plays' female characters exhibited more conventional behav-

FIG. 8.4. "Final Call for Reserves." From *Southern Punch*, June 25, 1864. Courtesy of the Library of Virginia.

iors or, like in *Going to the Camp Lee; or, The Petticoat Captains* (1863), which turned on cross-dressing women enlisting in the military, used the idea for amusement.[67]

On the Confederate stage, young women's engagement in military affairs represented a phase along their path to the altar. These ideas and Federal cavalry raids in March and May 1864 formed the context for the *Southern Punch*'s cartoon "Final Call for Reserves" (fig. 8.4). The scene is filled with elderly men and women wearing serious expressions and kepis over their civilian dress. Kepis, a part of the Confederate uniform, show the wearer's engagement in military service. The men press weapons into women's hands as, in the background, ranks of armed women wearing similar outfits march toward the right. While the hoopskirts of the central figure sweep the ground, the skirts of those women already carrying arms are shortened to reveal their bloomers. Their visibility hinted that arming women made them more radical and therefore less feminine.[68] Wordplay surrounding motherhood created weak puns in the text accompanying the cartoon, suggesting that bearing children would be a more effective role for women in the nation.

This cartoon ignored the thousands of Confederate women who already worked for the cause. It suggested that these well-dressed women were not already serving their nation and insinuated what Confederates such as nurse Kate Cumming already believed. After a day of nursing sick and wounded soldiers in early January 1864, she wrote in her journal, "I cannot help but lose my temper when I see so many idle women unwilling to do any little thing for these heroes."[69] While Confederate illustrated journals rarely celebrated or even noted women like Kate Cumming, they regularly ridiculed those whom Cumming described as "idle."

LESS THAN PATRIOTIC WOMEN

The scene in *Southern Punch*'s cartoon "Unpleasant Present, Unpleasanter Future" turned an ostensibly personal subject of finding a husband into a critique of women (fig. 8.5).[70] The well-dressed Juliet and Charlotte discuss issues of the day as they laze in a spacious and well-appointed room. Physiognomy hints at the right figure's acquisitiveness and melancholy character and the left's moral weakness. Their clothes and surroundings suggest that they are used to a life of ease, and their attitude points to an unpatriotic self-centeredness. They bemoan that the army's stripping the South of single men has interrupted courtship. (Juliet says, "Dear me! How very tiresome the days! Not a beau, except those I have arranged and re-arranged before my mirror!") In August 1862, North Carolina's *Fayetteville Observer* predicted that single soldiers would be "naturally drawn towards those [women] who, while they were away, suffering in camp, remembered to work for their comfort," but in reality, the growing cost in killed and maimed suggested that there would not be grooms enough for Southern brides.[71] The cartoon implied that only women who labored for the cause deserved marriage.

From the beginning of the war, Confederate leaders and thinkers associated success with a united effort by the entire population.[72] However, evidence of self-interest appeared on many Confederate streets. While most people dressed in recycled clothes, some men and women appeared wearing expensive goods run through the blockade. Their presence reminded people that profiteering was occurring and that some ship holds carried luxuries rather than war materiel.[73] Their dress rejected Confederate concepts of self-sacrifice. Even more worryingly, Confederates learned that some women actively encouraged men to avoid military service.[74] These instances compromised the image of women unified in their efforts for Confederate success. While the government and public sources used entreaty to dissuade these behaviors, the Confederate visual culture used ridicule.

An instance appeared in the September 1863 issue of the *Bugle Horn of Liberty;* in it "The Model Lady" depicted a woman dressed in ample flowing ribbons, hoopskirt,

FIG. 8.5. "Unpleasant Present, Unpleasanter Future." From *Southern Punch,* Dec. 13, 1863. Courtesy of the Library of Virginia.

petticoats, and patterned material (fig. 8.6). In other times, her modish costume may have attracted little attention. But Confederate audiences knew that the ideal woman dressed plainly in homespun, calico, recycled, or homemade materials.[75] Clad in the "last new fashion," this "model lady" looked to her own interests rather than her nation's well-being (the caption says she "puts her children out to nurse and tends lapdogs;—lies in bed till noon"). To emphasize her shortcomings, her physiognomy conveys an ungenerous nature, shallow character, and a naturally weak disposition.[76] The finery worn by the characters in "Unpleasant Present" and "Model Lady" suggests wealth. Such images represented attacks on both those upper-class women whom Drew Gilpin Faust described as practicing "noblesse" without "oblige" and those who profited from the war.[77]

The war disrupted prewar patterns of wealth, and in the Confederate South, dress alone no longer represented slave-based wealth. In late 1863, Richmond's *Daily Examiner* reported the emergence of a "blockade aristocracy" in the city similar to the "shoddy grandees of Boston and New York. *Proh pudor!*"[78] "Vulgar and illiterate, but shrewd and unscrupulous," wrote Richmond's *Dispatch* in April 1864, terming them the "shoddy-ocracy."[79] The *Southern Punch* cartoon "A Belle of Wet-zel" pictured two female members of this group, "returning from a fashionable Soiree in Richmond given by one of the Shoddy-ocracy" (fig. 8.7).[80] Each woman's face lent darker undertones to this seemingly innocuous scene in which two single women stand in the rain, having returned from a party. Their small mouths, long vertical noses, heavily lidded eyes, and low foreheads—features used by artists to depict prostitutes—all suggest the women's lustful, slow, and acquisitive natures. The resemblance not only implied the source of their wealth but reminded viewers that, according to the press, prostitutes had led Richmond's April 1863 bread riot.[81] When society related

FIG. 8.6. "The Model Lady." From *Bugle Horn of Liberty*, Sept. 1863. Courtesy of the Library of Congress.

a woman's status to her distance from sexuality, the prostitute's trade gave her little status in respectable society. Cartoons like these sent a message to Confederate women that frivolity and fine dress indicated social and moral ruin. Elie, a woman from Mobile, Alabama, advised banishment as the only remedy for these "frail sisters," lest the country face moral collapse.[82]

In the Confederate South, the slave owner class shared the trappings of wealth with the nouveaux riches. J.H.H.'s October 1863 cartoon about Mrs. Simpson and "her old Irish servant" Bridget O'Nail illustrated the changed paradigm (fig. 8.8). The character of Mrs. Simpson represented wealthy women refugees and Bridget O'Nail the parvenu ("See I'm been afther specalatin a bit' an' be the soul o' me I have so much o' yer Confederate money that I don't know what to do with it"). While dressed alike, their faces emphasized their disparity. Mrs. Simpson's forehead and nose showed her gentle and flexible character, whereas Bridget O'Nail's small celestial nose and its diminutive size compared to her forehead showed her weakness of mind and self-conceit. In short, the artist used O'Nail's selfish character and ethnicity as a differentiator between prewar and wartime wealth.

If women like O'Nail threatened the Confederacy's social order, females who jeopardized its ability to defend the nation posed an even greater threat. "A (Vain) Vane Aspir(e)ation" appeared in the May 1864 issue of the *Confederate Spirit, and Knapsack of Fun* (fig. 8.9). A well-dressed woman, carrying an umbrella, acts as a weather vane. On one level, the image suggests that vain women are blown by the wind. However, the inclusion of the points of the compass as well as the figure's orientation lead to other meanings. Union inroads into the South brought Southern women into contact with Northerners, and they looked to these Yankees for provisions, company, and trade.[83] "Vain Aspiration" presented these women's loyalty as unfixed and easily shifted to the North. The true Confederate woman would remain

FIG. 8.7. "A Belle of Wet-zel." From *Southern Punch,* May 14, 1864. Courtesy of the Library of Virginia.

FIG. 8.8. "Mrs. Simpson, an Exile from Tennessee," by "J.H.H." From *Bugle Horn of Liberty,* Oct. 1863. Courtesy of the Rare Book, Manuscript and Special Collections Library, Duke University.

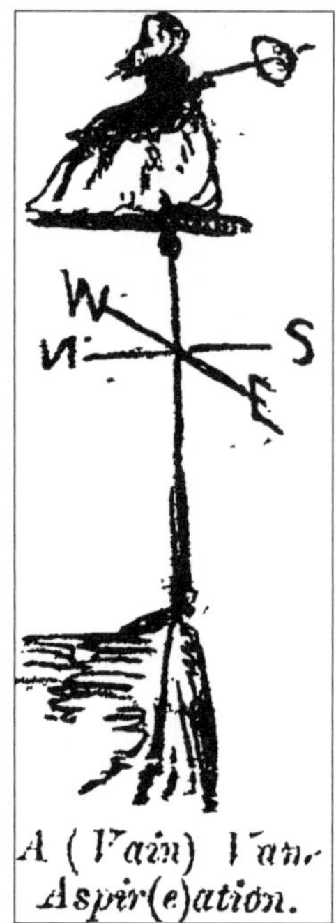

FIG. 8.9. "A (Vain) Vane Aspir(e)ation." From *Confederate Spirit, and Knapsack of Fun*, May 1864. Courtesy of Princeton University.

steadfast in her allegiance to the nation and encourage a similar attitude in other members of society.

Desertion and avoiding conscription plagued American Civil War armies.[84] It became increasingly clear that women played a role in Confederate soldiers' decision to abandon the cause. After he saw ten deserters executed, a soldier correspondent of Virginia's *Petersburg Daily Express* wondered, "Are the women of our bleeding Confederacy doing their whole duty?" He articulated concerns that women's negative influence weakened the army's strength.[85] Addressing Confederate women in his August 1, 1863, amnesty for soldiers absent without leave, President Jefferson Davis closed with a request for his "country's women" to use "their all-powerful influence" to ensure soldiers did their "duty to their families, to their country and their God." To do these things would "add one crowning sacrifice to which their patriotism has so freely and constantly afforded their country's altar."[86] The concerted urgings of all women could also sustain the nation.

Confederate graphic artists joined in these efforts by lambasting women who attempted to stop men from doing their duty. The cartoon "The Great Subject of the Day," from the *Confederate Spirit, and Knapsack of Fun*'s February 1864 issue, depicted the type of woman who ignored Davis's call (fig. 8.10). It showed a young woman, Jane Maria, responding to the recent news of the Confederate Congress abandoning the system that allowed conscripts to buy a substitute ("Just to think; that Congress talks of putting in the army all who have substitutes, and my Charles Augustus will have to leave so soon and go to fight those horrid Yankees!"). Her dress and surroundings suggest that her husband is a man of wealth, who has avoided military service.[87] While the older woman in the scene busily sews, Jane Maria leisurely reads. The older woman contributes to others; the younger one focuses on herself. Jane Maria drops her newspaper upon realizing the impact of Congress's decision on her life.[88] While her dress, apart from the suggestion of a hoop, is appropriately restrained, her low forehead conveys her weak intellect and her thin lips her ungenerous nature.[89] The cartoon announced that only the simple and self-centered would not willingly give their men to the nation.[90]

FIG. 8.10. "The Great Subject of the Day." From *Confederate Spirit, and Knapsack of Fun,* Feb. 1864. Courtesy of Princeton University.

FIG. 8.11. "Going to Kill-patrick." From *Southern Punch,* Mar. 26, 1864. Courtesy of the Library of Virginia.

The scene of *Punch*'s March 1864 woodcut cartoon "Going to Kill-patrick," set during the recent Union raid on Richmond, more blatantly imagined the sort of women who attempted to stop men doing their duty (fig. 8.11).[91] It depicted an older, bespectacled armed and uniformed man's attempt to leave a room while women use emotional and physical force to stop him. Through their snub noses, sloped low foreheads, and prominent lower lips, the artist conveyed to the viewers that these were women with low intellect, corporeal desires, and weak character.[92] Presumably, Confederates who saw the image knew of Union general Judson Kilpatrick's recent raid on Richmond that aimed at freeing thousands of Federal prisoners, torching property, and assassinating Confederate leaders. Richmond's *Dispatch* announced that when faced with "danger and death," Confederate women showed "spirit and courage."[93] Through this woodcut, *Punch* showed women who put personal interest ahead of the Confederate nation.

THE DOMESTIC SPHERE'S MOVING BOUNDARIES

Frail sisters proved easy and popular targets for Confederate cartoons. However, illustrations in Confederate periodicals did not present coherent or consistent models for women. This is evident in the February and March 1864 issues of the South's oldest journal, the *Southern Literary Messenger*. In February, it reprinted an article, "Confederate Women and the War," from Mobile's *Advertiser and Register*. The piece chastised women who bowed "to fashion's shrine" while the nation writhed "in agony" because doing so supported extortioners and blockade-runners.[94] A mere month later, the *Southern Literary Messenger* presented its sole wartime engraving—a delicately drawn fashion plate of two fashionably dressed women preparing to go out, standing before a mirror (fig. 8.12). Their finery suggests an overseas source. While the portrait of a man dressed in uniform suggests an absent male family member, the mirror insinuates the critical male gaze to be met on the street. Through this representation, the editor advocated the very qualities he had condemned a month earlier.

This incongruity is present in the portraits of the only three Confederate women—Belle Boyd, Ida Vernon, and Lucy Pickens—depicted in wartime engravings. Portraits of Boyd and Vernon show how far the bounds of femininity had extended (figs. 8.13 and 8.14).[95] The *News* based Boyd's portrait on a carte de visite by Richmond photographer David Cowell. Although her dress is restrained, her long hair worn back and the light background emphasize the feminine form that helped the seventeen-year-old Virginian gain military intelligence about the Union forces. While newsprint informed Confederates of Boyd's venture outside of her sphere, this image comforted them that her actions had not affected her gender.

The *Illustrated News*'s selection of actress Ida Vernon represented the extent to which war altered Confederate concepts of womanhood. In 1861, Richmond's *Dispatch* had told readers that the "young lady is quite naturally and properly averse to appearing on stage."[96] However, beginning with the amateur tableaux vivants staged by ladies' societies, Confederate experience transformed this belief. A year later, when

Fig. 8.12. *Fashions for March 1864*, by George Dunn, printed by George Dunn & Co., reprinted from *Le Bon Ton, Journal de Modes, and Monthly Reports of Paris Fashions*, Feb. 1863. From *Southern Literary Messenger*, Mar. 1864. Courtesy of Louisiana State University Libraries, Special Collections, Baton Rouge.

discussing tableux vivants, the *Dispatch* informed Confederates that they provided a "good example of a combination of refined amusement with the most timely and patriotic philanthropy."[97] Acceptance of women in Confederate theater took a little longer.

In the early part of the war, male actors dominated reports of Confederate plays, but as the war absorbed many more quality leading men into the army, female actors

FIG. 8.13. "Miss Belle Boyd, the Rebel Spy," by Eugene Crehen. From *Southern Illustrated News*, Oct. 18, 1862.

like Vernon assumed a greater profile. Already a seven-year stage veteran in 1861, when the eighteen-year-old Vernon began work in Richmond, Virginia, she proved herself a talented performer.[98] In August 1863, Vernon headed North and left New York on August 13, 1863, seemingly en route to California but in actuality headed to Europe.[99] Ten months later, the *Richmond Examiner* announced that "a favorite actress of the South" had returned to the Confederacy.[100]

Vernon returned with a portfolio of new and "absorbing" theatrical works that led to what Richmond's *Daily Whig* termed "a kind of dramatic revival."[101] Ready to forget their trials, her audience welcomed the escapist fare she had brought back. Thanks to these pieces and her acts of philanthropic patriotism, she found great favor among Southerners.[102] Her portrait as Leah from *Leah, the Forsaken*, a work she had smuggled into the South, featured in a September 1864 issue of the *Illustrated News*. The engraving became the second of two identified portraits of Southern women that the *News* published. The reasons they published it are not clear. Certainly the play's themes of the refugee experience, Vernon's celebrity, and her patriotic benevolence were relevant.[103] Regardless, it is a flattering portrait. Shown in profile, it displayed a physiognomy befitting a Confederate: noble and powerful yet cheerful and possessing both high intellect and generosity.

The portraits of Boyd the spy and actress Vernon represented the extent to which

FIG. 8.14. "Miss Ida Vernon as Leah, the Forsaken," by John W. Torsch. From *Southern Illustrated News*, Sept. 3, 1864. Courtesy of Emory University.

wartime eroded the domestic sphere's border. However, the decision to include Lucy Pickens's head on three Confederate banknotes showed other factors at play within the Civil War South (see fig. 1.4). The only real individual among the forty-three images of women that appeared on Confederate currency, her portrait suggested prominent service to the Confederate cause. Such was not the case. The evidence shows that apart from a few flag presentations, Pickens, the wife of South Carolina's first wartime governor, contributed nothing to the cause.[104] Rather than honoring service, the note's designers selected her image because of her close friendship with Confederate treasurer C. G. Memminger, and the novelty of her image made counterfeiting more difficult.[105] Their choice took and circulated an image of a Confederate socialite who practiced "noblesse without oblige" throughout the Confederacy.[106] It spoke of a society in which political favor and self-interest existed alongside patriotism—one that celebrated women if they were high enough on the social ladder even if they acted in ways that drew censure in others.

BLACK WOMEN

The depiction of Southern women in Confederate graphic arts lacked consistent values. Illustrators depicted them as variously victim or enactor, shallow or patriotic. The most consistent narrative gave them value in proportion to their involvement in the cause. However, the few flesh-and-blood women depicted had little in common with most Confederate women. Elite, actor, or spy, they may just as well have been the allegorical figures of Roman goddesses that featured on early war currency. By contrast, the handful of pictures of black women are much more consistent (see, e.g., figs. 3.5, 3.8, 3.9, 3.10, 3.12, and 3.14). Usually depicted with the physical characteristics and dress associated with the "Mammy" stereotype, they inhabit domestic scenes as loyal slaves or as extortioners' prey. While depictions of white women presented critiques and praise, those of black women conformed to the notion that they were benign and maternal domestic helpers.[107]

A major creation of proslavery propagandists, Confederates used this endlessly cheery and nurturing character in plays such as *Great Expectations; or, Getting a Promotion* (1863). The character of Aunt Sarah in this play is a gentle voice of reason when Mrs. Singleton throws caution to the wind and starts disposing of belongings before officials confirm her husband's promotion.[108] This stereotype showed not only a lack awareness of the enslaved but also that Confederates felt almost no threat from this section of their population.

An image exists that presents one hazard that black women posed: their sexuality. Slave owners cloaked their predatory behaviors by developing the idea of the seductive "Jezebel."[109] While this notion is absent from Confederate visual culture, one cartoon, "Shocking," from the August 1863 *Bugle Horn of Liberty*, came close to depicting the problematic ideas of interracial sex (fig. 8.15).[110] The iron rail fence and buildings set the scene in an upper-class residential street. A "venerable widower" named Mr. Tutt is walking. His small nose signifies poor self-control and shows that he is a man led by his passions. Before him is a woman who is, unbeknown to him, black. Her outfit contributes to his confusion. Instead of wearing the head wrap mandated as black women's badge of enslavement, she appears clad in fashionable bonnet and dress, carrying an umbrella.[111] Moreover, the cinched-waist bodice and hoopskirt of the outfit accentuate her figure. While the woman's reaction, "I b'long to Major Smif," could have suggested she is already another man's sex object, her round face is that of the benign Mammy character—an African American woman who, like every depiction of black women in the Confederate South, is content in bondage. Like other Confederate portrayals of enslaved women, it represents them as being more supportive of the system than male slaves.[112]

Black and white women presented ideological problems to the benevolent patriarchal system. While considered racially unequal, and whites could never have countenanced the equality of slave and white master, the paternalism of the system placed both the enslaved and white woman under the master's controlling hand. As antebellum proslavery thinker, George Fitzhugh, stated, weakness rather than racial

Mr. Tutt, a venerable widower, thinks he is just in the prime of his youth, pulls up his collar, and resolves that he will try matrimonial fortune "one more time," and will take the first opportunity that offers. He sallies forth, and is at once struck with the captivating figure of a female just then passing. "Great Heavens! what a form! he passionately exclaims. Only think of clasping it to my palpitating bosom, and calling it my own! Oh! fatal shaft!

Mr. Tutt's quick imagination at once suggest a romantic love affair, and he pursues the fascinating form. As they approach a shady retreat, he looks cautiously about to see if he is observed, and in the madness of a love beyond his control, clasps the angelic creature in his arms. A faint shriek! "Ah! mine, forever mine!" exclaims Tutt in a subdued, but earnest lovelike tone, as the object of his love turns her gaze upon him.

"No I isn't yours nudder—I ain't no runaway nigger—I 'longs to Major Smif, so I does.

Mr. Tutt in a deep reflective mood retraces his steps.

FIG. 8.15. "Shocking," by "J.H.H." From *Bugle Horn of Liberty,* Aug. 1863. Courtesy of the Library of Congress.

inequality created this situation. Men had the "duty of protecting the weak," and that involved "the necessity of enslaving" both women and slaves.[113] Consciously or not, in their anxiety to present black women as supporters of slavery, Confederate illustrators presented them as bearing similar trials and suffering as white women. William Washington's *The Burial of Latané* captured this notion. With mirrored stances and heads bent, black and white women are equally involved in the scene and its structure. Additionally, Washington made the black women's features appear more Caucasian than those of the male slaves. However, there are subtle differences between the women. Positioned on either side of the canvas, they have been separated by color, space, and attitude. The white women bow their heads more deeply than the female slaves. The poses of the enslaved denote reverence, whereas the mistresses mourn their gallant defender.

William Sheppard depicted a similar relationship between race and gender in his January 1865 design for the *Illustrated News*'s banner (see fig. 3.14). Placed in their own medallion at the pictorial and ideological center of the composition, black and white couples look toward their respective partners. To show each woman's inferiority, he places both in submissive stances in relation to their male partners. He shows the enslaved woman beside the fruits of her labor, while the white woman shows no sign of toil. The artist intended the scene to show the white soldier as "he lingers to rehearse those oft-repeated vows."[114] Sheppard's image shows the Confederate male's ideal woman. Her costume, without frivolous hoops, is restrained, and her broad vertical forehead and nose convey ideas of intellect and refinement. Her position, embracing the soldier and appearing to pass him a musket, shows her support of his efforts. However, although the *News* described most figures in vignettes, there is no mention of the white woman. She exists, like his uniform or rifle, as merely a male accessory. Sheppard's design suggested a gender status quo essentially unaltered by the war or the effects it wrought on Confederate women's lives.

The Confederacy's hypermasculinity determined that women would never be as visible as men. Images such as printer George Dunn's valentine "You Look at a Star from Two Motives," part of a series for Valentine's Day published in both 1864 and 1865, looked to an imagined postwar gender relationship (fig. 8.16). It showed men's desire to return to prewar gender norms of silent and "impenetrable" women. Yet war wrought transformations in women. Writing letters to politicians or encouraging men to withhold their military service made women more assertive. The physical objects women made and their presence in the Confederacy's visual culture gave them greater visibility. These created a complexity that gives Dunn's image a nostalgic quality. However, it also spoke to the reality that most power resided with men. The man is the active agent in this scene, chasing an elusive ideal woman with the aim of possessing her.

War brought Southern women into the public sphere. George Rable described the result as "change without change."[115] Visual and material culture reflected the tensions that resulted. Both sexes contributed to the visibility of Confederate womanhood. The objects women made or caused to be made contributed to a physical collective identity. For their part, male publishers, writers, artists, and illustrators captured and transmitted how Confederate men saw and valued women as war changed their world. Against the background of women as historical actors, this imagery pictured them often as abstract figures for celebration and critique.

The negative images of women captured and conveyed an increased rejection of suffering and sacrifice for the cause. They marked the growing Confederate awareness that other than "noble" women and those with a "self-denying spirit" existed within the South. Few images existed to counter such ideas. Rather, women's support of their nation became clear through the objects they made and their personifications onstage. These items and images aided Confederates in defining the ideal

FIG. 8.16. "You Look at a Star from Two Motives," by William Ludwell Sheppard (attributed). From *A Series of Comic Valentines* (Richmond, Va.: George Dunn, 1864). Courtesy of the Boston Athenaeum.

Confederate women and laid the foundations for the "unified home front" tenet of the Lost Cause myth. In doing so, former Confederates used selective memory and ignored their own encounters with the complexities created when Confederate women became more visible.

In late 1863, one Southern newspaper declared of Confederates, "A braver more war-like people probably never existed on the face of the earth . . . impetuous valor and patient endurance."[116] In the rush to establish and define their nation, Confederates spent intellectual energies in creating and making their people fit such ideals. Manufacturers, slaves, the races, the military, and women became subjects of examination and recipients of instructive critique. Above all, however, the Confederacy existed as a male entity. Men owned slaves, ruled women, and made politics and war. They also generated most of this visual and written commentary. Their position in society did not safeguard them from appraising eyes, especially as it quickly became apparent that not all Southern men shared the qualities valued by their fellow citizens. As with other sections of the Confederacy, these individuals and groups became the focus of public judgement and dictates. Among them can be discerned the Confederate paragon—the Confederate true man.

CHAPTER 9

Picturing Hierarchies of Manhood

Men of the South! the hour has come.
—ROBERT JOSELYN, "Gather! Gather!"

Reveries depicting both slave's and women's roles and behaviors made up a fraction of Confederate visual culture. The abundant representations of men mirrored their hegemony. These conveyed both American and more regional concepts of masculinity to Confederates. In particular, they described practices nineteenth-century Westerners thought separated manliness from simply being male. Explicitly, markers of masculinity included the capacity for independent action, citizenship, care of the weak, and assertiveness but also extended to the choice of clothing.[1] While men could demonstrate masculinity in many areas of life, war, ideologues long maintained, tempered and tested both the individual's and nation's manhood, and such was the case for the South. Ideas of manliness and nationalism combined in the Confederate States, and their written and visual discourse surrounding manhood reveals much of who they considered themselves to be as a people.

Confederates saw manhood as deeply involved in the conflict. However, this did not simply refer to the contest between men of the North and South. It also embraced men within the South. Certainly, Southerners used representations of Northern men to help define manhood, but they also did so through various types of men they found and described within their own borders. Moreover, their opinions were not fixed but responded to internal and external pressures generated by the four-year struggle. More particularly, a study of commercial visual mediums reveals that among the many varieties of manhood, Confederates came to value distinctive traits in their men. It shows that the image of manhood conveyed in paintings, photographs, and prints aligned with a hierarchy of masculinity also found in Confederate print media. Pictured on paper, produced onstage, and judged in word, the ideal of the Confederate male as more than a gallant patriotic protector of the South emerged. These representations depicted not only what Confederates believed constituted a true man but also the variety of beliefs and values current within the Confederate South.

Confederate images and representations of manhood derived from sociological and psychological contexts.[2] Similar to Confederate ideas of womanhood, their notions sprang from an American background. Unlike the canon of domesticity, male standards and role models varied. Writing from a small mountain town in Virginia, a correspondent discerned two classes of "true" Southern men. "Some men," he noted, "always decide and act quickly; others slowly, but not less surely."[3] One embodied action and the other reflection. The former showed the "martial" characteristics, which included a preference for militarism, adventure, dominance, aggression, and physical strength.[4] Conversely, the latter displayed the attributes of what Amy Greenburg terms the "restrained" man: Christian morality, a focus on the household, moderation, and considered judgment.[5] Regardless of nature, the writer stressed that both acted to support and preserve the Southern white way of life.

The relationship between manhood and the nation proved a fundamental one. Patriotism became its gauge, while contrast and comparison defined its boundaries. In similar fashion to race, industry, or womanhood, Confederate ideologues discerned opposites in their Northern brothers.[6] Although most differences between soldiers on each side, as Michael Barton's study into the character of Civil War soldiers shows, were more imagined than real, Confederates treated Yankees as their masculine antithesis and used them to compare and test their manhood.[7] Moreover, in the search for national identity, using gender rather than race sidestepped troublesome debates about the role of birthplace or heritage in determining what differentiated theirs from other nations. As Nathaniel Tyler of Richmond's *Daily Enquirer* wrote in early 1864: "This war has shown that many a Yankee was born in the South and many a good Southern man came to light in a region far less genial than ours. In this war the man who battles with us for our freedom is our brother."[8] To work for the autonomy of the South's great slave republic instantly raised an individual's character. Conversely, working against the South diminished it. Therefore, Confederates depicted such individuals as lesser men and counter-forms to Southern manhood.

American men believed in a bond between military service and manhood. As a result, depictions of soldiers generally provided the strongest instruments for conveying messages of masculinity. However, a willingness to hazard personal danger did not necessarily elevate their manhood. Rather, their status depended on the relationship between soldier and nation, whether they were attacking or defending it.

Therefore, being antagonists alone compromised Yankee soldiers' manliness. To this weakness, Confederates added other shortcomings. Of these, most related to the Yankees' inability to govern themselves.

THE ENEMY WITHOUT

Control was a principal element of manhood. In the antebellum period, evangelical movements heightened society's apprehension of the bodily and spiritual threats of vices. Furthermore, these ideas connected the ability to keep desires and feelings in check with masculinity.[9] Additionally, slaveholders saw the ability to manage passions or impulses as a mark of difference between white and black and male and female. Accordingly, in the hands of Confederate creatives, Yankees transformed into people unable to regulate their emotions or imaginations.

The Yankee character with unrestrained appetites or manner became a staple of the Confederate stage. The depictions of their rout at Manassas, featured in panoramic performances, showed a collective Yankee lack of self-control in battle. Plays such as Joseph Hodgson's *The Confederate Vivandiere,* James McCabe's *The Guerrillas,* and George W. Alexander's *The Virginia Cavalier* presented this failing within individuals. These works portrayed Yankees as unscrupulous, misguided, sensate, coarse-tongued, and lecherous cowards.[10] Similarly, other works portrayed Federals as less manly in different ways. For example, John Hill Hewitt's Federal officer Captain Bigelow in *The Scouts* is not only a cowardly libertine but is also described by a slave boy as "pompous, foppish, and rather effeminate."[11] Likewise, McCabe's April 1863 piece *The Maiden's Vow; or, The Capture of Courtland, Alabama* offered another typical instance. "Closely woven" to the "actual facts," the drama revolved around the successful July 25, 1862, Southern raid on the town of Courtland. McCabe intended the play to "show the Yankee in his true light."[12] The producers worried that the words and actions of the actors who portrayed Federal soldiers might concern audiences. Therefore, to prepare them, advertisements requested that spectators "not . . . be so unjust as to confound the actor with the part he plays."[13] Ultimately, words and deeds transformed actors into Yankees. On their stages, Southerners saw their enemies as men prey to base passions, instead of moral intellect, and reliant on physical strength to gain power and wealth.

These works contained no evidence of how or if players used gesture or makeup to enhance the text. Imagery provides more insight. Depictions of Yankees appeared in a range of visual media. Although rare in fine art, the graphic print industry provided a greater number of representations. Freed from fine art's gravitas, this medium could create and spread more overt pictures critiquing Yankee manhood.

FIG. 9.1. "The Yankee Cavalry Sent to Intercept General Stuart," by Susan Archer Talley. From *Southern Illustrated News*, Nov. 15, 1863.

Artists used a variety of devices to show Northern men's lack of moral and intestinal fortitude. Frequently, they depicted one Rebel battling many Union soldiers to contrast their men's comparative bravery. They also commonly adorned Northern soldiers with exaggerated military attire to show their love of puffery.[14] Additionally, they sometimes used the conventions of physiognomy to delineate Northerners' inner character. In Susan Archer Talley's cartoon "Yankee Cavalry Sent to Intercept General Stuart," uniform, accoutrement, and caricature emphasize the Federal troops' shortage of self-control (fig. 9.1). The only identified Confederate print produced by a woman, it presented a rare visualization of Yankees through feminine eyes.[15] In her cartoon, men dressed in splashy Union officers' uniforms cower behind rocks as a column of Southern horsemen pass by. Their elongated forms suggested flighty personalities, and their poor proportions pointed to their misshapen nature. Furthermore, their noses indicated melancholic dispositions. Along with these qualities, their long chins and faces showed their cunning and animal natures. The words attributed to the two speakers reinforce their nervousness but also suggest that the troops under their command have not followed them. Images such as Talley's enabled Confederates to picture their foes as insubstantial men.[16]

As the Union resolved to harden its prosecution of the war, Southerners believed that Yankees had unleashed their darker traits.[17] In August 1863, a North Carolina newspaper stated bluntly that the enemy was "only less savage than a Fijian in that he eats not his foe."[18] Similar ideas are depicted in "Sergeant Walter at Manassas,

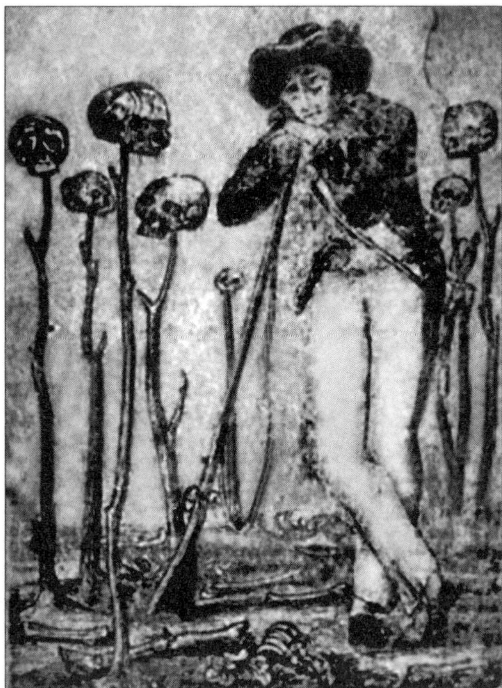

FIG. 9.2. "Sergeant Walter at Manassas, 1862." Damage and aging make it difficult to obtain a clearer version of this engraving. From *Illustrated Mercury*, Sept. 3, 1864. Courtesy of the North Carolina Department of Archives and History.

1862." Published in a September 1864 issue of the *Illustrated Mercury*, this pictured Yankee men's uncivilized nature for its audience (fig. 9.2). Featured on the first page of chapter 1 of Edward Edgeville's story *Castine; or, The Maid of Mirkland*, it shows the hero, Walter (later revealed to actually be Castine), on the battleground of First Manassas in July 1862. Walter's captain finds the soldier "leaning meditatively upon his musket in the midst of a golgotha" created by Union soldiers, who set Confederate skulls on sticks. "There is no deed too vile for his doing," Walter tells his commanding officer. The sergeant laments, "Is it not strange that men immortal, civilized, refined should be not only the worst foes to themselves, but the worst foes to their brothers?"[19] This image pictured the barbarism Confederates believed Yankees harbored.[20] Yet Northerners' baseness went beyond savagery. Even more damning for Confederates was their reaction to the seemingly God-endorsed institution of slavery.

In the white South, a man's response to black servitude provided an easy indicator of his manhood. Men upheld the laws safeguarding bondage and shielded those they thought weaker. Hence, Yankee efforts to undermine and destroy a system that Confederates believed protected slaves showed the North's degraded masculinity. Additionally, because they considered slavery a God-ordained institution, they be-

FIG. 9.3. "Masks and Faces—King Abraham before and after Issuing the Emancipation Proclamation." From *Southern Illustrated News*, Nov. 11, 1862.

lieved that those who opposed it were setting themselves against the Almighty. It is therefore unsurprising that the Confederate image makers targeted the North's leader, Abraham Lincoln, and his masculinity. Over the course of the war, they depicted him, among other characters, as a clown, a female teacher, a young black man, and even a drunken monkey.[21] Even as early as the end of 1861, some Confederates already likened Union leader Lincoln to the "Great Beast," Satan.[22] Undoubtedly, his issuance of the preliminary Emancipation Proclamation in September 1862, which ended bondage in Confederate states, confirmed it for others. *Illustrated News*'s November 1862 cartoon "Masks and Faces" visualized this idea (fig. 9.3). Dressed in tails, an entity with a satanic face stands alone in a landscape empty except for a gibbet. In one hand, he carries an empty watch chain; the other holds Lincoln's visage as a mask, and at his feet lies a scroll bearing "Jan. 1, 1863"—the date the decree came into effect. On seeing this cartoon, the editor of the *Chattanooga Rebel* proclaimed that its "truth is frightfully dramatic."[23] Lincoln's edict and his nation's intention to finish a system endorsed by the Divine confirmed many Confederates' opinion that amoral, unrestrained, and ungodly Yankees represented their ultimate opposite.

THE ENEMY WITHIN

Christian faith became increasingly tied to Confederate concepts of manhood. The view of the manly soldier as a Christian soldier arose to challenge religion's prewar feminine associations.[24] In June 1864, the editor of Richmond's *Enquirer* identified it as the key differentiator between Northern and Southern soldiers.[25] Individually, it formed an essential part of being a man. As a Georgian wrote in July 1862, when describing the "True Gentleman," religious "precepts govern his heart and control his actions."[26] Nationally, it fused with men's obligations as a citizen and defender of the weak and the Confederacy's spiritual purpose.[27] While biblical readings convinced the faithful that the Lord favored their cause, disasters and reverses led clergy and other ideologues to postulate why He denied them victories. Although some believed that the people's poor treatment of enslaved people or lack of religious observance prompted the Almighty's displeasure, others laid the blame for their chastisement by God on other behaviors by their countrymen and women.[28] They drew on biblical character Achan as an example of how a lone man can threaten a nation.[29] Achan pillaged goods set aside for the Creator and because of this the "Lord's anger burned against Israel" (Joshua 7:1). Could their misfortunes, Confederates ministers asked their congregations, be because there were similar men within the Confederacy? In an August 1863 sermon, leading churchman the Reverend Charles Minnigerode identified a long list of "Achans that troubleth our camp" who did not place Jehovah's rule before everything. "Who is he? Where is he?" he asked. Minnigerode found Achan in Southern men: leaders, entrepreneurs, cowards, sinners, "poor silly pretenders to fashion," those without faith, and those "who think a few prayers at Church will do."[30] Making patriotism akin to godliness meant that men who put anything ahead of duty to both God and country became national liabilities and objects of derision.

In February 1864, engraver and printer George Dunn released a series of twenty valentines.[31] Among pleasant pictures of Cupid, courtship, and ideal soldiers appeared less affirming caricatures such as "Croaker" (fig. 9.4).[32] Confederates labeled anyone who expressed worries or concerns about the progress of the war as a "croaker." In 1863, one Confederate described croakers as "degenerate and emasculated beings" and "libels upon manhood."[33] In keeping with these ideas, Dunn pictures Croaker's inhuman pessimism by exchanging his head with a raven's—the harbinger of woe.[34] The raven's sorrowful gaze meets the spectator's eye, as the figure's hand gestures toward a newspaper. Moreover, its surroundings reinforce the bleak outlook. An undertaker's hat sits on the table, and the few book titles visible on the library shelves are stories of disaster (*Gibbon's Decline and Fall [of the Roman Empire]*, *Last Days of Pompeii*, Goethe's *Sorrows of [Young] Werter*).[35] Finally, a bust of Diogenes, who preached the virtue of self-control, looks down with displeasure from the wall. In short, this card ridiculed those men unable to restrain their fears about the future of their national cause. As an August 1863 article stated, "A cheerful, hopeful, and determined spirit should pervade all." God's blessing and generals such as Lee, Johnston, and Beauregard, the writer wrote, ensured their success. Accordingly, when faced with reverses, Confederate men needed "Christian faith and manly endurance."[36]

FIG. 9.4. "Croaker," by William Ludwell Sheppard (attributed). From *A Series of Comic Valentines* (Richmond, Va.: George Dunn, 1864). Courtesy of the Boston Athenaeum.

Patriotism and religious observance both called on individuals to turn their focus away from the self. Indeed, many Confederate ideologues criticized men who placed their own interests ahead of their nation's and found examples in the world of commerce. Over time, inflation-ridden Southerners became sensitive to the idea that anyone who raised prices bore the taint of profiteering.[37] In June 1863, Virginia's Baptist Association worried that "self-interest and the love of money," traits of the Northern "wicked nation," were alive in the Confederacy.[38] Consequently, Confederates denounced profiteers more regularly than other men. Such behavior placed profits ahead of their country and relegated extortionists to the outer edges of manhood.[39] The cartoon "Recipe to Get Rid of Extortioners" depicted the type of men who profited from war in a similar manner (fig. 9.5). Full lips, claw-like fingers, and various types of nose indicate corporeal, bestial natures and weak or shrewd characters.

FIG. 9.5. "Recipe to Get Rid of Extortioners," by "H.A." or, if reversed, "A.H." (Armistead Hurdle?). From *Southern Illustrated News*, Sept. 19, 1863.

Their features emphasized their selfishness and lack of commitment to the cause. Furthermore, being burned at the stake suggests their godlessness. The approving smiles of the farmer, soldier, and gentleman seen in the background signaled that all men support their execution.[40]

If extortion weakened the nation's manhood, reunification threatened its very existence.[41] Pro-Union sentiment, disillusionment, and war-weariness led many within the Confederacy to desire and work for peace. Loyal Southerners abhorred this idea. An Alabama newspaper reported in August 1863, for instance, that Yankees were thieves, arsonists, and rapists. "Yet," it pointed out, "these are the people that reconstructions in North Carolina and elsewhere would have us united to again."[42] Furthermore, Southern leaders warned of its consequences. In late 1863, for example, North Carolina's governor, Zebulon Vance, cautioned that "submission" meant the "abolition of slavery, confiscation of property, and territorial vassalage." He added that anything short of "full and complete national independence" would "crucify afresh" the slain and put their "gallant soldiers to open shame."[43] The March 1864 engraving "Portraits of Leading North Carolina Reconstructionists" pictured how Confederates viewed those they believed threatened their cause (fig. 9.6).[44] Their

FIG. 9.6. "Portraits of Leading North Carolina Reconstructionists." From *Southern Punch*, Mar. 12, 1864. Courtesy of the Library of Virginia.

facial appearance revealed their personalities, and the engraving's identification as having been "sketched by our special artist" suggested the authenticity of these portrayals.[45] While the nose and mouth of the bespectacled individual on the left betray a well-formed persona, his sloping profile shows mental weakness. The flat faces of both men flanking the central leering figure suggest intelligence, but also acquisitiveness. The distortion and pose of the background form make it difficult to read whether it is one or two people. Only the middle body has a recognizable semblance. Barely discernible behind the cunning face and devil-like tufts of hair is the image of Raleigh's *Daily Standard* editor and gubernatorial candidate William W. Holden.[46] The similarity between the satanic features of this man and Lincoln in "Masks and Faces" implied that the men shared a similarly demonic nature; like Yankees, these men pursued reunification because they lacked intellect and religious morals and were greedy.

Yankees, the selfish and disloyal, stood outside what constituted the "true" Confederate man. The true "Southron" protected the Confederacy. These men exhibited both "martial" and "restrained" models of manhood. However, experience, example, and their American natures meant that restrained Confederate men became the ideal model of masculinity in the South.

Portrayals of disciplined heroic men appeared regularly in Confederate visual culture—for instance, James D. McCabe's "Arthur Douglas" in *The Guerrillas*. After Yan-

FIG. 9.7. "A Confederate Picket," by Conrad Wise Chapman. From *Southern Illustrated News*, Mar. 7, 1863.

kees killed his aged parents and burned his home, Douglas's comrade comments that "his grief is terrible, but still he does not weep."[47] The hero in J. J. Delchamps's play *Love's Ambuscade*, Edward Delafield, is not only self-controlled but also modest. On enlisting, Delafield refuses a commission because he does not feel worthy. However, in battle, as officers stand idly by, he rallies shaken troops and is subsequently made a colonel.[48] Some still imagery conveyed similar ideas. Conrad Wise Chapman's "A Confederate Picket" was one of few original images published in the *Southern Illustrated News* (fig. 9.7). Drawn from life at Drewry's Bluff, it depicted a picket, armed and equipped with what appears to be English-made materiel. The man cups an ear and appears to be caught rising in response to some disturbance to the right. Male characters such as Delafield, Douglas, and the picket showed more in common than just self-control; they were also all soldiers.

Charged with defending the nation, the South idolized its military forces. In late 1863, Richmond's *Daily Dispatch* described "the glorious and immortal army" as "the elite and flower, the intelligence, and manhood, of the Southern people."[49] Likewise, another editorial told readers that their armed forces contained "the cream of . . . the patriotism, the physical stamina, and the moral worth of the land . . . and fortitude of the Southern race." Soldiers, the *Richmond Dispatch* wrote in late 1863, understood the stakes for which they fought. For them, life had "no value without honor and independence."[50] Illustrations of any frontline soldier not only idealized their appearance but depicted their self-control. Confederates used caricature to ridicule both sexes in proportion to the devotion they exhibited to the war effort. On this scale, the men who fought represented both the heights and measure of masculinity.

MASCULINITY AND THE PRESENTATION OF SELF

From antebellum times, the Americans recognized the strong relationship between masculinity, citizenship, and soldiering. In the antebellum United States, this gave men license to exercise their fascination with "military raiment" and contributed to the profusion of uniformed companies that sprang up.[51] Despite these trends, not all Southern townships had organized volunteer units, and some of those extant languished.[52] Notwithstanding the aggressive posturing across the South, most companies, including the "Tullahoma Guards" and the "Floyd Rifles," adopted titles that suggest protection rather than attack. As troops went to war, their often unadorned service uniforms reflected a belief that plain dress revealed character.[53] Accordingly, self-disciplined, modest, and stoic gentlemen rejected the martial "plume, lace and cut" in favor of democratically restrained "plain attire."[54] Likewise, the moderate man joined to defend the cause, not to don flamboyant clothes, and some Confederates came to associate ostentatious garb with more impulsive and unsettled types of men and commented favorably on more plainly dressed troops.[55] Consequently, in many Southern minds, beautiful livery compromised rather than enhanced the manliness of the individuals wearing them. "A gentlemen," the *Southern Punch* told readers in early 1864, "looks anything but a gentleman even in a dress of the shabbiest description," and men who joined units with gaudy outfits became targets of derision.[56]

The disfavor of showy uniform expressed by some Confederates also revealed class tensions between slaveholder and non-slaveholder. Planters used civilian and military fashion as a marker of status as they attempted to exert paternalistic control over lower classes of black and white. This led to complex relations and performances as slave owners played the dual role of master and equal. Raised with egalitarian and republican values, other men resented those who dressed and acted like gentry, and war brought this tension to the surface.[57] In June 1861, for example, Private Harry Lewis judged his regiment's newly elected colonel solely on appearance. He wrote his mother: "Yesterday evening Colonel [Carnot Posey] mounted on his newly-bought steed and clothed in his flashing gray uniform with his tri-cornered continental hat, distinguished afar by a waving plume of red [Posey wore the regulation Mississippi dress], came on parade, I suppose for the purpose of showing off, but I think the horse is not as fine an animal as could be, nor that he is as fine a colonel as Jeff Davis was in Mexico."[58] In Lewis's estimation, a man who dressed for show was a poor judge of horse flesh and fell short as a soldier.

Confederates associated dressing up with other issues. Finely uniformed commissioned officers reminded new infantryman Frank L. Richardson of "the owners of slaves on plantations" who had "nothing to do but to strut about, dress fine and enjoy themselves."[59] Superiors in flashy apparel made social divisions patent and rankled the sensibilities of citizens raised in a democracy amid slavery. Confronted by individuals who appeared to consider themselves superior, Confederate soldiers commonly struck back using methods of charivari developed in prewar Southern society.[60] For a people with firm notions about the relationship between masculinity and presentation, some officers' flashy dress made them instant targets.[61] Chaplain Nicholas Davis wrote during the war of a Texas regiment's first colonel, who "came out to the camp . . . glittering with the tinsel of gold and bearing all the symbols of his rank." The display did not impress the Texans. After debating out loud: "What is it? Is it a man, a fish, or a bird?" one soldier decided, "A man—don't you see his legs?" "Well that may be a man," another replied, "but we don't call them men in Texas." His authority leveled the officer departed and "was never heard of by the 5th Texas again."[62] Troops such as these used baiting and ridicule to control those who attempted to use fine uniforms to exert authority.

Many Confederate generals showed awareness of their soldiery's distaste for flashy dress and wore costumes reminiscent of rural citizenry, such as farmers' coats, homespun jackets, or linen dusters, believing that respect rather than rank led volunteers to follow leaders.[63] This choice presented issues for officers. One veteran recalled that General James Longstreet usually dressed in a common overshirt and slouch hat, dress worn for shooting, and had "no mark of an officer about him." Apprehended as a straggler during an engagement, Longstreet's captor called him a "damned old hunting-shirt snoozer" when the general attempted to identify himself.[64] Commanders such as Longstreet understood that playing to the tastes of their men to gain greater connection with them was worth the occasional mistake.

Despite social pressures and military theories that advocated plainer dress, some individuals adopted showy outfits. While many reasons may have prompted them to do so, for many Confederates attracting the opposite sex was a significant factor. They had cause for this belief. Women featured prominently in Southern male constructions of masculinity.[65] Men looked to women for affirmation and considered finding and marrying a wife a clear marker of mature manhood. To be ignored by the opposite sex struck at their sense of manly worth. In this context, though the ideal of the plainly clad fighting man worked in theory, many soldiers understood that a fine uniform was more attractive than a coarse one. As one roughly garbed officer told another in late 1862, "It matters little how we are dressed at present; there are no ladies at our parades, or I might be tempted to makes an outlay in fine cloth and gold lace."[66] The idea of female's attraction to fine military dress found expression in the most common figure, other than the current national flag, to appear on Confederate sheet music covers.

Confederate music publishers used the front covers of sheet music to attract customers. On pieces such as the "No Surrender Song," "The Twinkling Stars Are Shining, Love," and "Virginian Marseillaise," at least two publishers, George Dunn and Eugene Crehen, featured a figure dressed alike and similar in appearance. The individual is of a goateed officer handsomely clad in a regulation dress Confederate uniform coat with plumed slouch hat. When young women were the primary consumers of these songs, displaying this figure suggests that the producers believed that men dressed like this attracted young women. Yet as the soldier's treatment of the Fifth Texas Infantry's first colonel suggests, not all were drawn to well-dressed officers.

In the army, private soldiers chided men who dressed like the figures featured on this sheet music. Away from the front, officers who wore this form of dress also faced criticism. The *Southern Punch* often took critical aim at what it called both "dandy officers" and the "female butterflies" attracted by their "mustard collars [denoting cavalry service] and gold braid sleeves." It even drew on this prose from earlier in the century to ridicule these men:

Florio, admired by silly girls
    Arranges his redundant curls
        Before a polished glass
Like Peter Bell among the trees,
    The solitary dandy sees
        A solitary ass.[67]

The dapper officer figured in a variety of print imagery. In cartoons or comic songs, it signified rear echelon staff officers—men concerned with appearance, the opposite sex, and other earthly pursuits. Some sought to defend these men. The president, one writer argued, determined the uniform, and when they "bedizen themselves with gold tinsel and buttons," they were merely following orders.[68] But when the War Department permitted officers to dress plainly and generals dressed in less ostentatious attire, such a defense may have seemed hollow.[69] Moreover, events occurred that suggested the real danger to the cause when men dressed and acted with less restraint.

The cavalry in the Army of Northern Virginia contained the greatest number of flashily dressed individuals. Many of them espoused chivalrous values to match their clothing. Michael S. Kimmel believes that "Confederate chivalry" belonged to the restrained manhood of the Christian gentleman. However, though most, if not all, of them were religious, Southern chivalry drew primarily on the works of Sir Walter Scott for models of male behavior before church teaching.[70] The high value they placed on militarism, bravery, and adventure suggests that they aspired to a martial model of manhood.[71] Successful raids made rebel cavalry leaders such as John Hunt Morgan, Wade Hampton, and Nathan Bedford Forrest heroes. Certainly, of all the nattily attired and dashing officers, Major General J.E.B. Stuart proved the ultimate beau idéal cavalier.[72] Events, including a series of episodes that occurred in the middle of 1863, showed that some Confederates saw dangers in men aspiring to this model in dress and behavior and tarnished General Stuart's reputation.

The victory at Chancellorsville in early May 1863 gave General Robert E. Lee space to plan the advance into Pennsylvania that culminated in the Battle of Gettysburg in early July. As the army readied for the campaign, generals organized a variety of parades. One of them took place on June 6, 1863, before five hundred women. In this event, thousands of mounted men and infantry from the Army of Northern Virginia marched and drilled. Witnesses noted that the "gold and yellow trappings" worn by the cavalry's "showy men" drew the attention of the hundreds of "light headed" ladies. As for the "tattered, worn and tired infantry," they "received not one smile."[73] Major General Stuart, a man described by Richmond's *Examiner* as "proud of his beauty, vain and foppish and fonder of admiration than he should be," commanded the cavalry.[74] His bearing as an archetypal cavalier, bold raids, and other actions earned Stuart fame. Within days, however, the Federal forces sullied Stuart and his men's standing.

In the foggy dawn of June 9, 1863, Union squadrons surprised Stuart and his troops near Brandy Station and only retreated after severely mauling the Rebels. Denied hard facts about the battle, Richmond newspapers concluded that another parade before women had distracted the cavaliers. Moreover, they imagined that the "plain" moderate Lee had warned the "vain" high-spirited Stuart to be on guard. This morality tale told Confederates that rather than the pomp of the "martial" male being the ideal, it was the "restrained" Christian gentleman to which Southerners should aspire.[75]

Besides this incident, the character of Confederate mounted soldiers came under increased attack from the press.[76] For example, infantry nicknamed them "Buttermilk Rangers" because they believed the mounted soldiers lived an easier life. Despite the continuance of the prewar pastime of knightly tournaments, articles appeared that couched these events in the language of distraction rather than nationalism.[77] Additionally, an article that described cavalrymen as "festive cavaliers" appeared in Confederate newspapers.[78] Meanwhile, across the South, their foraging became indistinguishable from theft to citizens and damaged morale. Successful and inspirational exploits of cavalry led by men such as Turner Ashby, Mosby, and Stuart ensured that such reports and experiences only eroded the cavalier's standing in the Confederate mind.

The idea of the impetuous and aggressive Southerner faced other pressures. While some called for a more offensive war, many speeches and tracts reminded them that they were fighting a defensive struggle to protect hearth and home.[79] As a winter of reverses followed the first flush of victories, ideologues responded by distancing their ideas of manhood from prewar notions of Southern élan. A soberer model of manhood gained prominence. "Our enemies," wrote one newspaperman in early 1862, "predicted that our men would make an impetuous rush in battle, and make for a time a great dash and display, but that they would soon become demoralized by inaction, and demonstrate an utter want of patience and stability. On the contrary, our men have hitherto shown a fortitude equal to their courage, and have patiently submitted to privations and delays."[80] In February 1862, Benjamin M. Hill extolled the soldiers' virtues of "duty and sacrifice" to the Georgia state legislature.[81] Around the same time, the *Richmond Dispatch* described true men as "patriots" able to "elevate themselves above the adversities of a day and look calmly and hopefully to that bright future" to be secured by "a union of true hearts and strong arms."[82] Plays such as Mrs. Maria J. Westmoreland's *Soldier's Trial; or, The Warning Voice*, from 1863, told of the "incentives to constancy and unswerving virtue."[83] Confederate imagery of soldiers cheerfully enduring hardships in the field illustrated the concepts of duty, endurance, and patience, which became more valuable to Southerners as they faced a protracted war. The belief in the justness of their cause and that Divine Providence guided the establishment of their nation sustained the true Confederate man.[84]

These ideas contributed to the manner in which Confederates depicted their troops. As a result, only a handful of pictures showed Rebels on the attack. Instead, pictures of soldiers generated by government and commercial bodies showed them in less aggressive poses. Arguably, the most visible of these appeared on the more than 3.4 million T-49, T-56, and T-65 Confederate one hundred–dollar notes issued by the Treasury from April 1863 (see fig. 1.4). Printed and circulated over the last year of the war, Keatinge and Dunn's design for the note featured a vignette and two portraits. On the right-hand side, the vignette shows a pair of fully equipped soldiers, in the center Lucy Pickens, and on the left former secretary of war George Washington Randolph. The infantrymen, representing youth and age, rest watchfully atop a hill, gazing toward the left. Physiognomically, these are noble and moral men. Although armed and equipped, they do not seek a fight. Rather, they scan the distance. On the other side of Pickens, Randolph's stare shares the same focal point. In contrast, Pickens looks toward the opposite direction. It is an image that presents all men engaged in a single purpose: the watchful defense of Southern womanhood.

RESTRAINED MANHOOD AS ICONOGRAPHY AND ICON

The concept of restrained manhood defending women and property permeated Confederate thought and is present in the development and final design of their great seal. In April 1862, Congress formed a committee to decide on the device. In autumn 1862, its deliberations generated the first of two alternative designs, both of which featured men defending women, rather than seeking to dominate others.[85] However, neither one captured the people's hearts and minds. Politicians believed both designs were too clearly set in the wartime present instead of a peaceful Confederate future.[86] When an Alabama senator proposed a more martial equestrian "cavalier" figure, critics rebuffed it.[87] The *Southern Illustrated News*, for example, objected to it on social rather than political grounds. "We are not all Cavaliers," it argued, "and we have no patrician order." In its place, the *News* suggested a view of Thomas Crawford's statue of George Washington that sat on the grounds of Richmond's capitol. In the *News*'s opinion, Washington represented "the loftiest development of a Southern man."[88]

Adopting this beloved American brought with it ideas attractive to Southerners. In popular mythology, Washington characterized restrained rather than martial manhood.[89] The catalog of anecdotes surrounding America's first president, from the mythic cutting down of the cherry tree to his loyal defense of union with Britain (until forced to defend his homeland), demonstrated his moderation.[90] Additionally, the *News* reminded readers, his ownership and effective management of "vast numbers" of slaves made him "the very model of a Southern man."[91] Washington's presence on the Confederate seal provided a compelling combination of heritage, history, and manhood.

Psychologically, the use of a real figure provided a powerful pattern of masculinity for Confederate men.[92] Moreover, Crawford's Washington, adopted soon afterward by Congress as the great seal's centerpiece, made temperate and patriotic manhood a national ideal. Yet as a symbol of Southern manhood, Washington lacked the emotional and nationalistic impact of two flesh-and-blood heroes from the Confederacy's short history: Generals Stonewall Jackson and Robert E. Lee. Both men came to epitomize restrained Confederate masculinity.

The myth of Stonewall Jackson embraced both his combat successes and his personality. In his simple and single-minded Protestant way of life, Confederates found reason for God granting him victories and a model of disciplined and moderate manhood. In late April 1863, David Cowell sat Stonewall before his camera. The surviving portrait showed the general in three-quarter profile dressed in a newly presented general's uniform, unarmed, without accoutrements, and wearing a steely expression. While a death mask of Jackson, made by Frederick Volck, revealed the general's hooked nose and lumpy forehead, Cowell chose an angle that hid the general's irregular features and instead emphasized his high forehead and made his nose look straighter.[93] To physiognomists, a high forehead and straight nose indicated nobility, intellect, and generosity. Since Confederates believed in the truthfulness of photographs, Cowell's portrait suggested an accurate depiction of the man.[94]

Many producers of imagery regularly drew on Cowell's photograph. It received its greatest and most valuable use, however, on the five-hundred-dollar bill (T-64). On this Treasury note, artists Keatinge and Dunn twinned it with Crawford's Washington to create a powerful symbol of national identity and masculinity. Washington appears under the Second National flag and laurel wreath, enclosed within a stand of arms and a belt of knowledge bearing the nation's motto (fig. 9.8). Additionally, the designers turned his head to face Jackson's portrait, creating a relationship between two Southern heroes. To Confederates, the bill pictured twin Southern exemplars: men who not only achieved successes in American struggles but did so while managing their emotions. Nevertheless, one Confederate personality stood larger than Jackson and Washington as a model of manhood.[95]

More than a record of military success made Robert E. Lee a Confederate hero.[96] His morals, manner, and pedigree matched or excelled those of Jackson and Washington in Southern minds.[97] While membership in Virginia's planter elite and gallant Revolutionary War forebears suggested a cavalier inheritance, his Christian convictions and enculturation in the patrician gentility determined that Lee valued restraint over martial manhood.[98] In late 1862, Peter Alexander of Savannah's *Republican* called him "a wise man, a good man" and the "Washington of our revolution." In Alexander's widely republished report, he stressed Lee's modesty and faith. He reported that when told by an officer of the army of the people's belief in him, Lee stated his unworthiness for such esteem. Furthermore, his choice of clothing also

FIG. 9.8. $500 *Treasury Note—Type-64*, by Edward Keatinge. Printed by Keatinge and Ball, Columbia, S.C., Apr. 1864. Courtesy of Pierre Fricke, https://www.buyvintagemoney.com.

reflected this character: "Exceedingly plain in his dress, one looks at his costume in vain for those insignia of rank for which most officers have such a weakness." Alexander summed up the Virginian as "withal and above all, a humble Christian."[99] According to a fellow officer, he was "the best and greatest man on the continent."[100] While a Georgian described him as "the representative man of a young, vigorous and Christian nation," an 1864 article described him as "our great chieftain, our hero patriot, our Christian soldier."[101] Another report explained that "the soldier cannot forget to behave himself in such presence."[102] Altogether, when measured against masculine ideals of the nineteenth century, Lee's intellect, Christian values, and gentlemanly qualities befitted him as a model man.[103]

Additionally, his physical aspect did much to recommend him to the people. "What a noble face and head," a journalist heard among cheers and shouts from Lee's soldiers in April 1864.[104] "The picture of a soldier," wrote Mary Boykin Chesnut in her diary.[105] His "well-shaped, squarely built head" with high forehead and "handsome nose," likened by one journalist to Napoleon's, showed his intellectual power and force of personality, and his mouth showed his "iron will."[106] Confederates wanted pictures of their hero, and unlike Jackson, it required little license to make his appearance conform to their expectations.

Men such as Lee and Jackson who put faith and country far ahead of self-interest became models for the ideal Confederate man. Yet Lee's behavior showed that despite what he said, he was not without vanity. In word and by reputation, Lee eschewed self-promotion and any hint of egotism. In his letters, he regularly professed his dislike or disinterest for having his picture made and made self-ef-

FIG. 9.9. *General R. E. Lee*, by Edward Caledon Bruce, 1864. Engraving. Reproduced courtesy of the Carter family.

facing comments about the results.[107] Nevertheless, the general found time to seat himself before at least four artists and five photographers during the war. Finally, in late 1864, Lee permitted "all artists to amuse themselves with photographs and give wide range to their fancies."[108] With and without this permission, artists produced a minimum of four paintings, eleven photographic portraits, a photograph of Edward Valentine's statuette of Lee, and other reprographic forms.[109] Overall, the images presented Lee as calm and collected.

This is seen in the portrait of Lee that Virginian Edward Caledon Bruce (1825–1900) developed in late 1864 (fig. 9.9).[110] Finished during the winter of 1865, it hung in Virginia's state capitol for the last months of the war.[111] Although the original painting disappeared from public view early in the twentieth century, copies of

FIG. 9.10. "General Robert Edmund Lee," by John W. Torsch. From *Southern Illustrated News*, Oct. 17, 1863.

the painting and oil studies survive. In contrast to other artists, Bruce worked up the final piece from studies and sketches. In 1866, a Northern journalist called it a "strikingly exciting picture." Descriptions of the portrayal provide some indication of details, such as colors, not visible in the reproductions. Clad in "plain gray uniform," unadorned by all but three small stars of a colonel on his collar, Lee rests on the scarlet lining of his military cloak, which is draped over the wheel of a cannon with a barrel marked "U.S.," holding his hat in one hand and binoculars in the other. He wears the sword and belt given to him by the ladies of Baltimore. While the three-quarter view of his head remained constant in every version, after trialing a variety of styles, Bruce determined to use a tighter and less painterly style around his face to suggest calm self-assurance. Meanwhile, wisps extend from the head and beard as if statically charged by the swirling "sulphurous canopy" that rings his head. At his feet lay tree branches freshly severed by battle, a red Zouave cap, a broken musket, a Union-fired Schenckl cannon shell, and the leg of a body projects from beneath the cannon. Regardless of the maelstrom, the courier behind him fighting to check Lee's "iron gray charger," Lee fixes a relaxed gaze toward the spectator's right. Altogether, he is a composed and collected figure amid chaos.[112]

This sense of a man in control amid turmoil reflected what *London Times* reporter Francis Lawley described in late 1862 as the "serenity, or, if I may so express it, the unconscious dignity of General Lee's courage, when he is under fire."[113] John Torsch insinuated this demeanor in a woodcut he produced for the *Southern Illus-*

FIG. 9.11. Detail of *General Robert E. Lee,* by Daniel T. Cowell, 1862. Scan from *The Photographic History of the Civil War* by Francis Trevelyan Miller (New York: Review of Reviews, 1911).

trated News (fig. 9.10). Published in an 1863 issue of the paper and reused in *The War and Its Heroes,* it became among the most widely distributed printed Confederate images of the man.

Like most *Illustrated News* portraits, Torsch based his engraving on a photograph of Lee (fig. 9.11). In selecting the image, the *News* had three contemporary photographic portraits to choose from: two seated and one full-length. While all presented a restrained image of Lee, each did so differently. The standing, or "Boots and Spurs," photograph portrayed the Lee of the battlefield. Standing contrapposto with his hand resting on his sword, his coat unbuttoned at the collar, and binoculars slung over this shoulder, he is a man of action.[114] The seated portraits depict two Lees. One shows him seated facing to the left with his uniform stiffly buttoned to the chin; in the other, he faces right and wears his coat unbuttoned. This last image, dated from before the September 1862 Maryland campaign, became acknowledged as the most popular photo of the Virginian.[115] The *News* gave Torsch this image to engrave.

The text that accompanied Torsch's engraving claimed that after Lee assumed control of the Army of Northern Virginia, in 1862, "his is the calm, broad, military intellect that reduced the chaos . . . to form and order."[116] The Marylander's portrait illustrated this version of Lee. He emphasized Lee's office by adding a wreath to the three stars that he commonly wore (indicating the rank of colonel), making Lee wear the badge designated for general officers. Moreover, he also reworked the Virginian's physical appearance in subtle ways, deepening the creases around his eyes and detailing the texture and contour of his hair. A comparison with Torsch's other works shows that he lavished greater attention on these areas than in other portraits.[117] His eye wrinkles age Lee, and the flips of hair make him look tousled and windswept. His unbuttoned coat and other features contrast with his resolute and confident gaze.

Popular media's images of Lee and Jackson presented both as restrained and dutiful members of the military. They portrayed Confederate ideals of manhood that valued God-fearing soldiers focused on the defense of the South: family, community, and racial slavery. These images fed belief in their men's innate Christian qualities and reason for the Lord to favor their cause. However, setting any man on a pedestal concerned those convinced of the sacred nature of their national and holy mission. A week before the *News* published Lee's portrait, it warned Confederates that hero worship loosened their proper focus. "Worship," the writer intoned, "belongs of right to the man of Jesus Christ alone."[118] To Richmond's *Whig*, such behavior belonged North of the Mason-Dixon Line. "Idol-worship," it declared, "is indispensable to their existence, and they cannot give up one image until another is supplied."[119] There were heroes, clergy told Southerners, but not in celebrity. "The true hero," Reverend Minnegerode stated in August 1863, "is he who thus lives and thus labors—with God his reliance, his rule, his law, his meat,—to do his duty and perform his work; he who rules his spirit to do hardship, and curb the pride of will, and conquer every lower desire so that he may glorify God and save his Country."[120] In essence, ranged against godless, unmanly Yankees, this type of man ensured the Lord's favor and the nation's success.

Confederates saw a battle between contending masculinities as a part of the war. This view brought both costs and benefits. Demeaning and attacking their opponents proved a relatively simple task. It reinvigorated flagging spirits and helped to delineate and bolster a distinctly Confederate identity. However, issues similar to those that attended race emerged. Both were fanciful imaginings that had more self-congratulation and flattery than objectivity.

Confederate prejudices caused some unexpected omissions. For example, despite being praised for his service in Congress and in the press, no advertisement for or notice about images of Nathan Bedford Forrest's have been found within extant Southern newspapers.[121] Although this may represent a Confederate focus on the Eastern theater, service away from Virginia did not stop photographic studios, the *Southern Illustrated News*, or Lee Mallory from publishing or exhibiting portraits of less acclaimed Western generals.[122] In addition, Tennessee representatives noticed this bias in May 1864, when Congress reworded a resolution of thanks to "strike out" references to Forrest as "among the most renowned military chieftains of the age."[123] Maybe Confederate image makers avoided Forrest because alongside accounts of acts of gallantry, newspapers carried reports of his violence, and negative images of Confederate soldiers rarely appeared in imagery.[124] Such a reputation for lack of restraint may have led the creators of commercial imagery to believe Forrest less salable.

The examples of Stuart and Forrest not only speak to the ranking of Confederate masculinity but also reveal the inconsistencies of Confederate thought. Ardent Confederates convinced themselves of their people's unity, God's favor, the lessons of history, the superior morale and character of their military, and the certainty of ultimate victory.[125] Confederate imagery contributed to this wishful thinking. While restrained Christian soldiers provided an aspirational model, however, this ideal also marginalized men engaged in the manufacturing necessary to support the war effort. Likewise, it made concern over the Confederacy's situation unmanly. Moreover, those men drawn to martial or cavalier display found themselves devalued compared to their more restrained compatriots. As with so much of the Confederacy, the effort to define themselves revealed the nation's complexity and the obstacles they faced in achieving a unified populace.

The Civil War crushed Southern manhood. Confederate ideologues, in words and images, held that brave, hardy, self-sacrificing, and controlled Christians would surely vanquish their foe. But in the Southron's most important test, being able to defend their homes and human chattel, Southern manhood failed. Moreover, the role of black troops compromised white Southern men's preeminence as defenders of society. Confederate depictions of manhood masked the grim and fundamental problem the war revealed—the inability of Confederate men to control the enemy, slaves, women, and their own fates.[126]

Epilogue

Confederate official and commercial bodies created objects and images throughout the war. Those instituted by government reflected contemporary models of nationalism. Through them, the administration attempted to present theirs as a modern nation. However, apart from establishing gray as the shade for the national uniform, the Confederate government struggled to create a consistent and manifest symbology. The domestically produced weapons and accouterments that often bore the government's initials were crudely made. The designs of the national flag and Treasury notes changed, and soldiers and officers wore uniforms of various patterns. Also, although the government-issued jackets had the potential to achieve a consistent national icon, soldiers' variable loyalties, each clothing depot's different cuts, and supply problems compromised their impact. In sum, the government struggled to present imagery and objects that presented their nation as stable and consistent.

Commercial producers contributed a range of objects, experiences, and imagery to the Confederate marketplace. These representations delivered the ideas of endurance, insiders and outsiders, and Confederate exceptionalism. Carried by Confederate print culture in a visual format, they contributed to a sense of intellectual and emotional unity among wartime Southerners. Imagery presented another escapist avenue for Confederates as their nation's future grew bleaker. Like the written word, these artifacts pictured a chimeric world of stability and substance. Faced with the unpalatable evidences of failure, they helped softened reverses and shored up the belief among Southerners that they were achieving their national goal.

Confederate producers of visual or material culture operated within a challenging context of a small, predominantly agricultural population and underdeveloped industries. The South entered the war with little artistic or artisanal capital. Later, enlistment in the army or departure from the Confederacy further depleted the number of available skilled artists and craftsmen. Every creative endeavor faced shortages of expert manpower and materials needed to produce large amounts of high-quality work. However, regardless of growing difficulties, inflation, and diminishing national fortunes, some producers continued their efforts to attract audiences to the end of the war. These efforts show that American capitalism existed within the South.

Confederate visual and material output by the government and business pictured the Civil War through the distorting lens of Confederate prejudices. Analyzing its depictions reveals that the manner of representation, perhaps predictably, reflected the creator's opinion of the subject's perceived relationship to the cause. In doing so, it magnified factors that justified faith in eventual Southern independence, such as military superiority and the enslaved's loyalty. It also minimized those issues, such as black troops and insufficient war materiel, that directly threatened the positive views of the Confederate world it presented.

Despite its jingoistic intentions, Confederate imagery also contributed to the divisions and delusions Confederates experienced during the war. It helped blind them to slavery's inhumanity and propped up Confederates' wishful thinking about military, social, and economic successes. In attempting to differentiate, affirm, or censure themselves, they drew dividing lines in their society. Delineating insiders and outsiders according to gender and ethnicity within the population encouraged greater distance between these groups and the cause.

An overarching weakness present in Confederate creation was its inaccuracy. This failing extended more deeply than the precision of physical representations. In the 1940s, Wilbur Cash observed that white Southerners were "so long trained to believe what they like to believe" that they readily convinced themselves that their opinions were fact.[1] Confederate imagery demonstrates this characteristic in the Civil War South. Imagery such as "Reconstruction," from a September 1864 issue of the *Southern Illustrated News* (fig. E.1), shows this quality. According to a reporter from the *Macon Daily Telegraph*, it depicted "a rebel with his title REBEL in large letters across his shoulders, a ball and chain to his ankles, a spade in one hand, a broom in the other with a negro master over him."[2] The imagery created a compelling scene. The rebel's ragged pants and worn shoes suggest both his poverty and soldiering past. His Union guard's enlarged lips imply his lascivious nature. Worse yet, a laughing black child mocks the Confederate veteran's situation. Informed by stereotypes, the cartoon imagined the reversal of power many Confederates believed loss meant—slavery and a society not just reordered but upended. It was a future that only existed in their apprehensions.

The history of the postwar South indicates that ideas present in Confederate visual culture continued into Southerners' postwar world. While Confederate de-

FIG. E.1. "Reconstruction," by "Casey." From *Southern Illustrated News*, Sept. 24, 1864. Courtesy of the Boston Athenaeum.

feat ended legal slavery in the United States, it made little change to the ideas that had led to its establishment. Rather, the Lost Cause mythology aided Southerners in maintaining a view of slavery as a benign and bucolic black occupation, white Southerners as born masters, and the system as harmonious and productive. Further, the embryonic pseudoscience that Confederates such as Vice President Alexander Stephens embraced developed into scientific theories that poisoned humanity for more than a century. And finally, as the Northerners and Congress lost interest in Reconstruction or at least in halting efforts by ex-Confederates to assume political roles in the South, white Southerners reclaimed their hegemony. While the region was no longer slave based, the recovery of control by former Confederates ensured that social, political, and economic shackles would bind not the former Rebels but Southern African Americans for another century.

In 1992, Drew Gilpin Faust challenged historians studying Confederate identity to investigate its iconology.[3] In responding to the call, this study finds that Confederate visual and material culture recorded a complex Confederate identity. The artifacts and resources within my reach not only recalled the obstacles that the Confederacy faced but also embodied many of the values around which white Southerners attempted to build a nation. Present among these articles are the Lost Cause's foundational myths, such as fractured ideas of race and rights, heroes, sacrifice, and an imagined South. The diversity of thought present within these visibly manifests the "kaleidoscope of gray" identified and discussed by Anne Rubin.[4] More than 150 years later, these artifacts are more than relics; they are provocative and emotionally charged representations of the nation from which they came. Ian Binnington suggests that "Confederate Americanism" underpins Southern ideas of being American.[5] This possibility makes these items avenues for understanding the South in both the past and present. The scope for using iconological sources to better grasp Confederate identity is still expanding. Certainly, this study has benefited from the efforts of archives and libraries to digitize their collections. Their labors have greatly enriched access to the materials that have formed the basis of this work, filling gaps in the evidence and providing new perspectives. These ongoing endeavors and recent scholarship using printed materials show that a great opportunity for further investigation and deeper understanding of Confederate identity remains.[6] They suggest the scope and merit in using sources such as imagery and objects to better discern the values of gray within the Confederate kaleidoscope.

APPENDIX

The Origins of Vignettes Used on Confederate Currency

Abbreviations:

NBNC—National Bank Note Company
SBNC—Southern Bank Note Company
H&L—Hoyer and Ludwig
M—Manouvier
K&B—Keatinge and Ball
JTP—James T. Paterson
BD—Blanton Duncanw

Type, amount, and printer	Vignette and portrait's previous use
1, $1,000, NBNC	Calhoun—Exchange Bank, Springfield, Vt., $5, 1854 Jackson—Tiverton Bank, Rhode Island, $5, 1859
2, $500, NBNC	Train—North Western Bank, Warren, Pa. Ceres—Corn Exchange Bank, De Soto, Neb., $2, 1860
3, $100, NBNC	*America*—Western Bank, Philadelphia, $5, 1861 Railroad train at station—American Bank of Baltimore, $3; Treasury Bank, Griggsville, Ill., Nov. 6 1860 Liberty—Bank of Sparta (Ill.), $1, June 1, 1860
4, $50, NBNC	Cotton Field Bank of Savannah (S.C.), $20, Jan. 1, 1861
5, $100, SBNC	Bank of Lexington (N.C.) $5 Justice—Derived, source uncertain Train rounding bend—Derived, source uncertain Minerva—Derived, source uncertain
6, $50, SBNC	Industry and Agriculture on cotton bale—Bank of Lexington (N.C.), Sept. 8, 1859, $5; Citizens' Bank of Louisiana at Shreveport, 1857, $5 Justice—Oneida Valley Bank (N.Y.), $3, 1855 Washington—Derived, source uncertain
7, $100, H&L	Ceres and Proserpine flying—Derived, source uncertain Washington—Derived, source uncertain

Type, amount, and printer	Vignette and portrait's previous use
8, $50, H&L	Tellus—Merchants' and Manufacturers' Bank, Columbus, Ga., $5, Nov. 1, 1854 Washington—widely used
9, $20, H&L	Sailing ship prewar—Derived, source uncertain
10, $10, H&L	Liberty and eagle—Bank of Hagerstown (Md.), $5, 1856 Hope and anchor—Eastern Bank, Bangor, Maine, $2, 1859
11, $5, H&L	Sailor and capstan—Farmers Bank, Wickford, R.I., from 1820 Liberty and eagle—Bank of Hagerstown (Md.), $5, 1856
12, $5, M	No vignettes
13, $100, H&L	Slave loading cotton—Mississippi and Alabama Railroad Company, 1838; Madisonville and Pearl River Turnpike Company (Miss.), Mar. 1, 1839 Sailor and anchor—Source not found
14, $50, H&L	Both prewar on notes delivered by Bank of Charleston (S.C.) Sailor and shipbuilder—Mechanics Savings Bank of Savannah, Ga., $50, 1859 Moneta—Bank of Cape Fear (N.C.), $5
15, $50, SBNC	Train—Westmoreland Bank of New Brunswick, Canada Liberty and eagle—Bank of Hagerstown (Md.), $5 1856 Justice—West River Bank, Jamaica, Vt., $50, 185[?] Hope, Morris County Bank, Morristown, N.J., July 18, 1852
16, $50, K&B	Jefferson Davis—Original
17, $20, H&L	Ceres between Commerce and Navigation—Bank of Washington (N.C.), $5, 1859 Liberty—Bank of Norwalk (Ohio), $1, Nov. 23, 1844
18, $20, H&L	Sailor and capstan—West Winfield Bank, West Winfield, N.Y., $10, 1859 Three-mast sailing ship—Monticello Bank, Charlottesville, Va., $2, May 1, 1861
19, $20, SBNC	Minerva—Broadway Bank, New York, $10, 1850s Navigation—Ship Builders Bank, Rockland, Maine, 1850s Blacksmith—City Bank of Columbus (Ohio), and the Coachatuate Bank, Boston, $3, 1850
20, $20, BD	Alexander Stephens—Original Industry, beehive, and Cupid—Original Hope with anchor and palmetto—version, Eastern Bank, Bangor, Maine, $2, 1859
21, $20, K&B	Alexander Stephens—Original Behind industry and agriculture—Original
22, $10, SBNC	Thetis—Commercial Exchange Bank, Terre Haute, Ind., $2

Type, amount, and printer	Vignette and portrait's previous use
	Native family—Farmers and Mechanics Bank, Rochester, New Hampshire, $1 Nov., 1, 18[?] Woman with corn—Bank of Cooperstown (N.Y.), $10
23, $10, K&B	John Elliott Ward, corn gatherer, wagon—Mechanics Savings Bank of Savannah (Ga.), $10
24, $10, K&B	R. Hunter—Original Child (Elwyn)—Derived, source uncertain
25, $10, K&B	R. Hunter—Original Hope with anchor—version, Eastern Bank, Bangor, Maine, $2, 1859 C. G. Memminger—Original
26, $10, K&B	R. Hunter—Original Hope with anchor—version Eastern Bank, Bangor, Maine, $2, 1859 C. G. Memminger—Original
27, $10, H&L	Liberty and eagle—Commercial Bank of Wilmington (N.C.), $5, June 1857 Train in square—Bank of Charleston (S.C.), $10, 1858
28, $10, JTP	*On left:* Commerce and Ceres seated with urn Train in square—Bank of Charleston (S.C.), $10, 1858
29, $10, BD	Slave picking cotton—Bank of Charleston (S.C.), $20, 1857 Canal, landscape in square—Derived, source uncertain
30, $10, BD	R. Hunter—Original Potato dinner—Bank of Charleston (S.C.), $5, 1843–60 Minerva, column—Original
31, $5, SBNC	Navigation—Merchants' County Bank of Erie County, Lancaster, Pa., $5, Mar. 1, 1844 Commerce, Agriculture, Justice, Liberty and Industry—Union Bank of Rochester (N.Y.), $5, 1853 Washington statue—Bank of Cold-Water, Coldwater, Mich., $5, Dec. 15, 1837
32, $5, K&B	Child portrait—Mechanics Savings Bank of Savannah (Ga.), $5, 1855 Blacksmith—Mechanics Savings Bank of Savannah (Ga.), $5, 1855
33, $5, K&B	C. G. Memminger—Original Minerva—Wisconsin Marine and Fire Insurance, Milwaukee, $10, July 4, 1847
34, $5, K&B	C. G. Memminger—Original Minerva—Wisconsin Marine and Fire Insurance, Milwaukee, $10, July 4, 1847
35, $5, H&L	Slaves loading cotton; white man leaning Indian figure—Bank of Charleston (S.C.), $5, Jan. 26, 1858; Bank of Saline (Mich.), 1837

Type, amount, and printer	Vignette and portrait's previous use
36, $5, JTP	Sailor—Bank of Savannah (Ga.), $2, 1859; Maritime Bank, Bangor, Maine, $2, 1855 Commerce on bale—Derived, source uncertain
37, $5, BD	C. G. Memminger—Original Sailor on cotton bales—Canal Bank, New Orleans, $100, Oct. 1, 1845 Justice and Ceres—Derived, source uncertain
38, $2, BD	J. P. Benjamin—Original Confederacy striking down Union—Original
39, $100, H&L	Milkmaid—Mechanics Savings Bank of Savannah (Ga.), $50, 1859 Train vignette—Bank of Columbus (Ga.), $5, 1856 Tioga County Bank, Tioga, Pa., $100, June 7, 1857
40, $100, JTP	Train—(diffused steam), Bank of Columbus (Ga.), $5, 1856; Tioga County Bank, Tioga, Pa., $100, June 7, 1857
41, $100, K&B	J. C. Calhoun—derived, source uncertain Cotton Field Bank of Savannah, $20 note, Jan. 1, 1861 *America*—reversed
42, $2, BD	J. P. Benjamin—Original Confederacy striking down Union—Original
43, $2, BD	J. P. Benjamin—Original Confederacy striking down Union—Original
44, $1, BD	Liberty—Original Steamship—West Winfield Bank, West Winfield, N.Y., $10, 1859 Lucy Pickens—Original
45, $1, BD	Liberty—Original Steamship—West Winfield Bank, West Winfield, N.Y., $10, 1859 Lucy Pickens—Original
46, $10, H&L	Commerce reclining on cotton bales—Bank of Chicago, $1, Nov. 2, 1852 R.M.T. Hunter—Original
XX-2 (47), $20, H&L	Liberty—Original R.M.T. Hunter—Original
XX-3 (48), $10	Ceres on Cotton Bales—North River Banking Company, New York, $3, 1840 R. M. T. Hunter—Original

Note:

Total number of vignettes: 104; number of those with antecedents: 67 (64%); total number of notes with reused vignettes: 36 of 49.

NOTES

Introduction

1. "Two Beautiful Paintings," *Richmond Enquirer,* March 2, 1865; "From Yesterday's Evening Edition," *Richmond Whig,* March 12, 1865.

2. Irishman Thomas Connolly recorded that he purchased both works for $9,000 on March 23, 1865. See Connolly, *Irishman in Dixie,* 61. The American Civil War Museum collection contains an albumen photograph (catalog no. FIC2009.03970) of a scene similar to *The Scout's Prize.* It clearly differs from the copy that Elder produced later in 1865—for example, the cavalryman is clean-shaven. However, it is undated.

3. Quigley, *Shifting Grounds,* 40–51, 70–72.

4. Stampp, "The Southern Road to Appomattox," in Stampp, *Imperiled Union,* 255–67; Escott, *After Secession;* Beringer et al., *Why the South Lost the Civil War.*

5. Faust, *Creation of Confederate Nationalism;* Gallagher, *Confederate War;* Rubin, *Shattered Nation;* Bernath, *Confederate Minds.*

6. Bonner, *Colors and Blood;* Binnington, *Confederate Visions;* Faust, "Altars of Sacrifice," 1200–1228; Boyd, *Patriotic Envelopes of the Civil War.*

7. Neely, Holzer, and Borritt, *Confederate Image,* 3.

8. Harvey, *Civil War and American Art,* 3.

9. "Fine Art," *Memphis Appeal,* July 5, 1861.

10. "Portrait of President Davis," *Memphis Appeal,* December 5, 1861; "Who Wants to See a Battle," *Memphis Appeal,* December 12, 1861; "President's Portrait," *Memphis Appeal,* December 29, 1861; "Lady's Studio," *Memphis Appeal,* February 8, 1862.

11. Elder repainted both works after the war. Comparing Elder's postwar version of *The Battle of the Crater* with the written account of the original indicates that at the least he altered some figures on the work's left side: missing is the principal figure of a Confederate soldier bayonetting a black soldier and a wounded Rebel falling over an African American Union infantryman. The alteration and written description make the 1869 rebel appear more defensive. See "Two Paintings," *Richmond Whig,* March 12, 1865; "The Crater—Elder's Picture," *Richmond Dispatch,* September 25, 1869.

12. Works that Confederates produced for private or personal consumption are not considered in this study.

13. The work of Maryland bound pro-Confederate artist Adelbert Volck, therefore, falls outside the scope of this work.

14. It is difficult to ascertain how fragmentary the evidence is. Works such as Blanton Duncan's

Pages from the Unpublished History of a Celebrated Financier do not appear to have been advertised. Frustratingly, few contemporary newspapers have complete files that might provide such notices. Only around half of George Dunn's 1864 series of valentines survive. A similar proportion of the over eighty photographs Jay D. Edwards produced and sold showing troops around Pensacola, Florida, in 1861 are extant. The chances of an example surviving are related to amount; one-off works, like paintings, are the least likely to have survived, then art or graphic prints, with sheet music and periodicals the most likely to still exist. However, with at least two-thirds of its issues lost, the *Confederate Knapsack* is an exception to this rule.

15. Hutchison, *Apples and Ashes.*

16. Watson, *History of Southern Drama,* 64–84; Irelan, *Enacting Nationalism,* xi–xv.

17. Binnington, *Confederate Visions;* Boyd, *Patriotic Envelopes of the Civil War;* Bonner, *Colors and Blood.*

18. Rable, *Civil Wars;* Rable, *Confederate Republic;* Rable, *Damn Yankees!;* Quigley, *Shifting Grounds;* Woodward, *Marching Masters;* Manning, *What This Cruel War Was Over.*

19. Harwell, "Brief Candle," 41–42, 44–45, 47. In addition to subscriptions and reading rooms that allowed access to periodicals, there is evidence that periodicals made it into camp, including an issue of Wisely's *The Confederate Spirit and Knapsack of Fun,* annotated "Julius S. Foscue, 7th Texas Infantry, Dalton Ga." (now in Perkins Library, Duke University). A Louisianan R. A. Pierson passed on copies of the *Southern Illustrated News* to his sister. See Reuben A. Pierson to William H. Pierson, February 2, 1863; and Reuben A. Pierson to Nancy C. Pierson, April 24, 1863, in Cutrer and Parrish, *Brothers in Gray,* 154, 187.

20. Invited to Charleston to paint General P.G.T. Beauregard's portrait, well-respected artist G.P.A. Healy found his work praised. However, four days later, he departed quickly after citizens threatened him with tarring and feathering because of his "northern feelings and anti-slavery sentiments." See Chambers, "Southern Artists in the Civil War," 71.

21. Comolli, "Machines of the Visible," 122.

22. Beegan, "Mechanization of the Image," 257–74; Varga, "Nineteenth-Century Mass Medium," 43–49.

23. Zhoray, *Fictive People,* 196.

24. Barnard, *Art, Design and Visual Culture,* 1–3, 18.

25. Harwell, "Brief Candle," 41–45; Bernath, *Confederate Minds,* 232.

26. Burke, *Eyewitnessing,* 187–88; Haskell, *History and Its Images.* By studying a wide range of historians from the past, Haskell, while showing the development of artworks as historic documents, shows the danger of using the study of images for personal ideologies or agendas, of assuming that images are strictly factual recordings of people, places, or events. Artworks contain ambiguities and cannot tell us everything about the people who made them,

27. Schlereth, *Material Culture Studies,* 39–40.

28. Prown, "Mind in Matter," 1–19; Fleming, "Artefact Study," 162–73; Tilley, *Reading Material Culture.*

29. Camille, "Simulacrum," 31–32.

30. Baudrillard, *Simulacrum and Simulation,* 1–22.

31. Sahlins, *Boundaries,* 271. See also Colley, *Britons,* 1–7.

32. Freud, *Joke and Its Relation to the Unconscious,* 99–102.

33. Wilson, *Jokes,* 228, 230; Nickels, *Civil War Humor.* Drawing on newspapers, periodicals, covers,

and sheet music, Nickels's exploration of humor identifies genres common to both North and South. While presenting a rich array of examples in their historic context, it rarely explores their function.

34. Faust, *Mothers of Invention,* 154–55.

35. Green and Brock, "Role of Transportation," 701–21.

36. See Burrows, "Sermon to the First Baptist Church," 3. Burrows asked: "Shall we all go and laugh and clap to the music and the dance, while the grasp of relentless foes is tightening upon the throats of our sons, and the armed heels of trampling hosts are bruising the bosom of our beloved land?"

37. Harwell, "Brief Candle," 41–87.

38. Cowling, *Artist as Anthropologist.*

39. Gabel, *Rails to Oblivion.* Even as Confederate national identity became more consolidated, the rail system began to fail. By June 1863, the government had engaged the foundries, mills, and machine shops necessary for keeping engines running and replacing worn wheels and rails with the production of war materiel. The encroachment of the Union army only hastened the destruction.

40. The historiography examining the Confederacy's strong relationship to religion includes: Faust, *Creation of Confederate Nationalism,* 22–40; essays by Kurt O. Berends, Paul Harvey, Daniel W. Stowell, Drew Gilpin Faust, Harry S. Stout and Christopher Grasso in Miller, Stout, and Wilson, *Religion and the American Civil War,* 111–46, 172–75, 187–207, 250–60, 313–59. Antebellum and wartime religion is explored in Fox-Genovese and Genovese, *Mind of the Master Class.* See also Stout, *Upon the Altar of the Nation;* Miller, *Both Prayed to the Same God;* Rable, *God's Almost Chosen Peoples.*

41. "Lutheran Church Fresco," *Augusta Chronicle and Sentinel,* June 8, 1861. Painted for St. Matthew's Lutheran Church by local men L. A. (or A. L.) Lankau (1832–80) and John W. Kreuger (1818–?), who both fled North in August 1863; "New Catholic Church," *Augusta Chronicle and Sentinel,* June 28, 1861; "Catholicism Was Founded Early in the State's History," *Augusta Chronicle and Sentinel,* May 12, 1935. Sculptor John P. Mullen ran these through the blockade for Most Holy Trinity Catholic Church; "Sacred Panorama," *New Orleans True Delta,* December 31, 1861. This work was displayed at the St. Vincent's Infant Asylum; "New Publications," *Richmond Enquirer,* September 2, 1862; "Panorama of Sacred History," *Raleigh Spirit of the Age,* July 13, 1863; "Andrew's Paintings," *Raleigh Weekly Standard,* July 15, 1863; "Masonic Hall," *Augusta Constitutionalist,* August 16, 1863. North Carolina artist J. P. Andrews painted this panorama; "Mr. Sanders' Paintings—Jeptha's [*sic*] Daughter and the Flight Zenobia," *Tuscaloosa Weekly Times,* August 21, 1861; "Salutatory," *Child's Index* 1, no. 1 (September 1862): 3. In their essay, "Civil War, Religion and Communication: The Case of Richmond," Harry S. Stout and Christopher Grasso find that in contrast to the image created by the religious press and official proclamations that religion had a "monolithic" influence, secular dailies increasingly challenged their views. In Miller et al., *Religion and the American Civil War,* 330–46; Stout, *Upon the Altar of the Nation,* 286–92.

42. Quigley, *Shifting Grounds,* 132–36; "The American Question in England," Richmond *Examiner,* April 6, 1863; Hubbard, *Burden of Confederate Diplomacy,* 140–50; "The Dismissal of the British Consuls—Official Correspondence," *Charleston Mercury,* October 19, 1863. See, e.g., "Non-Intervention," *Raleigh Mercury,* April 30, 1864. This cartoon presented the Confederacy as a wagon train and foreign nations as dime novel–marauding Native Americans picking over its wreckage.

43. "The Scout's Prize," *Richmond Dispatch,* December 22, 1865. Two versions of this work exist, both signed by Elder and dated 1865. The Commonwealth Club, Richmond, Va. which owns the postwar version of *The Battle of the Crater,*), holds one copy. In June 2015 Heritage Auctions, Dallas, sold an almost identical version under the title *Confederate Soldier with Captured Mount.* See lot no. 62794, 2015

June 19–21 Fine & Decorative Arts Including Estates Signature Auction—Dallas no. 5218, Heritage Auctions, https://fineart.ha.com/itm/other-art/john-elder-american-1833-1895-confederate-soldier-with-captured-union-mount-1865-oil-on-canvas/a/5218-62794.s?ic4=GalleryView-Thumbnail-071515; "The Crater—Elder's Picture," *Richmond Dispatch*, September 25, 1869.

44. McCarthy, *Detailed Minutiae of Soldier Life*, 3–7.

CHAPTER 1

Iconography of the Confederate Government

1. Smith, *National Identity*, 43; Quigley, *Shifting Grounds*, 131–33.

2. Rable, *Confederate Republic*, 64.

3. Rable, *Confederate Republic*, 16–19, 50–51, 56–57.

4. Nicola Marschall's name, despite his postwar accounts, does not appear in any contemporary record. See Cannon, "Genesis of the 'Stars and Bars.'"

5. "Wednesday, February 13th, 1861, Open Session," *Journal of the Open and Secret Sessions of the Provisional Congress, February 4, 1861–February 18, 1861*, chap. 7, vol. 5, War Department Collection of Confederate Records, Record Group 109, National Archives Building, Washington, D.C. (hereafter cited as RG109, NAB).

6. "Southern Congress," *New Orleans Picayune*, February 19, 1861. Of this exchange, the journal of the Provisional Congress only recorded that "after some discussion had thereon, Mr. Brooke withdrew same for the present."

7. "Southern Congress: Seventh Day," *New Orleans Picayune*, February 19, 1861.

8. Bonner, *Colors and Blood*, 51–53.

9. William P. Miles to General P.G.T. Beauregard, August 27, 1861, in Harrison, *Stars and Stripes and Other American Flags*, 337–38.

10. Bonner, *Colors and Blood*, 54.

11. Cannon, *Flags of the Confederacy*, 36–48.

12. Cannon, *Flags of the Confederacy*, 51–65; see also Madaus, *Battle Flags;* Madaus and Needham, "Unit Colors of the Trans-Mississippi Confederacy, Part I," 123–41; Madaus and Needham, "Unit Colors of the Trans-Mississippi Confederacy, Part II," 172–82.

13. Cannon, *Flags of the Confederacy*, 8.

14. Brown, *Confederacy's First Battle Flag*, 28–53.

15. "The Confederate Flag," *Shreveport News*, August 1, 1861.

16. "The Flag," *Richmond Dispatch*, August 26, 1861.

17. Bonner, *Colors and Blood*, 100–109.

18. The diary of Texas congressman Francis Barlow Sexton provides a day-by-day record. Estill, "Diary of a Confederate Congressman," in two parts: April 1935, 270–301, and July 1935, 33–65. The diary indicates that some members held the floor for hours. On August 25, 1862, Sexton wrote in frustration, "We are wasting so much time."

19. Estill, "Diary of a Confederate Congressman," July 1935, 64–65.

20. "The New Flag of the Confederate States," *Richmond Examiner*, May 9, 1863.

21. "Raising the Standard," *Richmond Examiner*, May 8, 1863.

22. "The New Flag," *Richmond Examiner,* May 7, 1863.

23. "Hoisting of the New Flag on the Capitol," *Richmond Enquirer,* May 15, 1863.

24. Escott, *Confederacy,* 10; Bonner, *Confederate Political Economy,* 34–39. Bonner finds that the number of secret sessions conducted by Congress contributed to this perception. Davis, *Look Away,* 345, 354–55, 363; editorial, *Charleston Daily Courier,* February 16, 1864.

25. "The New Flag," *Richmond Whig,* May 15, 1863.

26. Bonner, *Colors and Blood,* 115–19.

27. "Our Beautiful Flag," *Southern Punch,* February 20, 1864.

28. "The Proposed Flag," *Richmond Whig,* February 13, 1865.

29. Thian, *Documentary History,* 33–36.

30. Bradley T. Johnson, "The Several Confederate Flags," Richmond *Dispatch,* April 26, 1896.

31. "The New Confederate Flag," *Richmond Whig,* February 14, 1865.

32. Escott, *Confederacy,* 83–85; Davis, *Look Away,* 121; Rable, *Confederate Republic,* 29–30, 44–45, 77–80. See also "The Permanent Constitution of the Confederate States," *Augusta Constitutionalist,* April 9, 1861; "What the Morning Journals Say," *New Orleans Delta,* February 25, 1862.

33. "The Art of Sinking Dies," *New York Sun,* August 16, 1885.

34. "A National Coat of Arms," *Richmond Examiner,* March 29, 1862.

35. "The Confederate Seal," *Charleston News Courier,* June 13, 1904.

36. See "The Flag and Seal of the Confederacy," *Record of News, History and Literature,* June 18, 1863; "Messrs. Geo. Dunn & Co, Engravers &c.," *Southern Field and Fireside,* February 4, 1865; "A New Head," *Raleigh Mercury,* October 29, 1864. The correspondence to and from the Confederate Treasury shows no direction with regard to these designs.

37. Similar to the flag, there is no contemporary evidence to sustain the postwar claims of individuals such as artist Nicola Marschall or Lamar Fontaine as having played any part in designing or developing this uniform.

38. Francis S. Bartow to General A. R. Lawton, May 4, 1861, Montgomery, Ala., in *Calendar of Confederate Papers,* 171.

39. C. H. Slocum to Colonel A. C. Myers, New Orleans, May 4, 1861, and C. H. Slocum to Colonel A. C. Myers, New Orleans, May 6, 1861, both in chap. 5, vol. 1, Register of Letters Received by the Confederate Quartermaster Department, March–August, 1861, RG109, NAB; Colonel A. C. Myers to Captain J. M. Galt, Montgomery, Ala., May 24, 1861, chap. 5, vol. 13, Quartermaster Department—Letters and Telegrams Sent, March–September, 1861, RG109, NAB.

40. Colonel A. C. Myers to C. M. Slocum, Montgomery, Ala., May 6, 1861; and May 16, 1861, Circular, in Letters and Telegrams Sent by the Confederate Quartermaster Department, National Archives Microfilm Publication, M900, roll 1, RG109, NAB.

41. "City Intelligence," *New Orleans Delta,* June 16, 1861.

42. "The Confederate Uniform," *Savannah News,* reprinted in *New York Tribune,* July 2, 1898. On May 5, 1861, George Deas gave *Times* correspondent William Howard Russell the impression that he was quartermaster general of the Confederate Army. Russell, *My Diary,* 166; Major Larkin Smith to Henry C. Wayne, adjutant general of Georgia, May 23, 1861, Letters and Telegrams Sent by the Confederate Quartermaster Department.

43. Mollo, *Military Fashions,* 133.

44. *Uniform and Dress of the Army of the Confederate States,* 3–4.

45. De Leon, *Belles, Beaux and Brains,* 120–21; North, *Military Uniforms,* 59, 81; Mollo, *Military Fashions,* 166, 211.

46. Geertz, *Interpretation of Cultures,* 251. This "epochalism" is seen in chapters 1 and 2.

47. Colonel A. C. Myers to Major L. McLaws, Richmond, Va., June 12, 1861, chap. 5, vol. 13, Quartermaster Department—Letters and Telegrams Sent, March–September 1861, RG109, NAB.

48. Leslie Jensen to author, October 18, 2003. Jensen, curator of Arms and Armor at the West Point Museum, West Point Military Academy, is an expert in United States military clothing. He cites Duncan's plate as the only prewar or Civil War uniform pattern. According to Jensen, the influence of Duncan's tailor's plates is commonly seen in Confederate officers' uniforms.

49. "For Materials purchased and printing, preparing and binding colored plates of 'Dress and Uniform of Army,'" Blanton Duncan file, Confederate Papers Relating to the Citizens or Business Firms, (National Archives Microfilm Publication, M346, roll 236), RG109. Secretary of War George W. Randolph had approved payment of the bill for $2,839.

50. See "A New Work Uniform and Dress of the Confederate States Army," *Augusta Chronicle and Sentinel,* August 31, 1861; "A New Work Uniform and Dress of the Confederate States Army," *Nashville Republican Banner,* September 1, 1861; "A New Work Uniform and Dress of the Confederate States Army," *Macon Telegraph,* September 2, 1861; "A New Work Uniform and Dress of the Confederate States Army," *Little Rock Arkansas True Democrat,* September 12, 1861.

51. Ball, *Financial Failure and Confederate Defeat,* 112–19.

52. C. G. Memminger to Richard Jones, Montgomery, Ala., February 27, 1861, in Thian, *Correspondence of the Treasury Department,* 3. No engraver by this name has been found in either the New Orleans city directory or the 1860 U.S. Census.

53. C. G. Memminger to Samuel Smith, Montgomery, Ala., March 8, 1861, in Thian, *Correspondence of the Treasury Department,* 14.

54. *Report of the Director of the Mint,* 7–9; Todd, *Confederate Finance,* 12–14. According to a contemporary report, the mint in New Orleans did not issue any of the coinage it produced. See "One of the Last Slanders," *New Orleans Daily Crescent,* April 27, 1861.

55. Todd, *Confederate Finance,* 14–16; "Confederate Coinage," *Charleston Courier,* January 1, 1861.

56. Todd, *Confederate Finance,* 6. Confederate notes never became legal tender, despite debate in Congress and calls by members of the public.

57. Ball, *Comprehensive Catalog and History,* 27; Slabaugh, *Confederate States Paper Money,* 22.

58. "Seizure of Southern Property in New York," *New Orleans Daily Crescent,* April 26, 1861.

59. The draft constitution called for "no encouragement to domestic industry." The final Constitution, in art. 1, sec. 8, para. 1 and 3, denied the Confederate government the ability to protect industries through bounties or tariffs and blocked the appropriation of money to facilitate commerce. See Wilson, *Confederate Industry,* 3–5; Rable, *Confederate Republic,* 57.

60. "Treasury Report to the Confederate House of Representatives, March 14, 1862," In Thian, *Reports of the Secretary of the Treasury,* 64.

61. Majewski, *Modernizing a Slave Economy,* 140–41.

62. Binnington, *Confederate Visions,* 71. A study of *Thompson's Banknote and Commercial Reporter,* July 15, 1857 (which contains descriptions of the banknotes in circulation at this time), shows that Massachusetts banknotes contained more images of cotton and black Americans than those printed by banks across Alabama, Georgia, Louisiana, South Carolina, and Virginia. Fricke, *Collecting Confederate*

Paper Money. In addition to vignettes identified in this study, Fricke identifies another twelve reused vignettes (including two portraits of virulent anti-Confederates), 148, 186, 200, 208, 232, 282, 285, 344, 354, 364, 404, 422. Mihm, *Nation of Counterfeiters,* 260–66.

63. Lengyel, "Pictures Frozen in Time," 1–21.

64. Todd, *Confederate Finance,* 95–98. See, e.g., C. H. Stevens to C. G. Memminger, Charleston, S.C., August 31, 1861; M. Richardson to C. G. Memminger, Savannah, Ga., September 7, 1861; and "Bank Note Plates Received from S. Schmidt," October 26, 1861, all in Thian, *Correspondence with the Treasury Department,* 303, 319–20, and 406, respectively.

65. Ball, *Financial Failure and Confederate Defeat,* 112–19.

66. C. G. Memminger to Messrs. Furman, Sass, and Robinson, September 1, 1861 in Thian, *Correspondence of the Treasury Department,* 183–84.

67. George Dunn to J. D. Pope, Columbia, S.C., August 19, 1862, in Thian, *Correspondence with the Treasury Department,* 600.

68. "Five Dollar Confederate Note," *Charleston Mercury,* December 24, 1861.

69. Francis Trevelyan Miller, "Inside Workings of Governments during Wars," *Richmond Times-Dispatch,* March 31, 1912.

70. "Treasury Notes," *Richmond Whig,* August 9, 1861.

71. "Confederate Treasury Notes," *Salisbury Carolina Watchman,* September 5, 1861, reprinted from *Petersburg Express.*

72. *Augusta Chronicle and Sentinel,* reprinted in "Confederate Notes," *Macon Telegraph,* September 18, 1862.

73. "Bank Notes," *Tuscaloosa Observer,* reprinted in *Memphis Appeal,* August 24, 1862.

74. Lauer, "Money as Mass Communication," 111.

75. Tremmel, *Guide Book of Counterfeit Confederate Currency,* 2–21.

76. "Arrivals at Charleston Hotels," *Charleston Courier,* July 7, 1862. John Gemmell, William George Embleton, George Henry Keeling, William Gellatly, and J. McFarland accompanied Dunn. See "The Bermuda," *United States Reports, Cases Adjudged in the Supreme Court,* vol. 70 U.S. 3 Wall, docket 514 (1865): 515–59.

77. George Dunn to Joseph D. Pope, Columbia, S.C., August 19, 1862; Christopher G. Memminger to Joseph D. Pope, Richmond, Va., August 13, 1862; Christopher G. Memminger to Joseph D. Pope, Richmond, Va., November 3, 1862, all in Thian, *Correspondence of the Treasury Department* 600, 336, and 380, respectively. Keatinge was born in Dublin, Ireland, around 1830. New York City directories indicate that he worked there at points between the 1850s and late 1870s. He married Harriette Charlotte Harned (who became one of America's earliest doctors) about 1860. Around October 1861, he moved from New York to the South and returned there after the war, probably in 1867. He died in Manhattan on June 9, 1882.

78. Joseph D. Pope and S. G. Jamison to C. G. Memminger, September 6, 1862; *and* C. G. Memminger to Joseph D. Pope, September 15, 1862, Both in Thian, *Correspondence of the Treasury Department,* 620–21 and 353, respectively.

79. Joseph D. Pope to C. G. Memminger, November 3, 1862; and Joseph D. Pope to C. G. Memminger, December 10, 1862, both in Thian, *Correspondence with the Treasury Department,* 663 and 679–80, respectively.

80. S. G. Jamison to Christopher G. Memminger, secretary of Treasury, Columbia, S.C., December

24 1862, and June 26, 1863, Sanders G. Jamison file, Confederate Papers Relating to the Citizens or Business Firms, (National Archives Microfilm Publication, M346, roll 500), RG109.

81. Ball, *Financial Failure*, 114, 116, 117; Ball, *Comprehensive Catalog and History*, 15.

82. "The New Issue," *Raleigh Daily Progress*, January 5, 1863.

83. "A New Note," *Richmond Enquirer*, December 20, 1862.

84. "Improvement in Confederate Bills," *Charleston Mercury*, December 8, 1862.

85. "Expert," "Lithography and Counterfeiting—The Bank Bill Printing of the Confederate States—Interesting Account of Lithography," *Richmond Dispatch*, October 10, 1862.

86. Dinnie, *National Branding*, 68–69.

87. C. G. Memminger, "Report to the House of Representatives," August 18, 1862, *Reports of the Secretary of the Treasury Department of the Confederate States of America, 1861–'65* (Washington, D.C., 1878), 76.

88. C. G. Memminger endorsement on Joseph D. Pope to C. G. Memminger, April 4, 1863, in Thian, *Correspondence with the Treasury Department*, 74–75.

89. "New Currency," *Wilmington Journal*, April 5, 1864.

90. Keatinge and Ball to C. G. Memminger, Columbia, S.C., November 25, 1863, Letters Received by the Confederate Adjutant and Inspector General's Office, (National Archives Microfilm Publication, M474, roll 68), RG109. Born in Virginia in early 1861, Hunton joined a company that mustered into the Sixth Virginia Cavalry Regiment. He was detailed to the Engineer Bureau as a draftsman in November 1862. By 1874, his mental health led to his commitment to Virginia's Western State Hospital.

91. "An Hour with the Money Makers," *Richmond Enquirer*, March 23, 1864. Versions of this article appeared in many Confederate newspapers.

92. S. G. Jamison to C. G. Memminger, December 3, 1863, In Thian, *Correspondence with the Treasury Department*, 249–51.

93. "The New Issue," *Macon Telegraph*, April 8, 1864.

94. "An Hour with the Money Makers," *Raleigh Mercury*, May 14, 1864. Macon's *Telegraph* prediction that they would be called "Red Faces" was incorrect. See "The New Issue," *Macon Telegraph*, April 8, 1864. Around this time, the report, first published in Savannah's *Republican*, appeared in numerous Georgia newspapers.

95. "The New Issue," *Richmond Enquirer*, reprinted in *Columbus Enquirer*, March 18, 1864.

96. "The Treasury Department," *Richmond Examiner*, reprinted in *Columbia South Carolinian*, June 23, 1864.

97. "Paper Money," *Smith and Barrow's Monthly Magazine*, reprinted in *Augusta Chronicle and Sentinel*, February 12, 1865.

98. "The New Currency," *Richmond Examiner*, April 6, 1864.

99. "The Two Currencies," *Tuscaloosa Weekly Observer*, August 13, 1862.

100. "The Courts," *Richmond Enquirer*, August 19, 1863.

101. "Lost," *Richmond Enquirer*, April 23, 1863.

102. Bates, *Early Republic and Antebellum America*, 2:673–75.

103. "Small Change," *Richmond Enquirer*, July 11, 1861.

104. "Shinplasters," *Selma Reporter*, February 19, 1862.

105. "Look Out for Them," *Asheville News*, reprinted in *Raleigh State Journal*, March 31, 1863.

106. "N.C. Money in South-Carolina," *Raleigh Weekly Standard*, March 18, 1863. At around the same

time, the publishers of the *Atlanta Southern Confederacy* announced they would take bills from regular banks or the state railroad. See "We Won't Take Them," *Atlanta Southern Confederacy,* February 20, 1863.

107. "Observer" to the Editor, Coosawhatchie, S.C., March 6, 1863, *Raleigh Weekly Standard,* March 18, 1863. See also "Capt., Co. D. 61st N.C.T., to the Editor, James Island, March 15, 1863," *Raleigh Semi-Weekly Standard,* March 20, 1863.

108. "The Richmond *Enquirer*," *Augusta Chronicle and Sentinel,* May 31, 1862. Although not mentioned, the Union force's presence on the fringes of the city probably also prompted nervousness.

109. "Hoarded Specie Coming Out," *Richmond Enquirer,* March 3, 1864.

110. "An Hour with the Money Makers," *Richmond Enquirer,* March 23, 1864.

111. "Confederate Postage Stamps," *Yorkville Enquirer,* July 4, 1861.

112. "Postage Stamps," *Richmond Examiner,* reprinted in *Nashville Republican Banner,* September 17, 1861. See also "Postal Complaints," *Fayetteville Observer,* September 26, 1861.

113. "Letter from Richmond, October 7, 1861," *New Orleans Picayune,* October 18, 1861.

114. "Hermes," "Our Richmond Correspondence, October 11, 1861," *Charleston Mercury,* October 15, 1861.

115. "What the Morning Journals Say," *New Orleans Delta,* November 12, 1861.

116. "Postage Stamps," *Richmond Whig,* October 29, 1861.

117. "Burine," "The Issue of Postage Stamps," *Charleston Mercury,* November 20, 1861.

118. "Dixie," "Correspondence, Richmond, November 13, 1861," *Memphis Appeal,* November 18, 1861.

119. "Confederate Postage Stamps," *Augusta Chronicle and Sentinel,* December 12, 1861.

120. "Post Office Accommodations," *Charleston Courier,* December 2, 1861; "Postage Stamps," *Charleston Mercury,* December 9, 1861.

121. "The Confederate Post Office Department," *Memphis Appeal,* January 26, 1862.

122. Procter, *Not without Honor,* 134–40; "Congress—Another Duty," *Atlanta Southern Confederacy,* January 18, 1863.

123. "Postage Stamps and Treasury Notes," *Richmond Dispatch,* December 31, 1861.

124. "The New Postage Stamp," *Richmond Examiner,* reprinted in *Montgomery Weekly Advertiser,* April 29, 1863.

125. "Mr. Clisby, March 29, 1864," *Macon Telegraph,* March 31, 1864.

126. "Improved Condition of Our Postage Revenues," *Richmond Sentinel,* reprinted in *Raleigh Weekly Register,* May 27, 1863. See also "Postmaster General's Report," *Richmond Sentinel,* November 23, 1864.

127. *Report of the Postmaster General, July 1, 1862–June 30, 1863,* Post Office Department, Richmond, Va., December 7, 1863, 14; *Report of the Postmaster General, July 1, 1863–June 30, 1864,* Post Office Department, Richmond, Va., November 7, 1864, 3.

128. "Paper Money," *Smith and Barrow's Monthly Magazine,* reprinted in *Augusta Chronicle and Sentinel,* February 12, 1865.

129. "Postage Stamps," *Raleigh Confederate,* November 6, 1864.

130. "Sumter," "From Richmond, September 28, 1861," *Charleston Courier,* October 2, 1861.

131. McPherson, *Embattled Rebel,* 62–64, 82, 138, 205, 218.

132. "Hermes," "Letter from Richmond, April 28, 1863," *Charleston Mercury,* May 2, 1863, reprinted in *Natchez Courier,* May 13, 1863; *Atlanta Southern Confederacy,* May 5, 1863.

133. McCurry, *Confederate Reckoning,* 133–35.

134. Escott, *Confederacy*, 23; Rable, *Confederate Republic*, 154, 155–60, 300–301.

135. "The New Flag of the Confederacy," *Charleston Mercury*, March 6, 1862.

CHAPTER 2

Nativism and Depictions of Race

1. Roediger, *Wages of Whiteness.*

2. Gould, *Mismeasure of Man*, 62–104, 391–424; Barczewski, *Myth and National Identity*, 125–30; Kramer, *Nationalism in Europe and America*, 115–24.

3. Luse, "Slavery's Champions Stood at Odds," 379–412; Rubin, *Shattered Nation*, 32–34; Bonner, "Roundheaded Cavaliers," 34–59; Watson, *Norman and Saxons;* Quigley, "Patchwork Nation," 170–71; Bernath, "Confederate Minds," 48–100; Jimerson, *Private Civil War*, 124–25; 127–28; Phillips, *Diehard Rebels*, 41, 46, 53–60, 154; Rable, *Damn Yankees.*

4. Quigley, *Shifting Ground*, 130–31, 139–40.

5. Banton, *Idea of Race*, 48.

6. Gould, *Mismeasure of Man*, 26.

7. Spencer, *Race and Ethnicity*, xiv–xix, 1–2. See also Ormi and Winant, *Racial Formation in the United States*, 6; Jacobson, *Whiteness of a Different Color;* Rees, *Shades of Difference*, 30–50.

8. Bonner, *Colors and Blood*, 45–54. Although Bonner identified four designs related to racial slavery, correspondence of the Flag and Seal Committee shows five concepts that alluded to it—from J.M.F. Gaston, February 19, 1861; William M. Brantley, February 28, 1861; R. C. Ketchum, February 16, 1861; and Mr. Platt (as described by "Carolinian"), February 17, 1861, all in Thian, *Documentary History of the Flag and Seal;* William Porcher Miles, "Report of the Flag and Seal Committee," March 4, 1861, Provisional Congress of the Confederate States, 1st Sess., in Thian, *Documentary History of the Flag and Seal*, 4–5.

9. "The New Confederate Flag," *Savannah Morning News*, April 28, 1863; "The New Flag," *Savannah Morning News*, May 4, 1863.

10. Rubin, *Shattered Nation*, 20–28, 88–94; Bernath, "Confederate Minds," 48–100; Quigley, "Patchwork Nation," 224–32; Phillips, "Peculiar Defeat," 78–79; Rable, *Damn Yankees!*, 11–13, 86–90.

11. Moore, "Southern Civilization,"1—19; Watson, *Norman and Saxons*, 135–40; Bonner, "Roundheaded Cavaliers," 38–39.

12. Bonner, "Roundheaded Cavaliers," 34–59; Frost, *Never One Nation*, 110.

13. Chesnut, "Destinies of the South," 181–82.

14. Warwick, *Nasology.* Phrenology, the study of personality through the morphology of the skull, was another offshoot of this pseudoscience. It was enormously popular during the nineteenth century.

15. "Fun for the Camp: A Comic Medley," *Augusta Chronicle and Sentinel*, May 16, 1863.

16. Warwick, *Nasology*, 218—19.

17. For other examples of this type of nose being used on Yankees, see *Dissolving Views of Richmond, Scene 4th* (Columbia, S.C.: Blanton Duncan, 1862); "Yankee Cavalry Sent to Intercept Gen. Stuart," *Southern Illustrated News*, November 15, 1862; "Change of Masters," *Southern Punch*, September 19, 1863; "Yankee Army Battlefield Correspondent on the Battle-field," *Southern Punch*, October 31, 1863; "Gen. McClellan, the 'Little Napoleon' of the Yankee Army," *Confederate Spirit and Knapsack of Fun*, February 1864; "An Applicant for Official Favor," *Southern Punch*, March 10, 1864; "Recognition," *Southern Illustrated News*, September 5, 1863.

18. Blanton Duncan to C. G. Memminger, May 26, 1862, Blanton Duncan Files: Confederate Citizens and Business Firms Files (National Archives Microfilm Publication, M346, roll 263), RG109.

19. Bonner, "Roundheaded Cavaliers," 51–59.

20. *Richmond Enquirer*, July 11, 1863, cited in Bonner, "Roundheaded Cavaliers," 51. See also "Nights on the Rapidan—Number III," *Southern Illustrated News*, March 12, 1864.

21. Phillips, *Diehard Rebels*, 41, 46, 53–60, 154; Binnington, *Confederate Visions*, 95, 101–8.

22. Burton, *Melting Pot Soldiers;* Mahin, *Blessed Place of Freedom.*

23. See, e.g., "The City of Richmond," *Raleigh State Journal*, May 24, 1862; "The Prospects of the War," *Richmond Dispatch*, October 13, 1863; "Why the Hessians Enlist," *Eatonton Countryman*, September 29, 1862; Rable, *Damn Yankees!*, 37–40.

24. Warwick, *Nasology*, 19.

25. Cowling, *Artist as Anthropologist*, 80–83.

26. Act 2, scene 1, of Delchamps, *Love's Ambuscade*, 27.

27. See also Hodgson, *Confederate Vivandiere;* playbill, John H. Hewitt, *Scouts; or, The Plains of Manassas*, Augusta Concert Hall, A. Waldron, lessee and manager, February 16, 1863; McPherson, *Is Blood Thicker than Water*, 57–61.

28. "The Baltimore American," *Richmond Whig*, April 10, 1863; Rable, *Damn Yankees!*, 70–73.

29. Jimerson, *Private Civil War*, 124–25, 127–28.

30. Quoted in Lonn, *Foreigners in the Confederacy*, 419–20.

31. "Our Irish Soldiery," *Mobile Advertiser and Register*, reprinted in *Knoxville Register*, October 9, 1863; "Justice to Our Foreign-Born Citizens," *Savannah Daily Morning News*, November 27, 1862.

32. Bright, "Nothing to Fear from the Influence of Foreigners," 89–107.

33. Rogoff, "Is the Jew White," 201, 203–6.

34. Rosen, *Jewish Confederates*, 265–75; Rable, *God's Almost Chosen People*, 253–55.

35. Evans, *Judah P. Benjamin*, 198–210; Wilson, *Confederate Industry*, 67–82.

36. "The Catholic Church," *Richmond Enquirer*, May 29, 1863.

37. Rosen, *Jewish Confederates;* Winner, "Taking Up the Cross," 194–98.

38. In January 1865, a most notable Confederate attempted to depart for the North—the vociferous anti-Semite and Tennessee Confederate congressman Henry S. Foote.

39. Warwick, *Nasology*, 156–57.

40. "Shameful Extortion," *Southern Illustrated News*, February 14, 1863; "Important Discovery," *Southern Punch*, February 13, 1864; "No. 12. Anathema to One Who Hoards," *Series of Comic Valentines* (Richmond, Va.: George Dunn, 1864); "Now Ready," *Augusta Constitutionalist*, February 5, 1864; "Valentines," *Richmond Whig*, February 4, 1864.

41. *Richmond Enquirer*, July 11, 1863. See also "Foreigners in the War," *Richmond Enquirer*, February 9, 1864; "Shameful Extortion," *Southern Illustrated News*, February 14, 1863; "A Capital Fit," *Southern Punch*, April 30, 1864.

42. Luse, "Slavery's Champions Stood at Odds," 380–407; Gould, *Mismeasure of Man*, 62–104; Fredrickson, *Black Image in the White Mind*, 71–96.

43. Frederickson, *Black Image in the White Mind*, 53–58, 102–8; Genovese, *Roll, Jordan, Roll*, 298–303.

44. Blassingame, *Slave Community*, 114, 116, 133–34.

45. Joseph-Virey, *Natural History of the Negro Race*, 25.

46. Woodward, "Marching Masters," 160–61.

47. Jordan, *Black Confederates and Afro-Yankees,* 55, 151.

48. Mahar, *Behind the Burnt Cork Mask,* 1–2; Waterhouse, "Internationalisation of American Popular Culture," 1–11; Toll, *Blacking Up,* 103–44; Nickels, *Civil War Humor,* 115–16. Nickels finds Northern representation of black Americans were more racist and vitriolic; Savage, *Standing Soldiers, Kneeling Slaves,* 11–14.

49. Faust, *Creation of Confederate Nationalism,* 65, 67, 69.

50. *Mobile Register and Advertiser,* July 25, 1861; *Richmond Dispatch,* October 26, 1861, January 27, 1862; *Milledgeville Southern Union,* November 10, 1861; *Natchez Courier,* July 30, 1862; *Richmond Enquirer,* October 17, 1862; *Chattanooga Rebel,* July 30, 1863; *Columbus Times,* March 7, 1864; *Richmond Whig,* December 2, 1864. These are a small sample of newspapers citing professional minstrel troupes in the South.

51. Wiley, *Life of Johnny Reb,* 165–66.

52. Jordan, *Black Confederates and Afro-Yankees,* 55, 151.

53. Nielsen, "Captive Audience,"43–58. Nielsen's in-depth study indicates the popularity of theatrical troupes, and especially comedies, among prisoners. For information on Point Lookout Prisoner of War Camp, see "Point Lookout Prisoner of War Camp," American Civil War website, http://www.mycivilwar.com/pow/md-point_lookout.htm . For information on racial tensions between Confederate prisoners and black guards, see Woodward, "Marching Masters," 231–33.

54. Mahar, *Behind the Burnt Cork Mask,* 39. For information on Point Lookout Prisoner of War Camp, see "Point Lookout Prisoner of War Camp," American Civil War website, http://www.mycivilwar.com/pow/md-point_lookout.htm. For information on racial tensions between Confederate prisoners and black guards, see Woodward, "Marching Masters," 231–33.

55. The endmen's titles come from the instruments they play—Bones plays the bones and Tambo the tambourine.

56. "Theatricals in the Army," Gregg's Brigade, April 16, 1864, East Tennessee, *Southern Illustrated News,* May 7, 1864. For other examples of minstrel shows in Confederate armies, see "Fitz Lee's Minstrels," *Southern Illustrated News,* March 28, 1863; "Brown's Battalion Minstrels," *Houston Tri-Weekly Telegraph,* July 4, 1862.

57. *Southern Punch,* September 19, 1863. Conscription ravaged the popular "Ironclad" troupe. Tim Morris was conscripted while performing onstage. In late April 1864, authorities apprehended four members of the Ironclads troupe who were trying to escape to Union lines. See "Recapture of an 'Ironclad,'" *Richmond Dispatch,* July 7, 1864; "Ironclads Captured," *Richmond Whig,* April 29, 1864. The "Olio Minstrels," who performed during 1864 and 1865, were an all-women troupe. See "Richmond Varieties," *Richmond Dispatch,* September 12, 1864; Jordan, *Black Confederates and Afro-Yankees,* 151.

58. "Great Slaughter at Vicksburg—What Cruelty in Grant. Letter from Jackson, Mississippi, May 24, 1863," *Atlanta Southern Confederacy,* June 1, 1863.

59. Woodward, *Marching Masters,* 166–67.

60. "The Policy of Employing Negroes as Soldiers in the Confederate Army," *Montgomery Weekly Mail,* September 2, 1863.

61. Richard Stoddard Ewell to his wife, Elizabeth, July 20, 1862, in Hamlin, *Making of a Soldier,* 113.

62. Durden, *Gray and the Black.*

63. Woodward, "Marching Masters," 304–5.

64. Quoted in Beringer et al., *Why the South Lost the Civil War,* 386–87.

65. Thomas, *Confederacy as a Revolutionary Experience,* 127–32.

66. Most of these troops were former hospital orderlies. The "Jackson Battalion," under acting assistant surgeon Major Henry C. Scott of the Third Division Hospitals, left on March 11, 1865, for the front, where, according to Scott, the troops "acted with the utmost promptness and good will." Two more "Negro" companies from Chimbarazo Hospital served in Major Jackson Chambliss's battalion, on March 19, 1865, carrying a Confederate battle flag. See Wallace, *Guide to Virginia Military Organizations,* 187; Channing, *Confederate Ordeal,* 166–67.

67. *Richmond Whig,* March 20, 1865.

68. Advertisement for "Bud and Buckley's Minstrels," *Richmond Dispatch,* March 31 and April 1, 1865; "Amusements in Richmond," *National Republican,* March 28, 1865.

69. Fitzhugh, "Sociology for the South," 43–45; Frederickson, *Black Image in the White Mind,* 53–56, 259; Cartwright, "Negro Freedom," 651.

70. Boskin, *Sambo,* 54–63; Cash, *Mind of the South,* 117.

71. Frederickson, *Black Image in the White Mind,* 142–45.

72. Dew, *Apostles of Disunion,* 77–79.

73. Genovese, *Roll, Jordan, Roll,* 32–34.

74. "Letter from Logan, Meridian, July 3, 1864," *Jackson Mississippian* (Selma, Ala.), July 6, 1864; "Negro Hanging," *Jackson Clarion* (Meridian, Miss.), July 8, 1864. According to the *Clarion,* this was not "the first or third" instance of the enslaved insulting white women, but it was the first in which the culprit could be positively identified. An article on the history of the "Lynch Law" appears directly under this report.

75. Thomas J. Key, diary entry, April 10, 1864, quoted in McPherson, *For Cause and Comrades,* 109; Woodward, *Marching Masters,* 38–39.

76. Manning, *What This Cruel War Was Over,* 36–39, 173–76.

77. "Death Recalls Famous Painting," *Matthews Journal,* January 4, 1912.

78. See William D. Washington, *The Burial of Latané,* 1864, oil on canvas, 38 × 48" (96.5 × 121.9 cm), Johnson Collection, Spartansburg, S.C., http://thejohnsoncollection.org/william-washington-the-burial-of-latane/.

79. "The Burial of Latane," *Richmond Enquirer,* October 25, 1864; "Burial of Latane," *Richmond Examiner,* November 12, 1864; "Burial of Latane," *Richmond Whig,* November 12, 1864. Born 1833/1834 at "Clayton," his family home in the Shenandoah Valley, William DeHartnett Washington trained in Europe and then worked in Washington, D.C., from 1856 to 1860. There he helped found the Washington Art Association. In 1861, he returned to Virginia and, due to infirmity, only served for a short period. Later he set up a studio in Richmond and became part of the city's literary circle. On the fall of Richmond, Washington traveled to Europe. In 1869, he returned to an appointment as head of Department of Fine Arts at the Virginia Military Institute. He died suddenly on December 1, 1870. See Stevenson, *Confederate Soldier Artists,* 63–73; De Leon, *Belles, Beaux and Brains,* 285–92; Neely et al., *Confederate Image.* ix–xiii.

80. Faust, "Race, Gender, and Confederate Nationalism," 155; Harvey, *Civil War and American Art,* 14–15.

81. "The Burial of Latane," *Richmond Enquirer,* October 25, 1864.

82. In most accounts, if they are mentioned, these figures are described as "faithful." See, e.g., John R. Thompson, "The Burial of Latane," *Southern Literary Messenger* 34, no. 8 (August 1862): 475–76; "Burial of Latane," *Richmond Whig,* November 12, 1864.

83. "The Burial of Latane," *Richmond Enquirer,* October 25, 1864.

84. Cowling, *Artist as Anthropologist*, 61–63.

85. Jenkins, *Pro-Slavery Thought*, 246–49; Frederickson, *Black Image in the White Mind*, 57–58.

86. Kaplan "Miscegenation Issue," 274–83.

87. "Theatrical," *Richmond Examiner*, April 15, 1864; Genovese, *Roll, Jordan Roll*, 413–31; Weiner, *Mistresses and Slaves*, 92–93, 95–99.

88. Entry, April 10, 1864, in Cate, *Two Soldiers*, 70.

89. For additional examples related to miscegenation, see "Boston Miscegenators Welcomes an Odorous Sister," *Southern Punch*, June 11, 1864.

90. Cowling, *Artist as Anthropologist*, 62, 81–84, 94–95, 115–16.

91. "Theatrical," *Richmond Examiner*, April 15, 1864.

92. *Southern Illustrated News*, April 28, 1864; Theatrical," *Richmond Examiner*, April 15, 1864.

93. *Southern Punch*, April 26, 1864; *Southern Illustrated News*, April 23 and 30, 1864. Both sides used stories of illicit sex between blacks and whites as propaganda showing the sexual depravity of the other side. See Hodes, *White Women, Black Men*, 132–33.

94. Elder produced an altered version of this work in 1869 that totally reworked the painting's left half.

95. First quotation: "Remember Fort Pillow," *Richmond Dispatch*, August 2, 1864. Second quotation: "Petersburg, July 30, 1864," *Richmond Dispatch*, August 1, 1864.

96. "Beautiful Paintings," *Richmond Whig*, March 12, 1865.

97. Bonner, "Roundheaded Cavaliers," 59; Bernath, *Confederate Minds*, 59; Rable, *Damn Yankees*, 13–14; Frost, *Never One Nation*, 110.

98. Manning, *What This Cruel War Was Over*, 172.

CHAPTER 3
The Southern Defense of Slavery

1.*Richmond Magnolia Weekly*, December 27, 1862; McCabe, *Guerrillas*, 3; Harwell, "Brief Candle," 134; Fife, "Theatre during the Confederacy," 337; "Concert Hall Theatre," *Augusta Constitutionalist*, July 23–28, 1864; "Theatre," *Macon Telegraph*, September 24, 1864; "Theatre," *Macon Telegraph*, December 12, 1864.

2. See Phillips, "Central Theme of Southern History," 30–43; Stampp, *Peculiar Institution;* Elkins, *Slavery;* Genovese, *World the Slaveholders Made*, 118–246; Faust, *James Henry Hammond and the Old South;* Faust, *Creation of Confederate Nationalism*, 58–81; Freehling, *Reintegration of American History;* Manning, *What This Cruel War Was Over.*

3. For studies of Confederate literature and writing regarding slavery, see Fahs, *Imagined Civil War*, 27–28, 181–89, 253–54; Hutchison, *Apples and Ashes*, 70–71, 84–86, 116–17; Bernath, *Confederate Minds*, 102–5, 192, 196, 223.

4. For studies of imagery of slavery, see: Clytus, "Envisioning Slavery"; Cutter, *Illustrated Slave;* Savage, *Standing Soldier*, 26–27, 31, 41–45; Binnington, *Confederate Visions*, 3, 74–85.

5. Woodward, *Marching Masters*, 23–24.

6. "Census Data for 1860," Historical Census Browser, University of Virginia Library, Charlottesville, http://fisher.lib.virginia.edu/collections/stats/histcensus/php/state.php. This data indicates that 277,790

slaveholders (those who owned one or more slaves) lived in states that became part of the Confederate States of America.

7. Woodward, *Marching Masters*, 49.

8. The 1860 census reports that only around seven hundred enslaved Americans were listed as runaways. See *Population of the United States Census in 1860*, vi–xi, http://www.census.gov/prod/www/abs/decennial/1860.htm; Franklin and Schweninger, *Runaway Slaves*, 279–82.

9. Thrasher, *Slavery*. In this twenty-two-page pamphlet, Thrasher compiled all references to slavery in the Bible to show God's approval of the system.

10. Dew, *Apostles of Disunion*, 55–65.

11. James F. White and J.W.W. Drake to President Jefferson Davis, Auburn, Macon County, Ala., July 13, 1861, In Thian, *Correspondence with the Treasury Department of the Confederate States*, 198.

12. "The Author," preface to *The Old Plantation—A Poem by "The Wanderer"* (Turnwold, Ga.: Countryman Print, 1862), 4.

13. Binnington, "They Have Made a Nation," 48–95.

14. Smith, *Address to the Citizens of Alabama*, 19. Smith discusses slavery on three of the address's twenty-four pages.

15. Davis, *Look Away*, 102–5.

16. "Great News—Bella Horrida Bella," *Jacksonville Republican*, June 6, 1861.

17. Gallagher, *Confederate War*, 46–49; Davis, *Look Away*, 85–112. For example, George Bagby, the editor of *Southern Literary Messenger*, described the "Southern Cross" as the flag of the "Southern master and his African slave." See Bagby, "Editor's Table," *Southern Literary Messenger* 34, no. 1 (January 1862): 68.

18. Binnington, *Confederate Visions*, 3–4, 82–82. See also Binnington, "They Have Made a Nation," 11–12, 14, 99–100.

19. Chapman's extant wartime output consists of over thirty works, six of which include depictions of black people. William D. Washington produced around six works, two of which, *The Burial of Latané* (1864) and *Stonewall Jackson's Entry into Winchester* (ca. 1863), include black figures. John A. Elder is known to have painted at least five works, one of which, *J.E.B. Stuart and His Staff* (1863), includes an enslaved man. In addition, black Federal troops figured prominently in his *Battle of the Crater* (1865).

20. "Gamma," "Our Richmond Correspondence, January 1, 1864," *Mobile Advertiser and Register*, January 12, 1864. The report names one work, a sketch of Battery Beauregard, the oil version of which included enslaved men at work. Described as "really beautiful," the other works, "scenes in and around Charleston," included "the big gun [a Blakeley rifle] as it appeared . . . Fort Sumter . . . and the battery inside it—the cigar boat . . . Battery Beauregard and many other batteries."

21. Woodward, *Marching Masters*, 132, 143, 241; Hutchison, *Apples and Ashes*, 83–85. There is only one other instance of black people laboring in the foreground present in extant Chapman works: *Battery Marshall, Sullivan's Island, Dec. 4, 1863* (1864). Two works contain black figures holding horses: *Battery Bee, December 3, 1863*, and *White Point Battery, Charleston, December 24, 1863*. In both, however, the mounts are settled. Other works include groups of black laborers in the distance: the sketch and finished work for *White Point Battery, Charleston, December 24, 1863* (1864); *Battery Beauregard, November 22, 1863* (1864); and, *Fort Moultrie, November 11, 1863* (1864).

22. While the skin color of these figures is difficult to make out in the etching, Chapman repainted the work in 1867. In the collection of Amon Carter Museum of American Art, Fort Worth, Tex., the later work shows that Chapman painted these figures with dark-brown skin.

23. "Editorial Correspondence of the Courier," *Charleston Courier,* June 28, 1862; "Nellie Norton, or, Southern Slavery and the Bible," *Macon Telegraph,* January 13, 1864; Hutchison, *Apples and Ashes,* 53–55. The reclining black figure also appears in Chapman's *Camp of the Third Kentucky Confederate Infantry at Corinth, Mississippi* (ca. 1864). Similar to the *Fifty-Ninth Virginia* works, Chapman produced at least three versions of this scene. In the initial sketch, in the Richmond History Center collection, Chapman included only soldiers. The subsequent versions—one sold by Sotheby's New York, November 20, 2014, and the other brought to notice by Howard Holzer in a *Civil War Times Illustrated* article (34, no. 6 [February 1996]: 18)—both feature the reclining figure. Resting slaves also appear in his *Baggage Train Watering at a Stream* (ca. 1863–64), *Battery Haskel, March 4, 1864* (1864), and *Fort Sumter from Moultrie, Nov. 10, 1863* (1864).

24. Tise, *Proslavery.* Tise shows how this raft of ideas developed across America and was entrenched by 1860; see 3–11, 261–62, 356–62. Over the 1850s, this ideology entered more powerfully into popular culture through vehicles such as literature and banknote vignettes. Literature, such as Charles Jacobs Peterson, *The Cabin and Parlor; or, Slaves and Masters* (1852); Caroline E. Rush, *The North and the South; or, Slavery and Its Contrasts* (1852); and Caroline Lee Hentz, *The Planter's Northern Bride* (1854), presented sentimental and quixotic ideas of slavery. Studying prewar banknotes, Richard G. Doty found a pronounced increase in the amount, originality, and topicality of slavery-related imagery. See Doty, "The Color of Money: Background and Commentary," in Jones and Barbatsis, *Confederate Currency,* 41–43.

25. See Jordan, *Black Confederates and Afro-Yankees in the Civil War,* 218–19, 23; *Petersburg Express,* April 26, 1861, *Memphis Avalanche,* September 3, 1861; *Official Records of the Union and Confederate Armies in the War of Rebellion,* Washington, D.C.: Government Printing Office, 1880–1901, ser. 1, 6, 858; and "Act to Raise a Provisional Army of Tennessee," *Nashville Republican Banner,* June 7, 1861.

26. Wiley, *Southern Negroes,* 134; Yetman, *Voices from Slavery,* 99, 148, 165, 174, 181, 197, 202, 223, 230, 244, 260, 276.

27. Martin Jackson, quoted in Yetman, *Voices from Slavery,* 173. Martin was a member of Buchel's First Texas Cavalry Regiment.

28. Clytus, "Envisioning Slavery"; Cutter, *Illustrated Slave.*

29. Fitzhugh, "Times and the War," 12.

30. Fitzhugh, "Slavery for the South," 34–50.

31. Vlach, *Back of the Big House,* 15, 43, 44.

32. Nott "Natural History of the Caucasian and Negro Race," 227–28; Simms, "Morals of Slavery," 641–57.

33. Berry, *Slavery and Abolitionism,* 32–35.

34. Doty, *Pictures from a Distant Country,* 77–90. Doty finds the number of depictions of slavery ballooned after 1850. Doty sees a relationship between the growing tensions about slavery. However, the increase also coincided with a growth in the profits slave owners received for the goods their slaves produced.

35. Blanton Duncan to Christopher G. Memminger, May 21, 1862, "Enclosure #2," in Blanton Duncan file, *Confederate Papers Relating to Confederate Citizens or Business Firms,* (National Archives Microfilm Publication, M347, roll 263) RG109. During May 1862, Duncan, a thirty-six-year-old wealthy slaveholding Kentuckian, was engaged in an attempt to monopolize the Confederacy's security printing business.

36. In addition to the original that hangs in the U.S. Senate, White produced a number of versions

that appeared on numerous antebellum banknotes. "General Marion Inviting a British Officer to Share His Meal," *United States Senate Catalogue of Fine Arts*, http://www.gpoaccess.gov/serialset/cdocuments/sd107–11/pdf/268–271.pdf, included in the 1837 exhibition of the National Academy, New York, under the title "General Marion's Swamp Encampment," "Editor's Table," *Knickerbocker* 9, no. 6 (June 1837): 621; "Marion's Swamp Encampment," *Charleston Courier*, July 18, 1842; "General Marion Inviting a British Officer to Dinner," plates V-40165 and 46365, American Bank Note Archives, http://www.liveauctioneers.com/item/3011509 and https://www.liveauctioneers.com/item/3011510_1934-sweet-potato-dinner-proof-vignette-used-on-confed.

37. Frederickson, *Black Image in the White Mind*, 55–56. In proslavery thought, the "ideal slave" was seen as a high type of domesticated animal. Stories of loyal slaves received wide publication in Confederate newspapers. See "A Faithful Slave," *Richmond Dispatch*, August 2, 1861; "Fidelity of Some of Our Slaves," *Richmond Whig*, August 17, 1861.

38. "Group of Four Significant Die Proofs Related to the Civil War," Smillie Family Archives, Heritage Capital Corporation, https://currency.ha.com/itm/miscellaneous/group-of-four-significant-die-proofs-related-to-the-civil-war/a/3529–18415.s?ic4=GalleryView-Thumbnail-071515 .

39. Mihm, *Nation of Counterfeiters*, 12–14. Mihms discusses the relationship between confidence and worth of notes. Richard G. Doty, "The Color of Money: Background and Discussion," in Jones and Barbatsis, *Confederate Currency*, 42–43.

40. Woodward, "Marching Masters," 147–50.

41. Some sources suggest higher amounts—e.g., Jones, *Confederate Currency*. Artist John Jones identified around 122 Southern banknotes, from before to after the war, that depicted slavery. He used these as the basis for the 83 paintings depicting slavery that formed this exhibition. However, examining Gwynne and Day's *Descriptive Register of Genuine Banknotes* (1860) indicates that black people are identified in 47 vignettes (5.5%) carried on 41 of the 851 notes circulated by Southern banks. Additionally, states such as Massachusetts and Michigan also featured black people working.

42. The vignette of loading cotton on the T-13 Hoyer and Ludwig one hundred–dollar note is assumed to show black people working—but even at magnification, their ethnicity is not clear.

43. Slabaugh, *Confederate States Paper Money*. This work catalogs all money printed in the South during the war. Of the 282 different banknotes circulated by the States of the Confederacy, only 17 (6.3%) included images of black people. Exact figures for individual banks are not available, but examination of available samples suggests that black people appeared in a similar share as on Confederate and state notes.

44. Fahs, *Imagined Civil War*, 181–86.

45. Genovese, *Roll, Jordan Roll*, 72–75, 91. In his January 10, 1838, speech to the United States Congress, John C. Calhoun spoke of the "harmony" between action, labor, and capital that existed in slavery. See Calhoun "Speech on the Importance of Domestic Slavery," in McKitrick, *Slavery Defended*, 18–19.

46. Cited in Genovese, *Roll, Jordan, Roll*, 97–98. Thomas Roderick Dew, "Abolition of Negro Slavery" (1832), in Faust, *Ideology of Slavery*, 65–66. Joyner, *Down by the Riverside*, 231.

47. Fahs, *Imagined Civil War*, 181–86.

48. Faust, *Creation of Confederate Nationalism*, 63

49. Watson, *History of Southern Drama*, 82–84. James Dabney McCabe (1842–83) began writing *during* the Civil War and continued into the postbellum period. In 1869, McCabe considered *The Guerrillas* as among his "literary sins." See Davidson, *Living Writers of the South*, 346. Other "faithful slave"

characters include Joe in G. W. Alexander's *Virginia Cavalier* (see "Amusements," *Richmond Enquirer*, March 18 and May 18, 1863, February 24, 1864); Zeke in James D. McCabe's *Partisan Rangers; or, The Bushwacker* (see *Richmond Dispatch*, November 11, 1862); Napoleon Jackson in John Davis's *Roll of the Drum* (see "Athenaeum," *Atlanta Southern Confederacy*, April 30, 1863; "Theatre," *Augusta Constitutionalist*, February 14, 1863—in the show, the character sang the song "The Noble Flag That Bears the Southern Star," "Athenaeum," *Atlanta Southern Confederacy*, May 5, 1863); Jim Brown, "intelligent contraband," and Nelly, "a negro woman," in James D. McCabe's *Maiden's Vow; or, The Capture of Courtland*, *Richmond Dispatch*, April 15, 1863; *Charnel House*, *Southern Illustrated News*, April 25, 1863). Iline Fife also identifies Sable in J. H. Hewitt's *Vivandiere* and Uncle Abe in *The Scouts*. Additionally, Joe and Aunt Sarah in *Great Expectations*, and Ned and Brutus in *Major Jones' Courtship*. See "The Theatre during the Confederacy," 58, 249, 340, 440. In addition, there are a number of performances that may have included the trope of the faithful slave. Dr. Bircher's 1864 work *Parlor and Cabin* included cast and story line that led the April 30, 1864, *Southern Punch* to describe it as a "sterling" play "in defense of southern institutions and character" and "stinging satire on Yankee philanthropy of Beecher Stowe and Greeley." Early in 1861, a work entitled *The Great Southern Drama of Parlor and Cabin*, described as "a thorough vindication of Southern institutions," played in Richmond. See "How the War Began in This City," *Richmond Times-Dispatch*, April 9, 1911. *Miscegenation* featured Sam, "a Virginia Negro," whose participation in a "congenial" "grand plantation festival" indicated the superiority of the Southern system. See "Miscegenation in the Theatre," *Richmond Whig*, April 15, 1864. There was also Dinah in *Slasher and Crasher*. See *Richmond Dispatch*, November 22, 1864. Lee Mallory's *Pantechoptomon* featured the character of Asa. This is suggested by language and scenes listed in an existing synopsis, which describes the character "totin" wood, trying "Massa's gun," capturing a "contraband porker," discovering a Yankee expedition, engaging in a fistfight with a Yankee, capturing a Yankee in the Manassas rout before setting off after another. See "Pantechoptomon," *New Orleans Picayune*, December 7, 1861; "The War Illustrations," *New Orleans Delta*, December 18, 1861.

50. *Richmond Magnolia Weekly*, December 22, 1862; *Southern Literary Messenger* 35 (March 1863): 192; Harwell, *Confederate Belle-Lettres*, 23; Campbell, "Theater," 4:1589–90.

51. *Southern Illustrated News*, December 27, 1862. In the premiere performance, stage manager J. W. Thorpe played the role of Jerry. The *News* correspondent lamented that the capable stage manager Thorpe proved "unable to delineate negro character in proper style."

52. See announcement, "Concert Hall, A. Waldron lessee & manager . . . Monday evening, Feb'y 16th 1863," Emory University, Parrish and Willingham, in *Confederate Imprints*, 6620.

53. Variously named Joe, Jim, or Alexander Folkes, this figure was a "principal character" in G. W. Alexander's "Virginia Cavalier." See "Amusements," *Richmond Enquirer*, March 18 and May 18, 1863, and February 24, 1864.

54. *Great Expectations*, 8–9.

55. Harwell, "Brief Candle," 41–42, 44–45; Fife, "Theatre during the Confederacy," 202–4, 245, 274, 316, 368.

56. "Statistics of Georgia," *Richmond Whig*, November 4, 1864. As documented in a report of Georgia Baptists in the same paper, some Southerners worried that slave marriages were not respected. See James Henry Hammond, "Letter to an English Abolitionist" (1845), in Faust, *Ideology of Slavery*, 165–67, 173–76.

57. Frederickson, *Black Image in the White Mind*, 54, 56.

58. See Beegan, "Mechanization of the Image," 257—74. The historical record contradicts the impression that life was harmonious. See Ripley, *Slaves and Free Men in Civil War Louisiana*, 28–29, 42, 68.

59. Frederickson, *Black Image in the White Mind*, 54–56.

60. "The President's Message," *Richmond Whig*, November 9, 1864.

61. Wiley, *Southern Negroes*, 166–67; Faust, *Creation of Confederate Nationalism*, 61–75.

62. Beringer et al., *Why the South Lost the Civil War*, 337–67; Stampp, "The Southern Road to Appomattox," 11, 251–52, 255.

63. Faust, *Creation of Confederate Nationalism*, 56–62, 71–72; Woodward, "Marching Masters," 147–50. See also Davis, *Look Away*, 153; Ayres, *In the Presence of Mine Enemies*, 370–71, 373–74.

64. Freehling, *Reintegration of American History*, 231.

65. Examination of diaries and newspapers in Richmond, Va., for this period have failed to disclose an incident resembling this one.

66. For information on this untruth, see Richard Colfax, *Evidence against the Views of the Abolitionists, Consisting of Physical and Moral Proofs of the Natural Inferiority of the Negroes* (1833), cited in Fredrickson, *Black Image in the White Mind*, 49–50.

67. Cowling, *Artist as Anthropologist*, 79–86.

68. George Fitzhugh, "Sociology for the South," reprinted in McKitrick, *Slavery Defended*, 43–44.

69. Aptheker, *American Negro Slave Revolts*, 350–68; Stampp, *Peculiar Institution*, 130–40.

70. Joyner, *Down by the Riverside*, 104, 109, 110–14.

71. Genovese, *Roll, Jordan, Roll*, 499–512, 613–15.

72. Thomas, *Confederacy as a Revolutionary Experience*, 117–23.

73. "Murder," *Mobile Evening News*, reprinted in *Jackson (Selma, Ala.) Mississippian*, June 22, 1864. See also "Negro Sentenced to Be Hanged in Hanover," *Richmond Examiner*, September 3, 1864; "Richmond County Superior Court," *Augusta Chronicle and Sentinel*, October 29, 1863; Woodward, *Marching Masters*, 131, 146.

74. Ashworth, *Slavery, Capitalism, and Politics*, 1:1–4; Wiley, *Southern Negroes*, 175; Nolan, *Benjamin Franklin Butler*, 100–103.

75. Glathaar, "Black Glory," 142.

76. Historians estimate the number of enslaved people who ran away at anywhere between 200,000 and one million. See Woodward, "Marching Masters," 160–61. For examples of the handful of slaves who returned, see Wiley, *Southern Negroes*, 12, 230–32, 237–38; Jordan, *Black Confederates and Afro-Yankees*, 227–28; Vlach, *Back of the Big House*, ix–xi, 14–16.

77. Genovese, *Roll, Jordan, Roll*, 152–53.

78. Greenberg, *Honor and Slavery*, 48–49; Woodward, "Marching Masters," 134–38.

79. Genovese, *Roll, Jordan, Roll*, 452–55.

80. J. G. Richards (lyrics) and Charles L. Ward (music), "I'm Coming to My Dixie Home" (Louisville: D. P. Faulds, 1861), Wade Hall Collection of Southern History and Culture, William Stanley Hoole Special Collection Library, University of Alabama Libraries, Tuscaloosa. "We Have Received," *New Orleans Picayune*, April 18, 1861.

81. "Advertisements," *Macon Telegraph*, January 20, 1862.

82. Born in Strasbourg, Austria, in either 1803 or 1806 and educated in Paris, Wissler immigrated to America in 1849. 1861 found him employed by a New York printing company, who dispatched him and his family to Richmond, Va. A loyal Unionist when war started, he found employment, and virtual

imprisonment, designing and creating vignettes for many Confederate bonds and banknotes and commercial work. Initially, he worked as an "artist" for Hoyer and Ludwig and later worked for Blanton Duncan. After the war, the wealth he accrued from this work enabled him to purchase a farm in Macon, Miss. Later he returned North and took up residence and engraving in Camden, N.J., until his death on November 25, 1887. "Wissler—the Engraver for the Confederacy," *Wilson (North Carolina) Mirror,* December 7, 1887.

83. Davis, *Look Away,* 151–53. See, e.g., "The Negroes of Richmond," *Southern Punch,* August 29, 1864.

84. Woodward, *Marching Masters,* 128–29, 143–44, 152–55.

85. "Our New Masthead," *Southern Illustrated News,* January 14, 1865.

86. Born June 22, 1834, Torsch worked as a wood engraver in Baltimore for most of his life. In 1861 he slipped through Confederate lines and, though a soldier, became a leading engraver for the *Southern Illustrated News* up to January 1865. After the war, he served as a governor of the Maryland Confederate Soldier's Home. He was buried October 1, 1898, at Loudon Park Cemetery, Baltimore. See "Torsch, the Engraver," *Orange Court House Native,* June 5, 1868; "John W. Torsch," in Johnson, *Confederate Military History Extended Edition,* vol. 2: *Maryland,* 423–24; *Southern Illustrated News,* January 14, 1865.

87. Hutchison, *Apples and Ashes,* 84–85, 116–17; Bernath, *Confederate Minds,* 102–5. Bernath indicates that Confederates became less strident but more nuanced in their defense of slavery.

88. Cited in Gallagher, *Confederate War,* 23; Aptheker, *American Negro Slave Revolts,* 268; Blight, *Race and Reunion,* 208.

89. Genovese, *Roll, Jordan, Roll,* 97–98.

CHAPTER 4
Manufacturing and Southern Autonomy

1. *Manufactures of the United States in 1860,* 729, http://www2.census.gov/prod2/decennial/documents/1860c-01.pdf; McPherson, *Battle Cry of Freedom,* 9.

2. Majewski, *Modernizing a Slave Economy.* Majewski's study of the economies and economic ideologies of Civil War era Virginia and South Carolina shows that among contending ideas, many Southerners imagined a more than agricultural nation. Morgan, "Public Nature of Private Industry," 27–46; Wilson, *Confederate Industry;* Collins, "System in the South," 517–44; DeCredico, *Patriotism for Profit;* Bensel, "Southern Leviathan," 68–136; Luraghi, *Rise and Fall of the Plantation South,* 123–29; Thomas, *Confederacy as a Revolutionary Experience,* 134; Thomas, *Confederate Nation,* 212; Beringer et al., *Why the South Lost the Civil War,* 8–10; Goff, *Confederate Supply;* Dew, *Ironmaker to the Confederacy;* Vandiver, *Ploughshares into Swords;* Ramsdell, *Behind the Lines in the Southern Confederacy;* Ramsdell, "Control of Manufacturing by the Confederate Government," 231–49.

3. Bonner, *Confederate Political Economy,* 64–100.

4. Bonner, *Confederate Political Economy,* 126.

5. *Manufactures of the United States in 1860;* Cash, *Mind of the South,* 59–103; Bertelson, *Lazy South;* McPherson, *Battle Cry of Freedom,* 194–97; Springfellow, "Statistical View of Slavery," 536–46.

6. "Object of the War," *Richmond Dispatch,* May 3, 1861; "Letter from Lebanon, Virginia," Thomas C. M. Alderson to "Brother James," December 14, 1858, *Alderson Roots and Branches,* 6 (Decem-

ber 1994): 21–22, http://www.fridley.net/arb/arbv6n2.pdf; "Federal Falsehood and a Doctorate of Lying," *Southern Illustrated News*, March 13, 1863; "The Fall of Plymouth—A Specimen of Yankee Lying," *Raleigh Confederate*, May 2, 1864; "A South Carolinian," *Confederate*, 2, 8–21, 47–48, 54–59; "Yankee Lies," *Richmond Whig*, May 16, 1862. Southerners interwove these ideas with those that imagined Northerners as descendants of Puritans. See Watson, *Normans and Saxons*, 81–82.

7. "The Valley Mountain Fight," *Macon Weekly Telegraph*, December 20, 1861.

8. Quigley, *Shifting Grounds*, 64–65; Rable, *Damn Yankees*, 85–86. See also Fitzhugh, *Sociology for the South*, 226–58; "The W. B.," *Montgomery Weekly Mail*, December 31, 1862; "Independence," *Staunton Spectator*, February 16, 1864.

9. "F.Y.C.," "A Protective System Necessary," *Southern Monthly* 1 (February 1862): 406.

10. "Extortion by Southern Manufacturers," *Raleigh Semi-Weekly Register*, November 13, 1861.

11. Fox-Genovese and Genovese, *Mind of the Master Class*, 11–12, 138–37,146, 343, 672, 695; Genovese, *Political Economy of Slavery*, 21–22; Wright, *Political Economy of the Cotton South;* Bateman and Weiss, *Deplorable Scarcity;* Lebergott, "Why the South Lost," 58–74. Other writers to study Confederate manufacturing and supply discuss the mechanics. See also Ramsdell, *Behind the Lines in the Southern Confederacy;* Massey, *Ersatz in the Confederacy;* Goff, *Confederate Supply.*

12. Russell, *My Diary North and South*, 1:258–59.

13. Watson, *Normans and Saxons*, 73; "Free Trade vs. Protection," *Charleston Mercury*, April 9, 1862.

14. Potter, *Impending Crisis*, 456–57; Freehling, *Road to Disunion*, 19–22.

15. Art. 1, sec. 8, Constitution of the Confederate States of America, published in *Confederate Military History*, 374; Ball, *Financial Failure and Confederate Defeat*, 201–2.

16. From the *Lynchburg Virginian*, quoted in Current, "God and the Strongest Battalions," 15–16.

17. Franklin, *Militant South*, 231–36. Franklin indicates the push by Southern politicians for the increased armaments manufacturing.

18. "Georgia Cassimeres," *Columbus Sun*, November 15, 1860.

19. "Perote Guard," *Macon Telegraph*, February 18, 1860. See also Todd, "Notes on the Organization and Uniforms," 60. See also "Armed Men and Armaments of Natchez," *Concordia Intelligencer*, January 11, 1861; "Daniel Pratt to N. J. Fogarty and Others, February 1860," *Prattville Autauga Citizen*, February 23, 1860. While praising the popular movement, Pratt laments that manufacturers had "never received that encouragement that was due them." "Southern Orders," *Richmond Dispatch*, reprinted in *Prattville Autauga Citizen*, February 23, 1860.

20. Jones, *Agricultural Resources of Georgia*, 11.

21. Genovese, *Political Economy of Slavery*, 180–92; Wilson, *Confederate Industry*, xiii–xix, 17–18; McPherson, *Battle Cry of Freedom*, 94–100; Gregg, "Southern Patronage to Southern Imports and Domestic Industry," 102–4; Goldfarb, "Laws Governing the Incorporation of Manufacturing Companies," 415–16; Carlander and Majewski, "Imagining," 343–44.

22. "Company Uniforms," *Raleigh North Carolina Standard*, May 1, 1861.

23. "Good Advice for the South," *Augusta Chronicle and Sentinel*, May 29, 1861.

24. This was not a new idea. Since the late 1840s, James H. Hammond advocated the diversification of the Southern economy. History, he wrote, showed that "purely agricultural people have in all ages been the victims of rapacious tyrants." See Faust, *James Henry Hammond and the Old South*, 274–76.

25. "How to Help the Army," *Baton Rouge Advocate*, May 17, 1861. See also "We Must Develop Southern Industry," 497–99.

26. "Self-Dependence in Nations and in Individuals—International Law," *Southern Monthly* 2 (May 1862): 76.

27. Genovese, *Roll, Jordan, Roll*, 7–25; "Home Made Letter Paper," *New Orleans Picayune*, reprinted in *Augusta Constitutionalist*, October 3, 1861; *Memphis Appeal*, October 12, 1861; William Delony, "The Poverty of the South. Clinton, Louisiana, December 1861," *Southern Monthly* 2 (February 1862): 25–27. See, e.g., *Vicksburg Whig*, January 18, 1860; "Southern Industry," *Montgomery Advertiser*, May 12, 1864; "Benefits of the War," *Charleston Mercury*, December 6, 1861. For an opposing view, see "Southern Manufactures," *Lynchburg Virginian*, October 10, 1861.

28. "S.L.W.," "Letter from Virginia, November 10, 1861," *Memphis Appeal*, November 19, 1861. The apparent author, a twenty-one-year-old printer Solon L. Whittington, hoped for a war that would last long enough for total independence from the North. Killed in action at Chancellorsville, his service records indicate a young man of promise. See U.S. 1860 Federal Census, Mississippi, Marshall County, Ward 1, Holly Springs City, 5; Solon L. Whittington files, Seventeenth Infantry Regiment, Compiled Service Records of Confederate Soldiers Who Served in Organizations from the State of Mississippi (National Archives Microfilm Publication, M269, roll 262), RG109.

29. "The South a Yankee Colony!" *Richmond Dispatch*, August 13, 1861. See also Jay Carlander and John D. Majewski, "Imagining 'A Great Manufacturing Empire': Virginia and the Possibilities of Confederate Tariffs," *Civil War History* 49, no. 4 (2003): 343–44; *Natchez Courier*, October 19, 1861; "The Importance of Manufacturing Labor," *Richmond Dispatch*, March 28, 1862. See also "Letter from Richmond, November 8, 1861," *New Orleans Picayune*, November 16, 1861; *Macon Georgia Weekly Telegraph*, March 21, 1862; "Our Own Manufactures," *Augusta Chronicle and Sentinel*, June 19, 1861; *Milledgeville Confederate Union*, August 22, 1863; J.D.B. [James DeBow], "Notes of the War," *Charleston Mercury*, August 16, 1861; "Manufactures," *Galveston Weekly News*, June 24, 1863.

30. "Georgia Made Lager Beer," *Savannah Republican*, May 27, 1861; "Confederate Tea Ware," *Mobile Advertiser and Register*, September 11, 1861; "Charleston Made Matches," *Charleston Mercury*, September 11, 1861; "Palmetto Button Manufactory," *Charleston Mercury*, September 19, 1861; "A New Style of Letter Envelope," *Natchez Courier*, October 18, 1861; "Candle Manufactory," *Natchez Courier*, October 25, 1861; "Manufacture of Domestic Implements," *Natchez Courier*, December 6, 1861. For summaries of developments across the South, see also "What We Are Gaining by the War," *DeBow's Review* 32 (January–February 1862): 158–60; "What We Are Gaining by the War," *DeBow's Review* 32 (March–April 1862): 327–33.

31. "The Manufacture of Wooden Shoes," *Charleston Mercury*, January 4, 1862; "Lampblack Manufactory," *Charleston Mercury*, April 12, 1862; "A New Oil," *Charleston Mercury*, July 22, 1862; "Manufacture of Soap," *Charleston Mercury*, August 16, 1862; "Confederate Manufactured Writing Paper," *Mobile Advertiser and Register*, September 10, 1862; "Richmond, September 16, 1862," *Charleston Mercury*, September 20, 1862; "Black Lead Pencils," *Jackson (Selma, Ala.) Mississippian*, June 15, 1864.

32. *Macon Weekly Telegraph*, March 21, 1862; "The Benefits of War," *Charleston Mercury*, December 6, 1861; "Rifled Cannon—Southern Manufacture," *Charleston Tri-Weekly Courier*, August 13, 1861; "A New and Useful Article," *Augusta Constitutionalist*, December 11, 1861. See also "The War and the Manufacturing Interests of the South," *Charleston Mercury*, April 29, 1862.

33. "C. W. Brunner—Macon Button Factory," *Savannah Republican*, May 14, 1863. Brunner created machinery capable of making between thirty and forty thousand buttons or bone, wood or horn, per day. The *Republican* "appreciated the value of this enterprise" as a cheaper alternative to blockade goods. See "C. W. Brunner—Macon Bone; Wooden and Horn Buttons," *Savannah Morning News*, May 1, 1863.

34. *Macon Weekly Telegraph*, August 8, 1862. See also "Southern Oil Company," *New Orleans Daily Crescent*, June 17, 1861.

35. Fuller and Steuart, *Firearms of the Confederacy*, 284–87; Albaugh et al., *Confederate Handguns*, 23–38.

36. Walter Hodgkins to Captain Richard S. Cuyler, July 16, 1862, chap. 4, vol. 36, "Letters Received by Capt. Richard M. Cuyler, Ordnance Officer at Savannah and Macon, Georgia, April–June 1862," Confederate Ordnance Bureau Records, RG109, NAB.

37. Lieutenant R. Milton Gary to Captain Richard S. Cuyler, C.S. Arsenal, Belona, Va., chap. 4, vol. 4, "Letters Received, Macon (Georgia) Armory, July–September 1862," Confederate Ordnance Bureau Records, RG109, NAB.

38. Albaugh et al., *Confederate Handguns*, 30. Examining the smoldering remains of his township in November 1864, the seventy-five-year-old Griswold said, "If I were ten years younger I would start again." He died in September 1867.

39. "The New Orleans Rifle Factory," *New Orleans Bee*, August 5, 1861.

40. "Memphis Manufacture," *Memphis Appeal*, December 8, 1861. Leech and Rigdon used Colt's revolvers as a measure of their pistols' quality. See Leech and Rigdon to General John Pemberton, November 26 1862, Confederate Papers Relating to the Citizens or Business Firms (National Archives Microfilm Publication, M346, roll 579), RG109. See also "What Is Macon Doing," *Macon Weekly Telegraph*, February 7, 1862.

41. Rainer, " 'Sharp' Image," 102–5.

42. "Yankee and European Manufactures," *Richmond Dispatch*, August 17, 1863; "Chemical Writing Fluid," *New Orleans Picayune*, November 11, 1861; *Natchez Courier*, October 19, 1861; "F.Y.C.," "A Protective System Necessary," *Southern Monthly* 1 (February 1862): 407.

43. "City Intelligence—The Crenshaw Woollen Mill," *Richmond Enquirer*, October 17, 1861.

44. See, e.g., "The Military Resources of the South," *Richmond Examiner*, reprinted in *Raleigh Weekly Register*, May 27, 1863; "Independence," *Richmond Whig*, February 13, 1864; "Little Steps towards Southern Independence," *Augusta Constitutionalist*, May 28, 1864; "A Novelty—Home Manufactured Ice," *Augusta Constitutionalist*, June 28, 1864; "What the South Has Accomplished," "Our Future," *Macon Telegraph and Confederate*, September 30, 1864; *Macon Telegraph and Confederate*, December 12, 1864; "Resources Must Now Be Developed," *Richmond Whig*, reprinted in *Macon Telegraph and Confederate*, March 15, 1865.

45. "What We Are Gaining by the War," *De Bow's Review* 32 (January–February 1862): 158–60; "What We Are Gaining by the War—Continued," *De Bow's Review* 32 (March–April 1862): 327–33.

46. George Fitzhugh, "Conduct of the War and Complaints against It," *Richmond Dispatch*, September 30, 1861.

47. "New by Telegraph—Message of President Davis to the Congress," *Charleston Mercury*, November 20, 1861.

48. "Overton," "War Often a Necessary Instrumentality to Develop the Resources and Capacities of a People," *Augusta Chronicle and Sentinel*, January 11, 1863. God's hand was also seen in the industrial development of Macon, Ga. See "What Macon Is Doing," *Macon Weekly Telegraph*, February 7, 1862.

49. "Home Enterprise," *Southern Field and Fireside*, reprinted in *Augusta Constitutionalist*, December 15, 1861.

50. See, e.g., "Manufacturing Establishments in South Carolina," *Raleigh Register*, September 25, 1861; "Paper," *Augusta Chronicle and Sentinel*, January 18, 1862; James Vanvalkenburgh to the Editor, *Macon Telegraph*, January 29, 1862; "What the South Needs," *Augusta Constitutionalist*, March 29, 1862.

51. "Home Manufacture of Guns," *Holly Springs Herald*, reprinted in *Memphis Appeal*, October 8, 1861.

52. Sarah Morgan diary entry, September 24, 1862, in *Sarah Morgan*, 273.

53. Rubin, *Shattered Nation*, 50–52.

54. Gruber, *Confederate Papers*, 1–6.

55. Goff, *Confederate Supply*, 14–15, 29–32, 246.

56. Beringer et al., *Why the South Lost the Civil War*, 214–18.

57. Channing, *Confederate Ordeal*, 25.

58. Czekanski, "Notes on Accoutrement Makers," 48–51.

59. Jaffee, "Confederate Oilcloth Accoutrements," 32–35.

60. Anderson, *Memoirs*, 139–40. See also Keim, *Confederate General Service Accoutrement Plates*.

61. Gorgas, "Confederate Ordnance Department," 326.

62. "Notes of the War," *Charleston Mercury*, August 16, 1861.

63. "The Confederate States Armory," reprinted from *Richmond Enquirer*. *Greensborough Patriot*, May 5, 1864. The Augusta Powder Works, and its machine shops, was another significant center. Designed in a Gothic style and modeled on England's Waltham Abbey Powder Mills, its construction began in 1861. Though large, distinctive, and the most complex Confederate government building program, secrecy meant its operations received little notice in the Confederacy, and no published reports regarding its appearance have been found. See "The Twelve Pounder Napoleon Gun," *Charleston Mercury*, March 20, 1863; "Powder Works," *Augusta Weekly Constitutionalist*, May 6, 1863.

64. Edwards, *Civil War Guns*, 338.

65. Jackson, "Whistling Dixie," 28–34.

66. Daniels, *Cannoneers in Gray*, 16, 72, 74, 103; Daniels, *Soldiering in the Army of Tennessee*, 41–42; Glatthaar, *General Lee's Army*, 258–67, 286–87.

67. Daniel Harvey Hill in Vandiver, *Ploughshares into Swords*, 111–14.

68. Alexander, *Fighting for the Confederacy*, 60–62. See also "The New Twelve Pounder Gun," *Augusta Constitutionalist*, reprinted in *Natchez Courier*, March 28, 1863.

69. "Novel Feature of Falling Back on Our Own Resources," *Richmond Enquirer*, November 19, 1862. See also "Carbine Factory," *Meridian Clarion*, June 6, 1864.

70. "Mechanical Arts," *Yorkville Enquirer*, October 7, 1863.

71. Jensen, "Survey of Confederate Central Government Quartermaster Issue Jackets, Part 1," 107–20.

72. "Courtenay," *Charleston Mercury*, October 26, 1861. See also *New Orleans Delta*, November 22, 1861.

73. Goff, *Confederate Supply*, 71.

74. Morgan, "Public Nature of Private Industry," 45.

75. Rable, *Confederate Republic*, 192–93.

76. Wilson, *Confederate Industry*, 14.

77. Wilson, *Confederate Industry*, 32–38.

78. For Lower South amounts, see Wilson, *Confederate Industry*, 292. The remaining items in this note are from the Confederate Papers Relating to the Citizens or Business Firms (National Archives Microfilm Publication, M346), RG109. For Virginia amounts, see "Manchester Cotton and Woollen Manufactory," roll 652; "Kelly, Tackett and Ford," roll 539; "Danville Manufacturing Company," roll

224; "Scottsville Manufacturing Company," roll 912; "Crenshaw Woollen Mills," roll 208; "William Bell," roll 57; "Crawford and Young," roll 206; "Riverton Manufacturing Company," roll 868; "A. Thomas and Sons" (Holston Woolen Factory), roll 1019; "Samuel L. Larkin and Company," roll 570; "A. B. Tanquary," roll 1006; "J. T. O'Rork" (Staunton Woolen Factory), roll 760; and "Bonsack and Whitmore," roll 79. The total amounts of fabrics (tweeds, cassimere, jeans, and jerseys) recorded on receipts or contracts for these companies are: Manchester Woollen Mills—350,000 yards; Kelly, Tackett and Ford—244,000 yards; Danville Manufacturing Company—100,000 yards; Scottsville Manufacturing Company—277,000 yards; Crenshaw Woollen Company—218,000 yards; William Bell—approximately 9,000 yards; Crawford and Young—42,000 yards; Riverton Manufacturing Company—3,000 yards; Holston Woolen Factory—82,000 yards; Samuel L. Larkin and Company—2,200 yards; A. B. Tanquary—2,576 yards; Staunton Woolen Factory—28 yards; and Bonsack and Whitmore—15,000 yards. This amounted to a minimum of 1,359,776 yards of woolen fabric delivered to the Confederate Quartermaster's Department between September 1861 and March 1864. It is probable that these figures are conservative as not only are the records incomplete but the Eighth Census reported that in July 1860 another eighteen woolen mills existed in the counties that became Confederate Virginia. This number does not include North Carolina mills.

79. Wilson, *Confederate Industry*, 178–79.

80. Jensen, "Survey of Confederate Central Government Quartermaster Issue Jackets, Part 1," 110–11.

81. Goff, *Confederate Supply*, 247; Jensen "Survey of Confederate Central Government Quartermaster Issue Jackets, Part 1," 109–13; "Items from Louisville—Rebel Prisoners from Chattanooga," October 3, 1863; *San Francisco Bulletin*, November 4, 1863; "Fitzhugh Lee's Dash into Annandale," *Washington (D.C.) Chronicle*, June 28, 1863; Woodhead, *Echoes of Glory*, 81; Arliskas, *Cadet Gray and Butternut Brown*, 86, 92.

82. "The South—Their Army—Where Their Armies Are—Their Clothing Manufactories—Food. Washington, January 28, 1863," *St. Louis Republican*, reprinted in the *Cincinnati Enquirer*, February 5, 1863.

83. Quoted in Arliskas, *Cadet Gray and Butternut Brown*, 86. See also "From Tennessee, Camp of 2nd N.J. Cav. Near Memphis, December 8, 1864," *Bedford (Pa.) Inquirer*, December 23, 1864.

84. "Report of Inspection, Gracie's Brigade, April 18, 1864," Inspection Reports and Related Records Received by the Inspection Branch in the Confederate Adjutant and Inspector General's Office, 1863–65 (National Archives Microfilm Publication, M935, roll 2, 0034), RG109. See also "Officer Deport Quartermaster, September 11, 1863," *Selma Morning Reporter*, September 12, 1863.

85. John J. Knight to family, December 5, 1862, *Confederate Collection*, Tennessee State Archives, Nashville, John J. Knight File, box 9, folder 27; letter from Major Andrew Dunn, quoted in Daniels, *Soldiering in the Army of Tennessee*, 32; Abram M. Glazener to Lavinia B. Glazener, August 26, 1863, home.mchsi.com/~spbarber/web/html/glazener.htm.

86. "Office of the Clothing Department," *Richmond Examiner*, quoted in *Knoxville Daily Register*, February 3, 1863; Charles Seton Fleming to Margaret Seton Fleming, December 30, 1863, in Fleming, *Memoir of Captain C. Seton Fleming*, 90–91.

87. The quartermaster general and his office and department were immediately answerable to General Samuel Cooper, the secretary of war, the Confederate Congress, and ultimately, President Davis. See An Act: For the Establishment and Organization of a General Staff for the Army of the Confederate States of America, February 26, 1861," *Acts and Resolutions of the First Session of the*

Provisional Congress of the Confederate States, 62–63, http://docsouth.unc.edu/imls/proviscongress/session1.html.

88. See Benjamin Harrison McGuire to Lucy Carter McGuire, February 13, 1862, Camp Winder, Va., Byrd Family Papers, Virginia Historical Society, *Antebellum Plantation Records*, sec. M, pt. 3, sec. B, reel 5, 00560; *New York Herald*, August 12, 1861; from the *Statesville Express*, reprinted in March 11, 1864, edition of the *Mobile Register and Advertiser*. See also "Soldier Clothing," Middleton, Tenn., March 19, 1863," *Atlanta Southern Confederacy*. The Quartermaster's Department also delivered poorly made shoes to the army. In one batch of ten thousand shoes, sent to Lee's army during the crisis time of November 1862, over three thousand were returned as unfit due to poor construction, small sizes, and low sides. See Glatthaar, *General Lee's Army*, 215; Wilson, *Confederate Industry*, 71–74; "Appeals to the Women of the South," *Knoxville Register*, October 7, 1862; George K. Harlow to his father, mother, and family, February 1, 1864, quoted in Glatthaar, *General Lee's Army*, 355; "Clothing the Army," *Richmond Whig*, June 18, 1862; "Hermes," "Richmond Correspondence, October 8, 1862," *Charleston Mercury*, October 18, 1862; Peter W. Alexander, "Conditions of the Army," *Savannah Republican* and *Mobile Advertiser and Register*, October 23, 1862 (widely reprinted); "Correspondence, Richmond, October 13, 1862," *Mobile Weekly Advertiser*, November 1 1862; Andrews, *Footprints of a Regiment*, 184.

89. Ed —— to family, January 15, 1865, Los Indolons, Tex., "Civil War Miscellany," in Glatthaar, *Confederate Military Manuscripts*, ser. C. pt. 1, reel 11. Ed was a member of Rip Ford's Texas Cavalry Regiment, stationed near Brownsville.

90. "A," "Our Army Correspondence, Winchester, Virginia, October 12, 1862," *Mobile Weekly Advertiser and Register*, November 1, 1862. For similar expressions, see "Camp of 28th Virginia, Regiment, November 11, 1863," *Lynchburg Virginian*, November 24, 1863; "North Carolina Manufacturers," *Richmond Enquirer*, reprinted in *Fayetteville (N.C.) Observer*, August 29, 1864; "Who Is to Blame?" *Augusta Chronicle and Sentinel*, November 11, 1864.

91. "Our Army Correspondence, Camp Gracie, May 1, 1864," *Montgomery Advertiser*, May 11, 1864.

92. "Evils in the Clothing Department," *Richmond Enquirer*, November 3, 1863. Inspection reports of the Richmond Garrison do not support the correspondent's observations. See Inspection Reports for Richmond Department, 1863–64, Adjutant and Inspector General's Office.

93. "Our Suffering Army," *Richmond Whig*, November 10, 1862.

94. See Inspection Reports and Related Records Received by the Inspection Branch in the Confederate Adjutant and Inspector General's Office, 1863–65 (National Archives Microfilm Publication, M935, rolls 2–17), RG109.

95. "Anecdote of Gen. Hardee," *Augusta Chronicle and Sentinel*, October 11, 1863, reprinted in *Macon Telegraph*, October 17, 1863; "For the Standard, July 17, 1863," *Raleigh Semi-Weekly Standard*, July 24, 1863; "Defalcation," *Mobile Tribune*, January 3, 1864, reprinted as "Enormous Defalcation," *Charleston Mercury*, January 7, 1864; "Quartermasters," *Southern Watchman*, January 13, 1864; "Heavy Defalcation," *Richmond Enquirer*, January 13, 1864; see also Wilson, *Confederate Industry*, 66–81.

96. "Can Nothing Be Done . . . ," *Richmond Examiner*, June 17, 1864, reprinted as "The Treasury Department," *Columbia South Carolinian*, June 23, 1864.

97. "The Situation," *Atlanta Southern Confederacy*, March 25, 1863.

98. "The Situation," *Savannah News*, August 1, 1863.

99. "Quartermaster General," *Richmond Enquirer*, August 21, 1863.

100. *Confederate Spirit, or Knapsack of Fun* 1 (May 1864).

101. Harwell, "Brief Candle," 134.

102. *Great Expectations,* 3–6, 10–11. See also the figure "Major Fleecum QM" in "Mrs. Jeremiah Jenkins; or, A Hint for the Times," *Mobile Advertiser and Register,* December 27, 1863.

103. Wilson, *Confederate Industry,* 67–82.

104. *Columbus Sun,* January 20, 1864, quoted in Morgan, "Public Nature of Private Industry," 44.

105. Harry J. Raphael, Captain Assistant Quartermaster, Eighth Alabama Regiment Volunteers to Adjutant General Samuel Cooper, January 1, 1864, Harry J. Raphael file, Compiled Service Records of General and Staff Officers, and Non-Regimental Enlisted Men (National Archives Microfilm Publication, M331, roll 206), RG109.

106. Wilson, *Confederate Industry,* 103–5.

107. "How Is It?" *Raleigh Semi-Weekly Standard,* November 6, 1861. See also "War Speculation the Probable Cause of Ruin to Southern Manufactures," *Richmond Dispatch,* October 30, 1861.

108. "Cotton Manufactures," *Dallas Herald,* May 10, 1862.

109. "The Grant Factory," *Atlanta Southern Confederacy,* March 18, 1861; "William Gregg, President of the Graniteville Company, to the Editor," *Charleston Tri-Weekly Courier,* November 25, 1862; "Corporations Have No Souls," *Fayetteville Observer,* November 27, 1862; "Munificent Donation," *Athens Southern Banner,* November 4, 1863; "Patriotic," *Selma Morning Reporter,* January 1, 1863; "Cotton Spinner's Convention," *Atlanta Southern Confederacy,* May 17, 1863; "The Eagle Company," *Columbus Enquirer,* October 13, 1863; "Where Does It Come From?" *Atlanta Intelligencer,* November 13, 1863; *Savannah Republican,* December 15, 1863; *Mobile Register and Advertiser,* March 29, 1864; "Editorial Correspondence, Atlanta, Georgia, April 13, 1864," *Mobile Evening News,* April 16, 1864; "Augusta Manufacturing," *Mobile Tribune,* April 21, 1864; "The Eagle Manufacturing Company," *Augusta Chronicle and Sentinel,* reprinted in *Mobile Register and Advertiser,* April 26, 1864; "The Saluda Factory," *Columbia South Carolinian,* April 27, 1864.

110. "The Factories—Gov. Brown—The Bartow Petitioners—Dorcases, &c.," *Savannah Republican,* October 30, 1862.

111. "Manufacturers' Convention," *Columbus Enquirer,* June 25, 1864.

112. Corsan, *Two Months in the Confederate States,* 46–47, 53, 62–63, 65.

113. John B. Jones Diary, entry for May 2, 1863, *Rebel War Clerk's Diary,* 200; Faust, *Creation of Confederate Nationalism,* 41–57.

114. Massey, *Ersatz in the Confederacy;* Eklund, Jackson, and Thornton, ""Unintended Consequences," 187–205.

115. The actions and language of these groups are in keeping with those found by E. P. Thompson in "The Moral Economy of the English Crowd in the Eighteenth Century," *Past and Present,* February 1971. See "Jean" to the Editor, "Ladies Impress Cotton," Manassas, Bartow County, Ga., June 14, 1862, *Atlanta Southern Confederacy,* June 17, 1862; "Helping Themselves," *Columbus Weekly Enquirer,* November 11, 1862; "Rioting Women," *Atlanta Southern Confederacy,* April 16, 1863. According to the report, the women stole "finery." "Amazonian Display," *Augusta Constitutionalist,* April 11, 1863; *Columbus Weekly Enquirer,* April 21, 1863; "Female Highway Robbery," *Edgefield Advertiser,* May 6, 1863. Other incidents occurred in places as far apart as Mobile, Ala., Salisbury, N.C., and Richmond, Va. See also Faust, *Creation of Confederate Nationalism,* 52–55; Graham, "Women's Revolt in Rowan County," 131–47.

116. "Riots," *Turnwold Countryman,* April 21, 1863.

117. See "Corbett," "Letter from Richmond, October 7, 1861," *New Orleans Picayune,* October 17, 1861; "Extortion by Southern Manufacturers," *Raleigh Semi-Weekly Register,* November 13, 1861.

118. *Charleston Mercury,* April 14, 1862. See also "Southern Yankees," *South Western Baptist,* reprinted in *Jacksonville Republican,* November 7, 1861.

119. Corsan, *Two Months in the Confederate States,* 130.

120. Rable, "Despair, Hope and Delusion," 129–67.

121. "Our Future," *Macon Telegraph and Confederate,* September 30, 1864.

122. Reply of Major W.W.B. Cross to Hon. J. M. Leach, House of Representatives, inquiry January 10, 1865, *Register of Letters Received by the Confederate Quartermaster Department, October 1864–February 1865,* chap. 5, vol. 12; "Resources Must Be Developed," *Richmond Whig,* February 22, 1865, reprinted in *Macon Telegraph and Confederate,* March 15, 1865.

123. See Wilson, *Confederate Industry,* 128; Jensen, "Survey of Confederate Central Government Quartermaster Issue Jackets, Part 1," 110. See "Clothing for the Army of Tennessee," *Augusta Constitutionalist,* reprinted in the *Macon Telegraph and Confederate,* February 28, 1865. This article details the amounts of clothing distributed over the three months to February 1, 1865, and states that contrary to the "doleful wail" of "veracious and ugacious" writers, the army had "been amply supplied with clothing and that of the very best." Ironically, in the war's aftermath, ex-Confederates used these ample supplies to clothe themselves. "Dispatch from Danville, Virginia," *Macon Telegraph,* June 29, 1865; "Confederate Clothing," *Savannah Herald,* June 31, 1865, reprinted in the *Macon Telegraph,* July 1, 1865; *Macon Telegraph,* July 5, 1865.

CHAPTER 5
The Photographic and Graphic Print Industries

1. "Southern Literary Messenger," *Richmond Whig,* March 11, 1864. Since its first publication, in 1838, imagery had appeared on occasion in the *Messenger*. However, like that featured in its previous attempt (between June 1860 and 1861), it was produced in the North. The author has located three issues of the March 1864 *Messenger.* All three prints of the plate show no remaining trace of coloring.

2. Beegan, "Mechanization of the Image," 257–74; Barnhurst and Nerome, "Civic Picturing vs. Realist Photojournalism," 59–79.

3. "Lithographing, Engraving, Printing, and . . . ," *Nashville Union and American,* August 3, 1861. In 1860, Wagner was the sole lithographer in his section of Tennessee. In addition to printing, he offered his skills as a painter in oils and watercolors. Contracted by Blanton Duncan to print Treasury notes, Wagner left Nashville for Richmond, Va., in early 1862. See "Lithography," *Richmond Dispatch,* January 16, 1862.

4. *Manufactures of the United States of America in 1860,* cxxxii–cxlii, 82, 203, 438, 639, 717. There was one photographic establishment in North Carolina, two in Georgia, three in Virginia, and seven in Louisiana (all in New Orleans).

5. "Bank Note Engraving—Progress of Art in the South," *Richmond Dispatch,* January 1, 1862.

6. Lerner, "Money, Prices and Wages," 32–35.

7. By 1865, blockaders stopped one in every two blockade-runners. Nevins, *War for the Union,* 4:221–23.

8. "Another Paper Mill Burned," *Macon Telegraph,* June 2, 1863.

9. "Columbus Times—Rock Island Paper Mills," *Jackson Mississippian,* July 7, 1864.

10. "The Price of Paper," *Macon Telegraph,* February 2, 1864.

11. Ball, "Paper Mills in the Confederate South," 1–62.

12. Detlefsen, "Printing in the Confederacy," 53–69, 134–37. It is notable that when the *Richmond Whig* changed its typeface in late 1862, not only it but other newspapers noted and applauded the change. "The Richmond Whig," *Montgomery Advertiser*, December 14, 1862.

13. "Charleston Printing Ink Works," *Charleston Mercury*, May 5, 1863; Detlefsen, "Printing in the Confederacy," 102–9.

14. "Printing Ink," *Wilmington Journal*, August 20, 1864.

15. These included artists, letterers, steel engravers, transferrers, plate makers, and printers. See Keatinge and Ball, *Remarks on the Manufacture of Bank Notes*, 16. Thomas A. Ball (1822–76) was a Virginia merchant who worked in New York until June 1861. He went into partnership with Irish-born engravers Robert Leggett (1828–85) and Edward Keatinge. Leggett dissolved the partnership in March 1862 and soon after departed the South. Blanton Duncan incorrectly identified Leggett as "William."

16. "Confederate Printing Press Is a Curious Relic," *Richmond Times-Dispatch*, June 8, 1924; B. Duncan to C. G. Memminger, May 31, 1862, in Thian, *Correspondence with the Treasury Department*, 557.

17. J. D. Denegre to C. G. Memminger, May 18, 1861, in Thian, *Correspondence with the Treasury Department*, 107; C. G. Memminger to J. D. Denegre, May 25, 1861, in Thian, *Correspondence of the Treasury Department*, 93. The following documents can be found in Thian, *Correspondence with the Treasury Department:* J. D. Denegre to C. G. Memminger, July 8, 1861, 197; W. P. Reyburn to C. G. Memminger, July 24, 1861, 242–43; W. P. Reyburn to C. G. Memminger, July 29, 1861, 250–51; S. Schmidt to C. G. Memminger, August 29, 1861, 295; J. D. Denegre to C. G. Memminger, September 2, 1861, 306; J. D. Denegre to C. G. Memminger, September 9, 1861, 322–23; J. D. Denegre to C. G. Memminger, October 5, 1861, 361; C. G. Memminger to J. D. Denegre, October 14, 1861, 210–11. According to a 1950s history of the American Bank Note Company, at the end of 1862, Schmidt remitted seventeen thousand dollars (the net operating profits while under Confederate control) to the company. His pluckiness, loyalty, and integrity were so admired by the company's trustees that Schmidt retained his position as manager of this branch until the mid-1870s. Born in Germany in 1805, Carl August Solomon Schmidt arrived in 1841 in New Orleans, where he worked in the medallion, banknote, and bond engraving industry until his death on July 22, 1876. "Charles August Solomon Schmidt," *New Orleans Picayune*, July 26, 1876.

18. C. G. Memminger to J. E. White, August 15, 1861, in Thian, *Correspondence of the Treasury Department*, 175.

19. "A Noted Engraver," *Lawrence Journal*, November 27, 1887.

20. C. G. Memminger to J. P. Benjamin, Richmond, Va., January 10, 1862 (filed under "Menninger, C. G."), *Letters Received by the Confederate Adjutant and Inspector General's Office* (National Archives Microfilm Publication, M474, roll 50), RG109. Memminger wrote in response to a request from Blanton Duncan on the previous day. Blanton Duncan to C. G. Memminger, January 9, 1862, in Thian, *Correspondence with the Treasury Department*, 465. Born in 1840 in Virginia, Elam enlisted on March 27, 1861, in Memphis, in a company in the Ninth Mississippi Infantry Regiment. In March 1862, authorities arrested Elam for counterfeiting Confederate notes. On a spree, he and a partner broke into the offices of Hoyer and Ludwig, his employers, and pulled prints of one hundred–dollar bills. Through various means, he was never convicted. Previously, in August 1861, Memminger had arranged the discharge of lithographer Arthur C. Dabney from the Fifteenth Virginia Infantry to work for Hoyer and Ludwig. Over April and May 1862, at least five other soldiers—named as H. C. Lindell, George Hogle, Edward Schrempp, G. Hall, and Charles Carnahan—were detached to produce Confederate bonds and notes.

21. The letters cited in this note can be found in Letters Received by the Confederate Adjutant and Inspector General's Office (National Archives Microfilm Publication, M474), RG109. A. C. Dabney et al., employees of Hoyer and Ludwig, to J. P. Benjamin, Richmond, Va., March 6, 1862, roll 50; C. G. Memminger to G. W. Randolph, Richmond, April 24, 1862 (filed under "Menninger, C. G."), roll 50; S. Cooper to Colonel J. S. Preston, Richmond, Va., May 23, 1862, seeking exemption for Duncan's employees, and C. G. Memminger to G. W. Randolph, Richmond, Va., June 4, 1862, seeking exemption for Paterson's employees (filed under "Preston, Jno S."), roll 47. These lists contain the names of twenty-five civilians employed in producing Confederate notes and bonds. Hoyer and Ludwig employed a foreman, an artist, and twelve printers. Duncan listed an engraver and eleven printers, six of whom also appeared on Ludwig and Hoyer's list. Paterson listed a foreman, engraver/artist, polisher, ink grinder, and nine printers, seven of whom were formerly employed by Hoyer and Ludwig and three who also appear on Duncan's list.

22. Keatinge and Ball, *Remarks on the Manufacture of Bank Notes,* 30.

23. "An Hour with the Money-Makers," *Richmond Enquirer,* March 23, 1864; W. D. Nutt to P. Clayton, November 12, 1862, in Thian, *Correspondence with the Treasury Department,* 667–68.

24. "Confederate Bonds," *Los Angeles Times,* July 31, 1891.

25. C. G. Memminger to S. D. Morgan, October 26, 1861, in Thian, *Correspondence of the Treasury Department,* 225.

26. "Confederate Printing Press Is a Curious Relic," *Richmond Times-Dispatch,* June 8, 1924; "Lot 2369," Sale 52: The Westplex Sale, Schuyler Ramsey Philatelic Auctions, San Francisco, http://www.rumseyauctions.com/auctions/chapter/52/164.

27. Shaw, "Confederate Conscription and Exemption Acts," 379–82. In its final format, the February 17, 1864, act exempted, among others: "one editor for each newspaper," "such employees as said editor may certify on oath to be indispensable"; Confederate and state government public printers; and such journeymen as are "indispensable to perform the public printing." For more on the impact of exemptions, see "The Military Bill," *Richmond Dispatch,* February 17, 1864; Ellis, *Moving Appeal,* 71, 144, 278, 522.

28. "Col. Blanton Duncan," *Macon Telegraph,* January 21, 1862; "Col. Blanton Duncan's Lithographic Establishment in Columbia," *Charleston Mercury,* August 1, 1862.

29. C. G. Memminger to B. Duncan, April 7, 1862, in Thian, *Correspondence of the Treasury Department,* 281.

30. Ludwig Hoyer to President Andrew Johnson, June 26, 1865, Applications for Pardon Submitted to President Andrew Johnson by Former Confederates Excluded from Earlier Amnesty Proclamations, 1865–67, Confederate Amnesty Papers (National Archives Microfilm Publication, M1003, roll 63); Records of the Adjutant General's Office, Record Group 94, National Archives and Records Administration, Washington, D.C.

31. Duncan sold his printing business to Philip Clayton in the latter part of April 1863. The Treasurer rejected Clayton's offer to print notes and bonds for the government. See Sanders G. Jamison to Christopher G. Memminger, secretary of the Treasury, April 23, 1863, Sanders G. Jamison file, Confederate Papers Relating to the Citizens or Business Firms (National Archives Microfilm Publication, M346, roll 500), RG109. According to Duncan's application for amnesty, he fell ill during the summer of 1863 and left the Confederacy in early May 1864. See Blanton Duncan to President Andrew Johnson, August 7, 1865, Confederate Amnesty Papers (National Archives Microfilm Publication M1003, roll 25), RG94.

32. "Confederate Treasury Notes," *Charleston Mercury*, September 5, 1861.

33. These were produced by the presses of R. B. Howell in Savannah, Ga.; New Orleans's Pessou and Company and P. Werlein, Frederick Bornemann in Charleston, S.C.; Richmond's Hoyer and Ludwig; and the respective presses of O. Lederle and D. H. Huyett of Memphis, Tenn.

34. Boyd, *Patriotic Envelopes of the Civil War*, 30, 34, 38–39, 40–43, 51–52.

35. "Confederacy Flag Envelopes," *Augusta Constitutionalist*, March 16, 1861.

36. "Special Notices," *Richmond Dispatch*. August 23, 1862.

37. "The New Flag," *Richmond Examiner*, April 19, 1862; *Richmond Whig*, April 21, 1862. A self-promoter, described as a "humbug" by one contemporary North Carolina newspaper, in September 1863, after courting the Confederate government and winning the contract for Confederate medals of honor under questionable circumstances, Baumgarten left for Europe, only to resume his career in the North a year later. See "Contract for Buttons, Richmond, Virginia, August 17, 1861," Julius Baumgarten files, Confederate Papers Relating to the Citizens or Business Firms (National Archives Microfilm Publication, M346, roll 49), RG109; "North Carolina State Flag," *Raleigh Semi-Weekly State Journal*, January 18, 1862; Musick, "Mystery of the Missing Confederate Medals of Honor," 74–78.

38. Beegan, "Mechanization of the Image," 257–74.

39. "Interiors of Fort Sumter," *Charleston Tri-Weekly Courier*, April 16, 1861.

40. "The War," *New Orleans Daily Crescent*, May 14, 1861.

41. See, e.g., "City Intelligence," *Richmond Dispatch*, November 26, 1864; "Notice," *Fayetteville North Carolinian*, January 20, 1865.

42. See George S. Cook, D. T. Cowell, and Julian Vannerson files, Confederate Papers Relating to the Citizens or Business Firms (National Archives Microfilm Publication, M346, rolls 109 and 1051), RG109. Cowell's skills saw him detached from his company, in April 1864, to the Engineer Department's Photographic Establishment. The defense of Richmond and Petersburg caused an urgent need for the photographic maps he printed. See Colonel A. R. Rives to James A. Seddon, secretary of war, June 22, 1864; D. T. Cowell files, Third Local Defense Regiment, Compiled Service Records of Confederate soldiers Who Served in Organizations from Virginia (National Archives Microfilm Publication, M324, roll 396), RG109.

43. See General P.G.T. Beauregard to Surgeon J. J. Chisholm, September 27, 1863, *Endorsements, Department of South Carolina, Georgia, and Florida, September 1863–May 1864*,, chap. 2, vol. 187, 69, RG109, NAB. At Cook's request, Beauregard ordered ten ounces of silver nitrate from Surgeon Chisholm to make photographs of the effects of enemy fire on Fort Sumter. According to recipes, this amount would be enough for over one hundred photographs.

44. Eiserman, "We Have Had a Picture Taken," 44–47.

45. "Likeness of Stonewall Jackson," *Southern Illustrated News*, November 14, 1863; "Pictures of Confederate Generals," *Richmond Enquirer*, April 13, 1864; "Pictures of Confederate Generals," *Richmond Enquirer*, July 7, 1864. In Mobile, in late 1863, J. F. Stanton advertised that having secured an artist and blockade goods, his gallery was a place to have pictures made. "Blockade Ambrotype Goods," *Mobile Advertiser and Register*, December 23, 1864. In Montgomery, Ala., during December 1864, invalided young officer Captain George T. Shaw set up a studio and gallery. "A Place of Fashionable Resort," *Montgomery Mail*, December 3, 1864.

46. "Mr. David L. Clark," *Macon Telegraph*, April 23, 1864. Many Confederate newspapers carried this story over April 1864.

47. "The Human Face Divine," *Newbern Progress*, January 9, 1862.

48. Zeller, *Blue and Gray in Black and White,* 135–37.

49. "Likeness of Stonewall Jackson," *Southern Illustrated News,* November 14, 1863; "Stonewall Jackson," *Raleigh Semi-Weekly Standard,* May 26, 1863; "The South Victorious," *Raleigh Confederate,* May 25, 1864; "St. Valentine's Day" and "New Song," *Richmond Examiner,* February 4, 1864. In late 1863, a large photographic portrait of General Stonewall Jackson cost around ten times more than similar-size lithographs.

50. See advertisements for Blanton Duncan in *Augusta Chronicle and Sentinel,* May 15 and 20, 1862. Hoyer and Ludwig produced high-quality lithographs of President Davis and Vice President Stephens. "Tucker and Perkins," *Augusta Constitutionalist,* March 6, 1862.

51. Often incorrectly identified by other first names, from 1855 French-born Louis Eugene Napoleon Crehen lithographed imagery for Richmonders. He closed his business in September 1861 for a year, probably to work on Confederate currency. From then until after the war, his commercial illustrated work, sheet music, weeklies, books, and government jobs included the templates used to cut musket cartridges. His work earned him the respect of contemporaries and the title of "artist." See "Stonewall Jackson," *Richmond Dispatch,* September 11, 1862; "Lithography, Lithography," *Richmond Dispatch,* September 16, 1862; "Lithographer—Crehen," *Richmond Dispatch,* October 13, 1862. Technically and artistically skilled, Bornemann's work around South Carolina earned notice before the war. In the war's first year, he produced a number of works, including a now lost print of General Beauregard. In May 1862, the predatory Blanton Duncan stripped his shop of workmen, and Bornemann found employment engraving banknotes for James T. Paterson's printing company. For the next three years, until heart disease killed him, he worked for Patterson. See "The William Washington Monument," *Charleston Courier,* May 4, 1858; "A Card," *Charleston Courier,* October 22, 1853; "Portrait of Gen. Beauregard," *Charleston Mercury,* October 10, 1861. See also Samuel P. Mitchell's *Sketch of the County Occupied by the Federal and Confederate Armies on the 18th and 21st July 1861. Taken by Captain Samuel P. Mitchell, of 1st Virginia Regiment,* Museum of the Confederacy, Richmond, Va.; "Lithographic Establishment of J. T. Patterson's Co.," *Columbia South Carolinian,* August 13, 1862; F. W. Bornemann to C. G. Memminger, Charleston, S.C., May 13, 1862, in Thian, *Correspondence with the Treasury Department,* 538; "Obituary," *Charleston Courier,* June 3, 1865.

52. Lent and Simhi, "Northern Magazines in the South," 3, 986–87.

53. "C.C.B." to Editor, *Indianola Courier,* November 24, 1860.

54. "Editor's Table," *Southern Literary Messenger* 30, no. 6 (June 1860): 473.

55. "Our Reception," *Southern Monthly* 1 (October 1861): 162; "Opinions of the Press," *Southern Monthly* 1 (November 1861): 241–42.

56. S—, "For the True Democrat," *Little Rock Arkansas True Democrat,* November 21, 1861.

57. "Our Sanctum," *Southern Monthly* 1 (December 1861): 307–8.

58. Southern by "birth and feeling," Huyett worked in the North before joining the *Monthly.* In 1863, he worked as an assistant engineer with Captain Samuel Lockett around Jackson, Miss. See "Our Sanctum," *Southern Monthly* 1 (February 1862): 467; D. H. Huyett file, Confederate Papers Relating to the Citizens or Business Firms (National Archives Microfilm Publication, M346, roll 488), RG109.

59. Active in Memphis during the 1850–60s, O. Lederle's firm printed railroad bonds, public documents, maps, and some art prints. Lederle produced a lost lithograph of the "Battle of Belmont" in February 1862. See *Southern Monthly* 1 (February 1862): 472; *Southern Monthly* 1 (March 1862): 557; "Spirited Lithograph," *New Orleans Picayune,* February 15, 1862.

60. "Our Sanctum," *Southern Monthly* 1 (March 1862): 553; "The Rambler," *Southern Monthly* 1 (March 1862): 557–58.

61. In mid-1864, it may have been one of the "very imperfect lithographs" that James P. Douglas sent to his girlfriend. See James P. Douglas to Sallie White, June 16, 1864, in Douglas, *Douglas's Texas Battery,* 101.

62. "In Regard to Illustrations," *Southern Monthly* 1 (March 1862): 480.

63. "Our Sanctum," *Southern Monthly* 1 (April 1862): 626.

64. See "Prospectus," *Greensborough Patriot,* October 23, 1862; "Dissolution," *Richmond Dispatch,* December 6, 1864. Ayres was the twenty-six-year-old son of Richmond tobacco merchant Samuel Ayres and William H. Wade a twenty-five-year-old printer and former Confederate soldier. Ayres provided the capital and managed the business, and Wade acted as its editor and ran the printing office. See McCabe, "Literature of the War," 200–201.

65. "Southern Illustrated News," *Augusta Chronicle and Sentinel,* August 30, 1862.

66. Thompson, *Image of War,* 19–20.

67. Thompson, *Image of War,* 21–22; Patrick Leary, "A Brief History of the *Illustrated London News,*" *Gale Cengage Learning,* gale.cengage.co.uk/images/PatrickLeary.pdf.

68. New York–born King served a month in the Twenty-Fifth Virginia Infantry Battalion. After the war, he moved to his wife's hometown of New Haven, Conn., where he died on October 15, 1877. See "New Haven, Connecticut," *Hartford Courant,* October 17, 1877. Torsch, after a long career as an engraver, became active among Confederate veterans until his death. See "Captain John W. Torsch," in Johnson, *Confederate Military History Extended Edition,* 2:423–24; "The Death of Capt. J. W. Torsch," *Baltimore Sun,* October 3, 1898.

69. "Lieutenant Torsch," *Richmond Enquirer,* September 28, 1861.

70. "Notice to Correspondents," *Southern Illustrated News,* December 13, 1862.

71. "The News from Richmond," *Charleston Mercury,* September 12, 1862.

72. "Southern Illustrated News," *Columbia South Carolinian,* September 23, 1862.

73. "Completion of Our First Volume," *Southern Illustrated News,* June 27, 1863.

74. See advertisements, *Savannah Morning News,* November 1–3, 1862. Little is known of Campbell. Hurdle, a native of Alexandria, served with the Seventeenth Virginia Infantry Regiment. Wounded in August 1862, he convalesced in Richmond for a year before being discharged in August 1863. He died on December 1, 1865. McCabe, "Literature of the War," 200.

75. "Our Corps of Engravers," *Southern Illustrated News,* November 8, 1862; "New Banner," *Southern Illustrated News,* July 4, 1863.

76. "Southern Illustrated News," *Richmond Enquirer,* November 8, 1862.

77. "The Southern Illustrated News," *Atlanta Southern Confederacy,* March 19, 1863; "No Such Word as Fail," *Southern Illustrated News,* May 2, 1863; "The Drama," *Southern Illustrated News,* April 11, 1863.

78. In Fife, "Theatre of the Confederacy," 267.

79. "Evelyn," "Our Richmond Correspondence, May 29, 1863," *Mobile Advertiser and Register,* June 6, 1863.

80. "To Correspondents," *Southern Illustrated News,* August 28, 1863.

81. "Sudden Death in Saloon," *Richmond Examiner,* March 17, 1864.

82. "J.W.T." to the Editors, Winchester, Va., June 10, 1863, "Our Engraving," *Southern Illustrated News,* June 26, 1863.

83. "Southern Illustrated News," *Richmond Whig,* June 30, 1863.

84. "Lieut. Gen. Richard S. Ewell," *Southern Illustrated News,* July 4, 1863.

85. One batch, engraved before Petersburg, Va., "between picket firing and battery shelling," included a portrait of Lieutenant General Stonewall Jackson intended for use in a volume on the life of Jackson, written by "Dr. Dabney" and published by A. Morris of Richmond. See "The Arts," *Richmond Examiner,* August 25, 1864.

86. "Editor's Table," George William Bagby, *Southern Literary Messenger* 34 (October 1862): 581.

87. "Our Paper," *Southern Field and Fireside,* August 1, 1863.

88. Bernath, *Confederate Minds,* 151–210.

89. *Southern Field and Fireside,* May 30, 1863; "Alfred Maurice," *Augusta Constitutionalist,* July 21, 1864; "Wm. B. Campbell," *Savannah Morning News,* November 1–3, 1862; "W. B. Campbell," *Southern Punch,* February 6, 1864.

90. C. G. Memminger to Messrs. Fraser, Trenholm, and Co., October 9, 1861, in Thian, *Correspondence of the Treasury Department,* 201.

91. "Arrivals at Charleston Hotels," *Charleston Courier,* July 7, 1862. John Gemmell, William George Embleton, George Henry Keeling, William Gellatly, and J. McFarland also arrived then. See Chase and Supreme Court of the United States, *U.S. Reports: Bermuda,* 535.

92. Ball, *Comprehensive Catalog,* 15.

93. "English Engravers," *Richmond Whig,* May 1, 1863.

94. "English Engravers."

95. "Military Maps &c," *Richmond Enquirer,* July 18, 1863. In April 1864, Gellatly and his wife traveled north for supplies. In June 1864, they were captured on their return journey. See "To George Dunn and Co.," *Richmond Enquirer,* August 28, 1864.

96. "Making Rebel Money—An English Lithographer Tells How It Was Done," *New York Sun,* December 13, 1896.

97. "Walter Bowie, Report of Conscription, Columbia, South Carolina, September 21, 1864," Inspection Reports and Related Records Received by the Inspection Branch in the Confederate Adjutant and Inspector General's Office, 1863–65 (National Archives Microfilm Publication, M935, roll 2), RG109.

98. "The Confederate Spirit, and Knapsack of Fun," *Mobile Advertiser and Register,* October 17, 1863.

99. Blanton Duncan's printing house, e.g., copied Northern imagery. In 1863, it released an almost identical version of New York publishers Christopher, Morse, and Skippon's 1862 work, *Fun for the Camp: A Comic Medley.*

100. "Gen. John Morgan," *Bugle Horn of Liberty* (Griffin, Ga.) 1, no. 3 (October 1863): 8; "Bugle Horn of Liberty," *Augusta Constitutionalist,* October 16, 1863; J. C. Swayze, "A Vindication, Atlanta, October 13, 1863," *Atlanta Intelligencer,* October 15, 1863. Convalescing soldiers misinterpreted this burlesque and were so enraged by the "Morgan" satire that they rode the editor, John C. Swayze, out of town on a rail.

101. "Southern Literature and Art," *Mobile Advertiser and Register,* October 4, 1863.

102. "The New Issue," *Richmond Enquirer,* reprinted in *Columbus Enquirer,* March 18, 1864.

103. "The New Issue," *Columbus Enquirer,* April 10, 1864.

104. "Walter Bowie, Report of Conscription, Columbia, South Carolina, September 21, 1864," Inspection Reports from the Confederate Adjutant and Inspector General's Office (National Archives Microfilm Publication, M935, roll 2, 0757), RG109.

105. "The Hardtack," *Macon Telegraph,* May 5, 1864; "Our Vignette," *Hardtack* 1 (May 1864). A copy

of the first issue is in the collection of the Boston Public Library.

106. Middleton Michel to Thomas F. Wood, February 10, 1883, *North Carolina Medical Journal* 11 (February 1883): 75–76.

107. "The City," *Richmond Whig*, December 6, 1864; "Juvenile Children's Books," *Richmond Whig*, December 6, 1864.

108. "Just Published," *Augusta Constitutionalist*, February 28, 1865.

109. "New Music," *Richmond Dispatch*, February 14, 1865.

110. Hopley, *Life in the South*, 103–4.

111. Abel, *Confederate Sheet Music.*

112. "New Music," *Raleigh Conservative*, March 18, 1865.

113. Borrit et al., *Confederate Image*, 67.

114. Boyd, *Patriotic Envelopes of the Civil War*, 28–29.

115. Detlefsen, "Printing in the Confederacy," 124.

CHAPTER 6
The Meanings of Confederate Military Clothing

Epigraph: "The Jacket of Grey," by C. A. Ball, was first published after the war; the poem was featured on the front page of the *Confederate Veteran Magazine* 2 (March 1894).

1. Joseph, *Uniforms and Non-Uniforms*, 1.

2. Tonchi, "Signs of Order, Signs of Disorder," 196–98.

3. Joseph, *Uniforms and Non-Uniforms*, 10, 15, 18, 20–21, 23–24, 26, 37, 42, 49–50; Bonani, Frisa, and Tonchi, *Uniform: Order and Disorder*, 26, 147.

4. Russell, *My Civil War Diary*, quoted in Lord, *Uniforms of the Civil War*, 115–16; "Letter from Richmond, June 4, 1861," *Charleston Mercury*, June 12, 1861.

5. See Dedmondt, *Flags of Civil War South Carolina*, 66.

6. Joseph, *Uniforms and Non-Uniforms*, 26.

7. John Parker to Secretary of War J. P. Walker, Manatee County, Fla., April 30, 1861; see also Captain Edward Fitzgerald to Secretary of War J. P. Walker, April 4 and 9, 1861, both in Letters Received by the Confederate Secretary of War, March–May 1861 (National Archives Microfilm Publication, M437, roll 2), RG109.

8. "Regulations in Relation to Clothing for Volunteers, under Act of 30th August, 1861—War Department, Richmond, 10th October, 1861," *Richmond Examiner*, November 6, 1861.

9. Carp, "Nations of American Rebels," 24–28; Waldstreicher, *In the Midst of Perpetual Fetes*, 10; Savelle, "Nationalism and Other Loyalties," 914–16; Grodzin, *Loyal and the Disloyal*, 29; Potter, *South and the Sectional Conflict*, 48.

10. W. A. Love, "Company Records," *Confederate Veteran Magazine* 33 (February 1925): 50. This was not the only incident.

11. Stevens, *Reminiscences of the Civil War*, 8.

12. See "Georgia Troops in Augusta," *Augusta Chronicle and Sentinel*, April 28, 1861; "The Military Movements," *Augusta Constitutionalist*, May 2, 1861; "Additional Troops," *Augusta Chronicle and Sentinel*,

May 1, 1861; The "Confederate Light Guard" of Augusta, Ga., purchased dark-green nine-button fatigue jackets trimmed with yellow from the "Clinch Rifles." See art 6, sec. 8, "Revised By-Laws of the Clinch Rifles, April 1854"; and entry for April 20, 1861, both in *Clinch Rifles Minute Book*, Richmond County Historical Society, Augusta, Ga.

13. David, "Decorated Men," 5; Cunliffe, *Soldiers and Civilians*, 230; Kimball, *American City, Southern Place*, 190–92; Todd, *American Military Equipage*, vol. 2.

14. C. Vann Woodward, "John Brown's Private War," *Burden of Southern History*, 62–66; Freehling, *Road to Disunion: Secessionists Triumphant*, 213–15.

15. Selina Powell, to Henry (Charles L. Powell Jr.), Winchester, Va., ca.1859–60, Powell Family Papers, ser. D, box 2, folder 5, Earl Gregg Swem Library, William and Mary College, Williamsburg, Va.

16. Captain J. A. Strother to Adjutant General Henry C. Wayne, February 7, 1861, box 23, Adjutant General's Papers; see also W. W. Turner to Governor J. E. Brown, February 19, 1861, box 21, Governor's Incoming Correspondence; Captain A. M. Wallace to Governor J. E. Brown, January 11, 1861, box 21, Governor's Incoming Correspondence, all in Georgia Department of Archives and History, Atlanta.

17. Adjutant General Henry C. Wayne to Lieutenant Colonel J. K. Jackson, February 25, 1861, Adjutant General's Letterbook, no. 2, Georgia Department of Archives and History, Atlanta; Field, *Confederate Army*, 35–36.

18. "Alabama State Uniform," *Charleston Mercury*, February 15, 1861; "Mississippi Uniform," *Augusta Constitutionalist*, February 16, 1861.

19. Captain Bassett G. Lawrence to Governor Pettus, June 5, 1861, in Field, *Confederate Army*, 24; "Military Company," *Brandon Republican*, October 28, 1858; Ellis M. Myers to Quartermaster General William Barksdale, February 16, 1861, Record Group 9, vol. 3, Mississippi Department of Archives and History, Jackson, Military Requisitions.

20. See contents of box 27, Military Collections, Civil War Collection, Quartermaster Department Records, State Archives of North Carolina, Raleigh, North Carolina; "Letter from Pensacola," Fort Barrancas, April 6, 1861, *Fayetteville Observer*, May 2, 1861; Field, *Confederate Army*, 12–13.

21. "Letter from Pensacola."

22. De Leon, *Four Years in Rebel Capitals*, 116.

23. "From the 'Bass Grays' 7th Texas Infantry, Peterson Ky., November 1861," *Texas Republican*, December 7, 1861.

24. "Clothing the Soldiers," *Fayetteville Observer*, November 4, 1861. See also "Clothing Our Troops," *Fayetteville Observer*, November 27, 1862.

25. Joseph, *Uniforms and Non-Uniforms*, 18; Mollo, *Military Fashions*, 133. See also "Columbus, Kentucky," *New York Herald*, October 30, 1861; Military Collections, box 17, Civil War Collection, Quartermaster Records in the North Carolina Department of Cultural Resources, Division of Archives and History, Raleigh, Invoices from J. M. Holbrook to Quartermaster General I. E. Foster, June 1861 and December 24, 1861, "Receipts of Quartermaster General of the State of Georgia: 1861," Georgia Department of Archives and History, Atlanta; "Abstracts of Purchases, 1st Quarter 1861," Adjutant General's Financial Records, SG 1530, S+5224, Alabama Department Archives and History, Montgomery.

26. Thomas, *Confederacy as a Revolutionary Experience*, 44–45; Faust, *Creation of Confederate Nationalism*, 14; McPherson, *For Cause and Comrades*, 21, 104–6. See also "Correspondence from Virginia," *Montgomery Weekly Post*, May 15, 1861; P. D. Page to Secretary of War Leroy Pope Walker, Montgomery, Ala., June 9, 1861, Letters Received by the Confederate Secretary of War, May–June 1861 (National Ar-

chives Microfilm Publication, M437, roll 3), RG109; "Wise Legion," *Richmond Enquirer*, June 15, 1861; Cunliffe, *Soldiers and Civilians*, 52–54, 282–86; Day, *Down South*, 314–15.

27. "Correspondence from Virginia," Camp Pickens, Va., June 23, 1861, *Charleston Mercury*, June 26, 1861.

28. Guiseppe Garabaldi led an army (augmented by foreign volunteers) in an effort to liberate and unify what is now Italy from Austro-Hungarian and Bourbon control.

29. "Uniform," *Richmond Whig*, April 27, 1861.

30. Mollo, *Military Fashions*, 211.

31. "Company Uniforms," *Raleigh North Carolina Standard*, May 1, 1861.

32. "Volunteer Uniforms," *Rome Tri-Weekly Courier*, April 19, 1861 (widely cited). See also "Uniform for the Militia," *Richmond Whig*, April 16, 1861.

33. *Richmond Examiner*, March 28 and 29 and April 19, 1862.

34. Colonel A. C. Myer to Captain John M. Galt, Montgomery, Ala., April 19, 1861, chap. 5, vol. 13, Quartermaster Department—Letters and Telegrams Sent, March–September 1861, RG109, NAB. This outfit is very similar to that issued to Alabama troops from the Mount Vernon Arsenal, and its adoption may have been as a result of that establishment being turned over to Confederate control on April 8, 1861.

35. "Sealed Proposals, Quartermasters Offices, New Orleans, Louisiana, April 26, 1861," *New Orleans Daily Crescent*, April 27, 1861. This included blue flannel overshirts, thin woolen steel-gray trousers, and pliable leather stocks.

36. "Life in the Camp—No. III," Fort Morgan, Ala., April 6 [?], 1861, *Fayetteville Observer*, May 2, 1861. The details in the letter do not agree with the date and suggest a date of April 13, 1861. See Colonel A. C. Myers to Colonel W. J. Hardee, Montgomery, Ala., April 8, 1861, chap. 5, vol. 13, Quartermaster Department—Letters and Telegrams Sent, March–September 1861, RG109, NAB.

37. Jensen, "Survey of Confederate Central Quartermaster Jackets, Part 1," 110; Colonel A. C. Myers to Recruiting Officer Mount Vernon, Ala., Montgomery, May 2 1861; Colonel A. C. Myers to Captain John M. Galt, Montgomery, Ala., May 7, 1861; Colonel A. C. Myers to Captain John M. Galt, Montgomery, Ala., May 21, 1861, chap. 5, vol. 13, Quartermaster Department—Letters and Telegrams Sent, March–September 1861, RG109, NAB.

38. Colonel A. C. Myers to Captain J. M. Galt, Montgomery, Ala., May 24, 1861; Colonel A. C. Myers to Captain J. M. Galt, Richmond, Va., June 3, 1861; Colonel A. C. Myers to Captain J. M. Galt, Richmond, Va., June 5, 1861, chap. 5, vol. 13, Quartermaster Department—Letters and Telegrams Sent, March–September 1861, RG109, NAB.

39. "Clothing Bureau Richmond," *Raleigh North Carolina Standard*, August 31, 1861.

40. Colonel A. C. Myers to Major S. J. Smith, Richmond, Va., June 4, 1861, chap. 5, vol. 13, Quartermaster Department—Letters and Telegrams Sent, March–September 1861, RG109, NAB. In operation from early 1861 to October 1862, the Commutation System provided soldiers with twenty-one dollars initially and later twenty-five dollars every six months for clothing.

41. See Jensen, "Survey of Confederate Central Quartermaster Jackets, Part 1," 109–22; Jensen, "Survey of Confederate Central Quartermaster Jackets, Part 2," 162–71; Brooks, "Clothing the Tennessee Volunteer," 68–71; "Warm Clothing for Our Volunteers," *New Orleans Bee*, July 27, 1861; *New Orleans Bee*, August 12, 1861; "Wanted Immediately," *Richmond Dispatch*, August 17, 1861; Theodore Mandeville to Rebecca Mandeville, Grove Wharf, Va., August 27, 1861, Henry D. Mandeville and Family Papers,

Louisiana State University, in *Records of Antebellum Southern Plantations*, ser. 1, pt. 3, reel 4, frame 0820; "Louisianans on the Potomac," *New Orleans True Delta*, December 18, 1861; *Huntsville Southern Advocate*, September 18, 1861; Field, *Confederate Army*, 12–13; Bailey, "Clothing the Alabama Soldier," 28–29; Civil War Collection: Quartermaster Records, box 17, North Carolina Department of Cultural Resources, Division of Archives and History, Raleigh; Colonel Henry C. Wayne, Adjutant General, Georgia, to Colonel A. C. Myers, April 11, 1861, Adjutant General's Letterbook, no. 2, Georgia Department of Archives and History, Atlanta.

42. "Warm Clothing for Our Volunteers," *New Orleans Bee*, July 27, 1861.

43. Circular, "Clothing for the Soldiers," published in *Richmond Dispatch*, August 23, 1861; *Fayetteville Observer*, August 22, 1861; *Huntsville Southern Advocate*, August 28, 1861; *Mobile Tribune*, August 24, 1861.

44. "Clothing the Soldiers," *Richmond Examiner*, January 4, 1862.

45. "D," "From the Seat of the War in Virginia," Centreville, Va., November 15, 1861, *New Orleans Delta*, November 22, 1861.

46. "Malou," "Letter from Virginia," December 10, 1861, Richmond, Va., *New Orleans Daily Crescent*, December 17, 1861.

47. "The Confederate Flag," *Richmond Dispatch*, December 7, 1861.

48. Jensen, "Survey of Confederate Central Government Quartermaster Issue Jackets, Part 1," 109–22; Jensen, "Survey of Confederate Central Government Quartermaster Issue Jackets, Part 2," 162–71.

49. Troiani, "French Uniforms," 26; Jensen, "Survey of Confederate Central Government Quartermaster Issue Jackets, Part 2," 162–71.

50. McKee, "Notes on the Federal Issue Sack Coat," 50; Caldwell, *History of a Brigade*, 47.

51. "Notes on the Armies of the Confederate and Union Armies," in Underwood, and Buel, *Battles and Leaders of the Civil War*,4:768; Jensen, "Survey of Confederate Central Quartermaster Jackets, Part 1," 109–22; Jensen, "Survey of Confederate Central Quartermaster Jackets, Part 2," 162–71; Wilson, *Confederate Industry*, 310; *Savannah Republican*, May 24, 1864; *Mobile Register and Advertiser*, May 17, 1864. This figure does not include the Houston Depot in Texas or the thousands of articles of clothing constructed and issued by the states of North Carolina, Alabama, South Carolina, or Georgia.

52. "Issues of Clothing to Armies in the Field," in "Resources of the Confederacy, February 1865," *Southern Historical Society Papers* 2, no. 3 (September 1876): 120; Jensen, "Survey of Confederate Central Government Quartermaster Issue Jackets, Part 1," 110; Wilson, *Confederate Industry*, 128, 179.

53. "Report of Quartermaster W. R. Pickens of Alabama," *Selma Morning Reporter*, November 10, 1863.

54. See, e.g., Chapla, "Quartermaster Operations in the 42nd Virginia Infantry Regiment," 5–26.

55. Anderson, *Memoirs*, 161.

56. Hall, *Story of the 26th Louisiana Infantry*, 59–60; Tunnard, *Southern Record*, 220.

57. "The Soldier's Suit of Grey," *Augusta Constitutionalist*, April 7, 1864. A Confederate woman identified only as "Mildred" penned another poem using "grey" jackets as a symbol of Confederate soldiers. See "Mildred," "Grey Jackets," Tangipahoa, La., November 1863, reprinted in *Mobile Tribune*, November 23, 1863.

58. "The Soldier's Suit of Grey," Levy Sheet Music Collection, Johns Hopkins University, box 094, item 102, http://jhir.library.jhu.edu/handle/1774.2/4121.

59. Donald, "Confederate Soldier as Fighting Man," 296–307.

60. Entry for August 28, 1861, in Moore, *Life for the Confederacy*, 54.

61. W. D. Harris to Saphire E. Harris, September 21, 1861, Camp Davis, Lynchburg, Va., *Confederate Letters and Reminiscences*, 36.

62. "Petition to Governor Brown," [October] 1861, Confederate Collection, Georgia Department of Archives and History, Atlanta, M283/16, roll 74. See also a letter from a member of the Twelfth Georgia, August 19, 1861, in "Doles Cook Brigade," *Chattahoochee Historical Society Bulletin* 5 (November 1961): 49.

63. See, e.g., "Texas Rangers," *Nashville Patriot*, December 25, 1861; "Our Roanoke Island Correspondence, February 15, 1862," *New York Herald*, February 24, 1862; "Letter from Harrisburg, Pennsylvania, June 6 1862," *New Orleans Picayune*, July 12, 1862; "Rosser's Brigade of Cavalry," *Richmond Sentinel*, July 6, 1864; Musick, "Mystery of the Missing Confederate Medals of Honor," 74–76; "For the Army," *Richmond Dispatch*, January 5, 1865; Stout, "Buttons Made in the Confederacy," 246–47; Wiley, *Life of Johnny Reb*, 116–17; Harris, *Civil War Relics*, 12, 36, 62–63, 74, 80, 110–11, 115, 157, 182, 209; Woodhead, *Echoes of Glory*, 95, 117, 167; Coates, McAfee, and Troiani, *Don Troiani's Regiments and Uniforms*, 15, 206.

64. Kate Sperry, Winchester, January 16, 1862, "Kate Sperry's Diary, 1861–1866," in Andreae, *Virginia Country's Civil War* 1 (1983): 47.

65. Giles, *Rags and Hope*, 16. Relic collectors have recovered around sixty different Texas badge designs from Civil War campsites. See Ahlstrom, *Texas Civil War Artifacts*, 10–57.

66. "The Soldiers' Badge of Merit," *Richmond Whig*, May 5, 1864.

67. Faust, *This Republic of Suffering*, 118–22, 145–46.

68. John M. Tilley to family, February 23, 1862, Civil War Letters, letter 30, mf563, drawer 17, box 78, folder 2, Civil War Letters, Georgia Department of Archives and History, Atlanta.

69. Andrews, *Footprints of a Regiment*, 33.

70. Glatthaar, *General Lee's Army*, 167, 208, 209–10, 215–16, 355–57, 383, 431, 444–45, 448, 467.

71. Blackford, *War Years with J.E.B. Stuart*, 99.

72. "Supplies for the Army," *Richmond Enquirer*, November 13, 1862; Brigadier General A. R. Lawton to Mr. S. A. Miller, chairman of Special Committee on the Pay and Clothing of the Army, January 27, 1865, Official Records of the Union and Confederate Armies in the War of Rebellion, ser. 3, 3, 1039–40; S. A. Miller, *Report of Special Committee on the Pay and Clothing of the Army*, H.R. Rep. Confederate Congress, February 11, 1865, 5; Daniel, *Soldiering in the Army of Tennessee*, 31.

73. Goldsborough, *Maryland Line in the Confederate Army*, 125.

74. Field, *Confederate Army*, 5:36–37. See also David Pierson to Mary Catherine Pierson, July 19, 1862, in Cutrer and Parrish, *Brothers in Gray*, 105.

75. "Press Report—The President before Chattanooga, October 11, 1863," *Knoxville Register*, October 12, 1863. See also "Visit from the President to Bragg's Army," *Richmond Dispatch*, October 19, 1863.

76. George W. Morris to Mary E. Morris, March 9 1864, Bull's Gap, Tenn., in *Confederate Letters and Reminiscences*, 4:242–43.

77. "Peace," *Southern Illustrated News*, January 16, 1864; "Uniforms Desirable Not Essential," *Richmond Dispatch*, June 5, 1861; "General Washington's General Order, 1778"; "Suffering by War," *Mobile Tribune*, February 12, 1864.

78. Rubin, *Shattered Nation*, 51–52. According to his brother, soldier James Pierson misrepresented his poor dress in April 1863, despite having been issued a full uniform and also appropriating another full dress. The reason he showed "the darkest side of the case," his brother believed, was so his family could "appreciate the fact that he is soldiering." See David Pierson to William H. Pierson, April 3, 1862, in Cutrer and Parrish, *Brothers in Gray*, 171.

79. Evans, *Macaria*, 171. See also "Story of a Refugee: Chapter V," July 31, 1864, *Jackson (Selma, Ala.) Mississippian.*

80. "The Southern Confederacy. Special Correspondence, Culpeper Court House, November 14, 1862," *London Times*, December 27, 1862; Tichenor, "Fast Day Sermon," 94; Bishop Henry Champlin Lay, "The Devout Soldier: A Sermon Preached by Request to the Powatan Troop at Emmanuel Church, March 6, 1864," *Sermons*. See also "Like unto Us—How Precious the Sympathy of Christ with Human Infirmity," *Atlanta Southern Confederacy*, March 7, 1863; Faust, *Creation of Confederate Nationalism*, 22–23; Beringer et al., *Why the South Lost the Civil War*, 275–76; *Richmond Christian Observer*, January 23, 1862; Tally N. Simpson to Caroline V. Miller, July 18, 1863, in Everson and Simpson, *Far, Far from Home*, 258.

81. William D. Foley to James S. Foley, Tangipahoa, La., May 25, 1861, in author's collection.

82. Colonel A. C. Myers to E. Cain, Richmond, Va., July 1, 1861, vol. 5, chap. 13, Quartermaster Department—Letters and Telegrams Sent, March–September 1861. RG109, NAB.

83. Gallagher, *Confederate War*, 96–100.

84. Sorrell, *Recollections of a Confederate Staff Officer*, 51.

85. "Behold the Lilies of the Valley," *Richmond Examiner*, December 5, 1862.

86. "Uniforms of Officers," *New Orleans Picayune*, March 9, 1862.

87. "Uniform," *Richmond Enquirer*, July 19, 1862.

88. "Circular," War Department, Adjutant and Inspector General's Office, Richmond, Va., June 3, 1862; reprinted in "The Rebel Officers in Battle," *New York Times*, October 26, 1862.

89. Coates, McAfee, and Troiani, *Don Troiani's Regiments and Uniforms*, 170.

90. "An Act to Allow Commissioned Officers of the Army Rations and the Privilege of Purchasing Clothing from the Quartermaster Department," February 17, 1864, in Matthews, *Public Laws of the Confederate States of America*, 193.

91. General Order No. 28, March 4, 1864, Adjutant and Inspector General's Office.

92. "Remarks," Inspection of Cleburne's Division, Hardee's Corps, Army of Tennessee, Captain J. K. Dixon August 24, 1864, Inspection Records and Related Records Received by the Inspection Branch of the Confederate Adjutant and Inspector General's Office (National Archives Microfilm Publication, M935, roll 5, 0191), RG109. See also, "Remarks," Inspection of Bate's Division, Hardee's Corps, Captain C. Borsch, August 21, 1864, in Inspection Records (National Archives, Microfilm Publication, M935, roll 5, 0256), RG109.

93. "Remarks," Inspection of Tyler's Brigade, Bate's Division, Hardee's Corps, First Lieutenant J. S. Jones, August 23, 1864, Inspection Records and Related Records Received by the Inspection Branch of the Confederate Adjutant and Inspector General's Office (National Archives Microfilm Publication, M935, roll 5, 0284), RG109.

94. "A Panoramic View of the Rebel Army and Its General," *Cincinnati Commercial Tribune*, October 26, 1864.

95. "Appomattox Courthouse, April 12, 1865," in Coates et al., *Don Troiani's Regiments and Uniforms of the Civil War*, 170. The report found that rear echelon officers purchased most of the 31,940 yards of fine-grade cloth allocated for field officers.

96. "Officer's Pay," *Macon Telegraph*, December 10, 1864. This includes articles from *Montgomery Mail* and an unnamed Richmond newspaper.

97. Judith White McGuire, diary entry, March 7, 1862, *Diary of a Southern Refugee during the War,*

98–99. McGuire tells that one widowed mother of Confederate soldiers purchased overpriced Confederate gray from a store rather than more cheaply from the Quartermaster's Department because she felt she did not deserve it. "Letter from Rochester, Montgomery, Alabama, July 27 1864," *Mobile Tribune*, July 29, 1864.

98. "Juvenile Costume-Child's Cloak Made of Confederate Gray," *Southern Illustrated News*, January 17, 1863. The *Illustrated News* copied this figure from a fashion plate in the November 1862 issue of *Harper's New Monthly Magazine*. The *Harper's* overcoat was to be made of "light drab."

99. John Beauchamp Jones, diary entries, December 1, 1862; December 1, 4, and 13, 1864, in Miers, *Rebel War Clerk's Diary*, bk. 1, 200, 454, 456, 459; "Speculation and Extortion," *Huntsville Confederate*, April 2, 1863; "The Treasury Department," *Columbia South Carolinian*, June 23, 1864; Bill, *Beleaguered City*, 307.

100. "General Order No. 122, Section III," Adjutant and Inspector General's Office, Richmond, Va., September 11, 1863, *Richmond Enquirer*, September 16, 1863; Brigadier General A. R. Lawton to Mr. S. A. Miller, chairman of Special Committee on the Pay and Clothing of the Army, January 27, 1865, Official Records of the Union and Confederate Armies in the War of Rebellion, ser. 3, 3, 1039–40.

101. J. L. Wilson to Ellen Wilson, September 9, 1863, in *Confederate Letters and Reminiscences*, 9:217.

102. Wilson, *Confederate Industry*, 128.

103. Bonner, *Blood and Colors*, 121–23.

CHAPTER 7
Visualizing the War for the People

1. Lee to Davis, April 19, 1864, cited in Glatthaar, *General Lee's Army*, xiv.

2. Rubin, *Shattered Nation*, 123–26; Rable, "Despair, Hope and Delusion," 153–55; Phillips, *Diehard Rebels*, 170–76.

3. Gallagher, *Confederate War*, 127–55.

4. "Telegraphed Expressly for the Montgomery Messenger," *Montgomery Advertiser*, February 19, 1861.

5. "Amusements," *Richmond Dispatch*, April 12, 1861; "Amusements," *Richmond Whig*, April 16, 1861.

6. "Fort Sumter," *Charleston Courier*, April 16, 1861. Enterprising agents "testified to their fidelity" as they offered them for sale in places like Savannah, Ga. "Sumter, Moultrie and the Floating Battery," *Savannah Republican*, May 4, 1861.

7. "Fitz's Mammoth Panopticon," *Memphis Avalanche*, April 22, 1861.

8. "Panopticon of the South," *Memphis Appeal*, April 24, 1861.

9. "Panopticon of the South," *New Orleans Picayune*, July 30, 1861; "Panopticon of the South," *New Orleans True Delta*, July 30, 1861.

10. "Good Houses," *Nashville Gazette*, November 28, 1861.

11. Wallach, "Making a Picture," 29, 83–84, 90–91.

12. Reverend Chumley to the Editor, January 1862, *Augusta Constitutionalist*, February 28, 1862.

13. Davis, *Landscape of Belief*, 53–72; McGinnis, "Moving Right Along," 5–6, 121, 176–78; Oetterman, *Panorama*, 323–44.

14. "Grinevald's Pictures of the Battles of Charleston," *Charleston Mercury*, August 7, 1863. Described as "wonderfully definite and vivid," this featured three works: the April 1861 bombardment; the April 1863 battle between Fort Sumter and the monitors; and the bombardment of Fort Wagner. Little is

known of Grinevald. The first notice of him working as an artist is from Memphis, Tenn., in February 1853. By 1856, he had relocated to South Carolina, where he was active throughout the war. In June 4, 1862, he was listed as an engraver at James S. Paterson's printing establishment on a list of those exempted from duty forwarded by Treasury secretary Memminger to Secretary of War G. W. Randolph. In July 1865, the last notice of Grinevald appeared in a Columbia, S.C., newspaper.

15. "Great Victory," *Mobile Tribune*, August 6, 1861.

16. "Deaths," *New Orleans Picayune*, January 19, 1872; "Battlefield of Manassas," *New Orleans Delta*, August 6, 1861.

17. Harley, "Deconstructing the Map," 231–47; Crampton, "Maps as Social Constructions," 235–52; Short, "U.S. History through Maps and Mapmaking," 9:1–77.

18. "Mr. P. T. Eaton," *New Orleans Delta*, August 9, 1861.

19. "The Battle of Manassas Plains," *Nashville Patriot*, August 20, 1861.

20. Faust, *Creation of Confederate Nationalism*, 23–26.

21. These were J. C. Nott, "Position of Forces," *Mobile Evening News*, July 30, 1861, reprinted in *New York Herald*, August 8, 1861; Solomon Bamberger's *Map of the Battles on Bull Run, near Manassas;* James L. Bowen's *Battle Field of Young's Branch, or Manassas Plains, Battle Fought July 21, 1861;* and Samuel P. Mitchell's *Sketch of the Country Occupied by the Federal & Confederate Armies on the 18th & 21st July 1861.*

22. "The Genealogical Rank of Yankees as Human Animals," *Richmond Whig*, September 27, 1861; "Laus Deo," *Charleston Courier*, April 8, 1862; "Yankee Infamies, Big and Little," *Richmond Whig*, June 24, 1862; Bagby, "Editor's Table," 503–4; "The Difference," *Richmond Dispatch*, April 23, 1863; "Reticence—An Element of 'Defence and a Duty of Patriotism,'" *Record of News, History and Literacy* 1 (June 1863): 5; "Why We Always Beat Them," *Augusta Constitutionalist*, June 17, 1863; "How Do We Look," *Augusta Constitutionalist*, June 22, 1864; "Drunken Boast—Benhadad and Abraham Lincoln—Par Nobile Fratum," *Richmond Sentinel*, June 27, 1864; "The Future of Yankeedom," *Richmond Whig*, July 5, 1864; "Sennacherib and Our Yankee Foes," *Charleston Mercury*, July 27, 1864.

23. Parrish and Willingham list forty-five maps as having been published in the Civil War South. Of these, nine depicted specific battles: three of Manassas, two of Big Bethel, and single maps of Fredericksburg, Greenbrier River, Chickamauga, and Leesburg. See Parrish and Willingham, *Confederate Imprints*, 530–34. In addition to these maps, Southern newspapers contained advertisements or reports of the following: "Manassas by Mr. P. T. Eaton," *New Orleans Delta*, August 9, 1861; "Map of Battleground of Oak Hill," by Ellis and Moffett, *Memphis Appeal*, September 3, 1861; "Battle of Oak Hills," by Julius Baumgarten, Richmond, Va., *Richmond Dispatch*, November 11, 1861; "Battle of Bethel," by Julius Baumgarten, Richmond, Va., *Richmond Dispatch*, November 14, 1861; "Battles near Fredericksburg, May 1, 3, and 4, 1863," by Julius Baumgarten, Richmond, Va., *Richmond Enquirer*, June 12, 1863. In addition to these, Alfred Maurice engraved a series of maps for the *Augusta Constitutionalist:* "Map of Charleston Harbor," July 15, 1863; "Map of Gettysburg," July 22, 1863; "Map of the Battlefield of Chickamauga," October 3, 1863.

24. "Panopticon of the South," *New Orleans Picayune*, August 12, 1861; "Panopticon of the South," *New Orleans Delta*, August 12, 1861; "The Panopticon," *New Orleans Daily Crescent*, August 14, 1861; "The Panopticon," *New Orleans Daily Crescent*, August 20, 1861.

25. "Academy of Music," *New Orleans Delta*, December 17, 1861; "The Pan-tech-nop-to-mon," *New Orleans True Delta*, December 10, 1861; "Pantechoptomon," *New Orleans Picayune*, December 7, 1861. An advertisement states that act 3 of this show depicted the battle in four scenes: (1) "The first gun"; (2)

"To arms! The Washington Artillery in full play, Beauregard complimenting the boys, and dying horse and wounded soldier"; (3) "Capture of Sherman's Battery"; and (4) "The Yankees' Wonderful Run, Asa (a slave) gets another prize, and when last seen is in hot pursuit of more game."

26. "Bull Run and Bosphorous," *Memphis Appeal*, December 16, 1861; "A Splendid Work of Art," *Memphis Appeal*, December 5, 1861; "Burton's Southern Pictures," *Memphis Appeal*, December 13, 1861; "Burton's Southern Panorama," *Memphis Appeal*, December 8. 1861.

27. "Academy of Music," *New Orleans Picayune*, November 7, 1861; "Roll of the Drum," *Richmond Dispatch*, April 13, 1864. After its initial run, *Roll of the Drum* played in at least six Confederate cities until war's close. See "Roll of the Drum," *Mobile Register*, November 16, 1861; "Roll of the Drum," *Richmond Dispatch*, April 14, 1862; "Roll of the Drum," *Augusta Chronicle and Sentinel*, October 2, 1862; "Roll of the Drum," *Augusta Constitutionalist*, February 3, 1863; "Roll of the Drum," *Wilmington Journal*, June 12, 1863; "Roll of the Drum," *Richmond Dispatch*, April 12, 1864; "Roll of the Drum," *Macon Telegraph*, December 10, 1864; "Roll of the Drum," *Fayetteville North Carolinian*, December 17, 1864; "Roll of the Drum," *Wilmington Journal*, December 17, 1864.

28. Watson, *History of Southern Drama*, 77–78.

29. McPherson, *Battle Cry of Freedom*, 338; Hutchison, *Apples and Ashes*, 82, 118.

30. "Burton's Southern Moving Diorama," *Wilmington Journal*, May 22, 1862.

31. "The News from Richmond, September 15, 1862," *Charleston Mercury*, September 18, 1862.

32. "Engraving of the Virginia or Merrimac," *Mobile Evening News*, April 21, 1862.

33. The evidence contradicts the idea advanced by one historian that "no Confederate artist ever recorded its [the *Virginia's*] triumphs." Holzer, "Art of Ironclads," 47.

34. "Justice," *Augusta Constitutionalist*, April 27, 1862.

35. "Theatre," *Augusta Chronicle and Sentinel*, April 24, 1862.

36. "The Panopticon—An Excited Audience," *Augusta Constitutionalist*, April 26, 1862.

37. "War Illustrations," *Richmond Enquirer*. April 11, 1862.

38. Editorial, *Richmond Examiner*, January 1, 1863.

39. "The New Diorama," *Richmond Dispatch*, May 16, 1862; "Pantechnoptomon," *Richmond Examiner*, May 16, 1862; "Obituaries," *Richmond Dispatch*, September 27, 1862.

40. "Pantechnoptomon," *Augusta Constitutionalist*, December 12, 1862.

41. "Amusements," *Richmond Dispatch*, October 3, 1862.

42. "Theatre," *Mobile Register and Advertiser*, October 4, 1862.

43. "Odd Fellows' Hall," *Mobile Advertiser and Register*, April 19, 1863.

44. "New Panoramic Mirror at the Trinity Church," *Richmond Examiner*, April 2, 1863.

45. "New Paintings," *Richmond Examiner*, January 27, 1864. The piece was seven by three feet in size.

46. "Metropolitan Hall," *Richmond Whig*, July 10, 1863; "Theatre," *Montgomery Mail*, January 16, 1864; "Decided Hit," *Montgomery Mail*, January 19, 1864.

47. Jefferson Davis, "Message to the Fourth Session of the First Confederate Congress," Richmond, Va., December 7, 1863, *Compilation of the Messages and Papers of the Confederacy*, 345.

48. "From Fredericksburg," *Charleston Courier*, November 28, 1862.

49. "Defence of Vicksburg," *Macon Telegraph*, July 9, 1862.

50. "Vicksburg, Mississippi," *Southern Illustrated News*, November 8, 1862.

51. "Theatre," *Mobile Register and Advertiser*, October 25, 1862; "Grand Panoramic Mirror," *Wilmington Journal*, April 29, 1863.

52. "Advertisement," *Southern Illustrated News,* August 1, 1863.

53. "Bombardment of Vicksburg," *Augusta Chronicle and Sentinel,* August 28, 1863; "West and Johnston," *Southern Punch,* September 3, 1863. Vicksburg's Old Courthouse Museum holds one, if not the sole, example of this image.

54. "Just Three Years," *Richmond Examiner,* December 29, 1863; "Charleston and Fort Sumter," *Charleston Mercury,* January 1, 1864.

55. "The City of Charleston," *Augusta Constitutionalist,* July 2, 1864.

56. "Grand Panoramic Mirror," *Wilmington Journal,* April 29, 1863; "Lee Mallory's War Illustrations," *Richmond Enquirer,* August 8, 1863; "Grain's Panopticon," *Macon Telegraph,* June 30, 1864.

57. Bassham, *Conrad Wise Chapman,* 130. While Beauregard's self-promotion irritated President Davis, he fell out favor after taking an unauthorized leave from his army.

58. Lawrence B. Cohen's twenty-four-by-forty-inch painting *Ruins of Fort Sumter* showed Fort Sumter at sunrise, "every part perfect." To the fort's right, he set the picket monitor and made the blockading squadron look distant. "The Ruins of Sumter," *Charleston Courier,* January 15, 1864.

59. "Grinevald's Pictures of the Battles of Charleston," *Charleston Mercury,* August 7, 1863.

60. *Augusta Constitutionalist,* April 22, 1864; *Augusta Constitutionalist,* October 11, 1864.

61. "Gamma," "Our Richmond Correspondence, January 1, 1864," *Mobile Advertiser and Register,* January 12, 1864.

62. "Gamma," "Our Richmond Correspondence."

63. Account, August 1, 1863, George S. Cook file, Confederate Papers Relating to Business Firms and Citizens Files (National Archives Microfilm Publication, M346, roll 190), RG109R. He was paid for twenty-six copies of the photographs of the "Devils"; fifteen copies of *Fort Sumter,* and fifty-six copies of the monitors. In late September 1863, General P.G.T. Beauregard sent three large photographs and a set of stereoscopic photographs showing the damage done by enemy fire over the month of August 1863. See Lieutenant Colonel A. R. Rives to General P.G.T. Beauregard, October 14, 1863, Engineer Department—Letters and Telegrams Sent, 1861–1864, chap. 3, vol. 4, RG109, NAB.; Major General J. S. Gilmer to Lieutenant Colonel A. R. Rives, December 12, 1863, Confederate Engineer Department—Letters and Telegrams Sent, and Endorsements, Engineer Bureau, Department of South Carolina, Georgia and Florida, chap. 3, vol. 9, RG109, NAB.

64. "The Ironsides and Two Monitors Taken," *Charleston Courier,* September 9, 1863.

65. "The Bazaar," *Columbia South Carolinian,* January 18, 1865.

66. "Too Bad," *Augusta Chronicle and Sentinel,* March 25, 1865.

67. Binnington, *Confederate Visions,* 117–19; Sheehan-Dean, *Why Confederates Fought,* 119; Hutchison, *Ashes and Apples,* 118–19.

68. "Ladies Studio," *Memphis Appeal,* February 8, 1862.

69. "Painting on Porcelain," *New Orleans Picayune,* September 11, 1861.

70. "Galt—the Sculptor," *Columbus Sun,* December 6, 1861.

71. "Knoxville Art Association," *Knoxville Register,* October 19, 1862; "Confederate States Art Union," *Augusta Constitutionalist,* April 19, 1864.

72. "Confederate States Art Union."

73. "Hero Worship," *Southern Illustrated News,* October 10, 1863. See also "Our Milledgeville Correspondence," *Atlanta Southern Confederacy,* April 1, 1863. Stonewall Jackson's death prompted contemplation on this idea. See Stowell, "Stonewall Jackson and the Providence of God," 192–93, 195–96, 199.

74. "Grant and the Yankees," *Richmond Whig*, July 15, 1864. See also "In the Multitude of Counsellors There Is Safety," *Charleston Courier*, January 22, 1864.

75. "The Duty of the People," *Charleston Mercury*, August 11, 1863.

76. See, e.g., "Splendid Large Photographic Likenesses," *Charleston Courier*, August 6, 1861; "Portraits of Celebrities," *Augusta Chronicle and Sentinel*, September 3, 1861; "Christmas Presents," *Augusta Constitutionalist*, December 24, 1861; "Advertisement," *Savannah Morning News*, August 16, 1862; "Pictures of our Generals," *Richmond Enquirer*, August 14, 1863; "Advertisements," *Fayetteville Observer*, March 17, 1864; "Likenesses," *Wilmington Journal*, April 8, 1864; "Gallery of Confederate Generals," *Richmond Enquirer*, July 3, 1864; "A Place of Fashionable Resort," *Montgomery Mail*, December 3, 1864. In his studio "resort" in Montgomery, photographer George T. Shaw displayed not only leaders but also "many of Alabama's bravest sons who now sleep the sleep that knows no waking."

77. "Pictures of Our Generals," *Southern Illustrated News*, August 29, 1863; "Hero Worship," *Southern Illustrated News*, October 10, 1863.

78. "Our Paper," *Southern Field and Fireside*, August 1, 1863. In September 29, 1863, almost two months after its publication, *Southern Field and Fireside* presented its only other portrait, that of General Joseph E. Johnston.

79. "Mozart Hall," *Wilmington Journal*, March 2, 1864; "Mozart Hall," *Wilmington Journal*, March 11, 1864.

80. "Mozart Hall," *Wilmington Journal*, March 11, 1864; "Lee Mallory's War Illustrations," *Montgomery Mail*, April 24, 1864.

81. "Lee Mallory's War Illustrations," *Macon Telegraph*, April 2, 1864; "Lee Mallory's Illustrations," *Mobile Register and Advertiser*, May 10, 1864; "Novelty, Novelty," *Mobile Register and Advertiser*, May 12, 1864.

82. "Drama," *Southern Illustrated News*, November 11, 1864; "Montgomery Correspondence, September 26, 1864," *Mobile Tribune*, September 27, 1864; "Our Generals," *Fayetteville Observer*, March 17, 1864; "Lee Mallory War Illustrations," *Augusta Constitutionalist*, March 26, 1864.

83. "Mallory's War Illustrations," *Richmond Sentinel*, March 23, 1863; "Metropolitan Hall," *Richmond Enquirer*, June 19, 1863; "Great Southern Panorama," *Augusta Constitutionalist*, August 12, 1863; "New Panoramic Mirror at Trinity Church," *Richmond Examiner*, April 2, 1863.

84. "The Artist's Studio," *Southern Punch*, August 29, 1863; "General Robert E. Lee," *Charleston Mercury*, June 5, 1863; "Likeness of Gen. Lee," *Richmond Enquirer*, September 3, 1864; "Oil Painting of General Lee" and "Statuette of General Lee," *Richmond Examiner*, February 7, 1865, and *Staunton Spectator*, June 4, 1878; "House of Delegates," *Richmond Dispatch*, January 7, 1865; Crusan, "Confederate Civil War Photographers," 84. In early February 1865, photographs of Edward Valentine's statuette of Robert E. Lee circulated in Richmond. "Statuette of General Lee," *Richmond Examiner*, February 7, 1865; Hopkins, *Robert E. Lee in War and Peace*, 67.

85. Elder's work *Heroes of the Valley* is in the collection of Confederate Hall, New Orleans; Washington's *Jackson in Winchester* is in The Valentine, Richmond. *Richmond Whig*, November 12, 1863. Described as a full-length portrait by a "deaf artist," this work was probably by Edward C. Bruce. A photograph of this mounted work is in the collection of the Winchester-Frederick County Historical Society Collection, Winchester, Va.

86. "Stonewall Jackson," *Richmond Dispatch*, September 11, 1862; "General Thomas J. Jackson," *Southern Illustrated News*, September 13, 1862; "Southern Field and Fireside," *Augusta Constitutionalist*, August 6, 1863; "Obituary—Alexander Galt," *Richmond Dispatch*, January 21, 1863.

87. "Jackson Statue," *Richmond Enquirer*, July 3, 1863; "Jackson Statue," *Richmond Enquirer*, October 13, 1863.

88. "A Bust of Gen'l Jackson," *Richmond Enquirer*, August 26, 1863; "Glorious Old Stonewall," *Houston Tri-Weekly Telegraph*, June 19, 1863; "Stonewall Jackson," *Columbia South Carolinian*, March 11, 1864; "Gen'l Stonewall Jackson—Lithograph," *Charleston Mercury*, August 28, 1864. According to the *Mercury*, this portrait was "Executed by one of the original members of the Stonewall Brigade."

89. "The Five Hundred Notes," *Richmond Examiner*, March 29, 1864.

90. Manning, *What This Cruel War Was Over*, 217; Sheehan-Dean, *Why Confederates Fought*, 1–5.

91. "A Beautiful Picture," *New Orleans Daily Crescent*, November 18, 1861. The current whereabouts or status of this work is not known by the author.

92. "Who Wants to See a Battle," *Memphis Appeal*, December 12, 1861.

93. "A Splendid Work of Art," *Memphis Appeal*, December 5, 1861; "Burton's Southern Pictures," *Memphis Appeal*, December 8, 1861.

94. "Academy of Music," *New Orleans True Delta*, January 15, 1862; "Pantechnoptomon," *Savannah Republican*, October 30, 1862.

95. Grain served from 1861 to 1862 in a Tennessee artillery unit that served at the battle of Shiloh. George W Grain files, First Tennessee Heavy Artillery Regiment, Compiled Service Records of Confederate Soldiers Who Served in Organizations from the State of Tennessee (National Archives Microfilm Publication, M268, roll 86), RG109. "For One Night," *Columbus Enquirer*, November 16, 1864. The exceptions are a series of sacred panoramas displayed in New Orleans during Christmas 1861 and J. P. Andrews's series of twenty-four religious paintings entitled *Great Southern Panorama of Sacred History* that toured in the middle of 1863. See "Sacred Panoramas," *New Orleans True Delta*, December 31, 1861; "Panorama of Sacred History," *Wilmington Journal*, July 8 and 11, 1863.

96. In addition to those previously cited, the number also included "The Log Fort, or Woman's Heroism," "The Drama," *Richmond Dispatch*, January 1, 1862; "A Soldier's Trial, or the Warning Voice," *Southern Confederacy*, March 14, 1863; "Virginia Cavalier," *Richmond Enquirer*, March 18, 1863; "The Ghost of the Dismal Swamp," *Richmond Dispatch*, May 7 and August 6, 1864; "The Jayhawkers," *Savannah Republican*, May 11, 1863; "Battle of Leesburg, or Ball's Bluff," *Richmond Dispatch*, June 4, 1863; "Partisan Ranger, or the Bushwacker," *Richmond Dispatch*, November 9, 1863; "Courier, the Siege of Lexington," *Augusta Chronicle and Sentinel*, July 8, 1863; "Ghost of the Dismal Swamp, or, Marteau the Guerrilla," *Richmond Enquirer*, May 20, 1864; "Scenes of the War," *Richmond Sentinel*, June 18, 1864; "The Battle of Chickamauga," *Wilmington Journal*, November 28, 1864; "Old Warren, or the Scout of '61," *Macon Southern Confederacy*, April 6, 1865.

97. "In Southern Theaters during the War," *St. Louis Republic*, December 18, 1898.

98. Delchamps, *Love's Ambuscade*, 39–44.

99. McCabe, *Guerrillas*, 28.

100. Hodgson, *Confederate Vivandiere*, 20. The show premiered in Montgomery, Ala., during late January 1862. "The Confederate Vivandiere," *Montgomery Advertiser*, January 30, 1862.

101. "Theatre," *Savannah Morning News*, May 11, 1863. This work by John H. Hewitt, adapted from Bourcicault's *Siege of Lucknow*, depicted a Confederate garrisons' "stubborn resistance."

102. Faust, *This Republic of Suffering*, 6–7.

103. Delchamps, *Love's Ambuscade*, 43.

104. "Scenes of the Battle Field," *New Orleans Delta*, August 16, 1861.

105. "Pantechnoptomon," *New Orleans True Delta*, January 12, 1862; "War Illustrations," *Mobile Register and Advertiser*, April 26, 1863.

106. "War Illustrations," *Savannah Morning News*, November 10, 1862.

107. Davidson, *Cullings from the Confederacy*, 111–13.

108. "The Panopticon," *New Orleans Daily Crescent*, August 14, 1861; "War Illustrations," *Richmond Dispatch*, April 21, 1862.

109. The appearance of shows such as *The Angel of Death*, *The Ghost of Dismal Swamp*, Mallory's *Stereopticon*, and Professor St. Maux Bingham's *Phantasmagoria*, from late 1863, suggests audience's increased appetite for the metaphysical. See "Metropolitan Hall," *Southern Punch*, August 15, 1863; "New Richmond Theatre," *Richmond Sentinel*, November 11, 1863; Harwell, "Brief Candle," 71–74; "For the Bazaar," *Columbia South Carolinian*, January 18, 1865.

110. "Amusements," *Richmond Enquirer*, April 11, 1863.

111. McPherson, *For Cause and Comrades*, 140–41; Mitchell, *Civil War Soldiers*, 172.

112. Introduction to *The War and Its Heroes* (Richmond, Va.: Ayres and Wade, 1864), 11.

113. "Grand Panopticon," *Savannah Republican*, June 18, 1864.

114. "Theatre," *Montgomery Mail*, January 16, 1864; "Decided Hit," *Montgomery Mail*, January 19, 1864.

115. These included John A. Elder's *The Battle of the Crater* and a new the five-act war drama entitled *Scenes in the Present War*. *Richmond Dispatch*, June 16, 1864.

116. "War Illustrations," *Richmond Examiner*, September 4, 1863.

117. "Pantechnoptomon," *Richmond Examiner*, April 13, 1863; "Grand Panoramic Mirror," *Wilmington Journal*, April 29, 1863; "Grand Panoramic Mirror of the War," *Augusta Constitutionalist*, June 4, 1863.

118. Drama," *Southern Punch*, October 24, 1863; "Drama," *Southern Punch*, December 5, 1863.

119. These included smaller towns such as Greensboro, Ala., and Meridian, Miss. See "Burton's Panorama," *Greensboro Alabama Beacon*, January 1, 1864; "Burton's War Diorama," *Mobile Advertiser and Register*, January 31, 1864; "New Advertisements," *Meridian Clarion Ledger*, June 25, 1864.

120. Beringer et al., *Why the South Lost the Civil War*, 334–35.

121. Cumming, *Kate*, 271, 275. See also "News," *Troy Southern Advertiser*, April 28, 1865; Rubin, *Shattered Nation*, 123–26; Rable, "Despair, Hope, and Delusion," 153–55. Jason Phillips suggests that Confederate civilians found it harder than veterans to accept defeat. See Phillips, *Diehard Rebels*, 182.

122. Rable, "Despair, Hope, and Delusion," 129–55.

123. Phillips, *Diehard Rebels*, 144–46, 176–77.

124. Phillips, *Diehard Rebels*, 91.

125. Phillips, *Diehard Rebels*, 184–86.

126. Foster, *Gray Ghosts of the Confederacy*, 59, 117, 124–25, 136–37; Nolan, "Anatomy of the Myth," 11–34.

CHAPTER 8
Representations of Womanhood

Epigraph: Anya Jabour's work indicates that this dynamic existed beyond the playwright's imagination. See Jabour, *Scarlett's Sisters*, 268–71.

1. The literature on the experience of women in the Confederate South is substantial and presents insights into the diversity of women's experiences and thought. Faust's *Mothers of Invention* shows how women assumed great agency and visibility in the South. Clinton, *Stepdaughters of History*, reexamines

elite women's accounts of war, Southern women who stepped out of traditional gender roles, and the persistence of black women stereotypes. Silber, *Gender and Sectional Conflict,* finds parallels and contrast between the experience of women North and South. Jabour's work examines how young women in the South developed new standards of femininity during the war. Jabour, *Scarlett's Sisters,* 260–85. Ott's *Confederate Daughters* studies how young women in slaveholding families sustained their belief in prewar gender ideals and racial order. In her examination of the Confederacy's political outsiders, women and slaves, *Confederate Reckoning,* McCurry shows how these groups developed a degree of influence during the war. In *Scarlett Doesn't Live Here Anymore,* Edwards explores social mores and how black and white women tried to affect their destinies. See also Fahs, *Imagined Civil War,* 140–45. and Rable finds that Southern women's patriotism eroded and that most women found that gender roles remained unchanged. Rable, *Civil Wars,* 144–51, 288. Berlin finds that the failure of the Confederate government and armies to protect civilians from the North's increased targeting of civilians hastened the Confederate collapse. Berlin, "Did Confederate Women Lose the War," 168–88. Gallagher finds that many women continued to support the nation despite reverses. Gallagher, *Confederate War,* 5–6, 45, 75–80, 158–59, 163–67. Roberts finds that young Confederate women maintained loyalty by separating it from wartime reality. Roberts, *Confederate Belle,* 118.

2. Scott, *Southern Lady,* 80–102; Whites, *Civil War as a Crisis in Gender,* 3.

3. Rubin, *Shattered Nation,* 53–64.

4. "S. L." [Colonel Louis J. Dupre] to the Editor, "Women in the Quartermaster's Department, Richmond, Virginia, February 16 1863," *Knoxville Register,* February 21, 1863.

5. McCurry, *Confederate Reckoning,* 133–70, 359.

6. Studying the imagery in *Southern Punch* and *Southern Illustrated News* (the only illustrated periodicals with expensive runs) shows that *Punch* depicted women in 24 percent, black people in 11 percent, and men in 65 percent of engravings. The *News* included women in 16 percent, black people in 3 percent, and men in 81 percent of their illustrations. Of all the figures on Confederate currency, 39 percent were women (over 91 percent allegorical), 4 percent were black men and women, and 57 percent were white men.

7. A photographer, Mrs. E. Beachabard of New Orleans, operated over 1860–61, until her death in November 1861. Her extant known works depict soldiers. See Smith and Tucker, *Photography in New Orleans,* 100. In Memphis, in early 1862, Annie Perdue Sebring produced a portrait of General Sterling Price. "The Ladies Studio," *Memphis Appeal,* February 8, 1862.

8. Barker-Benfield, *Horrors of the Half-Known Life,* 9.

9. O'Brien, *Conjectures of Order,* 253–84.

10. "A Funeral in the South," *Alexandria Gazette,* January 24, 1856.

11. "Charitable Societies—The Clothing and Fuel Society," *Savannah Republican,* February 7, 1851; "The Ladies' Benevolent Society," *Mobile Register,* January 6, 1859.

12. Hutchison, *Apples and Ashes,* 65, 91–95.

13. Rable, *Civil Wars,* 15–17; Manning, *What This Cruel War Was Over,* 11–12; Clinton, *Stepdaughters of History,* 54–56; Massey, *Bonnet Brigades.*

14. Andrew S. Herron to Mrs. Samuel Skofield, June 3, 1861, *Baton Rouge Advocate,* June 4, 1861.

15. Cronin, "Patriotic Ladies and Gallant Heroines," 138–39.

16. *Atlanta Gate City Guardian,* February 26, 1861.

17. *Columbus Enquirer,* August 30, 1861.

18. Reprinted in *Memphis Appeal,* July 12, 1861.

19. Rubin, *Shattered Nation,* 55; Cronin, "Patriotic Ladies and Gallant Heroines," 141.

20. "The Ladies of Memphis," *Memphis Appeal,* June 14, 1861; "For the Eastern Clarion," *Paulding Eastern Clarion,* September 13, 1861; "The Needle and Thimble Brigade," *Memphis Appeal,* August 30, 1861; "Letter from Grace Hopper, New Orleans, May 5, 1861," *Baton Rouge Advocate,* May 9, 1861.

21. "The Soldier's Relief Association," *Charleston Courier,* December 9, 1864.

22. An English Officer [Fletcher], "Run through the Southern States," 499.

23. "The Ladies Volunteer Aid Association," *Augusta Constitutionalist,* October 10, 1862.

24. "Secretary's Report of the Ladies' Volunteer Association for the Month of February 1863," *Augusta Constitutionalist,* March 13, 1863. See also "What a Soldiers' Aid Society Has Accomplished," *Richmond Whig,* January 15, 1864.

25. Rable, *Civil Wars,* 140; Arliskas, *Cadet Gray and Butternut Brown,* 19–23, 48, 55.

26. J. W. Reid to family, November 6, 1861, *History of the Fourth Regiment S.C. Volunteers,* 56.

27. "Captain J. P. Andrews, Company G, Seventh Arkansas, to the Editor, March 5, 1864," *Macon Telegraph,* March 8, 1864.

28. McPherson, *For Cause and Comrades,* 131–42.

29. Phillips, *Diehard Rebels,* 88–90.

30. Cards to Ladies' Aid Societies from Camp near Grenada, January 17, 1863, *Natchez Courier,* February 3, 1863. See also Captain E. B. Millet to the ladies of Guadelupe and Caldwell Counties, December 30, 1864, *Houston Tri-Weekly Telegraph,* January 15, 1865; Ira R. Foster, "To the Women of Georgia," *Augusta Chronicle and Sentinel,* March 15, 1865.

31. Robert Bonner finds a similar dynamic arouse when the government assumed responsibility for issuing battle flags to army units. Bonner, *Colors and Blood,* 121–23.

32. E. J. Wiggins to Miss Julia A. Smith, Dalton, Ga., January 27, 1864; and H. T. Stringfellow to Miss Julia A. Smith, Dalton, Ga., March 20, 1864, both reprinted in McMillan, *Alabama Confederate Reader,* 351–52. Both Wiggins and Stringfellow (whose name does not appear on the muster roll of his regiment but does appear in the 1900 census of Confederate veterans) surrendered at the end of the war.

33. "Soldier's Relief Association of Charleston, Ninth Quarterly Report, October 20, 1863," *Charleston Mercury,* November 7, 1863.

34. "Fifth Quarterly Report of the Soldier's Relief Association of Charleston, October 21, 1862," *Charleston Mercury,* November 6, 1862.

35. "What Alabama Has Done for Her Soldiers," *Selma Morning Reporter,* October 11, 1863.

36. Fremantle, "1st June (Monday) 1863," *Three Months in the Southern States,* 155.

37. Kershaw's Brigade, April 5, 1864, Inspection Reports of McLaw's Division, Longstreet's Corps, Inspection Records and Related Records Received by the Inspection Branch of the Confederate Adjutant and Inspector General's Office (National Archives Microfilm Publication, M935, roll 2, 0075-0076), RG109.

38. "Army Correspondence, Jackson, Miss., June 28, 1863," *Atlanta Southern Confederacy,* July 6, 1863.

39. Mary E. Pope, "To the Women of the South," *Memphis Appeal,* April 21, 1861.

40. Faust, *Mothers of Invention,* 46–48; Rable, *Civil Wars,* 94–95. Research indicates that home production fell in the years leading up to the war.

41. *Tennessee Civil War Veterans Questionnaires.* Of the remaining respondents, 26 percent of the veterans either left the questions blank, stated that slaves did these jobs under the supervision of mis-

tresses, or, least frequently, said that no one made clothing in the house. See also "Coosa," "Communicated," *Montgomery Weekly Confederation*, July 5, 1861. This writer stated that before the war, between 75 and 80 percent of Southern men wore homespun winter clothing.

42. "Homespun," *Richmond Examiner*, December 9, 1862.

43. Cronin, "Patriotic Ladies and Gallant Heroines," 138–49.

44. "Blankets and Socks for the Soldiers," *Dalton Confederate*, reprinted in the *Mobile Tribune*, February 2, 1864; "The Needle and the Bayonet," *Augusta Chronicle and Sentinel*, March 30 1863; "True Patriotism," *Pensacola Gazette*, January 19, 1861, reprinted in *Charleston Courier*, January 23, 1861; "Convention of the Ladies of the State of Mississippi, Meridian, Mississippi, March 4, 1863," *Mobile Advertiser and Register*, March 22, 1863.

45. "Ladies Gun Boat," *Columbia South Carolinian*, February 1, 1863.

46. Whites's study of Augusta, Ga., suggests that some Confederate men believed this venture undermined traditional gender roles. See Whites, *Civil War as a Crisis in Gender*, 59–60.

47. Cronin, "Patriotic Ladies and Gallant Heroines," 149.

48. Watson, "Confederate Drama," 107–8.

49. Payment to Miss F. D. King for arresting and delivering Joshua West, a deserter from Company E, Twenty-Eighth Virginia Regiment of Infantry, Richmond, June 8, 1864, "Joshua West" file, Joshua West files, Twenty-Eighth Virginia Infantry Regiment, Compiled service records of Confederate soldiers who served in organizations from the State of Virginia (National Archives Microfilm Publication, M324, roll 750), RG109.

50. "Arrested by a Woman," *Richmond Examiner*, June 10, 1864.

51. Clinton, *Stepdaughters of History*, 40–41.

52. Berry, *All That Makes a Man*, 12–13, 44.

53. Catherine Clinton states that such women always faced rebuke or imprisonment. However, this was not always the case. See the stories of Amy Clarke in "A Female Soldier," *Charleston Mercury*, January 8, 1863; Mrs. Arnold, "Female Soldier," "Railroad Accident –A Sad Romance," *Atlanta Southern Confederacy*, March 6, 1862; *New Orleans True Delta*, reprinted in *Augusta Constitutionalist*, May 1, 1862; Mrs. Blalow, "A North Carolina Amazon," *Augusta Chronicle and Sentinel*, May 15, 1862; "A Female Soldier Boy," *Augusta Constitutionalist*, May 7, 1863; Mrs. Margaret Tolley, *Charlotte Democrat*, April 11, 1865. Some were arrested; see "A Female Soldier," *Columbus Enquirer*, September 23, 1863; "Sent Away," *Richmond Examiner*, July 16, 1863; "Female Soldiers," *Richmond Whig*, October 31, 1863; "Important Arrest," *Charlotte Democrat*, April 11, 1865.

54. See "Music," *New Orleans Picayune*, May 12, 1861; "Photographic Views," *New Orleans Sunday Delta*, May 26, 1861 (copies of two of these images can be found in folder 8, P-432/60, Samuel Henry Lockett Papers, Wilson Library, University of North Carolina at Chapel Hill; and in the Library of Congress, photographic collection, No. 7590-LC-B818–1145); "A Tableaux Vivants," *New Orleans Picayune*, December 7, 1861.

55. These were John Davis's "The Roll of the Drum" (1861–64); John H. Hewitt's "The Vivandiere" (1863) and "The Scouts; or, The Plains of Manassas" (1861–63); W. J. Hodgson's "The Confederate Vivandiere" (1862); and "The Vivandiere's Fortune" (1863). See Harwell, "Brief Candle," 65–66; Fife, "Theatre during the Confederacy," 334–36.

56. Watson, "Confederate Drama," 106–7; "The New Opera," *Savannah Morning News*, March 18, 1863.

57. Orr, "John Hill Hewitt," 58–62.

58. "Theatre," *New Orleans Picayune*, November 6, 1861; "Athenaeum," *Atlanta Southern Confederacy*, April 30, 1863.

59. Hodgson, *Confederate Vivandiere*.

60. Fife, "Theatre during the Confederacy," 140. Castine, the title character of Edward Edgeville's 1864 novel, represents another Confederate heroine who masqueraded as a soldier. However, she did so to avenge her sister's sexual assault by Union soldiers. See Fahs, *Imagined Civil War*, 250–55.

61. Cronin, "Daughters of the New Revolutionary War," 74–75. On Northern stages, similar plays concluded in the same fashion. See Gallman, *Defining Duty in the Civil War*, 219.

62. "The Yankee Doctress," *Richmond Examiner*, June 27, 1864; *Richmond Examiner*, May 26, 1864.

63. "Dr. Mary E. Walker," *Richmond Whig*, May 3, 1864; "Miss Mary E. Walker M.D.," *Southern Illustrated News*, May 14, 1864.

64. "A Female Soldier Boy," *Augusta Constitutionalist*, May 7, 1863.

65. McCabe, *Guerrillas*, 30.

66. "The Mobilization of Our Women," *Charlottesville Chronicle*, reprinted in *Wilmington Journal*, December 1, 1864. Also reprinted in *Augusta Constitutionalist*, December 16, 1864.

67. This show was based on Colin Henry Hazlewood's farce *Going to Chobham* (1853). Thomas Hailes Lacy, *Lacy's Acting Edition of Plays, Dramas, Farces and Extravagances, Etc., Etc., as Performed at the Various Theatres . . . .* (London: T. H. Lacy, 1854), 107–22.

68. "John Mitchell on the Fashions," *Macon Telegraph*, December 15, 1864, reprinted from *Richmond Enquirer*.

69. Cumming, *Kate*, 186.

70. "Unpleasant Present, Unpleasanter Future," *Southern Punch*, December 13, 1863; "War and Matrimony—Dreadful Reflections," *Southern Punch*, October 18, 1862. See also Faust, *Mothers of Invention*, 139–41; Jabour, *Scarlett's Sisters*, 281–86.

71. "Remember the Soldiers," *Fayetteville Observer*, August 25, 1862; "Public Meeting," *Macon Telegraph*, August 24, 1863.

72. "Message of President Davis, to the Provisional Congress of the Confederate States, Montgomery, Alabama, April 29, 1861," *Richmond Dispatch*, May 4, 1861; "Message of President Davis to the Congress of the Confederate States of America, Richmond, Virginia, July 20, 1861," *Richmond Dispatch*, July 22, 1861. As the war progressed, President Davis increasingly called for unanimity. See Jefferson Davis to the Congress of the Confederate States, Richmond, November 18, 1861, in Crist et al., *Papers of Jefferson Davis*, 7:412–21, transcribed from the signed copy amended by Davis in the National Archives, documents in the *Official Records*, ser. 4, 1:732–38; Jefferson Davis, Second Inaugural, transcribed from Rowland, *Jefferson Davis, Constitutionalist*, 5:198–203; "Speech of President Jefferson Davis in Columbia, South Carolina," *Charleston Courier*, October 6, 1864; "African Church Speech, February 6, 1865," *Richmond Sentinel*, February 8, 1865; "To the People of the Confederate States of America, Danville, Virginia, April 4, 1865," in Richardson, *Messages and Papers of the Confederacy*, 1:568–70.

73. Wise, *Lifeline of the Confederacy*, 107–20, 221–26.

74. McCurry, *Confederate Reckoning*, 125–32.

75. Rable, *Civil Wars*, 94–95; Faust, *Mothers of Invention*, 221–22; Silber, *Gender and the Sectional Conflict*, 48–50. Silber shows that this dynamic also affected the North.

76. Cowling, *Artist as Anthropologist*, 81–83.

77. Faust, "Moment of Truth," 138.

78. "If Some Student of the Occult Sciences . . . ," *Richmond Examiner,* November 26, 1863. *Proh pudor* translates as "for shame" and "shoddy" from a Northern term used to describe cheaply and poorly made war materiel.

79. "Description of Life in New York City," *Richmond Dispatch,* April 20, 1864.

80. "A Belle of Wet-Zel," *Southern Punch,* May 7, 1864. Wetzel was a small district on the outskirts of Richmond; there is no indication of why the artist chose this locale beyond a play on words. The *Southern Punch* copied this cartoon from the engraving *The Great Social Evil,* published in the January 10, 1857, issue of London's *Punch* and represented prostitutes in London's Haymarket.

81. Cowling, *Artist as Anthropologist,* 81–83, 113–19; Barber, "White Working Women in Confederate Richmond," 210–11.

82. "For the Register and Advertiser," *Mobile Evening News,* April 16, 1864.

83. Rubin, *Shattered Nation,* 215–17.

84. Gallagher, *Confederate War,* 31–33; Rable, *Civil Wars,* 87–89. Over 320,000 Union and 150,000 Confederate soldiers either deserted or hid from conscription. Rubin, *Shattered Nation,* 75–79.

85. "Petersburg," "From Gen. Lee's Army–September 6, 1863," *Petersburg Express,* reprinted in *Savannah Morning News,* September 16, 1863; Silber, *Gender and the Sectional Conflict,* 45.

86. "Sydney," "A Solemn Warning to the Wives of Soldiers—A Military Execution," *Selma Reporter,* reprinted in *Savannah Morning News,* February 13, 1863; "The Women and the War—To the Editor of the *Richmond Examiner,*" reprinted in *Fayetteville Observer,* September 7, 1863. See also "To the Soldiers of the Confederate States, Richmond, Virginia, August 1, 1863," *Augusta Chronicle and Sentinel,* August 16, 1863, reprinted across the South.

87. Rubin, *Shattered Nation,* 69–72. See also Moore, *Conscription and Conflict in the Confederacy;* Escott, *After Secession,* 63–64, 80–88.

88. Faust, *Mothers of Invention,* 154–57, 175.

89. Cowling, *Artist as Anthropologist,* 81–83.

90. Rubin, *Shattered Nation,* 71–72.

91. Long, "Jeff Davis Must Be Killed," 70–83. See also George E. Pond, "Kilpatrick and Dahlgren's Raid to Richmond," in Johnson and Buel, *Battles and Leaders of the Civil War,* 4:95–96; "More on the Raid," *Richmond Dispatch,* March 5, 1864; "The Enemies' Latest Schemes," *Richmond Dispatch,* March 8, 1864.

92. Cowling, *Artist as Anthropologist,* 81–83. These women's features are those commonly used to denote Irish or the poor in American and English illustrated papers.

93. "The Women of the Confederacy," *Richmond Dispatch,* March 11, 1864.

94. "Confederate Women and the War," *Southern Literary Messenger* 38 (February 1864): 217.

95. Boyd also figured as the sole woman in Lee Mallory's 1864 *Stereopticon*—this despite the notices announcing that the performance included "women of the South." See "Mozart Hall," *Wilmington Journal,* March 11, 1864. An 1862 photograph circulated of the "oppressed and heroic" spy Mrs. Rose O'Neal Greenhow by Henry E. Dibble of Julian Vannerson's Gallery, commissioned by the editor of Charleston's *Courier.* However, it did not make it into Mallory's show. See "Mrs. Rose Greenhow," *Charleston Courier,* June 19, 1862.

96. "Tableaux Vivants," *Richmond Dispatch,* December 30, 1861.

97. "Tableaux Vivants," *Richmond Dispatch,* November 15, 1862. See also Faust, *Mothers of Invention,* 26–28.

98. "Ida Vernon to Celebrate," *Lexington Herald,* September 2, 1906; "News from the South," *New York Herald,* December 12, 1861; "Items from the Rebel States," *San Francisco Evening Bulletin,* February 13, 1863.

99. "Passengers for California from New York, August 13, 1863," *San Francisco Evening Bulletin*, September 5, 1863; "Richmond Theatre," *Richmond Dispatch*, August 15, 1864.

100. "City Intelligence—Theatrical," *Richmond Examiner*, June 16, 1864.

101. *Richmond Examiner*, August 17, 1864; "Theatre," *Richmond Whig*, September 8, 1864.

102. "Correspondence," *Richmond Whig*, December 28, 1864; "Half a Century on Stage," *Boston Globe*, April 9, 1910.

103. "The Drama," *Southern Illustrated News*, September 3, 1864.

104. "The Pickens Family," *Columbia State*, January 31, 1910; "Presentation of a Flag to the Holcombe Legion, Adams' Run, June 2, 1862," *Charleston Courier*, June 4, 1862. See also Burton and Burton, "Lucy Holcombe Pickens," 1:273–98.

105. Blanton Duncan to C. G. Memminger, June 9, 1862, Blanton Duncan files, in Gruber, *Confederate Papers Relating to Citizens or Business Firms*, M346, roll 263), RG109; Joseph D. Pope to C. G. Memminger, January 27, 1863, in Thian, *Correspondence with the Confederate Treasury Department*, 14.

106. "The Issue of Treasury Notes," *Charleston Mercury*, November 12, 1862; "The New Currency," *Augusta Constitutionalist*, April 7, 1864.

107. Clinton, *Stepdaughters of History*, 84–86; White, *Ar'n't I a Woman*, 29–61; Frederickson, *Black Image in the White Mind*, 53–58, 102–16.

108. Unknown author, *Great Expectations*, 8–9. According to advertising written by a "citizen of Richmond," black female parts occurred more rarely than male. In addition to Aunt Sarah, the following parts have been found: Aunt Nelly, "a Negro woman," in James D. McCabe's "The Maiden's Vow, or the Siege of Courtland," *Richmond Dispatch*, April 15, 1863; Dinah, in Richard D. Ogden's "Miscegenation: or, A Virginia Negro in Washington," *Richmond Dispatch*, April 13, 1864; Dinah, in "Slasher and Crasher," *Richmond Dispatch*, November 22, 1864.

109. White, *Ar'n't I a Woman*, 29–61; Frederickson, *Black Image in the White Mind*, 53–58, 102–16.

110. Piacentino, "Confederate Disciplines of Momus," 251.

111. Genovese, *Roll, Jordan, Roll*, 558–59. In Charleston, S.C., a law forbidding black women from wearing veils helped men in "making the most proper distinction" between black and white women. See "Letter from Charleston, March 3, 1863," *Mobile Register*, March 8, 1863.

112. White, *Ar'n't I a Woman*, 77–90.

113. Weiner, *Mistresses and Slaves*, 56, 58–59.

114. "Our New Heading," *Southern Illustrated News*, January 14, 1865.

115. Rable, *Civil Wars*, 288.

116. "The Future of the Confederacy," *Knoxville Register*, October 3, 1863.

CHAPTER 9
Picturing Hierarchies of Manhood

1. See Wicks, *Wildmen and Warriors*, 11. The story of Charles Waters shows the boundaries of Confederate ideas of gender; arrested and investigated for wearing women's clothing, the press described Waters as an "it." See "The 'What Is It' in Town!" *Augusta Chronicle and Sentinel*, September 9, 1862. No record of trial or his subsequent history has been found.

2. McPherson, *For Cause and Comrades*, 151–53: Glatthaar, *General Lee's Army*, 228–34; Rotundo,

American Manhood, 3, 10–13, 16, 18, 21; Rotundo, "Learning about Manhood," 36–39. Rotundo identifies the three types: "Christian gentleman," "masculine primitive," and "masculine achiever." Michael Kimmel describes the "genteel patrician," a model that includes many of the values of the Christian gentleman, and the "self-made man" includes qualities akin to the masculine achiever. Kimmel's "heroic artisan" and Rotundo's masculine primitive are unique. Kimmel, *Manhood in America,* 16–17.

3. "P" to the editor, Parkersburg, Va., March 21, 1861, "Correspondence of the Richmond Dispatch," *Richmond Dispatch,* April 4, 1861.

4. Franklin, *Militant South,* ix, 33–62; Greenburg, *Manifest Manhood,* 11–12; This type relates to the values associated with "primal honor" that Wyatt-Brown identifies in Southern male behavior. Wyatt-Brown, *Southern Honor,* 70–79.

5. Greenburg, *Manifest Manhood,* 11–12. This type relates to the strand of "gentility" that Wyatt-Brown identifies in Southern behavior. Wyatt-Brown, *Southern Honor,* 70–79.

6. Quigley, *Shifting Grounds,* 142; Friend, "Crushing of Southern Manhood," 25–27.

7. Barton, *Goodmen,* 37–39; Potter, *Impending Crisis,* 448–84; Phillips, *Diehard Rebels,* 55–57; Rable, *Damn Yankees!* Rable's study into Confederate imaginings of their enemy indicates the breadth and complexity of Southern beliefs.

8. "Foreigners and the War," *Richmond Enquirer,* February 9, 1864.

9. Barton, *Goodmen,* 65–67, 72–75, 79–80; Censer, *North Carolina Planters and Their Children,* 16; Green, "Stout Chaps Who Can Bear the Distress," 174–84.

10. Watson, *History of Southern Drama,* 74–84; Bernath, *Confederate Minds,* 208–9; "The Roll of the Drum," *New Orleans Picayune,* November 7, 1861; "The Confederate Vivandiere," *Montgomery Advertiser,* January 30, 1862; "Virginia Cavalier," *Richmond Dispatch,* March 18, 1863. A number of Northern and Southern works presented President Lincoln with similar characteristics. See Irelan, "Lincoln the Yankee Goon," 59–74.

11. Quoted in Mullenix, "Performing Confederate Nationalism," 40.

12. "New Broad Street Theatre," *Richmond Examiner,* April 15, 1863. It played in Richmond April 13–15, May 30, and November 10, 1863. "Amusements—New Richmond Theatre," *Richmond Examiner,* April 13, 1863.

13. "Amusements—New Richmond Theatre"; "New Broad Street Theatre," *Richmond Examiner,* April 15, 1863; "The New Richmond Theatre," *Richmond Dispatch,* April 13, 1863.

14. See, e.g., "New 'Military' Order," *Augusta Constitutionalist,* June 12, 1863. The newspaper reported that despite losing the battle of Chancellorsville, the North intended issuing a medal to its soldiers.

15. "Letters from Richmond, November 14, 1862," *Charleston Mercury,* November 18, 1862.

16. Cowling, *Artist as Anthropologist,* 33, 49, 59, 81, 85.

17. "War Meeting," *Prattville Autauga Citizen,* February 13, 1862. See also "Yankee Outrages in North Carolina," *Montgomery Weekly Advocate,* August 26, 1863. See Grimsley, *Hard Hand of War.*

18. "Jacta alea est," *Wilmington Journal,* August 6, 1863.

19. Edward Edgeville, "Castine, or The Maid of Mirkland," *Illustrated Mercury,* September 3, 1864.

20. A print entitled *Grand Federal Menagerie* that originated in New Orleans after Federal troops reclaimed it in April 1862 portrayed General Benjamin Butler as a hyena scavenging among the graves of dead Confederate heroes. Reproduced in both lithograph and carte de visite format, it made its way into the Confederacy. The *Southern Illustrated News,* April 30, 1864, included a version with the title

"Butler the Beast at Work." See "Lithograph of Butler," *Houston Tri-Weekly Telegraph,* December 5, 1862; "The Great Hyena of This War," *Natchez Courier,* February 7, 1863.

21. For these images, see "Master Lincoln Gets a New Toy," *Southern Illustrated News,* February 28, 1863; "Abraham Lincoln—Grand Vizier U.S.," *Bugle Horn of Liberty,* August 1863; "President of the Misceg–United States," in "It Must Come," *Hard Tack* (May 1864); "Aunt Aby," in "Hungry Government School in Lincolnia," *Southern Punch,* July 9, 1864. See also "School Master Lincoln and His Boys," *Southern Illustrated News,* January 31, 1863.

22. "The Devil Quoting Scripture," *Charleston Mercury,* December 11, 1861; Mr. Clark and Mr. William P. Chilton of Alabama, in "Report of the Judiciary Committee to the Confederate Congress, October 1 1862," reprinted in *Richmond Dispatch,* October 2, 1862, quoted in *Richmond Dispatch,* October 14, 1863.

23. Quoted in the *Southern Illustrated News,* November 29, 1862. Lincoln is also depicted as the Devil in "Abduction of the Yankee Goddess Liberty," *Southern Punch,* November 14, 1863.

24. Berends, "Wholesome Reading Purifies and Elevates Man," 117–18; Stout, *Upon the Altar of the Nation,* 132–36, 288–92.

25. "A Contrast," *Richmond Enquirer,* June 4, 1864. This was not universal. Richmond newspapers debated the role of religiosity in national affairs. See Stout and Grasso, "Civil War, Religion and Communication," 313–59.

26. "L.L.V.," "The True Gentleman: Respectfully Dedicated to Dr. T. S. Powell of the Atlanta Medical College," *Literary Companion,* reprinted in *Macon Telegraph,* July 26, 1862.

27. "Southern Patriotism," *Richmond Dispatch,* May 6, 1862; Faust, *Creation of Confederate Nationalism,* 22—40; "The History and Philosophy of Yankee Fanaticism," *Atlanta Southern Confederacy,* May 29, 1863.

28. Rable, *God's Almost Chosen Peoples,* 283–90.

29. "Achans," *Salisbury Watchman,* reprinted in *Fayetteville Observer,* March 27, 1862; "Are There Any Achans amongst Us?" *Raleigh Spirit of the Age,* May 4, 1863; James N. Bethune, "To the People of the Southern Confederacy," *Columbus Sun,* reprinted in *Memphis Appeal,* January 2, 1864; "Be Not Discouraged," *North Carolina Christian Advocate,* reprinted in *Raleigh Confederate,* January 24, 1864.

30. "Fast Day: Sermon Given at St. Paul's Church," *Richmond Enquirer,* August 24, 1863.

31. "Valentines," *Richmond Whig,* February 4, 1864; "St. Valentine's Day," *Richmond Whig,* February 9, 1864; "Now Ready," *Augusta Constitutionalist,* February 5, 1864.

32. "Local Intelligence," *Richmond Enquirer,* February 9, 1864.

33. "A Chapter on Croakers," *Richmond Dispatch,* July 17, 1863. See also "Our Cause," *Houston Tri-Weekly Telegraph,* August 17, 1863; "A Chapter on Croakers," *Richmond Dispatch,* July 17, 1863; "The Spirit of the Army," *Richmond Dispatch,* September 3, 1863.

34. Cowling, *Artist as Anthropologist,* 61–63. See also "The Women of the South," *Augusta Constitutionalist,* February 27, 1862.

35. Confederate author O. Garth Jr. used one of these books, Goethe's *The Sorrows of Werter,* as the title of a satirical work that mocked Confederate shirkers. See "A Humorous Publication," *Richmond Whig,* June 22, 1864.

36. "The Duty of the Time," *Army Messenger,* reprinted in *Macon Telegraph,* August 31, 1863.

37. Faust, *Creation of Confederate Nationalism,* 49–51.

38. *Address of the Baptist General Association of Virginia,* 2, 6; Rable, *God's Almost Chosen People,* 251–52.

39. Roland, *Confederacy*, 42, 44–45; "Southern Patriotism," *Richmond Dispatch*, May 6, 1862; "What Has Seizing Done," *Atlanta Southern Confederacy*, March 6, 1863. The play *Wanted a Substitute; or, The Extortioners*, by "two gentlemen of this city," paired self-preservation and greed. See "In Active Preparation," *Richmond Dispatch*, October 16, 1863.

40. "The Voice of the Patriotic Dead," *Prattville Autauga Citizen*, May 19, 1862; "Letter from Atlanta," *Augusta Constitutionalist*, January 21, 1864; "The Correspondence of the Constitutionalist. Wilmington, North Carolina, January 24, 1864," *Augusta Constitutionalist*, January 27, 1864.

41. Commager, *Defeat of the Confederacy*, 163–70; Wilson, *Confederate Industry*, 60–62, 64, 202–3.

42. "Yankee Outrages in North Carolina," *Montgomery Weekly Advocate*, August 26, 1863.

43. "Governor Vance to the North Carolina Legislature," *Raleigh North Carolina Standard*, November 24, 1863. For result, see "North Carolina Legislature," *Richmond Dispatch*, December 1, 1863.

44. McPherson, *Battle Cry of Freedom*, 598.

45. Beegan, "Mechanization of the Image," 257–74.

46. William Holden's campaign for governor on a platform of negotiated peace failed.

47. McCabe, *Guerrillas*, 17.

48. Delafield, *Love's Ambuscade*, 2, 30, 38, 40–41.

49. "Our Chief Dangers," *Richmond Dispatch*, October 9, 1863.

50. "The Spirit of the Army," *Richmond Dispatch*, September 3, 1863.

51. Higginbotham, "Martial Spirit in the Antebellum South," 4.

52. See, e.g., "Noxubee Rifles," *Macon Beacon*, September 12, 1860; "Noxubee Rifles," *Macon Beacon*, January 9, 1861.

53. "Plain Clothing of the Confederates," *Richmond Dispatch*, March 7, 1862. See also Franklin Lafayette Riley, diary entry, December 10, 1861, in Riley, *Grandfather's Journal*, 55.

54. Wyatt-Brown *Southern Honor*, 48, 97, 103.

55. "Movement of Troops," *New Orleans Picayune*, April 11, 1861. For more on the relationship between the nature of the uniform and the character of the soldier, see "The Military," *Charleston Mercury*, June 1, 1861; "North Carolina Troops," *Petersburg Express*, quoted in *Winston-Salem Western Sentinel*, August 9, 1861; "Victory Follows Victory," *Nashville Union and American*, August 17, 1861.

56. "Caught a Tailor," *Southern Punch*, April 2, 1864; Fletcher, *Rebel Private*, 54; "Movement of Troops," *New Orleans Picayune*, April 11, 1861.

57. Freehling, *Road to Disunion*, 40–50; Boney, *Southerners All*, 13–24, 63.

58. Harry Lewis to Mrs. Nancy Lewis, June 26, 1861, Camp Clark, Corinth, Miss., in Evans, *16th Mississippi Infantry*, 8.

59. Frank Liddell Richardson to Francis DuBose Richardson and Bethia Liddell Richardson, Camp Moore, September 4, 1861, Southern Historical Collection, University of North Carolina, Chapel Hill. See also Donald, "Confederate as Fighting Man," 299. "S.D.G.," "Camp in the Woods of Scott County, Mississippi, July 28, 1863," Greenville *Southern Enterprise*, August 8, 1863.

60. Wyatt-Brown *Southern Honor*, 289, 444; Herrera, "Self-Governance and the American Citizen Soldier," 23, 26–27; Davis, *Look Away*, 241–44; Moore, *Conscription and Conflict*, 68, 74; McPherson, *Battle Cry of Freedom*, 611–12.

61. See diary entry for June 28, 1863, Fremantle, *Three Months in the Southern States*, 244; Fletcher "Run through the Southern States," 501.

62. Davis, *Campaign from Texas to Maryland*, 18. As James Jay Archer, the original colonel of the Fifth

Texas, continued to serve until promoted to general for gallantry, it is possible that Davis's story was apocryphal.

63. Herrera, "Self-Governance and the American Citizen Soldier," 23–27. See, e.g., "Camp Jones, Manassas, August 20, 1861," *Raleigh North Carolina Standard,* August 28, 1861; "Jackson, Mississippi, May 31, 1863," *New Orleans Picayune,* June 26, 1863; Albert A. Nefi, "Fuss and Feathers versus Rough and Ready," *North and South Magazine* 6 (February 2003): 8–9; Campbell, "Fabric of Command," 261–90; Anonymous [Captain William Parker Snow], *Southern Generals,* 158, 166, 172, 184, 316, 375, 383, 473–74, 482.

64. Collins, *Chapters from the Unwritten History of the War between the States,* 157–58; Coates et al., *Don Troiani's Regiments and Uniforms,* 242–43.

65. Berry, *All That Makes a Man,* 11–12; Friend, "Crushing of Southern Manhood," 20. These find that women's approval, the thirst for a hero's fame, and the dread of seeming effeminate motivated Southern men.

66. *Battlefields of the South,* 308.

67. "Epigram," *Southern Punch,* October 17, 1863. This poem appeared in print in America as early as 1838 under the title "On a Dandy." *Florio* may refer to Giovanni Florio (1553–1625), at one time accused of immorality. However, his reputation was more for pedantry than preening. *Peter Bell* refers to a William Wordsworth poem penned in 1798 and published in 1819. The tale in poetry follows the progress of the dull and shallow Bell from the country to damnation. See also "Ornamental Warriors," *Richmond Dispatch,* October 6, 1862; "Correspondence of the Telegraph," *Macon Telegraph,* November 7, 1862; "Who Are Patriots?" *Milton Chronicle,* February 13, 1863; "Reform," *Montgomery Weekly Mail,* February 18, 1863; "Letter from Jackson, June 26, 1863," *Mobile Register,* reprinted in *Macon Telegraph,* July 4, 1863; "The Fashions," *Mobile Advertiser and Register,* December 3, 1863; "City Affairs of the Week" and "Mrs. Jeremiah Jenkins; or, A Hint for the Times," *Mobile Advertiser and Register,* December 27, 1863; "Cavalry Hardships," *Richmond Whig,* March 25, 1864; "Dandies," *Southern Illustrated News,* July 9, 1864; "A Rich Order, October 25, 1864," *Macon Telegraph,* reprinted in *Richmond Whig,* December 2, 1864.

68. "The Noble Army of Quartermasters," *Montgomery Advertiser,* July 11, 1864. See also "The Richmond Examiner on Confederate Uniform," *Richmond Examiner,* reprinted in *Mobile Advertiser and Register,* December 16, 1862. The author described those who wore "stars and bars, and stripes and wreaths and nameless sleeve configurations of lace," as forming the "Dandiacal Body" of Richmond's billiard halls and hotels, being pleasing to tailors, and accelerating the pulses of "bread and butter misses." However, they concluded that "what shall be denied the defenders of our country?"

69. "Circular," War Department, Adjutant and Inspector General's Office, Richmond, Va., June 3, 1862; also reprinted in "The Rebel Officers in Battle," *New York Times,* October 26, 1862.

70. Rose, *Victorian America and the Civil War,* 42–43, 61. Even non-churchgoers, like Wade Hampton, referred to God and His designs.

71. Kimmel, *Manhood in America,* 75; Osterweis, *Romanticism and Nationalism in the Old South,* 18, 77, 131, 194, 201–2. See also Censer, *North Carolina Planters and Their Children;* Anstruther, *Knight and the Umbrella,* 246–68.

72. "Tournament and Barbecue," *Charleston Mercury,* December 22, 1863; Osterweis, *Romanticism and Nationalism in the Old South,* 15–18, 43, 56, 9–93.

73. "From Tivoli," Culpeper Court House, June 6, 1863, to the Editor, *Atlanta Southern Confederacy,* June 15, 1863.

74. "The Cavalry," *Richmond Examiner,* May 12, 1863.

75. "General Lee Gives General Stuart a Warning Which Was Not Heeded," *Atlanta Southern Confederacy,* reprinted in *Mobile Advertiser and Register,* June 19, 1863; *Charleston Mercury,* June 17, 1863; *Memphis Appeal,* June 15, 1863. For a defense of Stuart, see Charles Brewer to the Editor of the *Charleston Courier,* June 24, 1863. See also Andrews, *South Reports the Civil War,* 303–4.

76. "Editorial," *Richmond Examiner,* June 12, 1863; "The Cavalry Service: What They Are Doing and What They Want," *Richmond Whig,* October 2, 1863; "The Cavalry of General Lee's Army," *Richmond Enquirer,* November 19, 1863; "War on Horseback," *Richmond Whig,* November 25, 1863.

77. "Cavalry and Infantry," *Wilmington Daily Journal,* March 8, 1864; "Correspondence of the Fayetteville Observer, June 3, 1863," *Fayetteville Observer,* June 15, 1863. The writer describes how boredom prompted a day for "Knights" to show off for women, dine, dance, and entertain. Evidence for around a dozen wartime events described as "Tournaments" exists from 1861–64. The accompanying reports indicate that they were used as entertainments for troops and local communities. Balls capped off some of the more extensive.

78. "Sallust," "From General Lee's Army, May 23, 1864," *Richmond Dispatch,* reprinted in *Augusta Constitutionalist,* June 3, 1864; See also "The Cavalry at Reams Station," *Richmond Enquirer,* reprinted in *Fayetteville Semi-Weekly Observer,* September 8, 1864.

79. Bonner, *Colors and Blood,* 72, 77–84.

80. "The Demands of the Crisis," *Richmond Dispatch,* February 2, 1862. See also "The Difference," *Selma Morning Reporter,* June 7, 1864.

81. "Response to the Legality of Conscription—An Address to the General Assembly of the State of Georgia at Milledgeville," *Atlanta Southern Confederacy,* February 8, 1862.

82. "The Times," *Richmond Dispatch,* February 24, 1862.

83. "Theatre," *Atlanta Southern Confederacy,* March 14, 1863. See also "Maria Jourdan Westmoreland," in Raymond, *Southland Writers,* i, 450–51.

84. "Our Special Army Correspondent, Port Royal, Virginia, January 1, 1863," *Atlanta Southern Confederacy,* February 8, 1863; *Address of the Baptist General Association of Virginia,* 3; Renfroe, *Model Confederate Soldier,* 4–5; "Meeting at Autauga," *Prattville Autauga Citizen,* April 16, 1863; C. K. M'C, "A Private in the Ranks," *Knoxville Register,* June 10, 1864; "Our Correspondence from the 8th Confederate Regiment of Cavalry, Middletown, Tennessee, March 27, 1863," *Atlanta Southern Confederacy,* April 3, 1863; "The Army," *Richmond Dispatch,* April 11, 1864; "Providence in This War," *Atlanta Register,* March 27, 1864, reprinted in *Montgomery Weekly Advertiser,* March 30, 1864.

85. "Confederate Congress, Friday, September 19, 1862," *Richmond Dispatch,* September 25, 1862; "Confederate Congress, Saturday, October 11, 1862," *Richmond Dispatch,* October 13, 1862.

86. "The News from Richmond, September 24, 1862," *Charleston Mercury,* September 29, 1862; "The Confederate Seal," *Charleston Mercury,* October 7, 1862; "The Seal of the Confederacy," *Charleston Mercury,* October 15, 1862.

87. "Confederate States Congress, Thursday, February 12, 1863," *Richmond Dispatch,* February 13, 1863.

88. "Our Flag and Seal," *Southern Illustrated News,* March 12, 1863; "The Seal," *Richmond Enquirer,* April 24, 1863; Savage, "Self-Made Monument," 226–27; Bauer, "Review of *The Construction and Contestation of American Cultures and Identities,*" 96.

89. See Weems, *Life of Washington;* Charles Butler, *The American Gentleman* (1839); Samuel Roberts

Wells, *How to Behave: A Pocket Manual of Republican Etiquette and Guide to Correct Personal Habits* (1856), cited in Ellison, "Gender of Transparency," 587. See also Smith-Rosenberg, "Surrogate Americans," 1325.

90. "Speech on the Slavery Question, Delivered to the Senate, March 4, 1850," in Calhoun, *Works of John C. Calhoun*, 4:561.

91. *Southern Illustrated News*, April 11, 1863; Bryan "George Washington," 56–57.

92. Wicks, *Wildmen and Warriors*, 11.

93. "A Bust of Gen'l Jackson," *Richmond Enquirer*, August 26, 1863. Volck sold copies of the bust and the death mask on Richmond's streets. A copy of the death mask is in the collection of The Valentine, in Richmond. A copy of the bust is in the American Civil War Museum collection. Additionally, Volck's brother created an etching of the death mask profile that is in the collection of the Smithsonian's National Portrait Gallery. See http://collections.si.edu/search/detail/edanmdm:npg_NPG.78.20?q=volck+-Jackson&record=2&hlterm=volck%2BJackson&inline=true.

94. Beegan, "Mechanization of the Image," 257–74; Barnhurst and Nerome, "Civic Picturing vs. Realist Photojournalism," 59–79.

95. Bonner, "Roundheaded Cavaliers," 52–59. It is notable that the passing of Major General Earl Van Dorn, who died at around the same time as Jackson, received little attention. Van Dorn was murdered by a jealous husband. Of the career soldier, snappy dresser, and charmer of women, a correspondent wrote, "Think of the universal respect paid to the memory of the lamented Jackson . . . a striking illustration of the difference between sin and righteousness." See "Van Dorn," *Atlanta Southern Confederacy*, May 21, 1863.

96. See Gallagher, *Confederate War*, 85–96; Gary W. Gallagher, "The Idol of His Soldiers and the Hope of His Country: Lee and the Confederate People," *Lee and His Generals*, 3–20.

97. "The Times," *Southern Illustrated News*, May 2, 1863; Bonner, *Blood and Colors*, 113–15.

98. Wyatt-Brown, *Southern Honor*, 105–11.

99. Peter W. Alexander, "General Robert E. Lee," for *Savannah Republican*, cited in *Richmond Dispatch*, December 13, 1862.

100. "R" to Editor, May 1, 1864, *Columbia South Carolinian*, May 10, 1864.

101. "Our Special Richmond Correspondence" (Richmond, May 9, 1863), *Atlanta Southern Confederacy*, May 14, 1863; "Gen. R. E. Lee," *Lynchburg Virginian*, reprinted in *Columbus Enquirer*, April 1, 1864.

102. "Gen. Robert E. Lee," *Charlottesville Chronicle*, reprinted in *Macon Telegraph*, June 13, 1864.

103. Gallagher, "Idol of His Soldiers," 3–20.

104. "R" to Editor, May 1, 1864, *Columbia South Carolinian*, May 10, 1864.

105. Mary Boykin Chesnut, July 3, 1861, diary entry, *Private Mary Chesnut*, 87.

106. "General Robert E. Lee," *Charleston Courier*, reprinted in *Eatonton Countryman*, October 20, 1862; Cowling, *Artist as Anthropologist*, 37–38, 49, 59, 67, 81–82, 113.

107. Meredith, *Face of Robert E. Lee*, 6.

108. R. E. Lee to M. C. Lee, December 30, 1864, in Dowdey and Manarin, *Wartime Papers of Robert E. Lee*, 880; Hopkins, *Robert E. Lee in War and Peace*, 67.

109. R. E. Lee to M. C. Lee, March 21, 1863; R. E. Lee to M. C. Lee, April 24, 1863; R. E. Lee to M. C. Lee, November 11, 1864; R. E. Lee to M. C. Lee, December 30, 1864, all in Dowdey and Manarin, *Wartime Papers of Robert E. Lee*, 416, 440, 873, 880; Meredith, *Face of Robert E. Lee*, 5–6; Hopkins, *Robert E. Lee in War and Peace*, 67; "The Artist's Studio," *Southern Punch*, August 29, 1863; "Virginia Legislature," *Richmond Dispatch*, January 7, 1865; Johnson, "Mr. J. Vannerson," 21.

110. "The Late Edward C. Bruce," *Baltimore Sun,* December 3, 1900. An oil sketch of General Lee's camp, dated October 1864, suggests that preparations began in the fall of 1864. Three of the eight to ten studies Bruce made of Lee indicate that he constructed the portrait from sketches. Although he dated the finished work 1864, newspaper accounts make it clear that it took him until late February 1865 to finish the piece. While the painting is lost, in June 1867, a man from Richmond, G. L. Bidgood, sold photographs of the work, and engravings also survive. See also Virginius Cornick Hall, *Portraits in the Collection of the Virginia Historical Society: A Catalog* (Charlottesville: Virginia Historical Society, 1981), 144.

111. "Bruce's General Lee," *Richmond Dispatch,* June 17, 1867. According to a report, the Virginia House of Delegates purchased this "admirable likeness of the great and beloved chieftain and patriot" for sixty-five thousand dollars. See "Mr. Cox," *Macon Telegraph and Confederate,* February 15, 1865.

112. "Fine Arts. Full-Length Portrait of Gen. Lee," *New York Vindicator,* reprinted in *Dallas Herald,* January 20, 1866.

113. "An English Account of the Battle of Fredericksburg," *Charleston Mercury,* February 9, 1863, reprinted from *London Times,* January 13, 1863.

114. The *London Illustrated News* used this as a basis for an engraving of Lee in its June 4, 1864, edition.

115. "Gen. Robert Edmund Lee," *Southern Illustrated News,* October 17, 1863.

116. "Gen. Robert Edmund Lee."

117. Torsch resolved Lee's hair into twenty-six different wisps; Ewell fourteen; Longstreet fourteen; G. W. Smith nineteen; W. Hampton eighteen; Samuel Cooper thirty-two. Lee's face shows a greater tonal range and textural complexity. See *The War and Its Heroes* (Richmond, Va.: Ayres and Wade, 1864).

118. "Hero Worship," *Southern Illustrated News,* October 10, 1863.

119. "Grant and the Yankees," *Richmond Whig,* July 15, 1864.

120. "Fast Day," *Richmond Enquirer,* August 24, 1863.

121. There are five known wartime photographs of Forrest: one back-marked M. Sancier, Mobile, Ala. (ca. 1864–65); a portrait (retouched) from 1862; and three undated others.

122. Western generals John Stuart Williams and Thomas C. Hindman, e.g., had their images published in the *Southern Illustrated News* and featured in Lee Mallory's 1864 show *An Hour with the Confederate Generals.* See "Mozart Hall," *Wilmington Journal,* March 11, 1864; *Southern Illustrated News,* April 11, 1863, and January 2, 1864. Additionally, Williams had his portrait included among Julian Vannerson's 1864 medallion *Generals of the C. S. Army: Plate No. 2.*

123. "Confederate States Congress, May 14, 1864," *Richmond Enquirer,* May 16, 1864.

124. Quote from "A Sketch of Gen. Forrest," *Augusta Constitutionalist,* June 24, 1864.

125. Rable, "Despair, Hope and Delusion," 129–55.

126. Friend, "Crushing of Southern Manhood," 30–33.

Epilogue

1. Cash, *Mind of the South,* 421.

2. "Reconstruction," *Macon Telegraph,* September 28, 1864.

3. Faust, "Race, Gender, and Confederate Nationalism," 148.

4. Rubin, *Shattered Nation,* 248.

5. Binnington, *Confederate Visions,* 148.

6. See, e.g., Hutchison, *Apples and Ashes;* and Bernath, *Confederate Minds.*

BIBLIOGRAPHY

PRIMARY SOURCES

Manuscripts

Alabama Department of Archives and History, Montgomery
Adjutant General's Financial Records SG1530; S+5224
Reports of Cases Argued before the Supreme Court of Alabama, Vol. 39 (1863)
Civil War and Reconstruction Newspapers,
http://digital.archives.alabama.gov/cdm/landingpage/collection/cwnp

Center for American History, University of Texas at Austin
Confederate Military Manuscripts—Civil War Miscellany

Earl Gregg Swemm Library, College of William and Mary, Williamsburg, Va.
Powell Family Papers

Georgia Department of Archives and History, Atlanta
Adjutant General Correspondence, 1861
Annual Report of the Quartermaster General of Georgia for the Fiscal Year Ending October 20, 1864
Confederate Collection
Governor's Incoming Correspondence, 1861
Receipts of the Quartermaster General of the State of Georgia

Louis R. Wilson Library, Southern Historical Collection, University of North Carolina, Chapel Hill
Frank Liddell Richardson Papers

Mississippi Department of Archives and History, Jackson
Record Group 9—Military Requisitions

National Archives and Records Administration, Washington, D.C.

1860 United States Census

1870 United States Census

Applications for Pardon Submitted to President Andrew Johnson by Former Confederates Excluded from Earlier Amnesty Proclamations, 1865–67. Confederate Amnesty Papers (M1003), Record Group 94

Record Group 109

Compiled Service Records of Confederate Soldiers Who Served in Organizations from the State of Mississippi (M269)

Compiled Service Records of Confederate Soldiers Who Served in Organizations from the State of Virginia (M324)

Compiled Service Records of Confederate Soldiers Who Served in Organizations from the State of Tennessee (M268)

Compiled Service Records of General and Staff Officers, and Nonregimental Enlisted men (M331)

Confederate Ordnance Bureau Records, "Letters Received, Macon (Georgia) Armory, July–September 1862," chap. 4, vol. 4 (online version available through the Archival Research Catalog [ARC identifier 23005248], https://catalog.archives.gov/id/12005248)

Confederate Ordnance Bureau Records, "Letters Received by Capt. Richard M. Cuyler, Ordnance Officer at Savannah and Macon, Georgia, April–June 1862," chap. 4, vol. 36 (online version available through the Archival Research Catalog [ARC identifier 12008774], https://catalog.archives.gov/id/12008774)

Confederate Papers Relating to the Citizens or Business Firms (M346)

Engineer Department—Letters and Telegrams Sent, 1861–64, chap. 3, vol. 5 (online version available through the Archival Research Catalog [ARC identifier 6925807], https://catalog.archives.gov/id/6925807)

Engineer Department—Letters and Telegrams Sent, and Endorsements, Engineer Bureau, Department of South Carolina, Georgia and Florida, chap. 3, vol. 9 (online version available through the Archival Research Catalog [ARC identifier 6274104], https://catalog.archives.gov/id/6274104)

Inspection Reports and Related Records Received by the Inspection Branch in the Confederate Adjutant and Inspector General's Office, 1863–65 (M935)

Letters Received by the Confederate Adjutant and Inspector General's Office (M474)

Letters Received by the Confederate Secretary of War (M437)

Letters and Telegrams Sent by the Quartermaster's Department, (M900)

Quartermaster's Department—Letters and Telegrams Sent, March–September 1861, chap. 5, vol. 13, https://catalog.archives.gov/id/29908648.

Quartermaster's Department—Letters and Telegrams Sent, October 1861–May 1865, chap 5, vol. 31, https://catalog.archives.gov/id/51432951.

Quartermaster's Department—Letters and Telegrams Sent, August 1864–January 1865, chap 5, vol. 20, https://catalog.archives.gov/id/29908898.

Register of Letters Received by the Confederate Quartermaster's Department, March–August 1861, chap. 5, vol. 1 (online version available through the Archival Research Catalog [ARC identifier 29908227], https://catalog.archives.gov/id/29908227)

North Carolina Department of Cultural Resources, Division of Archives and History, Raleigh

Civil War Collection—Quartermaster's Records

Governors' Papers—Zebulon Vance

Richmond County Historical Society, Augusta, Ga.

Clinch Rifles Minute Book

Tennessee State Archives, Nashville

Confederate Collection—John J. Knight File

University of Virginia Library, Charlottesville

Historical Census Browser, http://fisher.lib.virginia.edu/collections/stats/histcensus/php/state.php

Virginia Historical Society, Richmond

Byrd Family Papers

Government Publications

Chase, Salmon Portland, and Supreme Court of the United States. *U.S. Reports: Bermuda, The, 70 U.S. 3 Wall. 514.* 1865. Periodical. https://www.loc.gov/item/usrep070514/.

Manufactures of the United States in 1860: Compiled from the Original Returns of the Eighth Census. Washington, D.C.: Government Printing Office, 1865.

Official Records of the Union and Confederate Armies in the War of Rebellion. Washington, D.C.: Government Printing Office, 1880–1901.

Population of the United States Census in 1860: Compiled from the Original Returns of the Eighth Census. Washington, D.C.: Government Printing Office, 1864.

Published Confederate Primary Sources

Acts and Resolutions of the First Session of the Provisional Congress of the Confederate States, Held at Montgomery, Ala. Richmond, Va.: Enquirer Book and Job Press, 1861.

Address of the Baptist General Association of Virginia, June 4th 1863. Richmond, Va.: Baptists General Association, 1863.

Bagby, George B. "Editor's Table." *Southern Literary Messenger* 34 (June 1862): 503–4.

Berry, Harrison. *Slavery and Abolition, as Viewed by a Georgia Slave*. Atlanta: M. Lynch, 1861.

Burrows, John Lansing. *Sermon to the First Baptist Church, February 8, 1863*. Richmond, Va., 1863.

Cartwright, Samuel. "Negro Freedom: An Impossibility under Nature's Laws." *DeBow's Review* 30, nos. 5–6 (May–June 1861): 651.

Concert Hall (Augusta, Georgia), A. Waldron Lessee and Manager, Monday Evening, Feb'y 16th, 1863. Augusta, Ga.: Office of the Constitutionalist, 1863.

Cowper, R. Lynden. *Poem: Confederate America*. Raleigh, N.C.: Book and Job Office Steam-power Press, 1864.

Davis, Nicholas A. *The Campaign from Texas to Maryland with the Battle of Fredericksburg*. Richmond, Va.: Presbyterian Committee of Publication of the Confederate States, 1863.

Delchamps, J. J. *Love's Ambuscade; or, The Sergeant's Stratagem: A War Drama in Three Acts*. Mobile, Ala.: A. G. Horn, 1863.

Edgeville, Edward. *Castine; or, The Maid of Mirkland*. Raleigh, N.C.: William B. Smith, 1865.

Evans, Augusta Jane. *Macaria; or, Altars of Sacrifice*. Richmond, Va.: West and Johnson, 1864.

Fitzhugh, George. "The Times and the War." *DeBow's Review* 31, no. 1 (July 1861): 10–14.

Great Expectations; or, Getting Promoted. Richmond, Va.: Charles H. Wynne, 1864.

Gregg, William. "Southern Patronage to Southern Imports and Domestic Industry, Chapter XI." *DeBow's Review, Agricultural, Commercial, Industrial Progress and Resources* 30 (January 1861): 102–4.

Hodgson, Joseph. *The Confederate Vivandiere; or, The Battle of Leesburg*. Montgomery, Ala.: John M. Floyd, 1862.

Keatinge and Ball. *Remarks on the Manufacture of Bank Notes and Other Promises to Pay*. Columbia, S.C.: F. G. DeFontaine and Company, 1864.

McCabe, James Dabney, Jr. *The Guerrillas: An Original Domestic Drama, in Three Acts*. Richmond, Va.: West and Johnston, 1863.

Miller, S. A. *Report of Special Committee on the Pay and Clothing of the Army*. House of Representatives, Confederate Congress, February 11, 1865.

Moore, J. Quitman. "Southern Civilization; or, The Norman in America." *DeBow's Review* 32, nos. 1–2 (January–February 1862): 1–19.

The New Richmond Theatre. Richmond, 1863.

Overall, John W., ed. *The Punch Songster: A Collection of Familiar and Original Songs and Ballads*. Richmond, Va.: Punch Office, 1864.

Public Laws of the Confederate States of America, Passed at the Second Congress: 1864. Edited by James M. Matthews. Richmond, Va.: R. M. Smith, 1864.

Records of Antebellum Southern Plantations from the Revolution through the Civil War. Frederick, Md.: University Publications of America, 1988.

Renfroe, J.D.D. *A Model Confederate Soldier: Being a Brief Sketch of the Reverend Nathaniel D.*

Renfroe, Lieutenant in a Company of the 5th Alabama Battalion, of General A. P. Hill's Division; Who Fell in the Battle of Fredericksburg, December 13, 1862. Documenting the American South. University Library, University of North Carolina at Chapel Hill. http://docsouth.unc.edu/imls/renfroe/menu.html.

Reports of the Secretary of the Treasury Department of the Confederate States of America, 1861–'65. Washington, D.C., 1878.

Smith, J. Henry. *A Sermon Delivered at Greensboro, North Carolina.* Greensboro, 1862.

Smith, Robert Hardy. *An Address to the Citizens of Alabama on the Constitution and Laws of the Confederate States of America.* Mobile: Mobile Daily Register Press, 1861.

Thrasher, John B. *Slavery: A Divine Institution.* Port Gibson, Miss.: Southern Reveille, 1861.

Tichenor, Isaac Taylor. "Fast Day Sermon, August 21 1863." In *Isaac Taylor Tichenor: Home Mission Board Statesman,* edited by Jacob Smiser Dill, 89–108. Nashville: Sunday School Board, 1908.

Timrod, Henry. "Ethnogenesis." In *War Songs of the South,* edited by William G. Shepperson, 63. Richmond: West and Johnson, 1862.

Uniform and Dress of the Army of the Confederate States; or, General Orders No. 9. Adjutant and General's Office, Richmond, Virginia, June 6 1861. Richmond: Charles H. Wynne, 1861.

The War and Its Heroes. Richmond: Ayres and Wade, 1864.

"We Must Develop Southern Industry." *DeBow's Review* 30, no. 4 (April 1861): 497–99.

Other Primary Sources

A Calendar of Confederate Papers with a Bibliography of Some Confederate Publications: A Preliminary Report of the Southern Historical Manuscript Commission. Prepared by Douglas Southall Freeman. Richmond: Confederate Museum, 1908.

Alexander, Edward Porter. *Fighting for the Confederacy: The Personal Recollections of General Edward Porter Alexander.* Chapel Hill: University of North Carolina Press, 1989.

Anderson, Ephraim McDonald. *Memoirs: Historical and Personal; Including the Campaigns of the First Missouri Brigade.* 1868. Reprint, Dayton: Press of Morningside Bookshop, 1972.

Andrews, William H. *Footprints of a Regiment: A Recollection of the 1st Georgia Regulars, 1861–1865.* Atlanta: Longstreet Press, 1992.

Anonymous [William Parker Snow]. *Southern Generals.* New York: Richardson Publisher, 1867.

Barber, Flavel Clingan. *Holding the Line: The Third Tennessee Infantry, 1861–1865.* Edited by Robert H. Ferrell. Kent: Kent State University Press, 1994.

Battlefields of the South: From Bull Run to Fredericksburg: With Sketches of Confederate Commanders, and Gossip from the Camps. By an English Combatant. Lieutenant of Artillery on the Field Staff. New York: John Bradburn, 1864.

Blackford, W. W. *War Years with J.E.B. Stuart.* New York: Charles W. Scribner, 1945.

Brevard, Keziah Goodwyn Hopkins. *A Plantation Mistress on the Eve of the Civil War: The Diary of Keziah Goodwyn Hopkins Brevard.* Edited by John Hammond Moore. Columbia: University of South Carolina Press, 1996.

Caldwell, J.F.J. *The History of a Brigade of South Carolinians, Known as "Gregg's" and Subsequently "McGowan's" Brigade.* Philadelphia: King and Baird, 1866.

Calhoun, John C. *The Works of John C. Calhoun.* Vol. 4. Edited by Richard K. Crallé. New York: D. Appleton, 1851.

Chesnut, Mary Boykin. *The Private Mary Chesnut: The Unpublished Civil War Diaries.* Edited by C. Vann Woodward and Elisabeth Muhlenfeld. New York: Oxford University Press, 1984.

Collins, Robert Marvin. *Chapters from the Unwritten History of the War between the States; or, The Incidents in the Life of a Confederate Soldier in Camp, on the March, in the Great Battles, and in Prison.* 1893. Reprint, Dayton: Press of Morningside Bookshop, 1982.

Connolly, Thomas. *An Irishman in Dixie: Thomas Connolly's Diary of the Fall of the Confederacy.* Columbia: University of South Carolina Press, 1988.

Confederate Letters and Reminiscences, 1861–1865. Atlanta: Georgia Division, United Daughters of the Confederacy, 1995–2000.

Corsan, William C. *Two Months in the Confederate States: An Englishman's Travels Through the South.* Edited by Benjamin H. Trask. Baton Rouge: Louisiana State University Press, 1996.

Crist, Lynda L., et al., eds. *The Papers of Jefferson Davis,* vol. 9. Baton Rouge: Louisiana State University Press, 1997.

Cumming, Kate. *Kate: The Journal of a Confederate Nurse.* Edited by Richard Barksdale Harwell. 1958. Reprint, Baton Rouge: Louisiana State University Press, 1998.

Cutrer, Thomas W., and T. Michael Parrish, eds. *Brothers in Gray: The Civil War Letters of the Pierson Family.* Baton Rouge: Louisiana State University Press, 1997.

Davis, Jefferson. "Message to the Fourth Session of the First Confederate Congress, Richmond, Va., December 7, 1863." In *A Compilation of the Messages and Papers of the Confederacy: Including the Diplomatic Correspondence, 1861–1865,* edited by James D. Richardson, 1:345–85. Nashville: United States Publishing Company, 1905.

Day, Samuel Phillips. *Down South; or, An Englishman's Experience at the Seat of the American War.* London: Hurst and Blackett, 1862.

De Leon, T. C. *Belles, Beaux and Brains of the 60's.* 1907. Reprint, New York: Arno Press, 1974.

———. *Four Years in Rebel Capitols: An Inside View of Life in the Southern Confederacy, from Birth to Death.* 1890. Reprint, New York: Collier Books, 1962.

Dowdey, Clifford, and Louis H. Manarin, eds. *The Wartime Papers of Robert E. Lee.* 1961. Reprint, New York: Da Capo, 1987.

English Officer, An [Charles Henry Fletcher]. "A Run through the Southern States." *Cornhill Magazine* 7, no. 40 (April 1863): 495–515.

Evans, Robert G., ed. *The 16th Mississippi Infantry: Civil War Letters and Reminiscences.* Jackson: University of Mississippi Press, 2002.

Everson, Guy R., and Edward H. Simpson, eds. *Far, Far from Home: The Wartime Letters of Dick and Tally Simpson, 3rd South Carolina Volunteers.* New York: Oxford University Press, 1994.

Fleming, Francis P. *A Memoir of Captain C. Seton Fleming: Illustrative of the History of the Florida Troops in Virginia during the War between the States.* Jacksonville, Fla.: Times-Union Publishing, 1884.

Fletcher, William A. *Rebel Private: Front and Rear. Memoirs of a Confederate Soldier.* 1908. Reprint, New York: Dutton Signet, 1995.

Fremantle, Arthur James Lyon. *Three Months in the Southern States, April–June 1863.* Lincoln: University of Nebraska Press, 1991.

Gorgas, Josiah. "The Confederate Ordnance Department." *The Confederate Soldier in the Civil War,* 326. 1897. Reprint, Fairfax, Va.: Fairfax Press, n.d.

Hall, Winchester. *The Story of the 26th Louisiana Infantry in the Service of the Confederate States.* Gaithersburg, Md.: Butternut Press, 1984.

Hamlin, Percy Gatling. *The Making of a Soldier: The Letters of General Richard Stoddard Ewell.* Richmond, Va.: Whittet and Shepperson, 1935.

Hopley, Catharine C. *Life in the South: From the Commencement of the War.* 1863. Reprint, New York: DaCapo Edition, 1974.

Johnson, Robert Underwood, and Clarence Clough Buel, eds. *Battles and Leaders of the Civil War.* 4 vols. 1889. Reprint, Edison, N.J.: Castle Books, n.d.

Jones, John Beaucamp. *A Rebel War Clerk's Diary.* 1866. Reprint, Baton Rouge: Louisiana State University Press, 1993.

Lane, Mills, ed. *Dear Mother, Don't Grieve about Me. If I Get Killed I'll Only Be Dead: Letters from Georgia Soldiers in the Civil War.* Savannah: Beehive Press, 1977.

Lay, Henry Champlin. *Sermons, 1861–1865.* Transcript of MS no. 418, Southern Historical Collection, Wilson Library, University of North Carolina at Chapel Hill. *Documenting the American South,* University of North Carolina Library, University of North Carolina at Chapel Hill, 1999. http://docsouth.unc.edu/imls/layhenry.html.

McCarthy, Carlton. *Detailed Minutiae of Soldier Life in the Army of Northern Virginia, 1861–1865.* Richmond: Carlton McCarthy and Company, 1882.

McGuire, Judith White. *Diary of a Southern Refugee during the War.* New York: E. J. Hale and Son, 1867.

McMillan, Malcolm C., ed. *The Alabama Confederate Reader.* Tuscaloosa: University of Alabama Press, 1963.

Morgan, Sarah. *Sarah Morgan: The Civil War Diary of a Southern Woman.* Edited by Charles East. New York: Touchstone Edition, 1992.

Moore, Robert A. *A Life for the Confederacy: As Recorded in the Pocket Diaries of Pvt. Robert A. Moore, Co. G, 17th Mississippi Regiment, Confederate Guards, Holly Springs, Mississippi.* Edited by James W. Silver. Jackson, Miss.: McCowat-Mercer Press, 1959.

Moxley-Sorrell, G. *Recollections of a Confederate Staff Officer.* New York: Neale Publishing Company, 1905. http://docsouth.unc.edu/imls/niles/.

Reid, J. W. *History of the Fourth Regiment S.C. Volunteers from the Commencement of the War until Lee's Surrender.* Greenville, S.C.: Shannon and Company, 1891.

"Resources of the Confederacy, February 1865." *Southern Historical Society Papers* 2, no. 2 (August 1876): 85–105.

"Resources of the Confederacy, February 1865." *Southern Historical Society Papers* 2, no. 3 (September 1876): 113–28.

Richardson, James D., ed. *A Compilation of the Messages and Papers of the Confederacy.* 2 vols. Nashville: United States Publishing Company, 1904.

Riley, Franklin Lafayette. *Grandfather's Journal: Company B 16th Mississippi Infantry Volunteer: Harris Brigade, Mahone's Division, Hill's Corps, Army of Northern Virginia, May 27, 1861–July 15, 1865.* Edited by Austin C. Dobbin. Dayton: Morningside Press, 1988.

Rowland, Dunbar, ed. *Jefferson Davis, Constitutionalist: His Letters, Paper, and Speeches.* Jackson: J. J. Little and Ives, 1923.

Russell, William Howard. *My Diary North and South.* Edited by Fletcher Pratt. 1863. Reprint, New York: Harper and Brothers, 1958.

Simpson, Edward H., and Guy R. Everson, eds. *Far, Far from Home: The Wartime Letters of Dick and Tally Simpson, 3rd South Carolina Volunteers.* New York: Oxford University Press, 1994.

Stevens, John W. *Reminiscences of the Civil War.* Hillsboro, Tex.: Hillsboro Mirror Press, 1902.

The Tennessee Civil War Veterans Questionnaires—Compiled by Gustavus W. Dyer and John Trotwood Moore. 5 vols. Edited by Colleen Morse Elliot and Louise Armstrong Moxley. Easley, S.C.: Southern Historical Press, 1985.

Thian, Raphael P. *Correspondence with the Treasury Department of the Confederate States of America, 1861–'65.* Washington, D.C.: Privately published, 1880.

———. *Correspondence of the Treasury Department of the Confederate States of America, 1861–'65.* Washington, D.C.: Privately published, 1879.

———. *Documentary History of the Flag and Seal of the Confederate States of America, 1861–'65.* Washington, D.C.: Privately published, 1880.

Tunnard, William H. *A Southern Record: The History of the 3rd Regiment Louisiana Infantry.* Baton Rouge: Printed for the author, 1866.

"William D. Washington, VMI Obituary, December 1870." *VMI Archives: An Online Historical Research Center.* http://www.vmi.edu/archives.aspx?id=18461.

Wirt, Armistead Cate, ed. *Two Soldiers: The Campaign Diaries of Thomas J. Key, CSA, December 17, 1863–May 17, 1865 and Robert J. Campbell, USA, January 1, 1864–July 21, 1864.* Chapel Hill: University of North Carolina Press, 1938.

Confederate Newspapers and Periodicals

Advertiser (Edgefield, S.C.)

Advertiser and Register (Mobile, Ala.)

Albany Patriot (Albany, Ga.)
Arkansas State Gazette (Little Rock)
Arkansas True Democrat (Little Rock)
Autauga Citizen (Prattville, Ala.)
Beacon (Greensboro, Ala.)
Bee (New Orleans)
Brandon (Miss.) Republican
Bugle Horn of Liberty (Griffin, Ga.)
Camden (S.C.) Confederate
Carolina Watchman (Salisbury, N.C.)
Charleston (S.C.) Mercury
Charleston (S.C.) Tri-Weekly Courier
Charlotte (N.C.) Democrat
Child's Index (Macon, Ga.)
Clarion (Jackson and Meridian, Miss.)
Columbus (Ga.) Daily Times
Columbus (Ga.) Enquirer
Concordia (La.) Intelligencer
Confederate Spirit, and Knapsack of Fun: A Humorous Monthly, Devoted to Wit, Humor, and the Spirit of the Times (Mobile, Ala.)
Countryman (Eatonton, Ga.)
Daily Advocate (Baton Rouge, La.)
Daily Avalanche (Memphis)
Daily Bulletin Winchester (Va.)
Daily Chronicle and Sentinel (Augusta, Ga.)
Daily Citizen (Vicksburg, Miss.)
Daily Constitutionalist (Augusta, Ga.)
Daily Delta (New Orleans)
Daily Dispatch (Richmond, Va.)
Daily Huntsville Confederate (Huntsville, Ala.)
Daily Intelligencer (Atlanta)
Daily Mississippian (Jackson, Miss.; Selma, Ala.)
Daily National Republican (Washington, D.C.)
Daily News (Savannah, Ga.)
Daily Picayune (New Orleans)
Daily Richmond Enquirer (Richmond, Va.)
Daily Sentinel (Richmond, Va.)
Daily Sun (Columbus, Ga.)
Daily Telegraph and Confederate (Macon, Ga.)
Daily True Delta (New Orleans)

Dallas Herald

DeBow's Review, Agricultural, Commercial, Industrial Progress and Resources (New Orleans and Columbia, S.C.)

Eastern Clarion (Paulding, Miss.)

Fayetteville (N.C.) Observer

Fayetteville (Tenn.) Observer

Galveston (Tex.) Weekly News

Greensborough (N.C.) Patriot

Hardtack (Atlanta)

Holly Springs (Miss.) Southern Herald

Illustrated Mercury (Raleigh, N.C.)

Indianola (Tex.) Courier

Jacksonville (Ala.) Republican

Knoxville Daily Register (Knoxville, Tenn., and Atlanta, Ga.)

Lynchburg Daily Virginian (Lynchburg, Va.)

Macon (Ga.) Daily Telegraph (Macon, Ga.)

Macon (Miss.) Beacon

Magnolia Weekly (Richmond, Va.)

Memphis (Tenn.) Daily Appeal

Milton (N.C.) Chronicle

Mobile (Ala.) Daily Tribune

Mobile (Ala.) Evening News

Mobile (Ala.) Register and Advertiser

Mobile (Ala.) Weekly Advertiser

Montgomery (Ala.) Daily Advertiser

Montgomery (Ala.) Daily Mail

Montgomery (Ala.) Weekly Advocate

Montgomery (Ala.) Weekly Mail

Montgomery (Ala.) Weekly Post

Nashville (Tenn.) Union and American

Natchez (Miss.) Daily Courier

New Orleans Commercial Bulletin

New Orleans Daily Crescent

North Carolina State Journal (Raleigh)

Petersburg (Va.) Daily Express

Record of News, History and Literature (Richmond, Va.)

Republican Banner (Nashville, Tenn.)

Raleigh (N.C.) Semi-Weekly Standard

Richmond (Va.) Daily Whig

Richmond (Va.) Examiner

Rome (Ga.) Tri-Weekly Courier
Savannah (Ga.) Daily Morning News
Savannah (Ga.) Republican
Selma (Ala.) Morning Reporter
Sentinel (Richmond, Va.)
South Carolinian (Columbia)
Southern Advertiser (Troy, Ala.)
Southern Advocate (Huntsville, Ala.)
Southern Banner (Athens, Ga.)
Southern Confederacy (Atlanta)
Southern Enterprise (Greenville, S.C.)
Southern Field and Fireside (Augusta, Ga.)
Southern Illustrated News (Richmond, Va.)
Southern Literary Messenger (Richmond, Va.)
Southern Monthly (Memphis, Tenn., and Grenada, Miss.)
Southern Punch (Richmond, Va.)
Southern Union (Milledgeville, Ga.)
Southern Watchman (Athens, Ga.)
State Journal (Raleigh, N.C.)
Statesville (Ala.) Express
Staunton (Va.) Spectator
Texas Republican (Marshall)
Tri-Weekly Telegraph (Houston)
Vicksburg (Miss.) Daily Whig
Weekly Enquirer (Columbus, Ga.)
Weekly Mississippian (Jackson, Miss.)
Weekly Raleigh (N.C.) Register
Weekly Telegraph (Macon, Ga.)
Wilmington (N.C.) Daily Journal
Winchester (Va.) Republican
Yorkville (S.C.) Enquirer

Other Newspapers and Periodicals

Alderson Roots and Branches (San Francisco)
Atlanta Constitution
Birmingham (Ala.) News
Blackwood's Edinburgh Magazine (UK)
Boston Daily Globe

Butte (Mont.) Weekly Miner
Cincinnati Commercial
Confederate Veteran Magazine (Nashville)
Daily Evening Bulletin (San Francisco)
Daily Wabash Express (Terre Haute, Ind.)
Evening News (San Jose, Calif.)
Harper's Weekly Magazine of Civilization (New York)
Lawrence (Kans.) Daily Journal
Lexington (Ky.) Herald
Los Angeles Times
Louisville Courier (Louisville and Bowling Green, Ky.)
New Orleans Times
New Orleans Times-Picayune
New York Herald
New York Sun
New York Times
North Carolina Medical Journal (Wilmington)
St. Louis (Mo.) Republic
Times (London)
Vermont Watchman and State Journal (Montpelier)
Virginia Medical Journal (Richmond)
Washington (D.C.) Herald
Winchester (Va.) Journal

SECONDARY SOURCES

Abel, E. Lawrence. *Confederate Sheet Music.* Jefferson, N.C.: McFarland and Company, 2004.

Albaugh, William A., III, Hugh Benet Jr., and Edward N. Simmons. *Confederate Handguns: Concerning the Guns, the Men Who Made Them, and the Time of Their Use.* Philadelphia: Riling and Lentz, 1963.

Anderson, Benedict. *Imagined Communities: Reflections on the Origin and Spread of Nationalism.* New York: Verso, 1991.

Anderson, Patricia. *The Printed Image and the Transformation of Popular Culture, 1790–1860.* London: Oxford University Press, 1991.

Andreae, Christine. "Kate Sperry's Diary, 1861–1866." *Virginia Country's Civil War* 1 (1983): 43–75.

Andrews, J. Cutler. *The South Reports the Civil War.* Pittsburgh: University of Pittsburgh Press, 1985.

Anstruther, Ian. *The Knight and the Umbrella: An Account of the Eglinton Tournament, 1839.* London: Geoffrey Bles, 1963.

Aptheker, Herbert. *American Negro Slave Revolts.* 1943. Reprint, New York: Columbia University Press, 1971.

Arliskas, Thomas M. *Cadet Gray and Butternut Brown: Notes on Confederate Uniforms.* Gettysburg: Thomas Publications, 2006.

Ashworth, John. *Slavery, Capitalism, and Politics in the Antebellum Republic,* vol. 1: *Commerce and Compromise.* Cambridge: Cambridge University Press, 1995.

Avery, Kevin J. "Movies for Manifest Destiny: The Moving Panorama Phenomenon in America." *The Grand Moving Panorama of Pilgrim's Progress.* Portland, Maine: Montclair Art Museum, 1999.

Ayers, Edward L. *In the Presence of Mine Enemies: War in the Heart of America, 1859–1863.* New York: W. W. Norton, 2003.

Bailey, Michael M. "Clothing the Alabama Soldier." *Camp Chase Gazette* 11 (November 1983): 28–29.

Ball, Donald B. *Comprehensive Catalog and History of Confederate Bonds.* Port Clinton: BNR Press, 1998.

———. *Financial Failure and Confederate Defeat.* Urbana: University of Illinois Press, 1991

———. "Paper Mills in the Confederate South: Industrial Archaeology of a Forgotten Industry." *Ohio Valley Historical Archaeology: Journal of the Symposium on Ohio Valley Urban and Historic Archaeology* 17 (2002): 1–68.

Banton, Michael. *The Idea of Race.* London: Tavistock Press, 1977.

Barbatsis, Gretchen, and John W. Jones. *Confederate Currency: The Color of Money, Images of Slavery on Confederate and Southern Currency.* West Columbia, S.C.: New Directions, 2002.

Barber, E. Susan. "Cartridge Makers and Myrmidom Viragos: White Working Class Women in Confederate Richmond." In *Negotiating Boundaries of Southern Womanhood, Dealing with the Powers That Be,* edited by Janet L. Coryell, 199–214. Columbia: University Press of Missouri, 2000.

Barczewski, Stephanie L. *Myth and National Identity in Nineteenth Century Britain: The Legends of King Arthur and Robin Hood.* London: Oxford University Press, 2000.

Barker-Benfield, G. J. *The Horrors of the Half-Known Life: Male Attitudes toward Women and Sexuality in Nineteenth-Century America.* New York: Routledge, 2000.

Barnard, Malcolm. *Art, Design and Visual Culture: An Introduction.* Hampshire, UK: Palgrave Macmillan, 1998.

Barnhurst, Kevin G., and John Nerone. "Civic Picturing vs. Realist Photojournalism: The Regime of Illustrated News, 1856–1901." *Design Issues* 16, no. 1 (Spring 2000): 61–65.

Barrett, Frank J., and Stephen M. Whitehead, eds. *The Masculine Reader.* Cambridge: Polity Press, 2001.

Barton, Michael. *Goodmen: The Character of Civil War Soldiers.* University Park: Pennsylvania State University Press, 1976.

Bassham, Ben L. *Conrad Wise Chapman: Artist and Soldier of the Confederacy.* Kent: Kent State University Press, 1998.

Bateman, Frederick, and Thomas Weiss. *A Deplorable Scarcity: The Failure of Industrialization in the Slave Economy.* Chapel Hill: University of North Carolina Press, 1981.

Bates, Christopher G., ed. *The Early Republic and Antebellum America: An Encyclopedia of Social, Political, Cultural, and Economic History.* New York: Routledge, 2015.

Baudrillard, Jean. *Simulacrum and Simulation.* 1981. Reprint, Ann Arbor: University of Michigan Press, 1994.

Bauer, Ralph. "Review of *The Construction and Contestation of American Cultures and Identities in the Early National Period.*" *South Atlantic Review* 65, no. 3 (Summer 2000): 96.

Beegan, Gerry. "The Mechanization of the Image: Facsimile, Photography, and Fragmentation in Nineteenth-Century Wood Engraving." *Journal of Design History* 8, no. 4 (1995): 257–74.

Beers, Henry Putney. *The Confederacy: A Guide to the Archives of the Confederate States of America.* Washington, D.C.: National Archives Trust Board, 1986.

Bensel, Richard. "Southern Leviathan: The Development of Central State Authority in the Confederate States of America." *Studies in American Political Development* 2 (Spring 1987): 68–136.

Berends, Kurt O. "Wholesome Reading Purifies and Elevates Man: The Religious Military Press and the Civil War Crisis." In *Religion and the American Civil War,* edited by Randall M. Miller, Harry S. Stout, Charles Reagan Wilson, 111–46. New York: Oxford University Press, 1998.

Berlin, Jean V. "Did Confederate Women Lose the War: Deprivation, Destruction and Despair on the Homefront." In *The Collapse of the Confederacy,* edited by Mark Grimsley and Brooks D. Simpson, 168–90. Lincoln: University of Nebraska Press, 2001.

Bernath, Michael T. "Confederate Minds: The Struggle for Intellectual Independence in the Civil War South." Ph.D. diss., Harvard University, 2005.

———. *Confederate Minds: The Struggle for Intellectual Independence in the Civil War South.* Chapel Hill: University of North Carolina Press, 2010.

Berringer, Richard E., Herman Hattaway, Archer Jones, and William N. Still Jr. *Why the South Lost the Civil War.* Athens: University of Georgia Press, 1986.

Berry, Stephen W. *All That Makes a Man: Love and Ambition in the Civil War South.* New York: Oxford University Press, 2003.

Bertelson, David. *The Lazy South.* New York: Oxford University Press, 1967.

Bill, Alfred Hoyt. *The Beleaguered City: Richmond, 1861–1865.* New York: Alfred A. Knopf, 1946.

Binnington, Ian. "Promoting the Confederate Nation: The *Southern Illustrated News* and the Civil War." In *Virginia's Civil War,* edited by Peter Wallenstein and Bertram Wyatt-Brown, 113–22. Charlottesville: University of Virginia Press, 2005.

———. "They Have Made a Nation: Confederates and the Creation of Confederate Nationalism." Ph.D. diss., University of Illinois at Urbana-Champaign, 2004.

———. *Confederate Visions: Nationalism, Symbolism, and the Imagined South in the Civil War.* Charlottesville: University of Virginia Press, 2013.

Blassingame, John W. *The Slave Community.* New York: Oxford University Press, 1972.

Blight, David W. *Race and Reunion: The Civil War in American Memory.* Cambridge: Belknap Press of Harvard University, 2001.

Boney, F. M. *Southerners All.* Macon: Mercer University Press, 1991.

Bonner, Michael Brem. *Confederate Political Economy: Creating and Managing a Southern Corporatist Nation.* Baton Rouge: Louisiana State University Press, 2016.

Bonner, Robert B. "Roundheaded Cavaliers? The Context and Limits of a Confederate Racial Project." *Civil War History* 48, no. 1 (March 2002): 34–59.

Bonner, Robert E. *Colors and Blood: Flag Passions of the Confederate South.* Princeton: Princeton University Press, 2002.

Boskin, Joseph. *Sambo: The Rise and Demise of an American Jester.* Oxford: Oxford University Press, 1986.

Boyd, Steven R. *Patriotic Envelopes of the Civil War: The Iconography of Union and Confederate Covers.* Baton Rouge: Louisiana State University Press, 2010.

Bright, Eric W. "Nothing to Fear from the Influence of Foreigners: The Patriotism of Richmond's German-Americans during the Civil War." Master's thesis, Virginia Polytechnic Institute and State University, Richmond, 1999.

Brooks, Ross. "Clothing the Tennessee Volunteer, 1861." *Military Collector and Historian* 46, no. 2 (Summer 1994): 68–71.

Brown, Kent Masterton. *The Confederacy's First Battle Flag: The Story of the Confederate Cross.* Gretna, La.: Pelican Publishing, 2014.

Bryan, William A. "George Washington: Symbolic Guardian of the Republic, 1850–1861." *William and Mary Quarterly* 7, no. 1 (January 1950): 53–63.

Burke, Peter. *Eyewitnessing: The Uses of Images as Historical Evidence.* Ithaca: Cornell University Press, 2001.

Burton, Georganne B., and Orville V. Burton. "Lucy Holcombe Pickens: Belle, Political Novelist and Southern Lady." In *South Carolina Women: Their Lives and Times,* edited by Marjorie Julian Spruitt, Valinda W. Littlefield and Joan Marie Johnson, 1:273–98. Athens: University of Georgia Press, 2009.

Burton, William L. *Melting Pot Soldiers: The Union's Ethnic Regiments.* Ames: Iowa University Press, 1988.

Bynum, Victoria E. *Unruly Women: The Politics of Social and Sexual Control in the Old South.* Chapel Hill: University of North Carolina Press, 1992.

Calhoun, John C. "Speech on the Reception of Abolition Petitions." In *Slavery Defended: The Views of the Old South,* edited by Eric L. McKitrick, 13–14. Englewood Cliffs, N.J.: Prentice-Hall, 1963.

Camille, Michael. "Simulacrum." In *Critical Terms for Art History,* edited by Robert S. Nelson and Richard Schiff, 31–32. Chicago: University of Chicago Press, 1996.

Campbell, Edward D. C. "Fabric of Command: R. E. Lee, Confederate Insignia, and the Perception of Rank." *Virginia Magazine of History and Biography* 98, no. 2 (April 1990): 261–90.

———. "Theater." In *Encyclopedia of the Confederacy,* edited by Richard N. Current, 4:1589–90. New York: Simon and Schuster, 1993.

Cannon, Devereaux D. *The Flags of the Confederacy: An Illustrated History.* Memphis: St. Lukes Press, 1988.

———. "The Genesis of the 'Stars and Bars.'" *Raven: A Journal of Vexillology* 23 (2005): 1–26.

Carlander, Jay, and John D. Majewski. "Imagining 'A Great Manufacturing Empire': Virginia and the Possibilities of Confederate Tariffs." *Civil War History* 49, no. 4 (December 2003): 334–52.

Carnes, Mark C., and Clyde Griffen, eds. *Meanings for Manhood: Constructions of Masculinity in Victorian America.* Chicago: University of Chicago Press, 1990.

Carp, Benjamin L. "Nations of American Rebels: Understanding Nationalism in Revolutionary North America and the Civil War South." *Civil War History* 48, no. 1 (March 2002): 24–28.

Carwardine, Richard J. *Evangelicals and Politics in Antebellum America.* Knoxville: University of Tennessee Press, 1997.

Cash, Wilbur J. *The Mind of the South.* New York: Vintage Books, 1941.

Censer, Jane Turner. *North Carolina Planters and Their Children, 1800–1860.* Baton Rouge: Louisiana State University Press, 1984.

Chambers, Bruce W. *Art and Artists of the South: The Robert P. Coggins Collection.* Columbia: University of South Carolina Press, 1984.

Channing, Steven A. *Confederate Ordeal: The Southern Home Front.* Alexandria, Va.: Time-Life Books, 1986.

———. "Slavery and Confederate Nationalism." In *From the Old South to the New: Essays on the Transitional South,* edited by Walter J. Fraser Jr. and Windred B. Moore Jr., 219–25. Westport: Greenwood Press, 1981.

Chapla, John D. "Quartermaster Operations in the 42nd Virginia Infantry Regiment." *Civil War History* 30, no. 1 (March 1984): 5–26.

Chesnut, James. "The Destinies of the South." *Southern Quarterly Review* 23, no. 13 (January 1853): 181–82.

Clinton, Catherine, ed. *Southern Families at War: Loyalty and Conflict in the Civil War South.* New York: Oxford University Press, 2000.

———. *Stepdaughters of History: Southern Women* and *the American Civil War.* Baton Rouge: Louisiana State University Press, 2016.

Clytus, Radiclani. "Envisioning Slavery: American Abolitionism and the Primacy of the Visual." Ph.D. diss., Yale University, 2007.

Coates, Earl J., Michael McAfee, and Don Troiani. *Don Troiani's Regiments and Uniforms of the Civil War.* Mechanicsburg, Pa.: Stackpole Books, 2002.

Cobb, Thomas R. R. *An Inquiry into the Law of Negro Slavery.* 1858. Reprint, New York: Negro University Press, 1968.

Colley, Linda. *Britons: Forging the Nation, 1707–1837.* New Haven: Yale University Press, 1992.

Colligan, Mimi. *Canvas Documentaries: Panoramic Entertainments in Nineteenth Century Australian and New Zealand.* Carlton South, Victoria: Melbourne University Press, 2002.

Collins, Stephen G. "System in the South: John W. Mallet, Josiah Gorgas, and Uniform Production at the Confederate Ordnance Department." *Technology and Culture* 40, no. 3 (July 1999): 517–44.

Commager, Henry Steele. *The Defeat of the Confederacy.* Princeton: Van Nostrand, 1964.

Comolli, Jean-Louis. "Machines of the Visible." In *The Cinematic Apparatus,* edited by T. de Laurentis and S. Heath, 121–42. London: Macmillan, 1980.

Coryell, Janet L. *Negotiating Boundaries of Southern Womanhood: Dealing with the Powers That Be.* Columbia: University of Missouri Press, 2000.

Cott, Nancy F. *The Bonds of Womanhood: "Women's Sphere" in New England, 1780–1835.* New Haven: Yale University Press, 1977.

Cowling, Mary E. *The Artist as Anthropologist: The Representations of Type and Character in Victorian Art.* Cambridge: Cambridge University Press, 1989.

Cramer, Janet M., and Hazel Dicken-Garcia. "Images of Women in Civil War Newspapers: Leave the 'Proper Sphere.'" In *The Civil War and the Press,* edited by David B. Sachsman, S. Kittrell Rushing, Debra Reddin van Tuyll, and Ryan B. Burkholder, 257–74. New Brunswick, N.J.: Transaction Publishers, 2000.

Crampton, Jeremy W. "Maps as Social Constructions: Power, Communication and Visualisation." *Progress in Human Geography* 25, no. 2 (2001): 235–52.

Cronin, Mary M. "Daughters of the New Revolutionary War: Representations of Confederate Women and Gun Culture in the Confederate Press, 1861–1864." *American Journalism* 28, no. 4 (2011): 55–80.

———. "Patriotic Ladies and Gallant Heroines: Images of Confederate Women in Southern Newspapers, 1861–65." *Journalism History* 36, no. 3 (Fall 2010): 138–49.

Crusan, Ronald L. "Confederate Civil War Photographers: Propagators of the Hero Myth." Master's thesis, Old Dominion University, 1995.

Cunliffe, Marcus. *Soldiers and Civilians: The Martial Spirit in America, 1775–1865.* Boston: Little, Brown, 1968.

Current, Richard N. "God and the Strongest Battalions." In *Why the North Won the Civil War,* edited by David Donald, 21–37. Baton Rouge: Louisiana State University Press, 1960.

Curtis, Lewis P. *Apes and Angels: The Irishman in Victorian Caricature.* 1971. Reprint, Washington, D.C.: Smithsonian Institution, 1996.

Czekanski, Thomas. "Notes on Accoutrement Makers: Magee and George of New Orleans." *Camp Chase Gazette* 24, no. 1 (October 1996): 48–51.

Daniels, Larry J. *Soldiering in the Army of Tennessee: A Portrait of Life in a Confederate Army.* Chapel Hill: University of North Carolina Press, 1991.

David, Alison Matthews. "Decorated Men: Fashioning the French Soldier, 1852–1914." *Fashion Theory* 7, no. 1 (March 2003): 3–38.

Davidson, James Wood. *Living Writers of the South.* New York: A. M. Carleton, 1869.

Davidson, Nora Fontaine M., comp. *Cullings from the Confederacy, 1861–1866.* Washington, D.C.: Rufus H. Darby, 1903.

Davis, John. *Landscape of Belief: Encountering the Holy Land in Nineteenth-Century American Art and Culture.* Princeton: Princeton University Press, 1996.

Davis, William C. *Look Away: A History of the Confederate States of America.* New York: Free Press, 2003.

DeCredico, Mary A. *Patriotism for Profit: Georgia's Urban Entrepreneurs and the Confederate War Effort.* Chapel Hill: University of North Carolina Press, 1990.

Dedmondt, Glenn. *The Flags of Civil War South Carolina.* Gretna, La.: Pelican Publishing, 2000.

Descriptive Register of Genuine Banknotes. New York: Gwynne and Day, 1860.

Detlefsen, Ellen Gay. "Printing in the Confederacy, 1861–1865." Ph.D. diss., D.L.S. Columbia University, 1975.

Dew, Charles B. *Apostles of Disunion: Southern Secession Commissioners and the Causes of the Civil War.* Charlottesville: University Press of Virginia, 2001.

———. *Ironmaker to the Confederacy: Joseph R. Anderson and the Tredegar Ironworks.* New Haven: Yale University Press, 1966.

Dinnie, Keith. *National Branding: Concepts, Issues, Practice.* Oxford: Butterworth-Heinemann, 2008.

Donald, David. "The Confederate as a Fighting Man." In *Essays on the Civil War and Reconstruction,* edited by Irwin Unger, 308–25. New York: Holt, Rinehart and Winston, 1970.

Doty, Richard G. *Pictures from a Distant Country: Seeing America Through It Paper Money.* Atlanta: Whitman Publication, 2013.

Douglas, Lucia R. *Douglas's Texas Battery, CSA.* Tyler, Tex.: Smith County Historical Society, 1966.

Durden, Robert F. *The Gray and the Black: Confederate Debate on Emancipation.* Baton Rouge: Louisiana State University Press, 1972.

Edwards, Laura F. *Scarlett Doesn't Live Here Anymore: Southern Women in the Civil War Era.* Urbana: University of Illinois Press, 2000.

Edwards, William B. *Civil War Guns: The Complete Story of Federal and Confederate Small Arms; Design, Manufacture, Identification, Procurement, Issue, Employment, Effectiveness and Post-War Disposal.* Harrisburg, Pa.: Stackpole Company, 1962.

Eiserman, Rick. "We Have Had a Picture Taken." *Civil War Times* 50 (August 2011): 44–47.

Eklund, Robert B., Jr., John D. Jackson, and Mark Thornton. "The 'Unintended Consequences' of Confederate Trade Legislation." *Eastern Economic Journal* 30, no. 2 (Spring 2004): 187–204.

Elkins, Stanley M. *Slavery.* Chicago: University of Chicago Press, 1959.

Ellis, B. G. *The Moving Appeal: Mr. McClanahan, Mrs. Dill and the Civil War's Great Newspaper Run.* Macon: Mercer University Press, 2003.

Ellison, Julie. "The Gender of Transparency: Masculinity and Conduct of Life." *American Literary History* 4, no. 4 (Winter 1992): 584–606.

Escott, Paul D. *After Secession: Jefferson Davis and the Failure of Confederate Nationalism.* Baton Rouge: Louisiana State University Press, 1978.

———. *The Confederacy: The Slaveholders' Failed Venture.* Santa Barbara: Praeger, 2010.

Estill, Mary S., ed. "Diary of a Confederate Congressman, 1862–1863." *Southwestern Historical Quarterly* 39, no. 1 (July 1935): 33–65.

Evans, Eli N. *Judah P. Benjamin: The Jewish Confederate.* New York: Free Press, 1988.

Fahs, Alice. *The Imagined Civil War: Popular Literature of the North and South, 1861–1865.* Chapel Hill: University of North Carolina Press, 2001.

Faust, Drew Gilpin. "Altars of Sacrifice: Confederate Women and the Narratives of War." *Journal of American History* 76, no. 4 (March 1990): 1200–1228.

———. *The Creation of Confederate Nationalism: Ideology and Identity in the Civil War.* Baton Rouge: Louisiana State University Press, 1988.

———, ed. *The Ideology of Slavery: Proslavery Thought in the Antebellum South, 1830–1860.* Baton Rouge: Louisiana State University Press, 1981.

———. *James Henry Hammond and the Old South: A Design for Mastery.* Baton Rouge: Louisiana State University Press, 1982.

———. "Moment of Truth: A Woman of the Master Class in the Confederate South." In *Slavery, Secession and Southern History,* edited by Robert L. Paquette and Louis A. Ferleger, 126–39. Charlottesville: University Press of Virginia, 2000.

———. *Mothers of Invention: Women of the Slaveholding South in the American Civil War.* Chapel Hill: University of North Carolina Press, 1996.

———. "Race, Gender, and Confederate Nationalism: William D. Washington's *Burial of Latané.*" *Southern Review* 25, no. 2 (Spring 1989): 297–307.

———. "Slavery in the American Experience." *Before Freedom Came: African-American Life in the Antebellum South,* edited by Edward D. C. Campbell Jr., with Kym S. Rice, 1–20. Richmond: Museum of the Confederacy, and Charlottesville: University Press of Virginia, 1991.

———. *Southern Stories: Slaveholders in Peace and War.* Columbia: University of Missouri Press, 1992.

———. *This Republic of Suffering: Death and the American Civil War.* New York: Alfred A. Knopf, 2008.

Field, Ron. *The Confederate Army, 1861–1865: Florida, Alabama, and Georgia.* Oxford: Osprey Publishing, 2005.

———. *The Confederate Army, 1861–1865: South Carolina and Mississippi.* Oxford: Osprey Publishing, 2005.

———. *The Confederate Army, 1861–1865: Tennessee and North Carolina.* Oxford: Osprey Publishing, 2007.

Fife, Iline. "The Theatre during the Confederacy." Ph.D. diss., Louisiana State University, 1949.

Fitzhugh, George. "Sociology for the South." In *Slavery Defended: The Views of the Old South,* edited by Eric L. McKitrick, 34–50. Englewood Cliffs, N.J.: Prentice-Hall, 1963.

Fleming, E. McClung. "Artefact Study: A Proposed Model." In *Material Culture Studies in*

America: An Anthology, edited by Thomas J. Schlereth, 162–73. Lanham, Md.: AltaMira Press, 1999.

Foster, Gaines M. *Gray Ghosts of the Confederacy: Defeat, the Lost Cause, and the Emergence of the New South, 1865–1913*. New York: Oxford University Press, 1987.

Fox-Genovese, Elizabeth, and Eugene D. Genovese. *The Mind of the Master Class: History and Faith in the Slaveholders' Worldview*. New York: Cambridge University Press, 2005.

Franklin, John Hope. *The Militant South, 1800–1861*. 1956. Reprint, Urbana: University of Illinois Press, 2002.

Franklin, John Hope, and Loren Schweninger. *Runaway Slaves: Rebels on the Plantation*. New York: Oxford University Press, 1999.

Frederickson, George M. *The Black Image in the White Mind: The Debate on Afro-American Character and Destiny, 1817–1914*. New York: Harper and Row, 1971.

Freehling, William W. *The Reintegration of American History: Slavery and the Civil War*. New York: Oxford University Press, 1994.

———. *The Road to Disunion: Secessionists at Bay, 1776–1854*. New York: Oxford University Press, 1990.

———. *The Road to Disunion: Secessionists Triumphant, 1854–1861*. New York: Oxford University Press, 2007.

Friend, Craig Thompson. "The Crushing of Southern Manhood." In *Masculinities and the Nation in the Modern World: Between Hegemony and Marginalization*, edited by Pablo Dominguez Andersen and Simon Wendt, 19–38. New York: Palgrave Macmillan, 2015.

Freud, Sigmund. *The Joke and Its Relation to the Unconscious*. 1905. Translated and edited by Joyce Crick. London: Penguin, 2002.

Fricke, Pierre. *Collecting Confederate Paper Money: A Complete and Fully Illustrated Guide to Collecting All Confederate Note Types and Varities* [*sic*]. New York: R. M. Smythe and Company, 2005.

Frost, Linda. *Never One Nation: Freaks, Savages, and Whiteness in U.S. Popular Culture, 1850–1877*. Minneapolis: University of Minnesota Press, 2005.

Fuller, Claud E., and Richard D. Steuart. *Firearms of the Confederacy*. Lawrence, Kans.: Quarterman Publications, 1944.

Gabel, Christopher R. *Rails to Oblivion: The Decline of Confederate Railroads in the Civil War*. Fort Leavenworth, Kans.: U.S. Army Command and General Staff College Press, 2002.

Gallagher, Gary W. *The Confederate War: How Popular Will, Nationalism and Military Strategy Could Not Stave Off Defeat*. Cambridge: Harvard University Press, 1997.

———. *Lee and His Generals in War and Memory*. Baton Rouge: Louisiana State University Press, 1998.

———, ed. *The Third Day at Gettysburg*. Chapel Hill: University of North Carolina Press, 1994.

Gallman, J. Matthew. *Defining Duty in the Civil War: Personal Choice, Popular Culture and the Union Homefront*. Chapel Hill: University of North Carolina Press, 2015.

Geertz, Clifford. *The Interpretation of Cultures: Selected Essays*. New York: Basic Books, 1973.

Genovese, Eugene D. *The Political Economy of Slavery*. 1961. Reprint, New York: Pantheon Books, 1967.

———. *Roll, Jordan, Roll: The World the Slaves Made.* New York: Vintage Books, 1972.

———. *The World the Slaveholders Made.* Hanover, N.H.: Wesleyan University Press, 1988.

Glatthaar, Joseph T. "Black Glory: The African-American Role in Union Victory," in Gabor Borritt et al., *Why the Confederacy Lost.* New York: Oxford University Press, 1992.

———, ed. *Confederate Military Manuscripts: Holdings of the Centre of American History, University of Texas at Austin.* Bethesda, Md.: University Publications of America, 1998.

———. *General Lee's Army: From Victory to Collapse.* New York: Free Press, 2008.

Godzin, Morton. *The Loyal and the Disloyal: Social Boundaries of Patriotism and Treason.* Baton Rouge: Louisiana State University Press, 1956.

Goff, Richard D. *Confederate Supply.* Durham, N.C.: Duke University Press, 1969.

Goldfarb, Stephen. "Laws Governing the Incorporation of Manufacturing Companies by Southern State Legislatures before the Civil War." *Southern Studies: An Interdisciplinary Journal of the South* 24, no. 4 (Winter 1985): 415–20.

Gould, Stephen J. *The Mismeasure of Man.* London: Penguin Books, 1996.

Graham, Christopher A. "Women's Revolt in Rowan County." *The Columbiad: A Quarterly Review of the War between the States* 3, no. 1 (Spring 1999): 131–47.

Grattin, Kali Brinton. "The Todd Sisters Living in Selma during the Civil War." Honors diss., University of Georgia, 2010.

Goldsborough, W. W. *The Maryland Line in the Confederate Army, 1861–1865.* Baltimore: Guggenheimer Weil and Company, 1900.

Green, Jennifer R. "Stout Chaps Who Can Bear the Distress: Young Men in Antebellum Military Academies." In *Southern Manhood: Perspectives in Masculinity in the Old South,* edited by Craig Thompson Friend and Lorri Glover, 174–84. Athens: University of Georgia Press, 2004.

Green, Melanie C., and Timothy C. Brock. "The Role of Transportation in the Persuasiveness of Public Narratives." *Journal of Personality and Social Psychology* 79, no. 5 (2000): 701–21.

Greenberg, Amy S. *Manifest Manhood and the Antebellum American Empire.* Cambridge: Cambridge University Press, 2005.

Greenberg, Kenneth S. *Honor and Slavery: Lies, Duels, Noses, Masks, Dressing as a Woman, Gifts, Strangers, Humanitarianism, Death, Slave Rebellions, the Proslavery Argument, Baseball, Hunting, and Gambling in the Old South.* Princeton: Princeton University Press, 1996.

Grimsley, Mark. *The Hard Hand of War: Union Military Policy toward Southern Civilians, 1861–1865.* New York: Cambridge University Press, 1995.

Gruber, Robert H. *Confederate Papers Relating to Citizens or Business Firms.* Washington, D.C.: National Archives Microfilm Publications, 1982.

Haig, Robin Andrew. *The Anatomy of Humour: Bio-Psychosocial and Therapeutic Perspective.* Springfield, Ill.: Charles C. Thomas Publications, 1988.

Hammond, James Henry. "Letter to an English Abolitionist." In *The Ideology of Slavery: Proslavery Thought in the Antebellum South, 1830–1860,* edited by Drew Gilpin Faust, 168–205. Baton Rouge: Louisiana State University Press, 1981.

Harley, E. B. "Deconstructing the Map." In *Writing Worlds: Discourse, Text, and Metaphor in the Representation of Landscape*, edited by Trevor J. Barnes and James S. Duncan, 231–47. London: Routledge, 1992.

Harrison, Pelag Dennis. *The Stars and Stripes and Other American Flags*. Boston: Little, Brown, 1918.

Harvey, Eleanor Jones. *The Civil War and American Art*. New Haven: Yale University Press, 2012.

Harwell, Richard Barksdale. "Brief Candle: The Confederate Theatre." *Proceedings of the American Antiquarian Society*. Worcester, Mass.: American Antiquarian Society, 1971.

———. *Confederate Belle-Lettres: A Bibliography and Finding List of the Fiction, Poetry, Drama, Songsters, and Miscellaneous Literature Published in the Confederate States of America*. New York: Gordon Press, 1977.

Haskell, Francis. *History and Its Images: Art and the Interpretation of the Past*. New Haven: Yale University Press, 1993.

Hendrickson, Robert. *Sumter: The First Day of the Civil War*. Chelsea, Mich.: Scarborough House, 1990.

Herrera, Ricardo. "Self-Governance and the American Citizen-Soldier, 1775–1861." *Journal of Military History* 65, no. 1 (January 2001): 23–32.

Higginbotham, R. Don. "The Martial Spirit in the Antebellum South: Some Further Speculations in a National Context." *Journal of Southern History* 58, no. 1 (February 1992): 3–26.

Hodes, Martha Elizabeth. *White Women, Black Men: Illicit Sex in the Nineteenth-Century South*. New Haven: Yale University Press, 1997.

Holt, Thomas C. "Explaining Racism in American History." In *Imagined Histories: American Historians Interpret the Past*, edited by Anthony Molho and Gordon S. Wood, 107–19. Princeton: Princeton University Press, 1998.

Holzer, Harold. "The Art of Ironclads." *Civil War Times* 46 (March–April 2007): 42–49.

———. "Beyond Face Value: Slavery Iconography in Confederate Currency." *Beyond Face Value: Depictions of Slavery in Confederate Currency, A Project of the United States Civil War Center*. http://www.cwc.lsu.edu/cwc/BeyondFaceValue/images/index.htm.

Holzer, Harold, and Mark E. Neely Jr. *Mine Eyes Have Seen the Glory: The Civil War in Art*. New York: Orion, 1993.

Hopkins, Donald A. *Robert E. Lee in War and Peace: The Photographic History of a Confederate and American Icon*. El Dorado Hills, Calif.: Savas Beattie, 2013.

Horsman, Reginald. *Race and Manifest Destiny: The Origins of American Racial Anglo-Saxonism*. Cambridge: Harvard University Press, 1981.

Hubbard, Charles M. *The Burden of Confederate Diplomacy*. Knoxville: University of Tennessee Press, Knoxville, 2000.

Hutchison, Coleman. *Apples and Ashes: Literature, Nationalism and the Confederate States of America*. Athens: University of Georgia Press, 2012.

Irelan, Scott R. "Lincoln the Yankee Goon: An Early Public Image in Both Southern and Copperhead Dramatic Literature and Live Performance." In *Enacting Nationhood: Identity,*

Ideology and the Theatre, 1855–99, edited by Scott R. Irelan, 59–74. Newcastle on Tyne: Cambridge Scholars, 2014.

Jabour, Anya. *Scarlett's Sisters: Young Women in the Old South.* Chapel Hill: University of North Carolina Press, 2007.

Jackson, E. Larry. "Whistling Dixie: C. S. Richmonds." *North South Trader's Civil War* 18, no. 3 (March–April 1991): 28–34.

Jacobson, Matthew Frye. *Whiteness of a Different Color: European Immigrants and the Alchemy of Race.* Cambridge: Harvard University Press, 1998.

Jaffee, Robert M. "Confederate Oilcloth Accoutrements." *North South Trader's Civil War* 18, no. 1 (January–February 1991): 32–35.

Jenkins, William Sumner. *Pro-Slavery Thought in the Old South.* Gloucester: Peter Smith, 1960.

Jensen, Leslie D. "A Survey of Confederate Central Government Quartermaster Issue Jackets, Part 1." *Military Collector and Historian* 41, no. 3 (Fall 1989): 107–20.

———. "A Survey of Confederate Central Government Quartermaster Issue Jackets, Part 2." *Military Collector and Historian* 41, no. 4 (Winter 1989): 162–70.

Jimerson, Randall C. *The Private Civil War: Popular Thought during the Sectional Conflict.* Baton Rouge: Louisiana State University Press, 1988.

Johnson, Bradley T. *Confederate Military History Extended Edition*, vol. 2: *Maryland.* Edited by Clement G. Evans.1899. Reprint, Wilmington, N.C.: Broadfoot Publishing, 1987.

Johnson, Brooks. "Mr. J. Vannerson . . . Remarkably Successful in the Matter of Likenesses." *Chrysler Museum Journal* 1 (1994): 15–25.

Jones, James B., Jr. *Hidden History of Civil War Tennessee.* Charleston, S.C.: History Press 2013.

Jordan, Ervin L. *Black Confederates and Afro-Yankees in Civil War Virginia.* Charlottesville: University Press of Virginia, 1995.

Joseph, Nathan. *Uniforms and Non-Uniforms: Communication through Clothing.* New York: Greenwood Press, 1997.

Joseph-Virey, Julian. *The Natural History of the Negro Race. Extracted from the French.* Charleston, S.C.: D. J. Dowling, 1837.

Joyner, Charles. *Down by the Riverside: A South Carolina Slave Community.* Chicago; University of Illinois Press, 1985.

———. "The Life of Plantation Slaves." In *Before Freedom Came: African-American Life in the Antebellum South.* Richmond: Museum of the Confederacy, and Charlottesville: University Press of Virginia, 1991.

Kaplan, Sidney. "The Miscegenation Issue in the Election of 1864." *Journal of Negro History* 34, no. 3 (July 1949): 274–83.

Keim, Lon W. *Confederate General Service Accoutrement Plates.* Orange, Va.: Moss Publications, 1987.

Kimball, Gregg D. *Southern Place: A Cultural History of Antebellum Richmond.* Athens: University of Georgia Press, 2000.

Kimmel, Michael S. *Manhood in America: A Cultural History.* New York: Free Press, 1996.

Kramer, Lloyd. *Nationalism in Europe and America: Politics, Cultures and Identities since 1775.* Chapel Hill: University of North Carolina Press, 2011.

Lauer, Josh. "Money as Mass Communication: U.S. Paper Currency and the Iconography of Nationalism." *Communication Review* 11 (2008): 109–32.

Lavater, Joseph. *The Pocket Lavater; Or, The Science of Physiognomy.* New York: Van Winkle and Wiley, 1817.

Lebergott, Stanley. "Why the South Lost: Commercial Purpose in the Confederacy, 1861–1865." *Journal of American History* 70, no. 1 (June 1983): 58–74.

Lengyel, Christian M. "Pictures Frozen in Time: Determining Whether or Not Confederate Currency Vignettes Functioned as Proslavery Propaganda." *Past Tense: Graduate Review of History* (University of Toronto Department of History) 4, no. 1 (2016): 1–21.

Lent, John A., and Kohava Simhi. "Northern Magazines in the South." In *Encyclopedia of the Confederacy,* edited by Richard N. Current, 3:986–87. New York: Simon and Schuster, 1993.

Lerner, Eugene M. "Money, Prices and Wages in the Confederacy." *Journal of Political Economics* 63, no. 1 (February 1955): 32–35.

Levi, Harold. *The Lovett Cent: A Confederate Story.* Blairsville: Skeenah Gap Publications, 2013.

Long, David E. "Jeff Davis Must Be Killed: Lincoln and the Dahlgren Raid." *North and South: The Official Magazine of the Civil War Society* 9, no. 5 (October 2006): 70–83.

Lonn, Ella C. *Foreigners in the Confederacy.* 1940. Reprint, Chapel Hill: University of North Carolina Press, 2002.

Luraghi, Raimondo. *The Rise and Fall of the Plantation South.* New York: New Viewpoints, 1978.

Luse, Christopher A. "Slavery's Champions Stood at Odds: Polygenesis and the Defense of Slavery." *Civil War History* 53, no. 4 (December 2007): 379–412.

McCabe, James D. "Literature of the War: Confederate Publishing in the Sixties." *Southern Historical Society Papers* 42, no. 4 (October 1917): 200–201.

McCurry, Stephanie. *Confederate Reckoning: Power and Politics in the Civil War South.* Cambridge: Harvard University Press, 2010.

McDermott, John F. *The Lost Panoramas of the Mississippi.* Chicago: University of Chicago Press, 1958.

McGinnis, Karin Hertel. "Moving Right Along: Nineteenth Century Panorama Painting in the United States." Ph.D. diss., University of Minnesota, 1983.

McKee, Paul. "Notes on the Federal Issue Sack Coat." *Military Collector and Historian* 47, no. 2 (Summer 1995): 50–59.

McKitrick, Eric L., ed. *Slavery Defended: The Views of the Old South.* Englewood Cliffs, N.J.: Prentice-Hall, 1963.

McPherson, James M. *Battle Cry of Freedom: The Civil War Era.* Oxford: Oxford University Press, 1988.

———. *For Cause and Comrades: Why Men Fought in the Civil War.* New York: Oxford University Press, 1997.

———. *Is Blood Thicker than Water? Crises of Nationalism in the Modern World*. New York: Vintage Books, 1999.

———. *What They Fought For, 1861–1865*. Baton Rouge: Louisiana State University Press, 1994.

Madaus, Howard Michael. *The Battle Flags of the Confederate Army of Tennessee*. Milwaukee: Milwaukee Public Museum, 1976.

Madaus, Howard Michael, and Robert D. Needham. "Unit Colors of the Trans-Mississippi Confederacy, Part I." *Military Collector and Historian* 41, no. 3 (Fall 1989): 123–41.

———. "Unit Colors of the Trans-Mississippi Confederacy, Part II." *Military Collector and Historian* 41, no. 4 (Winter 1989): 172–82.

Mahar, William J. *Behind the Burnt Cork Mask: Early Blackface Minstrelsy and Antebellum Popular Culture*. Urbana: University of Illinois Press, 1999.

Mahin, Dean B. *The Blessed Place of Freedom: Europeans in Civil War America*. Washington, D.C.: Brassey's, 2003.

Majewski, John. *Modernizing a Slave Economy: The Economic Vision of the Confederate Nation*. Chapel Hill: University of North Carolina Press, 2009.

Manger, J. A., and James Walvin. *Manliness and Morality: Middle Class Masculinity in Britain and America: 1800–1940*. Manchester: Manchester University Press, 1987.

Manning, Chandra. *What This Cruel War Was Over: Soldiers, Slavery and the Civil War*. New York: Alfred A. Knopf, 2007.

Massey, Mary Elizabeth. *Bonnet Brigades: American Women in the Civil War*. New York: Alfred A. Knopf, 1966.

———. *Ersatz in the Confederacy: Shortages and Substitutes on the Southern Homefront*. Columbia: University of South Carolina Press, 1952.

Meredith, Roy. *The Face of Robert E. Lee*. New York: Charles Scribner's Sons, 1947.

Mihm, Stephen. *A Nation of Counterfeiters: Con Men, Capitalists and the Making of the United States*. Cambridge: Harvard University Press, 2007.

Mirzoff, Nicholas, ed. *The Visual Culture Reader*. London: Routledge, 1998.

Mitchell, Reid. *Civil War Soldiers*. New York: Viking Penguin, 1988.

Mohr, Charles L. *On the Threshold of Freedom: Masters and Slaves in Civil War Georgia*. Athens: University of Georgia Press, 1986.

Mollo, John. *Military Fashions: A Comparative History of the Uniforms of the Great Armies from the 17th Century to the Great War*. London: Barrie and Jenkins, 1972.

Moore, Albert Burton. *Conscription and Conflict in the Confederacy*. 1924. Reprint, New York: Hillary House Publishers, 1963.

Morgan, Chad. "The Public Nature of Private Industry in Confederate Georgia." *Civil War History* 50, no. 1 (March 2004): 27–46.

Mullenix, Elizabeth Reitz. "Performing Confederate Nationalism: Constructing Southern Identity at the Richmond Theatre." In *Enacting Nationhood: Identity, Ideology and the Theatre, 1855–99*, edited by Scott R. Irelan, 25–42. Newcastle on Tyne: Cambridge Scholars, 2014.

Musick, Michael P. "The Mystery of the Confederate Medals of Honor." *Military Collector and Historian* 23, no. 3 (Fall 1971): 74–78.

Neely, Mark E., Jr., Harold Holzer, and Gabor S. Boritt. *The Confederate Image: Prints of the Lost Cause.* Chapel Hill: University of North Carolina Press, 1987.

Nevins, Allan. *War for the Union, Volume 4: The Organized War to Victory, 1864–1865.* New York: Charles Scribner and Sons, 1971.

Nichols, James L. *The Confederate Quartermaster in the Trans-Mississippi.* Austin: University of Texas Press, 1964.

Nickels, Cameron C. *Civil War Humor.* Jackson: University Press of Mississippi, 2010.

Nielsen, Anna. "Captive Audience: Theatre Presentations at Johnson's Island Confederate Prisoner of War Camp." In *Enacting Nationhood: Identity, Ideology and the Theatre, 1855–99,* edited by Scott R. Irelan, 43–58. Newcastle on Tyne: Cambridge Scholars, 2014.

Nolan, Alan T. "Anatomy of the Myth." In *The Myth of the Lost Cause and Civil War History,* edited by Gary W. Gallagher and Alan T. Nolan, 11–34. Indianapolis: Indiana University Press, 2000.

Nolan, Dick. *Benjamin Franklin Butler: The Damnedest Yankee.* Novato: Presidio Press, 1991.

North, Rene. *Military Uniforms, 1686–1918.* London: Hamlyn Publishing Group, 1970.

Nott, Josiah C. "The Natural History of the Caucasian and Negro Race." In *The Ideology of Slavery: Proslavery Thought in the Antebellum South, 1830–1860,* edited by Drew Gilpin Faust, 206–38. Baton Rouge: Louisiana State University Press, 1981.

O'Brien, Michael. *Conjectures of Order: Intellectual Life and the American South, 1810–1860.* Vol. 1. Chapel Hill: University of North Carolina Press, 2004.

Oetterman, Stefan. *The Panorama: A History of a Mass Medium.* New York: Zone Books, 1997.

O'Leary, Cecilia Elizabeth. *To Die For: The Paradox of American Patriotism.* Princeton: Princeton University Press, 1999.

Ormi, Michael, and Howard Winant. *Racial Formation in the United States from the 1960s to the 1980s.* New York: Routledge, 1986.

Orr, N. Lee. "John Hill Hewitt, Bard of the Confederacy." *American Music Research Center Journal* 4 (1994): 31–75.

Osterweis, Rollin G. *Romanticism and Nationalism in the Old South.* New Haven: Yale University Press, 1949.

Ott, Victoria E. *Confederate Daughters: Coming of Age during the Civil War.* Carbondale: Southern Illinois University Press, 2008.

Parrish, T. Michael, and Robert M. Willingham Jr. *Confederate Imprints: A Bibliography of Southern Publications from Secession to Surrender.* Austin: Jenkins Publishing Company, 1987.

Pearl, Sharrona. *About Faces: Physiognomy in Nineteenth Century Britain.* Cambridge: Harvard University Press, 2010.

Phillips, Jason. *Diehard Rebels: The Confederate Culture of Invincibility.* Athens: University of Georgia Press, 2007.

———. "Peculiar Defeat: Warfare and the Confederate Culture of Invincibility." Ph.D. diss., Rice University, 2003.

Phillips, Ulrich B. "The Central Theme of Southern History." *American Historical Review* 34, no. 1 (October 1928): 30–34.

Piacentino, Edward J. "Confederate Disciples of Momus: *Bugle Horn of Liberty* and *The Southern Punch*." *Studies in American Humor* 4, no. 4 (1984–85): 249–61.

Pond, George E. "Kilpatrick and Dahlgren's Raid to Richmond." In *Battles and Leaders of the Civil War*, edited by Robert Underwood Johnson and Clarence Clough Buel, 4:95–96. New York: Century Company, 1884.

Potter, David M. *The Impending Crisis, 1848–1861*. New York: Harper Perennial, 1976.

———. *The South and the Sectional Conflict*. Baton Rouge: Louisiana State University Press, 1968.

Powell, Lawrence N., and Michael S. Wayne. "Self-Interest and the Decline of Confederate Nationalism." In *Old South in the Crucible of War*, edited by Harry P. Owens and James J. Cook, 32–33. Jackson: University Press of Mississippi, 1983.

Procter, Ben H. *Not without Honor: The Life of John H. Reagan*. Austin: University of Texas Press, 1962.

Prown, Jules David. "Mind in Matter: An Introduction to Material Culture Theory and Method." *Winterthur Portfolio* 17, no. 1 (Spring 1982): 1–19.

Przyblynksi, Jeannene M., and Vanessa R. Schwartz. *The Nineteenth Century Visual Culture Reader*. London: Routledge, 2004.

Quigley, Paul D. H. "Patchwork Nation: Sources of Confederate Nationalism, 1848–1865." Ph.D. diss., University of North Carolina, 2006.

———. *Shifting Grounds: Nationalism and the American South, 1848–1865*. New York: Oxford University Press, 2012.

Rable, George C. *Civil Wars: Women and the Crisis of Southern Nationalism*. Urbana: University of Illinois Press, 1989.

———. *The Confederate Republic: A Revolution against Politics*. Chapel Hill: University of North Carolina Press, 1994.

———. *Damn Yankees! Demonization and Defiance in the Confederate South*. Baton Rouge: Louisiana State University Press, 2015.

———. "Despair, Hope, and Delusion: The Collapse of Confederate Morale Re-Examined." In *The Collapse of the Confederacy*, edited by Mark Grimsley and Brooke D. Simpson, 129–67. Lincoln: University of Nebraska Press, 2001.

———. *God's Almost Chosen Peoples: A Religious History of the American Civil War*. Chapel Hill: University of North Carolina Press, 2010.Rainer, Joseph T. "The 'Sharp' Image: Yankee Peddlers, Southern Consumers, and the Market Revolution." In *Cultural Change and the Market Revolution in America*, edited by Scott C. Martin, 102–5. Lanham, Md.: Rowman and Littlefield, 2004.

Ramsdell, Charles R. *Behind the Lines in the Southern Confederacy*. Baton Rouge: Louisiana State University Press, 1944.

———. "The Control of Manufacturing by the Confederate Government." *Mississippi Valley Historical Review* 8, no. 3 (December 1921): 231–49.

Raymond, Ida. *Southland Writers: Biographical and Critical Sketches of Living Female Writers of the South*. Philadelphia: Claxton, Remsen and Haffelfinger, 1870.

Rees, Richard W. *Shades of Difference: A History of Ethnicity in America.* Lanham, Md.: Rowman and Littlefield, 2007.

Reynold, Donald E. *Editors Make War: Southern Newspapers in the Secession Crisis.* Nashville: Vanderbilt University Press, 1970.

Ripley, C. Peter. *Slaves and Free Men in Civil War Louisiana.* Baton Rouge: Louisiana State University Press, 1976.

Roberts, Giselle. *The Confederate Belle.* Columbia: University of Missouri Press, 2003.

Roediger, David R. *The Wages of Whiteness: The Making of the American Working Class.* London: Verso, 1991.

Rogoff, Leonard. "Is the Jew White? The Racial Place of the Southern Jew." *American Jewish History* 83, no. 3 (1997): 195–230.

Roland, Charles P. *The Confederacy.* Chicago: University of Chicago Press, 1960.

Rose, Anne C. *Victorian America and the Civil War.* New York: Cambridge University Press, 1992.

Rosen, Robert N. *The Jewish Confederate.* Columbia: University of South Carolina Press, 2000.

Rotundo, E. Anthony. *American Manhood: Transformations in Masculinity from the Revolution to the Modern Era.* New York: Basic Press, 1993.

———. "Learning about Manhood: Gender Ideals and the Middle Class Family in Nineteenth Century America." In *Manliness and Morality: Middle Class Masculinity in Britain and American, 1800–1940,* edited by J. A. Mangan and James Walvin, 35–51. Manchester: Manchester University Press, 1987.

Rubin, Sarah Anne. *A Shattered Nation: The Rise and Fall of the Confederacy, 1861–1868.* Chapel Hill: University of North Carolina Press, 2005.

Sahlins, Peter. *Boundaries: The Making of France and Spain in the Pyrenees.* Berkeley: University of California Press, 1989.

Savage, Kirk. "The Self-Made Monument: George Washington and the Fight to Erect a National Monument." *Winterthur Portfolio* 22, no. 4 (Winter 1987): 225–42.

———. *Standing Soldiers, Kneeling Slaves: Race, War and Monument in Nineteenth-Century America.* Princeton: Princeton University Press, 1997.

———. *The Civil War in Art and Memory.* Washington, D.C.: National Gallery of Art, 2016

Savelle, Max. "Nationalism and Other Loyalties in the American Revolution." *American Historical Review* 67, no. 4 (July 1962): 914–16.

Schlereth, Thomas J. *Cultural History and Material Culture: Everyday Life, Landscapes, Museums.* Ann Arbor: UMI Research Press, 1990.

Scott, Anne Firor. *The Southern Lady: From Pedestal to Politics, 1830–1930.* 1970. Reprint, Charlottesville: University of Virginia Press, 1995.

Sellers, Charles Grier, Jr. "The Travail of Slavery." In *The Southerner as American,* edited by Charles Grier Sellers Jr., 40–51. Chapel Hill: University Press of North Carolina, 1960.

Shaw, William L. "Confederate Conscription and Exemption Acts." *American Journal of Legal History* 6, no. 4 (October 1962): 379–82.

Sheehan-Dean, Aaron. *Why Confederates Fought: Family and Nation in Civil War Virginia.* Chapel Hill: University of North Carolina Press, 2007.

Short, John Rennie. "U.S. History through Maps and Mapmaking." In *Dictionary of American History*, edited by S. I. Kutler, 9:2–5. New York: Thomson-Gale, 2003.

Silber, Nina. *Gender and the Sectional Conflict*. Chapel Hill: University of North Carolina Press, 2008.

Simms, William Gilmore. "The Morals of Slavery." *Southern Literary Messenger* 3 (November 1837): 641–57.

Slabaugh, Arlie R. *Confederate States Paper Money*. Iola, Wis.: Krause Publications, 2000.

Smith, Anthony D. *National Identity*. Reno: University of Nevada Press, 1991.

Smith, Margaret Denton, and Mary Louise Tucker. *Photography in New Orleans: The Early Years, 1840–1865*. Baton Rouge: Louisiana State University Press, 1982.

Smith-Rosenberg, Carroll. "Surrogate Americans: Masculinity, Masquerade and the Formation of a National Identity." *Publications of the Modern Language Association of America* 119, no. 5 (October 2004): 1325–35.

Spencer, Stephen. *Race and Ethnicity: Culture, Identity and Representation*. New York: Routledge, 2006.

Stamper, Anita Miller, and Mary Edna Lorenz. *Mississippi Homespun: Nineteenth Century Textiles and the Women Who Made Them*. Jackson: Mississippi Department of Archives and History, 1989.

Stampp, Kenneth M. *The Imperiled Union: Essays on the Background of the Civil War*. New York: Oxford University Press, 1980.

———. *A Peculiar Institution: Slavery in the Antebellum South*. New York: Alfred A. Knopf, 1956.

———. "The Southern Road to Appomattox." *The Imperiled Union: Essays on the Background of the Civil War*. New York: Oxford University Press, 1980.

———. "The Tragic Legend of Reconstruction." In *Myth and Southern History*, vol. 1: *The Old South*, edited by Patrick Gerster and Nicholas Cords, 155–68. Urbana: University of Illinois Press, 1989.

Stevenson, Lauralee Trent. *Confederate Soldier Artists: Painting the South's War*. Shippensburg: White Mane Publishing Company, 1998.

Still, William N., Jr. *Iron Afloat: The Story of the Confederate Armorclads*. Columbia: University of South Carolina Press, 1985.

Stout, Harry S. *Upon the Altar of the Nation: A Moral History of the Civil War*. New York: Penguin Books, 2006.

Stout, Harry S., and Christopher Grasso. "Civil War, Religion and Communication: The Case of Richmond." In *Religion and the American Civil War*, edited by Randall M. Miller, Harry S. Stout, and Charles Reagan Wilson, 313–59. New York: Oxford University Press, 1998.

Stout, S. H. "Buttons Made in the Confederacy." *Confederate Veteran Magazine* 5 (June 1897): 246–47.

Stowell, Daniel W. "Stonewall Jackson and the Providence of God." In *Religion and the American Civil War*, edited by Randall M. Miller, Harry S. Stout, and Charles Reagan Wilson, 187–207. New York: Oxford University Press, 1998.

Taylor, William R. *Cavalier and Yankee: The Old South and American National Character.* Cambridge: Cambridge University Press, 1979.

Thomas, Emory M. *The Confederacy as a Revolutionary Experience.* Englewood Hills, N.J.: Prentice-Hall, 1971.

———. *The Confederate Nation, 1861–1865.* New York: Harper and Row, 1979.

———. "Reckoning with Rebels." In *The Old South in the Crucible of War,* edited by Harry P. Owens and James J. Cook, 12–28. Jackson: University Press of Mississippi, 1983.

Thompson, William F. *The Image of War: The Pictorial Reporting of the American Civil War.* Baton Rouge: Louisiana State University Press, 1959.

Tilley, Christopher. *Reading Material Culture: Structuralism, Hermeneutics and Post-Structuralism.* Cambridge: Basil Blackwell, 1990.

Todd, Frederick P. *American Military Equipage, 1854–1872.* New York: Chatham Square Press, 1983.

———. "Notes on the Organization and Uniform of South Carolina Military Forces, 1860–1861." *Military Collector and Historian* 3, no. 3 (September 1951): 58–64.

Todd, Richard C. *Confederate Finance.* Athens: University of Georgia Press, 1954.

Toll, Robert C. *Blacking Up: The Minstrel Show in Nineteenth Century America.* New York: Oxford University Press, 1974.

Tonchi, Stefano. "Signs of Order, Signs of Disorder." In *Uniform: Order and Disorder,* edited by Francesco Bonani, Maria Luisa Frisa and Stefano Tonchi, 10–50. Milan: Edizioni Charta, 2000.

Tosh, John. *A Man's Place: Masculinity and the Middle Class Home in Victorian England.* New Haven: Yale University Press, 1999.

Trachtenberg, Alan. *Reading American Photographs: Images as History, Mathew Brady to Walker Evans.* New York: Hill and Wang, 1990.

Tremmell, George B. *A Guide Book of Counterfeit Confederate Currency: History, Rarity and Values.* Atlanta: Whitman Publishing, 2007.

Troiani, Don. "French Uniforms, Clothing and Equipment in the Union Army, Part 2." *North South Trader's Civil War* 26, no. 3 (May–June 1999): 3–6.

Ural, Susannah J., ed. *Civil War Citizens: Race, Ethnicity and Identity in America's Bloodiest Conflict.* New York: New York University Press, 2010.

Vandergriff, Cara. "Petticoat Gunboats: The Wartime Expansion of Confederate Women's Discursive Opportunities through Ladies' Gunboat Societies." Master's thesis, University of Tennessee, 2013.

Vandiver, Frank E. *Ploughshares into Swords: Josiah Gorgas and Confederate Ordnance.* Austin: University of Texas Press, 1952.

Varga, Tunde. "A Nineteenth-Century Mass Medium in the Formation of Cultural Stereotypes." *Neohelicon* 32, no. 1 (April 2005): 43–49.

Vlach, John Michael. *Back of the Big House: The Architecture of Plantation Slavery.* Chapel Hill: University of North Carolina Press, 1993.

———. "Plantation Landscapes of the Antebellum South." In *Before Freedom Came: African-American Life in the Antebellum South*, 21–50. Richmond: Museum of the Confederacy, and Charlottesville: University Press of Virginia, 1991.

Waldstreicher, David. *In the Midst of Perpetual Fetes: The Making of American Nationalism, 1770–1820*. Chapel Hill: University of North Carolina Press, 1997.

Wallace, Lee A. *A Guide to Virginia Military Organizations, 1861–1865*. Lynchburg: H. E. Howard, Virginia, 1986.

Wallach, Alan. "Making a Picture of the View from Mt. Holyoke." In *American Iconology: New Approaches to Nineteenth-Century Art and Literature*, edited by David C. Miller, 80–91. New Haven: Yale University Press, 1993.

Warren, Robin O. "Acting Feminine in the South: Antebellum and Civil War Stages." Ph.D. diss., University of Georgia, 2005.

Warwick, Eden. *Nasology; Or, Hints towards a Classification of Noses*. London: Richard Bentley, 1848.

Waterhouse, Richard. "The Internationalisation of American Popular Culture in the Nineteenth Century: The Case of the Minstrel Show." *Australian Journal of American Studies* 4, no. 1 (July 1985): 1–11.

Watson, Charles S. "Confederate Drama: The Plays of John Hill Hewitt and James Dabney McCabe." *Southern Literary Journal* 21, no. 2 (Spring 1989): 100–112.

———. *The History of Southern Drama*. Lexington: University of Kentucky Press, 1997.

Watson, Ritchie Devon. "The Difference of Race: Antebellum Race Mythology and the Development of Southern Nationalism." *Southern Literary Journal* 35, no. 1 (Fall 2002): 1–13.

———. *Norman and Saxon: Southern Race Mythology and the Intellectual History of the American Civil War*. Baton Rouge: Louisiana State University Press, 2008.

Weems, Mason L. *The Life of Washington*. Edited by Marcus Cunliffe. Cambridge: Belknap Press, Harvard University, 1962.

Weiner, Marli F. *Mistresses and Slaves: Plantation Women in South Carolina, 1830–1880*. Urbana: University of Illinois Press, 1998.

Welter, Barbara. "The Cult of True Womanhood: 1820–1860." *American Quarterly* 18 (Summer 1966): 151–74.

White, Deborah Gray. *Ar'n't I a Woman? Female Slaves in the Plantation South*. New York: W. W. Norton, 1985.

Whites, LeeAnn. *The Civil War as a Crisis of Gender: Augusta, Georgia, 1860–1865*. Athens: University of Georgia Press, 1995.

Wicks, Stephen. *Wildmen and Warriors: Men, Masculinity and Gender*. Westport, Conn.: Bergin and Garvey, 1996.

Wiley, Bell I. *The Life of Johnny Reb: The Common Soldier of the Confederacy*. Baton Rouge: Louisiana State University Press, 1970.

———. *Southern Negroes, 1861–1865*. 1938. Reprint, New Haven: Yale University Press, 1965.

Wilson, Chris P. *Jokes: Form, Content, Use and Function*. London: Academic Press, 1979.

Wilson, Clyde N. "'Free Trade: No Debt: Separation of Banks': The Economic Platform of John C. Calhoun." In *Slavery, Secession and Southern History*, edited by Robert Louis Paquette and Louis A. Ferleger, 81–99. Charlottesville: University Press of Virginia, 2000.

Wilson, Harold S. *Confederate Industry: Manufacturers and Quartermasters in the Civil War*. Jackson: University Press of Mississippi, 2002.

Winner, Lauren F. "Taking Up the Cross: Conversion amongst Black and White Jews in the Civil War South." In *Southern Families at War: Loyalty and Conflict in the Civil War South*, edited by Catherine Clinton, 194–98. New York: Oxford University Press, 2000.

Wise, Stephen R. *Lifeline of the Confederacy: Blockade Running during the Civil War*. Columbia: University of South Carolina Press, 1988.

Woodhead, Edward Henry. *Echoes of Glory: Arms and Equipment of the Confederacy*. Alexandria: Time-Life Books, 1991.

Woodward, Colin Edward. "Marching Masters: Slavery, Race and the Confederate Army, 1861–1865." Ph.D. diss., Louisiana State University, 2005.

———. *Marching Masters: Slavery, Race and the Confederate Army in the Civil War*. Charlottesville: University of Virginia Press, 2014.

Woodward, C. Vann. *The Burden of Southern History*. Baton Rouge: Louisiana State University Press, 1960.

Wright, Gavin. *The Political Economy of the Cotton South: Households, Markets and Wealth in the Nineteenth Century*. New York: W. W. Norton, 1978.

Wyatt-Brown, Bertram. *Honor and Violence in the Old South*. New York: Oxford University Press, 1986.

———. *Southern Honor: Ethics and Behavior in the Old South*. New York: Oxford University Press, 1982.

Zeller, Bob. *The Blue and Gray in Black and White: The History of Civil War Photography*. Westport: Praeger Publications, 2005.

Yetman, Norman L., ed. *Voices of Slavery: 100 Authentic Slave Narratives*. Mineola, N.Y.: Dover Publications, 2000.

———, ed. *When I Was a Slave: Memoirs from the Slave Narrative Collection*. Mineola, N.Y.: Dover Publications, 2002.

Zboray, Ronald J. *A Fictive People: Antebellum Economic Development and the American Reading Public*. New York: Oxford University Press, 1993.

INDEX

Note: Page numbers in italic indicate illustrations.

A. E. Blackmar and Brothers, 113, 122, 157

abolitionism, 51, 57, 195; Confederates associate with Satan, 102, 192; and Northern print literature, 62, 102; Southern critiques of, 51, 56, 63–64, 72–73

accoutrement, 83, 190

African Americans: as contraband, 72; and enslavement, 57, 61–62, 68–69; escape, 72, 233n8; as soldiers, 46–47, 48–49, 53, 160; stereotypes of, 41–45, 47–48; women, 182

agriculture, 30. *See also* Confederate economy; slavery

Alexander, Edward Porter, 84

Alexander, George W. (writer/soldier)

—works: *The Virginia Cavalier*, 67, 189, 236n49, 236n53

Alexander, Peter W., 204–5, 244n88

American Revolution, 118, 167; Confederates draw parallels with their war, 37, 204; Francis Marion in, 64–65; generation of, as role models, 126

ammunition. *See* Ordnance Department

antebellum South. *See* Confederate currency/bond vignettes; graphic print industry; illustrated periodicals; manufacturing; masculinity; photography; racial theories; racism; women

Appomattox, 3, *121*, 129

Archer, John (engraver), 97, *123*

Arkansas True Democrat: praises *Southern Monthly*, 102

armaments. *See* manufacturing; Ordnance Department

Armistead, Robert W. (soldier/artist), 141

armored rams. *See* Confederate navy; CSS *Manassas;* CSS *Virginia;* naval engagements

Army of Northern Virginia, 16, 152; cavalry, 201; clothing, 122, 125, 129, 244n88; in popular culture, 53, 88, 152; in popular imagination, 52–53, 160; surrender of, 129

Army of Tennessee, 122, 126, 128, 246n123

Artist as Anthropologist, The (Cowling), 5

artists, 103, 152, 155, 162; critique women, 178; depict African Americans, 43, 66; shortage of, 108, 110; use devices to convey character, 5, 173;190. *See also by name*

Asheville News: on impact of counterfeit shinplasters, 27

Attack on Charleston by the Yankee Iron Clad Fleet, April 7th 1863, The. See under Grinevald, Augustus (artist/lithographer)

Augusta, GA: art in, 150; gender issues, 268n46, 271n1; Ladies Volunteer Aid Association, 164; photography in, 149, 150, 250n50; powder works, 242n63; printing in, 99, 112, 114; religious art in, 6, 221n41; theatrical productions in, 140

Augusta Chronicle and Sentinel: encourages Confederate industrialization, 79; on problems caused by Confederate currency designs, 22; on *Southern Illustrated News* as venture, 104

Augusta Constitutionalist, 236n49, 242n63, 246n123, 272n14

"Aunt Abby" (engraving), *67*, 67–68

authors. *See by name*
Ayres, E. H. See *Southern Illustrated News*
Ayres and Wade. See *Southern Illustrated News; War and Its Heroes*

badges, 120, 124–25, *125*, 127, 167
Ball, Douglas B., 20
Ball, Thomas. *See* Keatinge and Ball (banknote engravers)
banknotes, prewar, 21, 43, 64–65, 215–18, 224n62, 234n24, 234n36, 235n41. *See also* Confederate currency/bond vignettes; graphic print industry
Barton, Michael, 188
Bartow, Georgia, 91
Bartow, Francis S., 18
Baton Rouge Daily Advocate: advocates Confederate industrialization, 79
battle. *See* combat, depictions of
Battle Flag. *See* Confederate flag designs
Battle of the Crater, The (Elder). *See under* Elder, John Adams (artist)
Battle-Field of Fredericksburg (Key), *109*, 110
Baudrillard, Jean, 4
Baumgarten, Julius (engraver), 16, 100, 249n37, 260n23
Beauregard, P. G. T., 193, 262n57; as Confederate hero, 149; as instigator of Confederate imagery, 11–12, 146–48, 249n43, 262n63; depictions of, 99, 101–2, 149, 220n20, 250n51; on stage, 139, 261n25
"Belle of Wet-zel, A" (engraving), 173, *175*, 270n80
Benjamin, Judah P., 39
Benson, C. D. (music publisher), 94
Berlinger, Richard E., 2
Bernath, Michael T., 2, 3, 108, 238n87
Berry, Harrison, 63
Bible, 56, 138, 233n9. *See also* religion
bigotry. *See* Confederate identity; racism
Binnington, Ian, 21, 58, 214
blackface, *44*, *45*; as proslavery tool, 43–45
Blassingame, John W., 41, 43
Blessing, Tom (Solomon) (photographer), 101
blockade of Southern ports, 17, 94, 97, 139–40, 143; creatives enter through, 58; depictions of, 147, 262n58
—impact on: graphic print imagery, 111; manufacturing, 24; prices, 94; society, 90–91, 172–73, 178
—spurs: innovation, 101; manufacturing, 240n33; graphic print industry, 62. *See also* graphic print industry; manufacturing; naval engagements
Bonner, Michael, 77, 223n24
Bonner, Robert B., 37, 53
Bonner, Robert E., 10–11, 228n8, 267n31
Boyd, Belle, 178, *180*, 270n95
bread riots. *See* Confederacy—and civil disorder
Brooke, Walter, 10, 222n6
Brown, John, 117
Brown, Joseph E., 49
Bruce, Edward Caledon, 152, 153, 263n85, 278n110
—works: *General R. E. Lee,* 206–7, *206*, 278n111
Buckner, Simon B., portraits, *103*
Budd, John T. (artist/ showman), 145, 156
—works: *Dioramic Pantomorph,* 142, *159*
Buffalo Paper Mills, 97
Bugle Horn of Liberty, 108, 111, 252n100; on failings of men, 182, *183;* on failings of women, 172, *174*, *178*
Bull Run. *See* First Battle of Bull Run (Manassas)
Burial of Latané, The. See under Washington, William D. (artist)
Burton, William J. (artist/showman), 138, 154, *159*, 159–60
—works: Battle at the Head Passes diorama, 139; *Panic at Manassas,* 138
Butler, Benjamin F., 272n20

Cain, Edward (military tailor), 18, 127
Camille, Michael, 4
Camp, 59th Virginia Infantry at Diascund Bridge. See under Chapman, Conrad Wise (artist)

Camp Scene, Belle Plain, May 16 or 17, 1864 (photograph), *125*
Campbell, William B. (engraver), 105–6, 108, 251n74
cartoons, 5, 8, 105; as social tool, 66
—depicting: gender, 171, 172, 174; enslavement, 63, 70, 71, 72; European powers, 6, 221n42; "gunboat fever," 140; men's failings, 167, 200; profiteers, 90, 194; race, 34, 37, 39, 40, 47, 51, 56, 182; Reconstruction, 212, *213;* war, 132; women's failings, 173, 174, 176, 177, 270n80; Yankees, 6, 40, 47, 190, 192. *See also individual titles of cartoons*
Cartwright, Samuel, 49
Cash, Wilbur, 212
Castine; or, The Maid of Mirkland. See under Edgeville, Edward (author)
casualties, 132, 155–58; as sacrifice, 50, 139
cavaliers: Confederates as, 17, 34, 57, 201, 203. *See also* racial theories
cavalry. *See* Army of Northern Virginia; Army of Tennessee
Chapman, Conrad Wise (artist), 58–60, 146–47, 233nn19–23
—works: *Camp, 59th Virginia Infantry at Diascund Bridge, 59,* 59–60; "A Confederate Picket," 197; *The Fifty-Ninth Virginia Infantry—Wise's Brigade, 59*
Chapman, John Gadsby (artist/ engraver)
—works: *The Fifty-Ninth Virginia—Wise's Brigade,* 60, 61
Charleston, SC, *145;* and abolitionism, 220n20; art in, 146–47, 259n14, 262n58; defense of, 143, 145–49, *146, 148,* 166, 259n14, 262n58, 262n63; female slave clothing in, 271n111; photography in, 100–1, 134, 147–48, 150; prices in, 90, 165
Charleston Courier, 30, 270n95; on photographs of Fort Sumter, 100
Charleston Mercury, 28–29, 30; criticizes hero worship, 150; describes *Southern Illustrated News,* 105; on government's obligation to troops, 85; on Jackson lithograph, 264n88; on manufacturing's social impact, 91; praises quality of five-dollar bill, 22; on quality of fifth series issue Treasury notes, 24
Chattanooga Rebel, 192
Chesnut, James, 34
Chesnut, Mary, 205
Child, John V. (engraver), 97, 136–37
"Child's Cloak made of Confederate gray cloth" (engraving), 130, *130*
Child's Index, 6
children, 135, 150, 156, 171, 173; black, depictions of, 68, *69, 72, 212;* white, depictions of, *7,* 50–51, *130*
Christianity. *See* religion
civilians (Northern), depictions of, *52, 63, 133*
civilians (Southern)
—clothing: prewar, 268n41; reflects shortages, 90–99; use of Confederate gray, 129–30
—depictions of: females, *6, 25, 63, 130, 168–69, 171, 173–77, 179–81, 185;* males, *36, 39, 41, 44, 69, 70, 90, 168–69, 171, 183, 185, 194–96*
—relationship to: army, 132, 153–59, 164–65; government, 83, 87, 266n1
Clinton, Catherine, 163, 167, 265–66n1, 268n53
clothing. *See* civilians (Southern); military clothing
Clothing Bureau. *See* Quartermaster's Department
Cohen, Lawrence B., 262n58
coinage. *See* Confederate currency/coinage
Columbia, SC, 30, 98, 110, 111, 149, 166
Columbus, GA, 83, 163
Columbus Enquirer: on failings of seventh series Treasury note engraving, 111
Columbus Sun: encourages purchase of Southern-made goods, 78; on quartermasters, 89
combat, depictions of: in cartoons, 6, *7, 46, 136;* on currency, 24; in maps, 136–38, *137,* 260n21, 260n23; in paintings, 1, 53, 135, 150, *151,* 219n11, 259n14; in panoramic performances, 134–35, 138–42, 154–55, 260n25;

combat, depictions of *(continued)*
in photographs, 147–48; in prints, 250n59; as propaganda, 135, 159–60, 161; on stage, 139, 141, 155, 160, 260n27, 264n96. *See also* First Battle of Bull Run (Manassas); military events; naval engagements

Comolli, Jean-Louis, 3

commercial art. *See* graphic print industry

Confederacy: army/civilian relationship, 132, 153–59, 164–65; Christianity linked to, 56, 137, 150, 163, 188, 193, 205; and civil disorder, 91, 245n115; currency, 26–27; and dissent, 176–78, 195–96, *196*, 266n1; economic conditions in, 27, 56, 77–79, 89–91, 94, 95, 101, 165, 238n2; ersatz in, 82–83, 97; female patriotism in, 166–69, 180–81; flags of, 10–12; and literacy, 4, 94; and military clothing depots, 119–20, 122, 128, 162, 256n51; and military dress, 117, 124–25; nativism in, 38–41, 78; naval defense of, 139–43, 166; social order in, 56–57, 68, 167, 173, 181, 187; social pressures in, 6–7, 49, 72, 172–77; social tensions in, 38–40, 88, 198–99, 203; tensions due to shortages, 89–91. *See also* blockade of Southern ports; Confederate identity; Confederate ideology; female identity; gender roles; Jewish population; manufacturing; military clothing; racism; slavery

Confederate Americanism, 21, 214

Confederate army regulation dress, 115, 119–20; development of, 18–19; inaccurate description of, 126–27; newspapers advocate adoption, 119, 127. *See also* military clothing

Confederate cultural nationalism. *See* Confederate Americanism

Confederate currency/bond vignettes, 215–18, 224n62, 234n24; antebellum, 21, 234n34, 234n36; limitations of, in conveying national messages, 24; martial, 23, 24–25, *123*, *142*, 203; North vs. South, 34, *35*; portraits, 23, 24, 203; selection of, 21–23, 64; of slavery, *42*, 43, 58, 64, *64*, 65, *65*, 234n24, 235n41, 235n42, 235n43

Confederate currency/coinage, 20, 27, 224n54; counterfeiting, 20, 22–23, 24, 27–28, 98, 181, 247n20; criticisms of, 22, 24, 26, 28, 98, 111; design of, 23–25, 28, 64, 181, 223n36, 237n82; emotional attachment to, 26; nicknames for, 25, 226n94; production, 96, 98, 248n21, 250n51, 260n14; shinplasters, 26–27; use of, 26; variety of, 26, 98. *See also* Confederate currency types; Confederate currency/bond vignettes; Confederate economy; graphic print industry

Confederate currency types: Type-29, *42*, 43; Type-30, *64*, 64; Type-31, 22; Types-38/42/43, 34–35, *36*, 98, *99*; Type-41, *65*, 65; Type-49, 24, *25*; Type-54, 98, *99*; Type-64, 17, 23, 153, 204, *205*; Type-68, 24–25

Confederate economy: agriculture, 17, 56; industrialization, 77–78, 81–84; inflation, 27, 94, 101; social impact of, 89–92, 128, 162, 194

Confederate flag and seal committee, 10, 12, 16, 31, 33, 203, 228n8

Confederate flag designs: first national, 11, *11*, 12, *141*, *143*; second national, *11*, 12–14, 33, *147*, *148*, 204, *205*; third national, *11*, 15, 223n30; "battle flag," 11–12, 16, 112, *133*; Southern Cross, 12

Confederate government: centralization of control, 30, 85–86, 89–90, 91, 221n39; congressmen and, 12, 14, 40, 222n18; obligation to clothe troops, 85; and profiteering, 89–90, 90, 130; and support of graphic print industry, 96–98, 110, 248n27; and support of manufacturing, 78

—Congress, 12–13, 14, 16, 49, 176, 210, 222n7, 223n24; finance and, 20, 23, 132, 224n56; Provisional, 10, 11; soldiers' clothing and, 85, 125, 128, 129

—iconography: currency, 20–25; flags, 10–14; military uniform, 18–19; postage stamps, 29–30; seals, 15–17. *See also* Confederate Post Office; Confederate seals; Confederate Treasury Department; Confederate War Department; Davis, Jefferson; Memminger, Christopher;

Ordnance Department; Quartermaster's Department
Confederate gray, 87–88, 129–30, 259n97; meanings, 130–32. *See also* civilians (Southern); military clothing; Quartermaster's Department
Confederate Great Seal, 6, *15*, *205*; design, 16–17, 203–4; use of, 17; Confederate iconography within, 17, 58
Confederate iconography. *See* Confederate army regulation dress; Confederate currency/coinage; Confederate flag designs; Confederate Great Seal; Confederate postage stamps; Confederate seals
Confederate identity: army embodying, 127, 130, 132–33, 153–54, 188, 198; manufacturing and, 79–82, 84–85, 86, 91, 130; marketplace and, 90–91, 111; national, 24, 33, 137, 163, 204, 209, 214; patriotism and, 164, 188, 193; state loyalties, 11, 117, 124. *See also* Confederacy; Confederate Americanism; Confederate ideology; First Battle of Bull Run (Manassas); religion; Vicksburg, MS
Confederate ideology, 3; culture of invincibility, 139, 143, 158–60; fear of dependency, 76, 79, 195, 198; international recognition, 6, *7*, 221n42; Lee and Jackson and, 204–5; people's unity, 153–54, 159–60; and prewar America, 10–12, 17, 21–22; religion and, 126, 137–38, 150, 162, 193, 209; and resolution, 29, 34, 143–45; sacrifice, 50, 126, 144, 202; soldiers' resolve, 146–47, 126, 202; superiority, 79–80, 135, 139, 161; tensions in, 84, 160, 172, 176, 181–82, 184, 203. *See also* Confederacy; Confederate Americanism; female identity; First Battle of Bull Run (Manassas); male identity; racism; religion; slavery; truthfulness; Yankees
Confederate imagery, 2–6, 219n14; and plagiarism, 111–12, 252n99, 259n98, 270n80. *See also* Confederate currency/bond vignettes; *imagery by subject, artist, or type*
Confederate navy: ironclads in popular imagination, 139–43, 147. *See also* naval engagements
Confederate Ordnance Department. *See* Ordnance Department
"Confederate Picket, A." *See under* Chapman, Conrad Wise (artist)
Confederate Picket Post near Charleston, S.C., A. See under Cook, George S. (photographer)
Confederate Post Office, 28–30
Confederate postage stamps: criticisms of, 28–29; portraits used on, 29–30; shortages of, 29, 30; usage, 29, 30
Confederate Provisional Congress [1861], 10, 30, 222n6
Confederate Quartermaster's Department. *See* Quartermaster's Department
Confederate regulation uniform. *See* Confederate army regulation dress
Confederate seals: Justice Department, *16*; Patent Office, *16*; Post Office, *16*; Provisional Government, *16*; Treasury Department, *16*; War Department, *16*. *See also* Confederate Great Seal
Confederate Spirit, or Knapsack of Fun, 93, 107, 108, 111, 220n19, 228n17; on failings of women, 174, *174*, 176, *177*; on profiteering, *90*; racial stereotypes in, 51, 52
Confederate stamps. *See* Confederate postage stamps
Confederate States Art Union. *See* East Tennessee Art Association
Confederate States Medical and Surgical Journal, 108
"Confederate States Steamer Virginia, The." *See under* Hoyt, John K. (artist/soldier)
Confederate theater. *See* theater
Confederate Treasury Department, 20–26, 30, 42, 64, 96–98, 110, 111. *See also* Confederate currency/coinage; Memminger, Christopher
Confederate troops: C.S. Zouave Battalion, 168; Regulars, 119
Confederate uniform. *See* military clothing
Confederate Variety's. See under Omenhauser, John J.
Confederate Vivandiere, The. See under Hodgson, Joseph (playwright)

Confederate War Department, 18–19, 116, 119–20, 201. *See also* Confederate seals
Cook, George S. (photographer), 100–1, 146, 147–48, 249n43, 262n63
—works: *View from Fort Sumter Parapet, 148; A Confederate Picket Post near Charleston, S.C.,* 61, *62; Interior View of Fort Sumter, 148*
Cook Brothers (gun makers), 80
Corsan, W. C., 90, 91
Cotton Fields. See under Smillie, James D.
counterfeiting. *See under* Confederate currency/coinage
courtship. *See* gender relations
Cowell, David T. (photographer), 100, 101, 153, 249n42
—works: Belle Boyd carte de visite, 178; Jackson portrait, 204, *205;* Robert E. Lee portrait, 208
Cowling, Mary, 5
Crater, Battle of the, 53
Crawford, Thomas, 203
Crehen, Eugene (lithographer/artist), 101, 106, 110, 200, 250n51
—works: illustration of infantry officers' uniforms, *18,* 109; "Just Before the Battle Mother," 112, *113; Southern Illustrated News* masthead, *145;* "Miss Belle Boyd, the Rebel Spy," 178, *180*
Crenshaw Woolen Mills, 81, 243n78
"Croaker." *See under* Dunn, George (engraver)
Cronin, Mary, 166
CSS *Alabama,* 17, 261n37
CSS *Chicora,* 143, 166
CSS *David,* 147
CSS *Manassas,* 139
CSS *Palmetto State,* 143, 166
CSS *Virginia,* 139–40; depictions of, *75, 141,* 142, *143;* and "gunboat fever," 140, 166
culture of invincibility. *See* Confederate ideology
Cumming, Kate, 160
currency. *See* Confederate currency/coinage

Dallas Herald: calls on manufacturers to justify high prices, 89
Davis, Jefferson, 116, 132, 144, 176, 269n72; photographs of inauguration, 100, 133–34; in popular opinion, 30, 149, 199; on priorities for supplying military forces, 83; sees God's support of Confederacy, 81; use of portrait, 16, 30, 99, 102, 150, 216, 219n10, 250n50
Davis, John (actor/writer/manager)
—works: *The Roll of the Drum:* battle reunites couple, 139; loyal slave in, 236n49; popularity of, 261n27; Southern man wins Northern woman, 168–69
Davis, Nicholas, 199, 274n62
Dawson, Francis W., 38
De Bow, James D. B., 102
Deas, George, 18, 223n42
death, 155–58, 169; depictions of, 139, *157, 158. See also* casualties
Delchamps, J. J.
—works: *Love's Ambuscade:* combat in, 155; "good death" in, 155; female patriotism in, 162; male restraint in, 197; Northern inferiority in, 37
dependency, white fear of. *See under* Confederate ideology; manufacturing
dioramas. *See* theater
domestic sphere. *See* gender roles
dress. *See* civilians (Southern); military clothing
"Drummer Boy of Shiloh, The" (sheet music). *See under* Grinevald, Augustus (artist/lithographer)
Duncan, Blanton (printer), 97, 98, 101, 234n35, 248n31; describes design for Confederate Treasury note, 64; quality of work, 24, 98; relationship with C. G. Memminger, 39
—works printed by: *The Attack on Charleston by the Yankee Iron Clad Fleet April 7th 1863,* 146, *147;* "The Drummer Boy of Shiloh," 156, *157; Fun for the Camp,* 34, *35;* "I'm Coming to My Dixie Home," 73, *74;* Treasury notes, 34, *36, 42,* 64, *99; Uniform and Dress of the Army of the Confederate States, 18,* 19, 224n48
Dunn, George (engraver), 23, 110, 200, 203, 219n14, 222n30
—works: *Vignette* (Confederate ironclad sinking

Union vessel), *143;* "Croaker," 193, *194; Fashions for March 1864,* 93, *179;* "You Look at a Star from Two Motives," 184, *185*

East Tennessee Art Association, 150
economic development. *See* manufacturing
Edgeville, Edward (author)
—works: *Castine; or, The Maid of Mirkland,* 191, *191,* 269n60
Edwards, Jay Dearborn (photographer), 100, 168, 219n14
Elam, George W. (engraver), 97, 247n20
Elder, John Adams (artist), 152, 153, 160, 233n19, 263n85
—works: *The Battle of the Crater,* 1, 8, 53, 160, 219n11, 221n43, 233n19, 265n115; *The Scout's Prize,* 1, 8, 219n2, 220n43
emancipation, 192; in cartoons, *52;* Confederate myths about, 51–52, 55, 63, 72–74
Emancipation Proclamation, 192
enemy stereotypes. *See* Yankees
engraving. *See* graphic print industry
entertainment. *See* escapism; theater
escapism, 3, 5, 43, 141, 143, 152, 158, 160, 180, 211
Escott, Paul D., 2, 13
Europe, 6, 19, 61, 111, 180
European nationalism, 32–33, 118
Evans, Augusta Jane (author)
—works: *Macaria,* 126
Ewell, Richard S., 48, 107; portraits, *107*
"Exodus of Israelites," *41*
extortion and speculation, 90–91, 182; by civilians, 172–74, 178, 194; depictions of practitioners of, *41, 90, 174, 175, 195;* and greed, 77–78; manufacturers criticized for, 89; Quartermaster's Department and, 88–90; sinful nature of, 194; and Yankees, 91
Ezekiel, Moses Jacob, 40

fabrics. *See* homespun textiles; manufacturing
Fahs, Alice, 66
Fashions for March 1864. See under Dunn, George (engraver)
Faust, Drew, 2, 66, 173, 214, 265n1
Fayetteville Observer, 276n77; on women involved in war work, 172
female identity: benevolence, 163–65; martial, 167–71; men's attempts to affect, 162–63, 169, 172–79; sexual, 170, 171, 173–74, 182; societal expectations of behavior and, 163, 164, 178–79, 183–84; societal expectations of dress and, 167, 170, 172–4, 178, 182, 184
Fifty-Ninth Virginia Infantry, The—Wise's Brigade. See under Chapman, Conrad Wise (artist); Chapman, John Gadsby (artist/engraver)
"Final Call for Reserves" (engraving), 171, *171*
fine arts. *See* painting; sculpture
First Battle of Bull Run (Manassas), 11, 135; Confederate myths about, 135–38; depicted in maps, 102, 137–38; depicted on stage, 138–39, 154, 169, 189; in popular imagination, 137–39, 153–54
Fitz, John D. (showman)
—works: *Panopticon of the South,* 134, 138, 155–56, *159*
Fitzhugh, George, 62, 70, 81, 182
Flag and Seal Committee. *See* Confederate Flag and Seal Committee
flags, military use of, 11–12. *See also* Confederate flag designs
Foley, William D., 127
Foote, Henry S., 40, 229n38
Forrest, Nathan Bedford, 160, 201, 210
Fort Pillow, 160
Fort Sumter, 100; depictions of Confederate defense of 1863–64, *75,* 145–49, *147, 148,* 262n58; depictions of Union defense of 1861, 134–35
Frank Leslie's Illustrated Weekly, 102, 104–5
Fremantle, Arthur, 165
Freud, Sigmund, 5
Fun for the Camp, 252n99; racial stereotypes in, 34, *35*

Gallagher, Gary, 2, 266n1
Galt, Alexander (sculptor), 149, 153, 263n86
Gate City Guardian: on women and war effort, 163

Gellatly, William (engraver), 225n76, 252n95
—works: *Battle-Field of Fredericksburg, from General Lee's Headquarters on the Road, 109,* 110
gender relations: attraction, 182, 200–1; courtship and marriage, 169, 172, 200; enslaved, 67, 73, 236n56; interracial, 37–38, 51–52, 232n93; making connections, 165, *183;* male identity and, 200; normative notions, 184–85; prewar, 163; Yankees and, 37, 51, 169, 174, 189. *See* also female identity; male identity
gender roles, 266n1, 268n46; clothing and, 169–70, 271n1; religion and, 163; spheres, 163, 167; women's right to protection, 182–83, 202
General Marion Inviting a British Officer to Share His Meal (White), 64, *64*
General R. E. Lee. See under Bruce, Edward Caledon
"General Robert Edmund Lee." *See under* Torsch, John W. (engraver/soldier)
Gen'l E. Kirby Smith. See under Shaver, Samuel M.
Georgia troops: Capt. John A. Strother's Muscogee Mounted Rangers, 20th Georgia Infantry, 117; Sidney Brown Infantry, 6th Georgia, 124; 1st Georgia Regular Infantry, 125; 3rd Georgia Infantry, 116, 117; 4th Georgia Infantry, 116, 117; 15th Georgia Infantry, 124–25
Gettysburg campaign. *See* military events
Glorious Turtle Ram Fight (Burton), 139
"Going to Kill-patrick!" (engraving), 177–78, *177*
"Good death." *See* death
Gorgas, Josiah, 83
Gould, Stephen J., 33
government. *See* Confederate government
Gow, James L. (engraver), 99–100
Grain, George W. (artist/showman), 145–46, 152, 154–55, 160, 264n95
—works: Fort Pillow scene, 160; *Panoramic Mirror, 142, 159; Grain's Panopticon, 159*
graphic print industry: art prints, 99, 250n59; circulation of, 5–6; and Confederate currency, 96, 98; colored printing, 93; demand for sheet music, 112–14; economic impacts on, 101; engravers/engraving, 95–96, 247n20; ephemera, 99–100; equipment, 95–97; ersatz, 97, 101; government support of, 96, 111; high point of, 108–11; historians' estimation of, 114; lithographers/lithography, 97–98, 101–4; materials, 97; pre-war, 94; processes employed, 95; quality of, 111–12; shortages of skilled labor, 94, 111–12; types of, 95; U.S. blockade effect on, 94–95. *See also* Confederate currency/coinage; illustrated periodicals; patriotic envelopes; photography; *producers by name*
Great Britain, 6, 7, 118, 197
Great Expectations (play), 67, 88, 236n49, 271n108
Great Southern Naval Victory in Hampton Roads (Mallory), 141–42
"Great Subject of the Day, The" (engraving), 176–77, *177*
"Great Victory—Taken on the Spot by Our Own Artist" (engraving), 136, *136*
Greenburg, Amy, 188
Greenhow, Rose O'Neal, 270n95
Grinevald, Augustus (artist/lithographer), 110, 153, 259n14
—works: *The Attack on Charleston by the Yankee Iron Clad Fleet, April 7th 1863,* 146, *147;* "The Drummer Boy of Shiloh," 156, *157;* Fort Sumter panorama, 135
Griswold, Samuel, 80
Griswold and Gunnison revolver, 81
Guerrillas, The. See under McCabe, James Dabney
gunboat fever. *See* CSS *Virginia*
gunboat societies, 166

Halpin, John (engraver), 97
Hammond, James Henry, 57, 66, 236n56, 239n24
Hampton Roads, Battle of. *See* naval engagements
Hardee, William, 11, 103, 119
Harpers Ferry raid, 117
Harper's Weekly, 102, 105
Haw, Mary Jane (author)
—works: *The Rivals,* 35–36, *36*

heroes, 126, 159–60, 172; Confederate concerns about, 150, 209; Davis and Beauregard as, 149; generals as, 149–53, 201, 204; on stage, 196–97
Hewitt, John Hill (playwright/composer)
—works: *The Jayhawkers*, 155; *The Scout; or, The Plains of Manassas*, 67, 139, 169, 189, 236n49; *The Veteran '76 and '62*, 167; *The Vivandiere*, 168, 236n49
Hodgson, Joseph (playwright)
—works: *The Confederate Vivandiere*, 155, 169, 189, 264n100
Holden, William W., 89, 196, 247n46
homespun textiles, 199, 267n41; and patriotism, 173. *See also* military clothing; women
honor, southern, 24, 198, 272n4
Hoyer, Ludwig. *See* Hoyer and Ludwig (printers)
Hoyer and Ludwig (printers), 14, 97, 98, 101, 247n21, 248n30; lose Treasury contract, 98; Treasury notes, 22, 235n42; work quality, 22, 98
Hoyt, John K. (artist/soldier)
—works: "The Confederate States Steamer Virginia," 140, *141*
Hunton, Henry, 24–25, 226n90
Hurdle, Armistead (artist), 105, 111, 251n74
—works: "Now Mars Walter," *36;* "Recipe to Get Rid of Extortioners," *195;* "Recognition," *7;* *Southern Illustrated News* banner, 145
Hutton and Freligh (publishers). See *Southern Monthly*
Huyett, David H. (illustrator), 103–4, 250n58

iconography: African Americans, 42–43, 44–47; government, 10–30; manhood, 203–9; martial, 120–24, 142–43; proslavery, 59–76; Union soldiers, 34–38. *See also* Confederate army regulation uniform; Confederate currency/coinage; Confederate flag designs; Confederate postage stamps
illustrated envelopes. *See* patriotic envelopes
Illustrated Mercury, 112; on Yankee barbarism, *191*
illustrated periodicals: Confederate desire for, 102, 107; and high-water mark of Confederate publishing, 108, 111; obstacles in production, 103–4, 106, 112; prewar history of, 104; quality of engravings, 111; Southern, as antidote to Northern, 102. *See also* graphic print industry; *individual titles*
"Illustration of the New Yankee Doctrine about the Darkey," 46, *47*
"I'm Coming to My Dixie Home" (sheet music). *See under* Wissler, Jacques (artist/lithographer)
imagery. *See* Confederate imagery
immigrants. *See* Confederacy; Jewish population; racism
"In Favor of the Prosecution of the War" (cartoon), *90*
independence, 144, 195; economic, 79–80, 82, 86; intellectual, 3, 102; masculine ideal, 187
industrialization/industry. *See* manufacturing
Interior View of Fort Sumter. *See under* Cook, George S.
ironclads. *See* Confederate navy; CSS *Manassas;* CSS *Virginia;* naval engagements

Jackson, Martin (former slave), 61
Jackson, Thomas J. "Stonewall," 153; as masculine ideal, 204; depictions of, 101, 105, 152–53, *205*, 250n49, 252n85, 277n93; as hero, 153; mourning death of, 14, 277n95; physiognomy, 204; portrait on banknote, *205;* responses to death, 153. *See also* Confederate ideology
"Jem Wells, of the New Richmond Theater" (Cave), 44, *44*
Jewish population, 38–41
Johnston, Joseph E., 11–12, 14, 149, 193, 262n78
Jones, John B., 90
Joseph, Nathan, 115, 116
"Just Before the Battle Mother." *See under* Crehen, Eugene (lithographer/artist)

Keatinge, Edward C. (engraver), 23, 24, 97, 225n77
—works: *Portrait of Judah P. Benjamin*, *99;* Jackson portrait, 204, 205

Keatinge and Ball (banknote engravers), 24, 65, 96, 110, 153, 247n15; Treasury notes, 23, 65, *203*, *205*
Kentucky troops, 117; 1st Battalion Infantry, 118
Key, John Ross (artist/engineer), 146
—works: *Battle-Field of Fredericksburg*, *109*, 110
Key, Thomas J., 49, 51
Kimmel, Michael S., 201, 271n2
King, James W. (artist), 105, 152, 251n68
Kirby Smith, E., 150, *151*
Knoxville Art Association. *See* East Tennessee Art Association
Knoxville Daily Register: on Army of Tennessee, 126

labor shortages: in graphic print industry, 94, 111–12
ladies' aid societies, 164, 165
ladies' gunboat movement, 166
Lauer, Josh, 23
Lawton, A. R., 86, 129
Lederle, Otto (lithographer), 103, 249n33, 250n59
—works: *Maj. Gen. S. B. Buckner*, *103*
Lee, Robert E., 49, 53, 110, 132, 201; depictions of, 149, 152–53, 205–6, *206*, *207*, *208*, 209; as masculine ideal, 204–5; as physiognomic ideal, 205. *See also* Confederate ideology
Lee's army. *See* Army of Northern Virginia
Lengyel, Christian M., 21
Lewis, Harry, 199
Lincoln, Abraham: caricatures of, 192, 272n10, 273n23; Confederate concerns about, 9, 57–58
lithography. *See* graphic print industry
"Lo! The Poor, Unhappy Slave" (engraving), 68, *69*
Lost Cause, 8, 213–13; origins of, 76, 114, 161
Louisiana troops: Washington Artillery, 138, 261n26; Wheat's Battalion Infantry, 127; Hays' Brigade, 158
"Louisianans of Hays' Brigade Burying the Dead on Malvern Hill" (engraving), *158*
Love's Ambuscade (Delchamps). *See under* Delchamps, J. J.
Lovett, George (engraver)
—works: Confederate Treasury seal, 16
"Lt. Gen. Thomas J. Jackson." *See under* Maurice, Alfred (illustrator/engraver)
Ludwig, Charles L. *See* Hoyer and Ludwig (printers)
Luraghi, Raimondo, 77

Macaria. *See under* Evans, Augusta Jane
Macon Daily Telegraph: on cartoon in *Southern Illustrated News*, 212; on *Hardtack*, 111–12; on the war's benefits, 91; on how people use postage stamps, 29; on improved quality of seventh series Treasury notes, 25
Macon Georgia Weekly Telegraph: on Yankee dishonesty, 78
magazines. *See* illustrated periodicals
Maiden's Vow, The; or, The Capture of Courtland, Alabama. *See under* McCabe, James Dabney
mail service. *See* Confederate Post Office
Majewski, John, 21, 238n2
male identity, 187; and apparel, 198–200, 271n1; Confederate conceptions of manhood, 176, 188, 191, 193; war as a test of manhood, 188–89. *See also* masculinity; patriarchy and paternalism
Mallory, Lee (artist/showman), 146, 210, 158, 160
—works: *Pantechoptomon (War Illustrations)*, 138, 154, *159*, 236n49; *Great Southern Naval Victory in Hampton Roads*, 141–42 ; *Stereopticon*, 151–52; *159*, 270n95; "The Wounded Officer and His Steed," 156–57
Manassas. *See* First Battle of Bull Run (Manassas)
Manning, Chandra, 3, 53
manufacturing, 3, 4; accoutrement, 83; armaments, 80, 82–84, 242n63; erstatz and, 79, 80, 82, 83, 95, 97; and Europe, 17, 79; government involvement in, 243n87, 244n59; impact of, 78, 82, 86, 87, 89, 165;

independence and, 78–79, 239n24; and the North, 57, 78–79, 80–81, 241n40; paper, 97; and patriotism, 81–82, 85; prewar, 77–78, 239n19; and profiteering, 86–87; quality of products, 81, 244n88; and shortages of goods, 79; slavery and, 80; and society, 27, 78, 89–91, 130, 210; as symbolic weapon, 78; textiles, 78, 89, 129–30, 166, 242n78; vignettes related to, 215–17; war's impact on, 77

—as symbol of: independence, 86, 91; God's influence, 81, 241n48; Southerners' skills, 79–81, 84, 91

maps, 100, 102, 136–38, 249n42, 250n59, 260n23. *See also by title*

marriage. *See* gender relations

masculinity: antebellum concepts of, 187–88; and cavalier type, 201–2, 203; and citizenship, 191, 198; Jackson as model of, 204; Lee as model of, 204–9; martial type, 200; military service and, 188–89, 198; religion and, 192–93, 277n95; restrained type, *170*, 203; tension between types, 201–2, 210; Washington as model of, 203

—degree of related to: dress, 198–200; fortitude, 193, 202; modesty, 197, 198, 204; patriotism, 188, 195–96; restraint, 139, 190–93, 196–98, 203; selflessness, 194

"Masks and Faces—King Abraham before and after issuing the Emancipation Proclamation" (engraving), 192, *192*

Maurice, Alfred (illustrator/engraver), 108, 260n23

—works: "Lt. Gen. Thomas J. Jackson," 151, *152*

McCabe, James Dabney (writer), 235n49

—works: *The Guerrillas:* 37, 55, 67, 155–56, 170, 189, 196; *The Maiden's Vow; or, The Capture of Courtland, Alabama*, 189, 271n108

McCarthy, Carlton, 8

McIntyre, Archibald C. (photographer)

—works: *Inauguration of Jefferson Davis*, 100, 133–34

McPherson, James, 164

mechanical reproduction. *See* Confederate currency/coinage; graphic print industry; illustrated periodicals; photography

melodrama. *See* theater

Memminger, Christopher, *39;* criticism of, 26, 39–40; portrait on currency, 217–18; role in providing currency, 20–24, 27, 96–98, 181, 248n31

Memphis, TN, 28, 144

Memphis Appeal: on Burton's diorama, 154; on failings of post office stamps, 29; on lack of quality Southern art before the war, 2; on *Panopticon of the South*, 134; on revolver's quality, 80

men. *See* gender relations; gender roles; male identity; masculinity; soldiers

Meridian, MS: lynching in, 49, 231n74

Miles, William Porcher, 10–12, 14

military clothing (Confederate enlisted men): associations with independence movements, 118; badges, 124–25, *125;* cavalry criticized for style of, 201–2; civilian use of, 129–30; commutation system and, 119–20, 255n40; Confederate regulation dress and, 119, 122; compared to U.S. clothing, 86, 120; construction of, 86, 120; government obligation to provide, 85, 122; headgear, 118, *125;* homemade, 165; in popular imagination, 123–24; initial soldier dress, 116–18; jackets, 119–24, *121, 123;* military science influences, 118; prewar, 78, 116–117, 198; problems with, 87, 125, 244n88; raggedness, 125–26; sociology and, 115–16; soldier responses to, 124–26; state issue, 117, 122; supply, 122, 246n123, 256n51; uniformity of, 119–20; women and, 162–66. *See also* Confederate army regulation dress; Confederate gray; Quartermaster's Department

—meanings of: indicates affiliations, 116–18, 124, 163–65; indicates character, 200–1; indicates favoritism, 87; indicates individuality, 124; indicates service, 122, 126

military clothing (Confederate officers): badges, 127, 275n68; generals, 199, 204–5; field, 127–29, *127*; regulation dress, *18*, use of, 127, 199, 201; staff, 87, 200–1, 258n95; women and, 200
military clothing (Union officers), *46*, *48*, 190, *190*
military events: Appomattox campaign (1865), 129; Early's Raid (1864), 132, *133*; Gettysburg campaign (1863), 88, 107, 201, 260n23; impact of depictions of, on civilians, 136–38; popularity of depiction of, among civilians, 158, 160; Knoxville evacuation, 150; Maryland campaign (1862), 16, 153, 209; Richmond raid (Union), 177–78. *See also* combat, depictions of; *engagements by name*
military forces: and Confederate prisoners of war, 45, 86, *125*; and Union prisoners of war, 37, 47–48, 178; women's interaction with, 176, 200–1
Minnis, George W., 101
Minnis and Cowell photographic studio, 50, 95, 105
minstrelsy. *See* theater
miscegenation. *See* race; racism
Miscegenation; or, Life of a Virginia Negro in Washington (play), 51–52, 236n49, 271n108
"Miscegenation; or, The 'Free American of African Descent' Enjoying His Long-Lost Freedom (engraving), 51, *52*, 72
"Miss Belle Boyd, the Rebel Spy." *See under* Crehen, Eugene (lithographer/artist)
"Miss Ida Vernon as Leah, the Forsaken." *See under* Torsch, John W.
"Miss Mary E. Walker, M.D." (engraving), *170*
Mississippi troops: Prairie Guards, 11th Mississippi Infantry, 116; 16th Mississippi Infantry, 199; Samuel Benton Relief Rifles, 18th Mississippi Infantry, 117
Mobile, AL: and civil disorder, 245n115; counterfeit shinplasters in, 27; crime in, 72; naval defenses, 143; photography in, 249n45, 278n121; theatrical productions in, 142, 152, 155, 156; trade in, 90; women in, 163, 174
Mobile Register: criticizes government's care of soldiers, 87; on *Confederate Spirit, and Knapsack of Fun*, 111; on Chapman paintings, 233n20; on failings of women, 178; on *Southern Illustrated News*, 106
"Model Lady, The" (engraving), 172–72, *174*, 269n76
money. *See* banknotes; Confederate currency/coinage
monogenesis. *See* racial theories
Montgomery, AL, 10, 15, 18; counterfeit shinplasters in, 27; photography in, 133–34, 249n45; post office at, 29; theatrical productions in, 160, 274n100
Montgomery, AL, congress. *See* Confederate Provisional Congress
Montgomery Weekly Mail, 48
morale, 135; army, 86, 129; civilian, 202; late war, 132, 160–61, 265n121; and manufacturing, 79–80, 91; and religion, 209; and resilience, 143–48, 186, 193, 202; of soldiers, 164; and visual culture, 5, 155; and the war, 132, 134–35
Morton, Samuel G., 41
"Mrs. Simpson, an Exile from Tennessee" (engraving), 174, *175*
munitions. *See* Ordnance Department
Myers, Abraham C., 39; Confederate uniform and, 18–19, 119, 127

Nashville, TN: effect of loss, on Confederacy, 121–22, 144; graphic printing in, 94, 246n3
Nashville Patriot, 137
Nashville Republican Banner: on post office stamps, 28
Nasology; or, Hints toward Classification of Noses (Warwick), 24, 228n14
National Bank Note Company, 65, 96, 215
nationalism: Confederate, 31, 127; European, 32, 33; Southern, 33–34, 77, 79. *See also* Confederate identity; Confederate ideology

naval engagements: Battle of Hampton Roads (1862), *75*, 139–40, *143*; battle of the Head Passes (1861), 139; Charleston Harbor (1863), 143, 166; depictions of, *75*, 139, 140–42, *143*, *144*; in popular imagination, 140, 166
naval vessels. *See by name*
nativism. *See* racism
New Orleans, LA, 144; art and, 149, 153–54; effect of loss on Confederates, 96, 121; manufacturing and, 80, 83; photography and, 100, 168, 246n4, 266n7; postmaster, 28; printing and, 20, 96, 137, 249n33, 272n20; "secession fever" in, 102
—theatrical productions in: 156, 168; panoramic, 138, 260n25; religious, 264n95
New Orleans Bee: on military clothing, 119; praises Confederate rifle's quality, 80
New Orleans Daily Crescent: describes painting of Confederate family, 153–54; on military clothing, 120, 255n35
New Orleans Daily Delta: and First Battle of Bull Run, 136; on Fitz's *Battle of Manassas*, 156; on Mallory's *War Illustrations*, 138; on lack of postage stamps, 29
New Orleans Picayune: on post office supplying stamps, 28; on military clothing, 127
Nixon, J. B., 35
North Carolina troops: issue uniforms, 117; 27th North Carolina Infantry, 126
Northerners: ancestry, 34, 53, 239n6; Confederate opinion of, 33–34, 51, 57, 190–192, 194; and counterfeiting, 24; depictions of, 1, 35, 52, 53, 63, 272n10; exploiting African Americans, 47, 69; racism among, 230n48; and Southerners, similarity, 37, 188; white workers, 32. *See also* Yankees
"Now Mars Walter." *See under* Hurdle, Armistead

Ogden, Richard D. (actor/writer/theater manager), 51–52, 72
Old Testament. *See* religion
Omenhauser, John J.
—works: *Confederate Variety's*, 44–45, *45*
Ordnance Department: Augusta powder works, 242n63; impact on war effort, 83; manufacture of ammunition and weapons, 84; quality of accoutrement, 83; quality of ammunition, 84; quality of weapons, 80, 84, *85*; success of, 82. *See also* accoutrement; revolvers; rifles
Overall, John W. (publisher), 40

Pages from the Unpublished History of a Celebrated Financier (engraving), 39–40, *39*
paintings, 135, 220n14; exhibition of, in Confederacy, 6, 50, 146, 149, 150; patriotic, 149; in prewar South, 2. *See also by title or artist*
panoramas. *See* theater
Pantechoptomon. *See* Mallory, Lee; theater
paper money. *See* Confederate currency/coinage
Paterson, James T. (printer), 97, 215; employees, 248n21, 250n51, 260n14; *The Soldier's Suit of Grey* (sheet music), *123*
patriarchy and paternalism: Calhoun and, 57; planters and, 198; proslavery, 68, 73, 76; women and, 182–83
patriotic envelopes, 99, 100
patriotism. *See under* manufacturing
Payne, Alexander Dixon, *128*
"Peace Movement North, The" (Casey), 132, *133*
Pelot, Alma A. (photographer), 100
periodicals. *See* illustrated periodicals
"Personification of the Yankee Proposition for the New Cartel of Exchange" (engraving), 47, *48*
Petersburg Daily Express: on soldier morale, 176
Phillips, Jason, 160, 265n121
photographers. *See by name*
photographic studios, 95. *See by name*
photography: cost of, 101, 250n49; in early war, 100; ersatz, 101; impact of inflation on, 101; Lee and, 206, 208, *208*; materials, 95, 100, 249n43, 249n45; persistence of in the Confederacy, 100, 101; prewar, 94, 246n4; processes, 61, 95; role in hero worship,

photography *(continued)*
150–51; and truthfulness, 68, 100, 148; types of, 262n63
—subject matter: Confederate military camps, 61, 62, 101, 154, 220n14; generals, 101, 149, 152–53, 204, 278n121; military theaters, 100, 147, 220n14; political, 133–34; women, 168, 178, 270n95
—use of: commercial, 100, 133–34; documentary, 249n43; in engraving, 68, 103, *107,* 208; military, 147–48, *148,* 249n42, 262n63; portraiture, 100, *208,* 249n45, 270n95; reprographic, 150, 219n2; in theatrical productions, 151–52, 210
physiognomy, 40, *41;* emphasizing racial stereotype, 51, 70, *70,* 71, *71;* indicating "in group" personality, 70, *70,* 75, *75,* 167, 180, 203–4; indicating "out group" personality, 34, *35,* 37, 51, *52,* 167, 172–73, 190
Pickens, Lucy Holcombe, 178; on bank note vignettes, 25, 181, 203, 218
Pickens, W. R., 122
plagiarism. *See under* Confederate imagery
planters, 17, 56
plays. *See* theater
polygenesis. *See* racial theories
Portrait of Judah P. Benjamin. See under Keatinge, Edward C. (engraver)
"Portraits of Leading North Carolina Reconstructionists" (engraving), 195–96, *196*
Posey, Carnot, 199
postal service. *See* Confederate Post Office
printing. *See* graphic print industry
prisoners of war. *See under* military forces
profiteering. *See* extortion and speculation; manufacturing; women
prostitution, 173, 270n80
Providence. *See* religion
pseudoscience. *See* racial theories

Quartermaster's Department, 243n87; civilians and, 130, 165, 259n97; contracts, 119, 255n35; in public opinion, 87–90; tax-in-kind, 85–86; textiles manufacturers and, 86, 89, 243n78. *See also* Confederate army regulation dress; Lawton, A. R.; military clothing; Myer, Abraham C.
—army clothing: *128;* described, 86, 119, 122; issues with, 244n88; and officers, 128–29; responsible for, 85; supply of, 119, 122, 246n123, 255n34, 256n51
Quigley, Paul, 3

Rable, George, 3, 184, 266n1, 272n7
racial theories: and Confederates, 34, 37, 38, 41; monogenesis, 41; physiognomy, 34, 37, 43, 270n92; as political tool, 32–33; polygenesis, 41; pseudoscience, 33; and Southern exceptionalism, 33–34, 198
racism, Confederate: and anti-Semitism, 38–40; in official Confederate iconography, 33; and fears of race mixing, 37, 49–52; and foreign-born Confederates, 38; in minstrel shows, 43–45; and performance of black troops, 46–47; and prejudice, 38–39; and stereotypes of African Americans, 41–51, 72; and stereotypes of Northerners, 34, 37, 51, 162; uses of, 33; violence and, 49. *See also* Yankees
"Ragged Rebel." *See* military clothing
railways. *See* transportation
Raleigh, NC, 23, 114, 221n21
Raleigh Daily Standard: on military clothing, 118, 119; *See also* Holden, William W.
Raleigh Weekly Standard: on manufacturers' profiteering, 89; and refusal of traders to take North Carolina notes, 27
Raphael, Harry J., 89
Reagan, John. *See* Confederate Post Office
"Recipe to Get Rid of Extortioners." *See under* Hurdle, Armistead
"Recognition." *See under* Hurdle, Armistead
Recruiting Unbleached Citizens of Virginia for the Confederate States Army (show), 49
Rees, Charles (photographer), 101
Reinhart, Benjamin Franklin (painter), 153–54
religion: and Confederates, 221n40, 273n25; art

and, 221n41; death and, 156, *157*; God's favor and, 193; views of extortion, 194–95. *See also* Bible; Confederate ideology

reprographic industries. *See* Confederate currency/coinage; graphic print industry; illustrated periodicals; photography

"Returned Prodigal, The" (engraving), 72–73, *73*

Revised Map of Manassas, A (engraving), 137–38, *137*

revolvers: Griswold and Gunnison, 80, *81*; Leech and Rigdon, 241n40; Schneider and Glassick, 80; on stage, 168

Richmond, VA: armory, 84; art in, 1, 50, 58, 146, 153; black Confederate troops in, 49; civil disorder in, 173; civilian clothing in, 90, 130; graphic print industry in, 100, 110; manufacturing in, 81, 84; photography in, 101, 150, 178; social divisions, 40, 90; Union raids on, 177–78; women in, 162, 167, 173

—theatrical productions in: burlesque 49; dramatic, 51–52, 88, 106, 180; panoramic, 134, 141–42, 156, 160

Richmond Dispatch: on Mallory's *War Illustrations,* 141–42; on graphic print industry, 94, 112; on manhood of Confederate soldiers, 198; on efforts to provide quality stamps, 29; on need for national uniform, 120; on resilience, 202; on war profiteers, 173; on women, 178–79; on Yankees, 81

Richmond Enquirer: advocates statue of Stonewall Jackson, 153; on Elder's *The Battle of the Crater,* 1; on effect of shinplasters, 27; on failings of Treasury notes, 26, 28, 111; on fifth series banknote quality, 24; on Mallory's *War Illustrations,* 158; on manhood, 188, 192; on military clothing, 127; praises Confederate-made carbine's quality, 84; praises *Southern Illustrated News,* 105; on race, 37, 41; on raising the second national flag, 13; on seventh series ten dollar Treasury note vignette, 25; on Washington's *Burial of Latané,* 50

Richmond Examiner: on commutation system, 119; on Confederate quartermasters, 88; on Confederate uniform, 275n68; on Confederates' religious tolerance, 40; on failings of Memminger, 26; on failings of Stuart, 201; on failings of seventh series Treasury notes, 26; on gray as national color, 119; on Ida Vernon, 180; on Mallory's *War Illustrations,* 160; on miscegenation, 51; on post office stamps, 28; on raising the second national flag, 13; on shortage of skilled engravers, 100; on war profiteering, 173; on women, 167

Richmond Sentinel: on postage stamps, 29

Richmond Whig: on achieving God's favor, 87; on black troops, 49; on Confederate currency, 22; on difference between Northerners and Southerners, 209; on Elder's *Battle of the Crater,* 1, 53; on engravings by Dunn and Company, 110; on engravings by Torsch, 108; on graphic printing, 93; on gray military clothing, 118; on Ida Vernon, 180; on organizing manufacturing, 91; promotes slavery, 68; on the second national flag, 14; on Southern racial superiority, 32, 38–39; on Washington's *Burial of Latané,* 50

rifles: Cook Brothers, 80; on stage, 155; Richmond armory, 84

riots. *See* Confederacy—and civil disorder

Rivals, The. See under Haw, Mary Jane

Rock Island Paper Mills, 95

Roediger, David, 32

Rogers, Arthur L., 14

Roll of the Drum. See under Davis, John (actor/writer/manager)

Rosecruz, Monti de (artist/showman), 140

Rubin, Anne, 2, 214

Sahlins, Peter, 4

Sambo stereotype. *See* racism

satanic symbolism, 192, *192*, 196, *196*, 273n23

Savannah, GA: graphic print industry in, 249n33; photographs of Fort Sumter sold in, 259n6; post office in, 29; theatrical productions in, 155

Savannah Daily News: on poor reputation of staff officers, 88
Savannah Morning News: on Hewitt's *Jayhawkers,* 155
Savannah Republican: on Lee, 204; on manufacturing and high prices, 89; relates industrialization to independence, 80, 240n33;
Schmidt, Samuel (Charles August Solomon) (artist/engraver), 96, 247n17
Schneider and Glassick (revolver manufacturers). *See* revolvers
Scott, Sir Walter, 33, 201
Scott, Winfield, 136, *136*
Scout, The; or, The Plains of Manassas. See under Hewitt, John Hill (playwright/composer)
Scout's Prize, The. See under Elder, John Adams (artist)
sculpture. *See* Galt, Alexander; Valentine, Edward; Volck, Frederick
Sebring, Annie Perdue (painter), 149, 266n7
Semmes, Raphael, 17
separate spheres. *See* female identity; gender roles; male identity
"Sergeant Walter at Manassas, 1862" (engraving), 191, *191*
sex/sexuality. *See* gender relations
Shaver, Samuel M. (artist), 150
—works: *Gen'l E. Kirby Smith,* 150, *151*
sheet music, 112–24, 200. *See also by title*
Sheppard, William L. (artist), 105, 112
—works: "Croaker" (attributed) *194; Southern Illustrated News* masthead, 75, *75,* 143, *144,* 183–84; "You Look at a Star from Two Motives" (attributed) 184, *185*
shinplasters. *See* Confederate currency/coinage
"Shocking" (engraving), 182, *183*
shortages. *See under* Confederacy; Confederate postage stamps; graphic print industry; manufacturing
"silent slave," 58
simulacra, Confederate images as, 4
slave owners, 17, 56
slave picking cotton vignette (engraving), *42*
slavery: African American experience of, 61–62, 72; Confederate attitudes toward, 61, 65–66, 75; Confederate concerns regarding, 56, 62, 71; depictions of, *42, 43,* 58–76; discrepancy between ideology and reality, 43, 68–69, 72; and economy, 56; "positive good," 57; racial theories and, 41, 43, 49, 53; religion and, 57, 68, 191–92, 233n9; and non-slaveholders, 17, 56–57; and secession, 9, 32, 57; and the South, 57–58; visibility of, 57, 75–76. *See also* Confederacy; Confederate ideology
—Confederate myths concerning: disloyalty, 47, 70; loyalty, 64–67; reciprocity, 67–69; slaves happier in the South, 55, 63–64, 72–74
"Slavery in the North—Slavery in the South" (engraving), 63, *63*
"Slaves Apprehend a Colored Correspondent of the New York Tribune" (engraving), 70, *70*
Smillie, James D.
—works: *Cotton Fields,* 65, *65*
Smith, Edmund Kirby, 150, *151*
Smith and Barron's Monthly Magazine: criticizes seventh series Treasury notes, 26
soldiers
—Confederate: African American, 46, 48–49; and camp life, *59, 60, 62;* cavalry, 202; conscripts, 122; as consumers of visual culture, 3, 67, 100, 110, 220n19, 251n61; desertion of, 175–76, 270n84; detached to print Treasury notes, 97, 98, 247n20; as extras on stage, 155; female, 268n53; home and, 165–66; infantry, in popular opinion, 39, 202–3; Lee and, 205; meaning of clothing of, 86, 87, 116–26, 163–65, 198–200; profiteering and, 130; reaction to accoutrements, 83; respond to black Union troops, 47–48; and slavery, 53, 79; violent acts on noncombatants, 49, 252n100. *See also* Confederacy; Confederate identity; Confederate ideology; military forces; slavery

—Union: African American, 53; Confederate opinion of, 34, 37, 53, 189–92; desertion of, 270n84; foreign-born, 34, 37
soldiers' clothing. *See* military clothing
Soldier's Suit of Grey, The (sheet music), 122, *123*
Soldier's Trial; or, The Warning Voice. See under Westmoreland, Maria J.
South Carolina troops: Kershaw's Brigade, 165; Palmetto Battery, 62
South Carolinian: on *Southern Illustrated News*, 105
South Rising in Its Might and Striking Down the North and Crippling the Eagle, The (engraving), 34–35, *36*
Southern Bank Note Company, 22, 96, 215
Southern Confederacy: on *Southern Illustrated News*, 105–6
Southern diorama. *See* Burton, William J. (artist/showman)
Southern Field and Fireside: and engravings, 107–8, 111, 263n78; and Jackson, 151, *152;* on patriotism, 82. *See also* Maurice, Alfred (illustrator/engraver)
Southern Illustrated News: banners/mastheads of, 75, *144*, 145, *145;* on black character, *46, 71;* characters in engravings, 266n6; circulation of, 105; on Confederate Great Seal, 203; contemporary public response to, 108, 111; on death in wartime, *158;* on Dr. Mary E. Walker, 170; on Ewell, 107; on fashion, *130;* genesis of, 104; on heroes, 150–51; on international recognition, *7;* on Lee, 209; and Lincoln, *192;* on men, *75, 195, 197;* on military struggle, *133;* production of, 105–6, 108 112; promotes slavery, 67–68, *75;* quality of engravings, 105, 111; on Reconstruction, *213;* staff, 105, 106, 108; welcomes closure of *Miscegenation* play, 52; on women, 75, *180, 181;* on Yankees, *190*. *See also engravings by title or artist*
Southern Literary Messenger: considers adding illustrations, 107; links slavery to Confederate flag, 233n17; on fashion, 178, *179;* prewar, 102, 246n1
Southern Monthly: contemporary descriptions of, 102; criticism of engravings, 103; on difficulties in producing pictorial journal, 103–4; and First Battle of Bull Run, 137–38, *137;* illustrations, 99, 102–3; relates industrialization to independence, 79
Southern nationalism. *See* Confederate nationalism
Southern Punch: anti-semitism in, 40, *41;* on black troops, *48;* on changes to second national flag, 14; characters in engravings, 266n6; criticism of engravings, 111; on failings of well-dressed officers, 200; on masculinity and clothing, 198; on men, *168, 169, 196;* portraits of military figures, 151; production of, 108, 112; promotes slavery, *63, 69, 70, 73*, 236n49; publication begins, 107; staff, 108; on women, *168, 169, 171, 173, 175, 177. See also engravings by title*
speculation. *See* extortion and speculation; manufacturing
Sperry, Kate, 124
Stampp, Kenneth, 2
stamps. *See* Confederate postage stamps
Stephens, Alexander, 24, 32, 150, 216, 250n50
stereotypes. *See* African Americans; women; Yankees
Stuart, J. E. B., 201–2, 233n19
supply. *See* military clothing; Ordnance Department; Quartermaster's Department

Talley, Susan Archer (writer/illustrator)
—works: "The Yankee Cavalry Sent to Intercept General Stuart," 190, *190*
tax-in-kind. *See under* Quartermaster's Department
Texas troops: Texas Polk Rifles, 5th Texas Infantry, 116; 1st Texas Infantry, 101; 5th Texas Infantry, 199; 7th Texas Infantry, 117
textile production. See manufacturing
textiles. *See* homespun textiles; manufacturing; Quartermaster's Department
theater: actors, 142, 155, 168, 179–80, 189;

theater *(continued)*
adaptations, 264n101, 269n67; audience, 4, 49, 67; audience experience, 134, 140, 156, 158–60, 189; blackface, 43, 44, *44*, *45*; concerns about propriety, 37; drama, 169, 180, 189, 235n49, 264n96, 265n115; minstrel shows, 43–45, 230n56, 230n57; musical, 168; panoramas, 134–35, 138–39, 140–42, 151–52, 154, 160; performance as instruction, 155 158; production, 155; promoting slavery ideology, 51–52, 66–67; similarities of Confederate with Union theatrical productions, 269n61; soldiers as extras, 155; tableaux vivants, 140, 178–79; theatrical performances, 51–52. *See also* escapism
Thomas, Emory, 72, 77
Torsch, John W. (engraver/soldier), 105–7, 209, 238n86
—works: *Southern Illustrated News* masthead, 75, *75*, *144*; Ewell engraving, 107, *107*, 278n117; "Miss Ida Vernon as Leah the Forsaken," 180, *181*; "General Robert Edmund Lee," *207*, 209
Tosi, Samuel (painter) 2
transportation, 6, 30, 160, 221n39
Treasury. *See* Confederate Treasury Department
Tredegar industrial complex, 77, 84
truthfulness, 4; art and, 142, 146, 149; and black people, 41; and manufacturing, 80; minstrel shows and, 43; photography and, 68, 100, 147–48, 259n6; symbolized in second national flag, 12; Yankees' lack of, 78, 81, 142. *See also* Confederate imagery
Tuscaloosa Observer: on failings of Confederate Treasury notes, 22
typography, 15–16, 102, 107, 133, 247n12

uniforms. *See* military clothing
Union naval blockade. *See* blockade of Southern ports
"Unpleasant Present, Unpleasanter Future" (engraving), 172, *173*

"(Vain) Vane Aspiration, A" (engraving), 174, *176*
Valentine, Edward (sculptor)
—works: statue of Lee, 153, 206, 264n84
Van Dorn, Earl, 277n95
Van Felson, Charles (engraver), 108
Vance, Zebulon, 195
Vernon, Ida (actor), 180–81
Vernon, V. E. W. (McCord) (writer)
—works: *The Warrior's Steed*, 158
Veteran '76 and '62, The. See under Hewitt, John H.
Vicksburg, MS: seige of, 144–45
Victorian culture: desire for visual stimulus, 94; pseudoscience and, 33, 41, 43
View from Fort Sumter Parapet. See under Cook, George S. (photographer)
vignettes. *See* Confederate currency/bond vignettes
Virginia Cavalier, The. See under Alexander, George W. (writer/soldier)
Virginia troops: 4th Cavalry Regiment, *128;* 59th Virginia Infantry, 58, *59*, *60;* Culpeper Minutemen, 13th Infantry Regiment, 118
Vivandiere, The. See under Hewitt, John H. (playwright/composer)
Volck, Andrew Frederick (sculptor)
—works: Jackson bust, 153, 277n93; Jackson death mask, 153, 204; Jackson statue, 153

Wade, William H. See *Southern Illustrated News*
Walker, Mary E., 169–70, *170*
Wallace, Allan, 134
war. *See* combat, depictions of
War and Its Heroes (Ayres and Wade), 159–60
Warrior's Steed, The. See under Vernon, V. E. W. (writer)
Warwick, Eden
—works: *Nasology; or, Hints toward Classification of Noses*, 34, 37
Washington, George, 29, 30, 169, 203; statue by Crawford, 17, 203
Washington, William D. (artist)

—works: *The Burial of Latané,* 50–51, 158, 183, 231n79, 231n81, 231n82, 233n19
Westmoreland, Maria J. (author)
—works: *Soldier's Trial; or, The Warning Voice,* 202
"What's Master's" (engraving), 70–71, *71*
White, John Blake
—works: *General Marion Inviting a British Officer to Share His Meal,* 64, 234n36
Wilmington, NC: art in, 264n95; photography in, 150
Wilmington Daily Journal: incorrectly identifies politicians on Treasury Notes, 24; on printing ink, 95
Wissler, Jacques (artist/lithographer), 237n82, 110
—works: "I'm Coming to My Dixie Home," 73, *74*
women: actors changed status of, 178–80; African American, 182–83; artists, 190, 266n7; comparison of depictions of black and white, 182–84; concerns about disloyalty, 172–78; as Confederate soldiers, 170; contradictory expectations for, 166–72, 178–81; depictions of, in currency and periodicals, 266n6; gunboat societies of, 166; inconsistency in acknowledgment of, 166–72; patriotism of, judged, 163–64, 166, 172–74, 176–77; prewar, 163; profiteering and, 173–74; refugees, 174; as Union soldiers, 169–70; and volunteer work, 163–66. *See also* female identity; military clothing
—as characters on stage, black, 67, 182, 235n49, 271n108
—as characters on stage, white, 37, 167, 168–69, 170
Woodward, Colin, 3
"Wounded Officer and His Steed, The." *See under* Mallory, Lee

"Yankee Cavalry Sent to Intercept General Stuart, The." *See under* Talley, Susan Archer
Yankees, 6; as Confederate opposite, 33, 126; as inhuman, 190–91, 272n20; religion and, 191–92; similarity of appearance to Southerners, 120; on stage, 34, 67, 181, 170, 189; transforming, to Confederate, 188, 189; transforming Confederate into, 91. *See also* Confederate identity
—traits: dishonest, 24, 53, 78, 81, 142; domineering, 89, 102; effeminate, 189; exploitative, 47, 48, 53; Godless, 138; greedy, 34, 78, 94, 136; lacking self-control, 33, 34, 138, 189, 190; lustful, 37, 52; physically weak, 37; shrewd, 24; showy, 27, 126, 138; spiteful, 145
"You Look at a Star from Two Motives." *See under* Sheppard, William Ludwell (artist)

"Zouave Mazourka" (sheet music), 168
zouaves, 168, 207